VOLUME ONE
ATOMIC ROBO AND THE **FIGHTIN' SCIENTISTS OF TESLADYNE**

publishers
PAUL ENS and SCOTT CHITWOOD

graphic design
PAUL ENS

ATOMIC ROBO VOLUME ONE: ATOMIC ROBO and the FIGHTIN' SCIENTISTS OF TESLADYNE

This volume collects ATOMIC ROBO #1 through #6 of the comic-book series originally printed by Red 5 Comics.

Published by
RED 5 COMICS
298 Tuscany Vista Rd NW, Calgary, Alberta, Canada, T3L 3B4

www.red5comics.com

To find a comics shop in your area, call the Comic Shop Locator Service toll-free at 1-888-266-4226

Fourth Printing:
ISBN-13: 978-0-9809302-0-7

Printed in Canada.

VOLUME ONE
ATOMIC ROBO AND THE FIGHTIN' SCIENTISTS OF TESLADYNE

WORDS
BRIAN CLEVINGER

ART AND COVER
SCOTT WEGENER

COLORS
RONDA PATTISON

LETTERS
JEFF POWELL

WWW.RED5COMICS.COM // WWW.ATOMIC-ROBO.COM

INTRODUCTION

In this day and age, I take comfort in knowing there are certain things I can still trust in life.

I trust there will always be cartoons on Saturday mornings. I trust that chocolate will always taste better with peanut butter. I trust that a cold beer will always be the perfect beverage after a hard day's work. And now there's something new I can trust...

I trust that any comic book released by Red 5 will be worth every penny!

Red 5 Comics was a company that seemed to come out of nowhere. They stealthily entered the market and made an immediate splash by publishing some of the best quality comics we've seen in years. Every single one of their titles has been a joy to hold and read from start to finish. From the covers, production values, and paper, to the writing, art, coloring and lettering, each one of their releases has been top notch from beginning to end.

And no comic is a better example of this then the one you now hold in your hands... Atomic Robo!

Want the premise in one sentence? Atomic Robo is a self-aware, wise-cracking, bad-ass robot created by Nikola Tesla who's now in the employ of the U.S. government and tasked with battling supernatural and unexplained threats to the planet's safety. How's that sound? Crazy, right? But let me tell ya, it works! The AR creative team pulls this series off in spades!

Where Brian Clevinger gets his ideas, I'll never know. And I don't know if I want to. But they explode onto the page and make you instantly fall in love with Robo. And while this is a slam-bang, action-packed comic, Brian also instills it with plenty of heart, especially in the way that Robo deals with the people around him. Yes, he's a robot, but he cares a hell of lot about life and the folks in his.

Scott Wegener was someone whose work I'd been following for a while now. He's the master of the simple line. At a quick glance, Scott's style is clean and open, but the more you look the more you see. The way he tells his story through the angles he chose and paces he puts his characters through are genius. There's a level of hidden detail that Scott brings to his craft that make him the perfect choice to bring Robo to life in this series.

Ronda Pattison's colors work in perfect harmony with Scott's line work. And Jeff Powell's balloons, for and effects complete this published package.

This creative collective has combined their amazing talents to bring to life an original character, one that's quite unique in today's comic industry, that everyone can read and enjoy. So go ahead, turn the page and see for yourself. You're so gonna love Atomic Robo!

Trust me.

C.B. Cebulski
New York City
April 16th, 2008

FROM THE CREATORS

I remember thinking, "He needs to look like a '58 Ford Edsel." In fact, Robo ended up looking like a 1950 Studebaker Commander, but that's neither here nor there.

Brian and I will both tell you that we have no idea what we are doing. Even now, well into work on Atomic Robo Vol.2, we are just making it up as we go along. What we do know is that Atomic Robo is something that we both care very deeply about. It is a shock and a joy to know that other people seem to think he's pretty alright, too.

Everyone always thanks their spouse. It's cliché, I know. But seriously, without Dorinda there is no way this could have happened. She took a leap of faith with me, and this career that most people don't have the intestinal fortitude to pull off. I love you for that. And to my daughter Emma; we weren't expecting company, but I'm so glad you stopped in.

Thanks to Phil Hester and Neil Vokes, for letting me cut my teeth on your books, and showing me that the real storytelling is in those first rough layouts that come from the gut. The rest is disturbingly similar to work. To Oeming, Powell, Pattison, Kube, the FOO crew, Yost, and Mauer (what the hell did you talk me into?!) And to Mike Mignola for keeping my interest in comics alive, at a time when I thought I was all done with them.

This book is for my dad. Thank you for showing me *Forbidden Planet*, *Body Snatchers*, *War of the Worlds*, and all the rest. I'm sure Mom wouldn't have approved.

Scott Wegener

First, I have to thank my parents. Their support and love of science, humor, and adventure made all of this possible.

Then there's Team Robo itself. Scott, Ronda, and Jeff. I don't know how it happened, but everyone working on this book is exactly who was needed to make Atomic Robo the best it could be (also, I'm working on it). The dedication, professionalism, and talent they bring to this project is simply incredible.

I'd like to thank Lydia, the unsung member of Team Robo. She helped to shape the Roboverse from the beginning and she continues to be my sounding board, critic, and inspiration. Also, I steal a ton of her ideas and no one will ever find out!

Lastly, this book is for the one person who is most responsible for Robo being what he is today, my grandfather, Michael J. Novosel, Sr.

Brian Clevinger

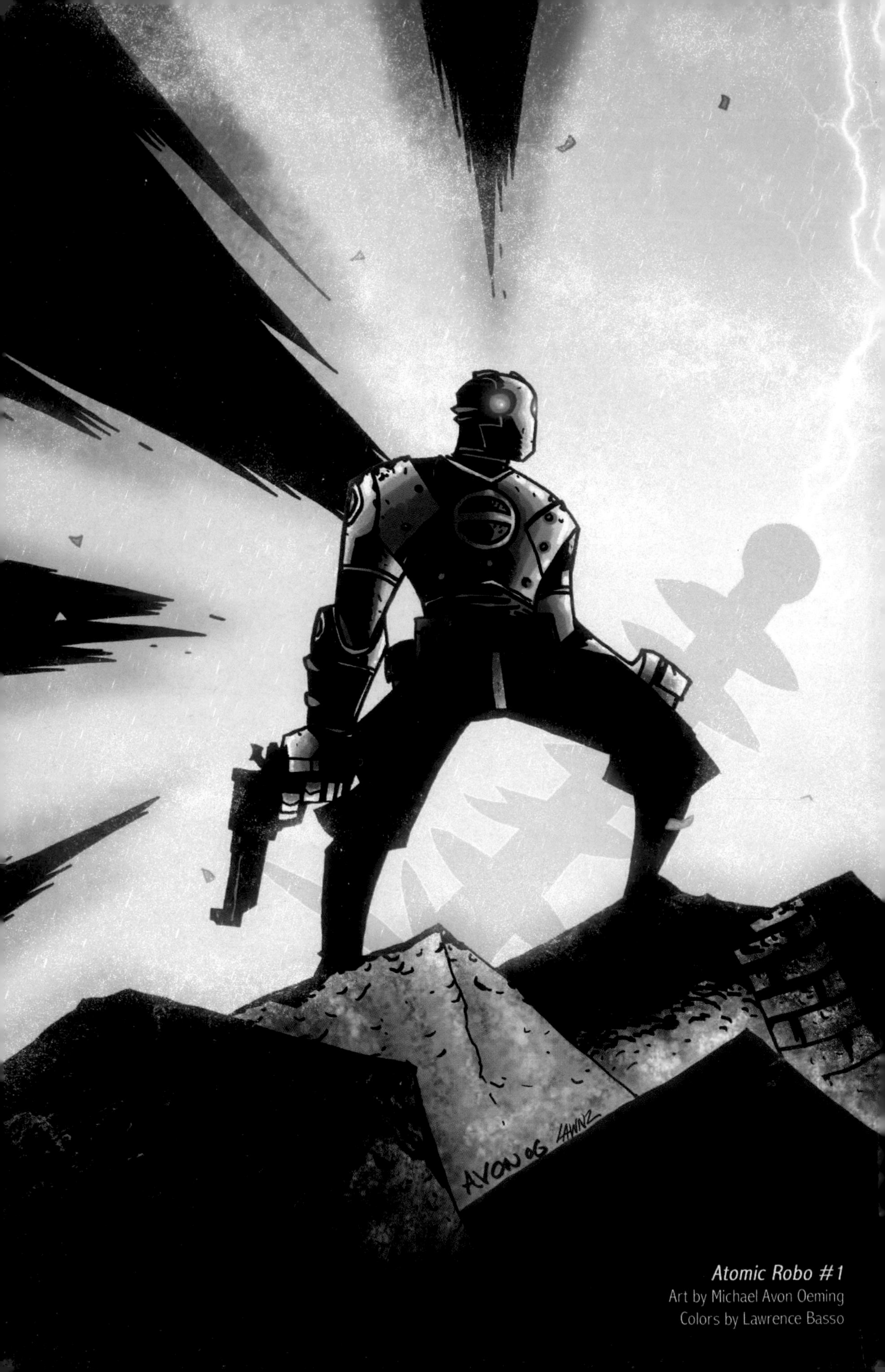
AVON 06
LAWNZ

Atomic Robo #1
Art by Michael Avon Oeming
Colors by Lawrence Basso

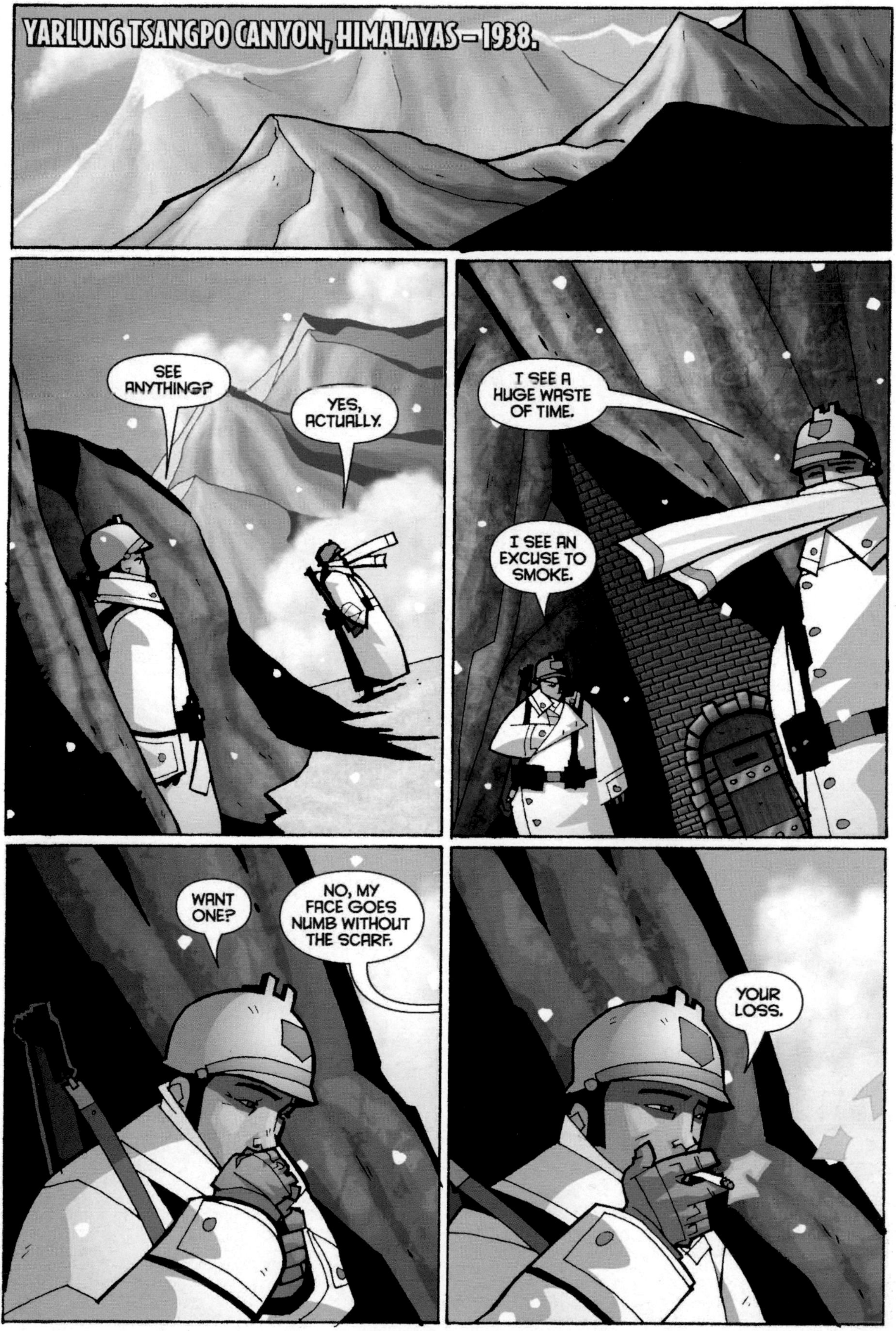
YARLUNG TSANGPO CANYON, HIMALAYAS – 1938.
SEE ANYTHING?
YES, ACTUALLY.
I SEE A HUGE WASTE OF TIME.
I SEE AN EXCUSE TO SMOKE.
WANT ONE?
NO, MY FACE GOES NUMB WITHOUT THE SCARF.
YOUR LOSS.

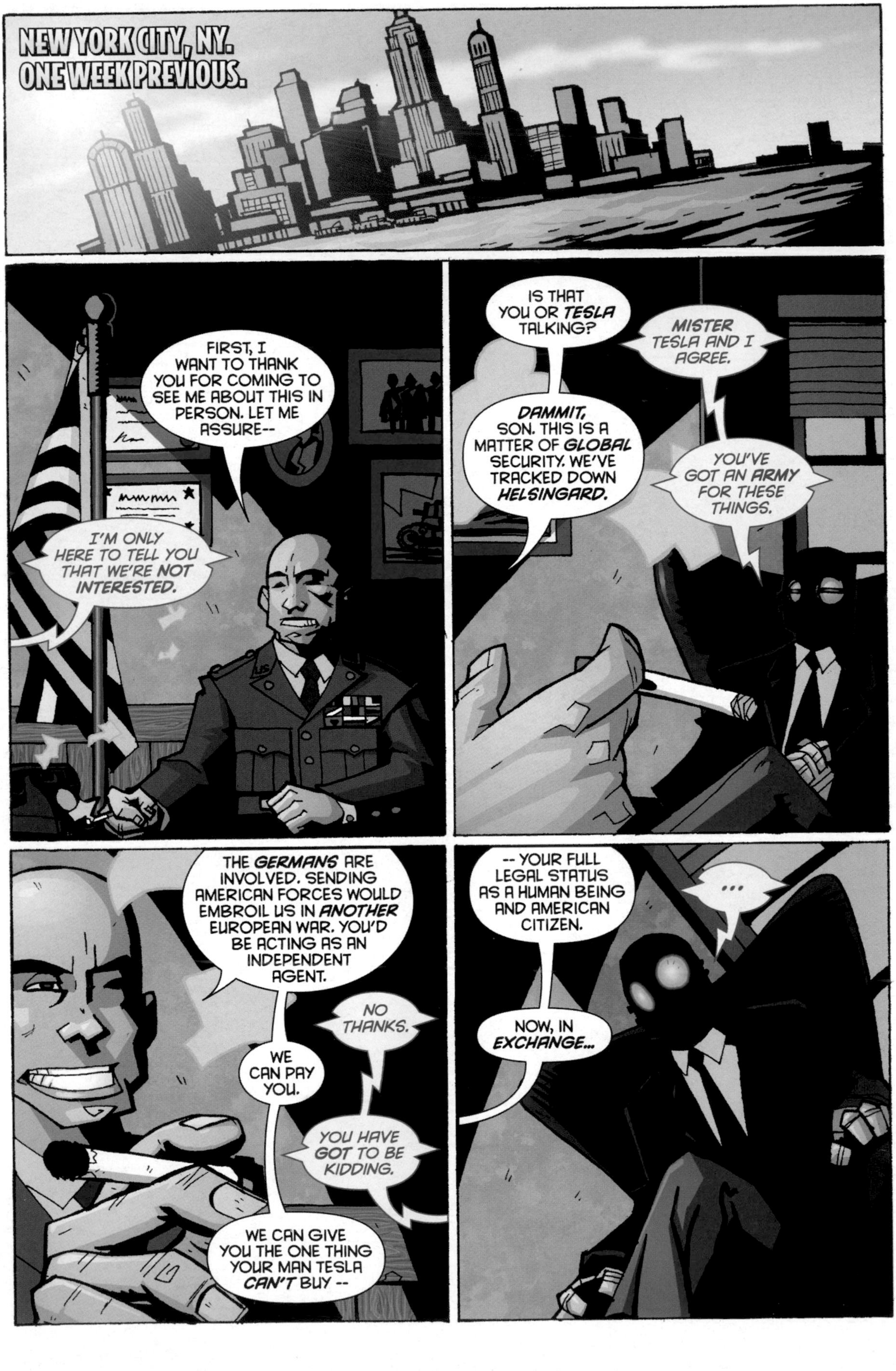
NEW YORK CITY, NY. ONE WEEK PREVIOUS.
FIRST, I WANT TO THANK YOU FOR COMING TO SEE ME ABOUT THIS IN PERSON. LET ME ASSURE--
I'M ONLY HERE TO TELL YOU THAT WE'RE NOT INTERESTED.
IS THAT YOU OR TESLA TALKING?
MISTER TESLA AND I AGREE.
DAMMIT, SON. THIS IS A MATTER OF GLOBAL SECURITY. WE'VE TRACKED DOWN HELSINGARD.
YOU'VE GOT AN ARMY FOR THESE THINGS.
THE GERMANS ARE INVOLVED. SENDING AMERICAN FORCES WOULD EMBROIL US IN ANOTHER EUROPEAN WAR. YOU'D BE ACTING AS AN INDEPENDENT AGENT.
NO THANKS.
WE CAN PAY YOU.
YOU HAVE GOT TO BE KIDDING.
WE CAN GIVE YOU THE ONE THING YOUR MAN TESLA CAN'T BUY --
-- YOUR FULL LEGAL STATUS AS A HUMAN BEING AND AMERICAN CITIZEN.
...
NOW, IN EXCHANGE...

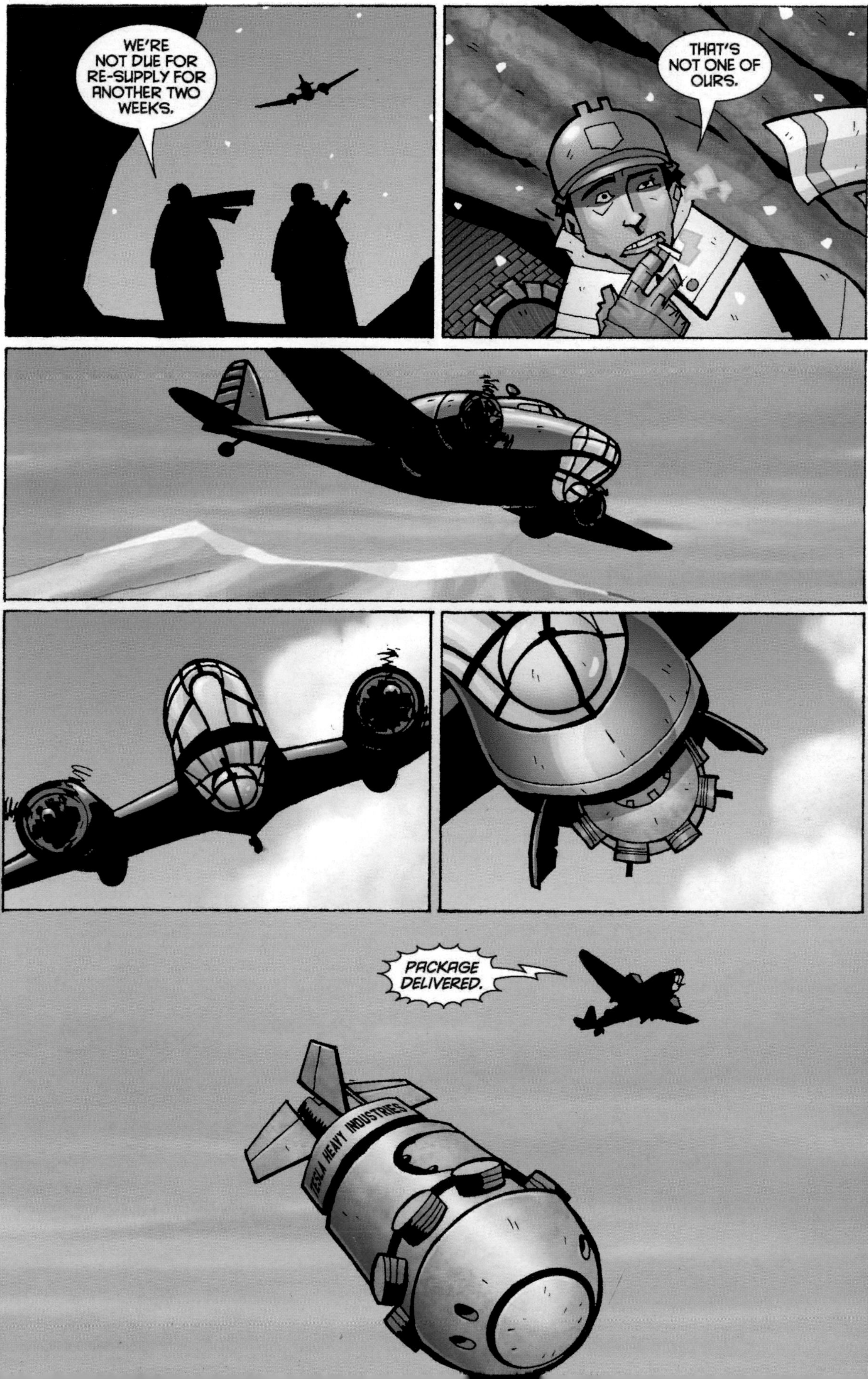
WE'RE NOT DUE FOR RE-SUPPLY FOR ANOTHER TWO WEEKS.
THAT'S NOT ONE OF OURS.
PACKAGE DELIVERED.
TESLA HEAVY INDUSTRIES

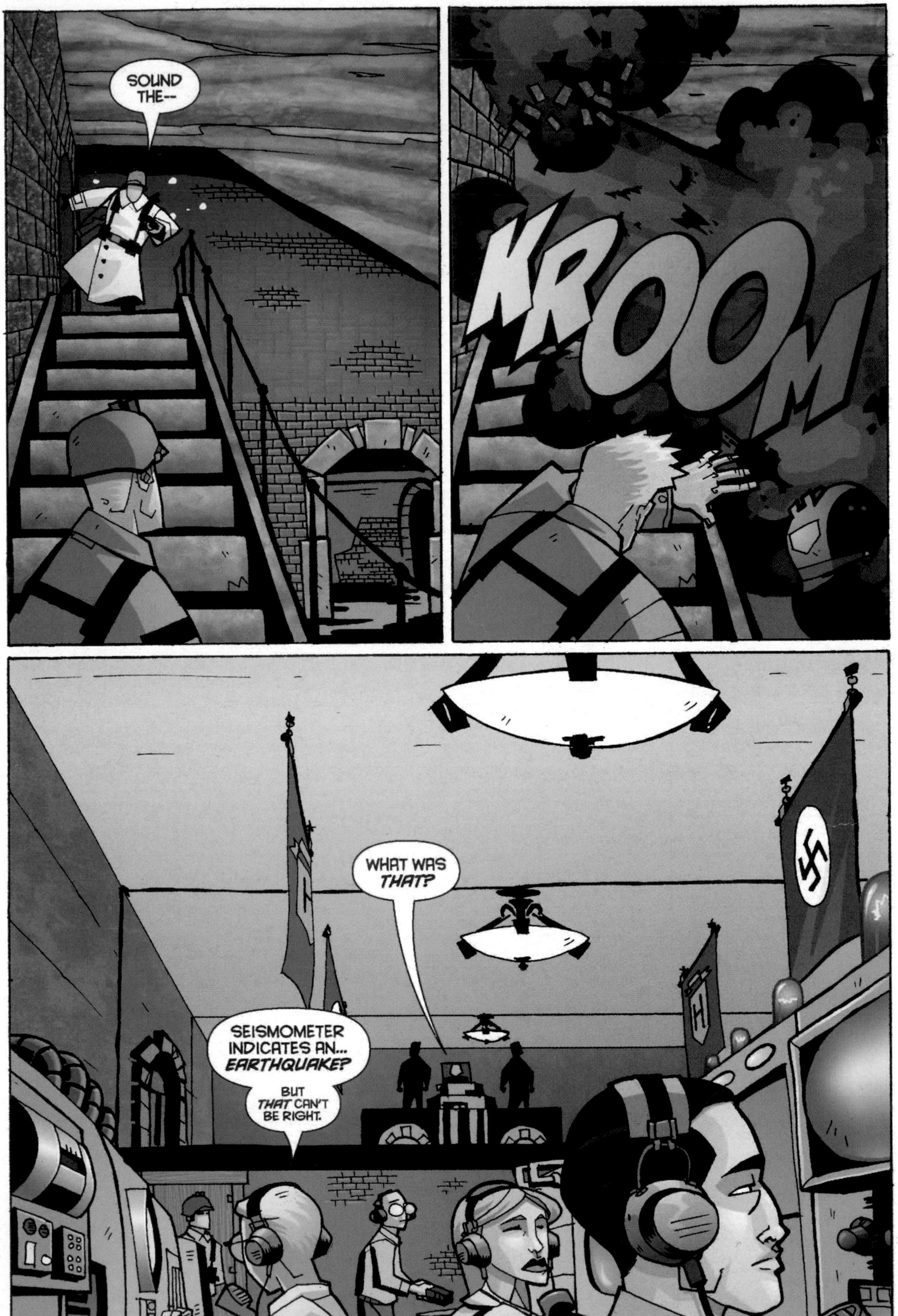
SOUND THE--
KROOM
WHAT WAS THAT?
SEISMOMETER INDICATES AN... EARTHQUAKE?
BUT THAT CAN'T BE RIGHT.

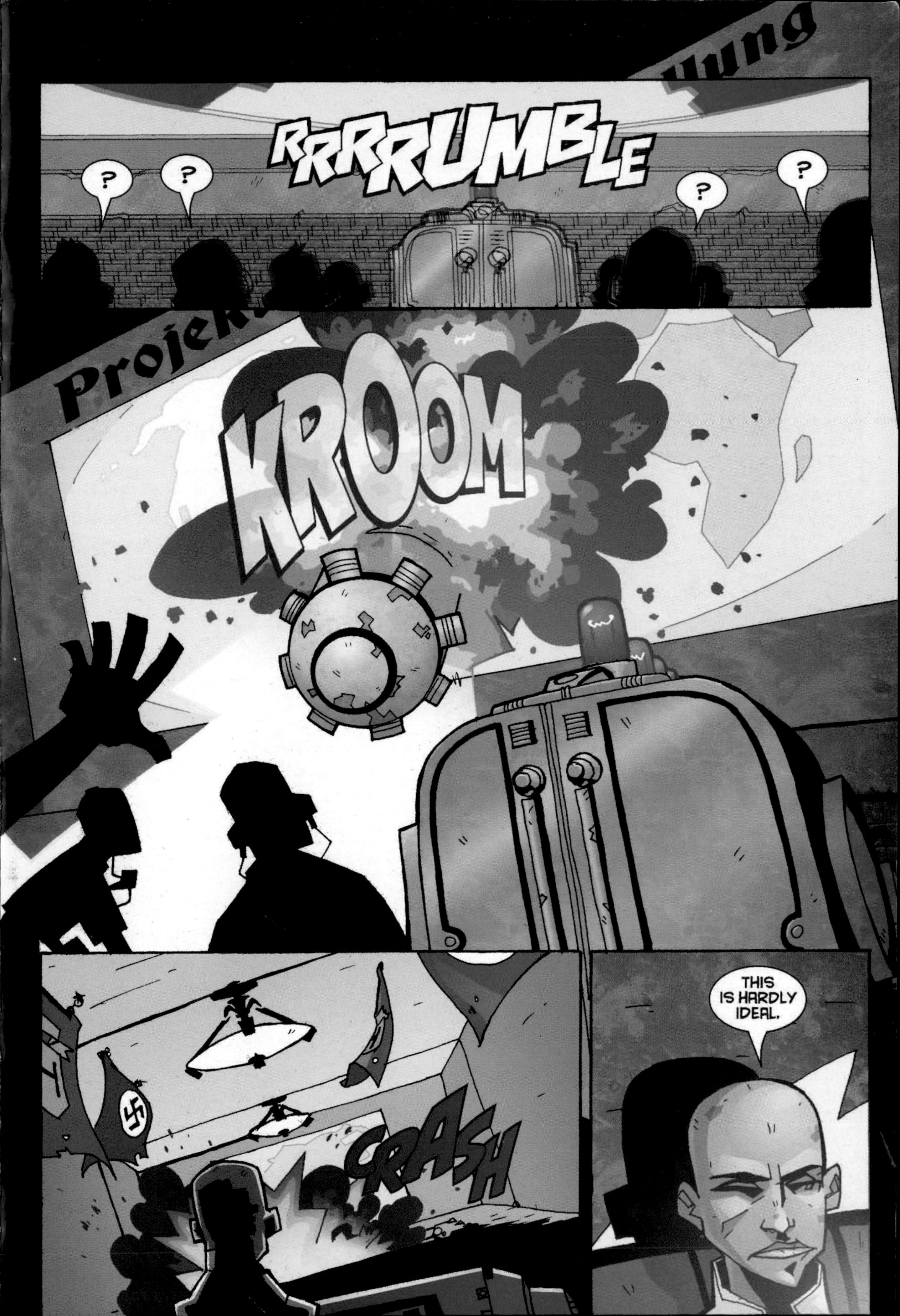

...llung
RRRRUMBLE
?
?
?
?
Projek...
KROOM
CRASH
THIS IS HARDLY IDEAL.

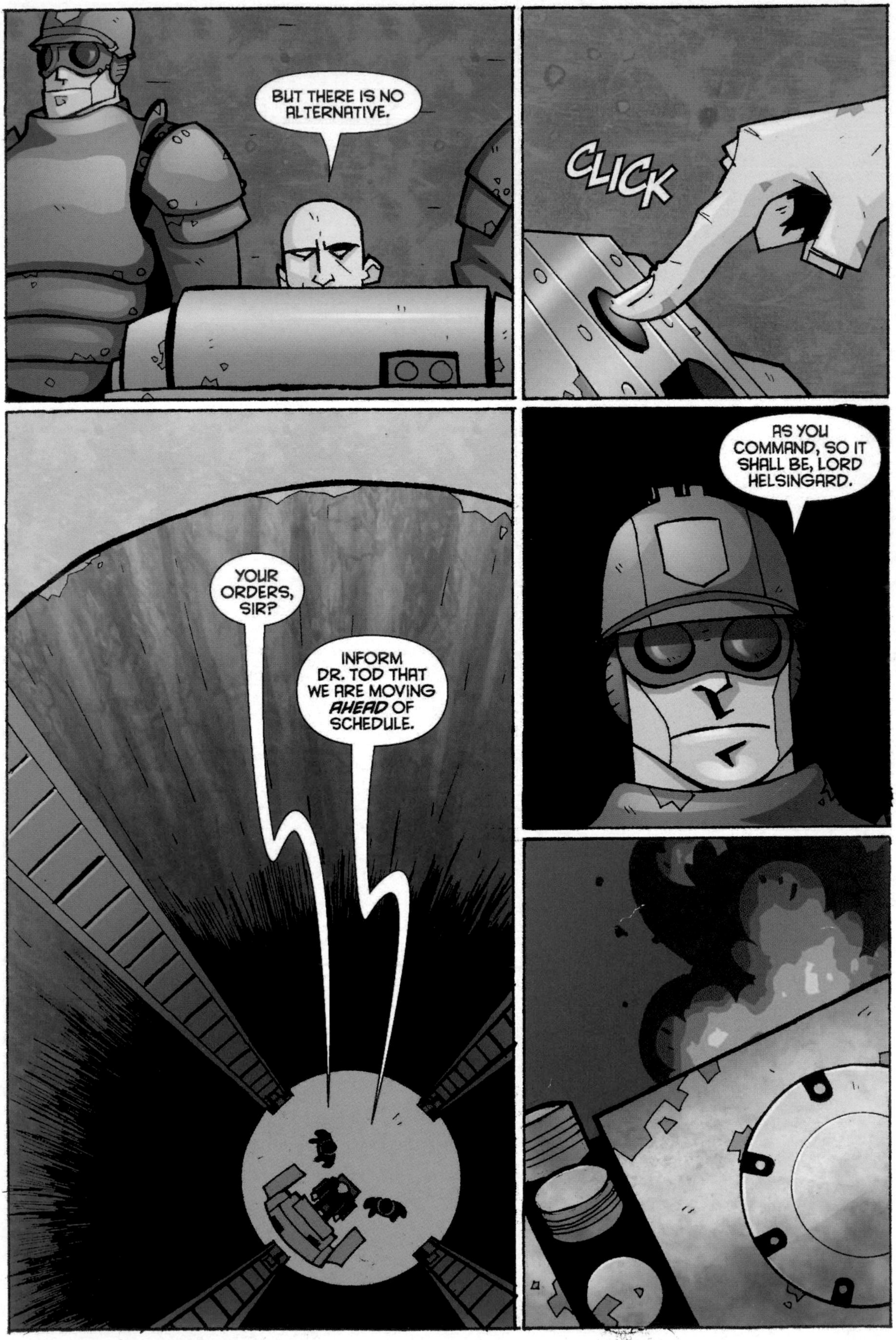
BUT THERE IS NO ALTERNATIVE.
CLICK
YOUR ORDERS, SIR?
INFORM DR. TOD THAT WE ARE MOVING AHEAD OF SCHEDULE.
AS YOU COMMAND, SO IT SHALL BE, LORD HELSINGARD.

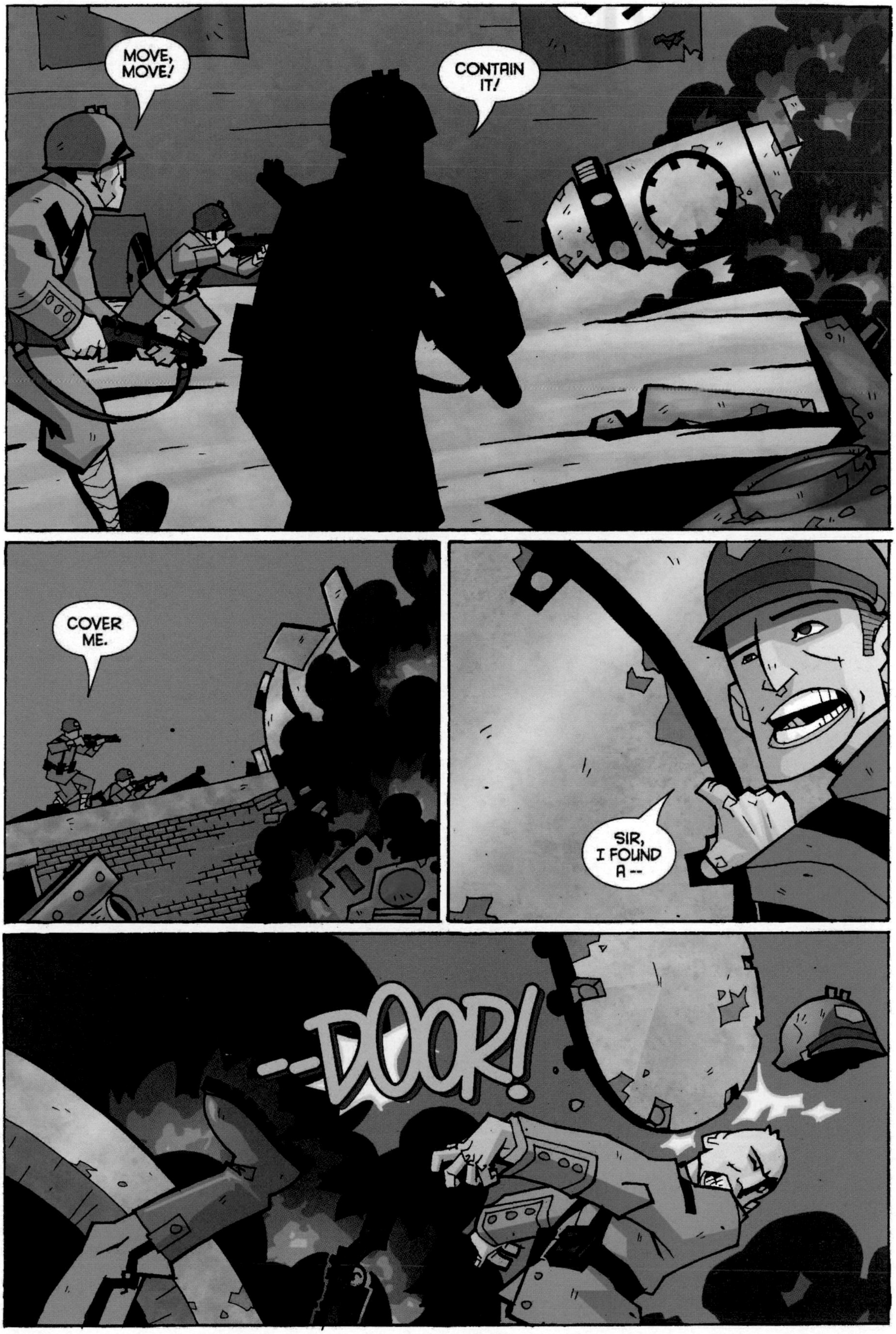
MOVE, MOVE!
CONTAIN IT!
COVER ME.
SIR, I FOUND A --
--DOOR!

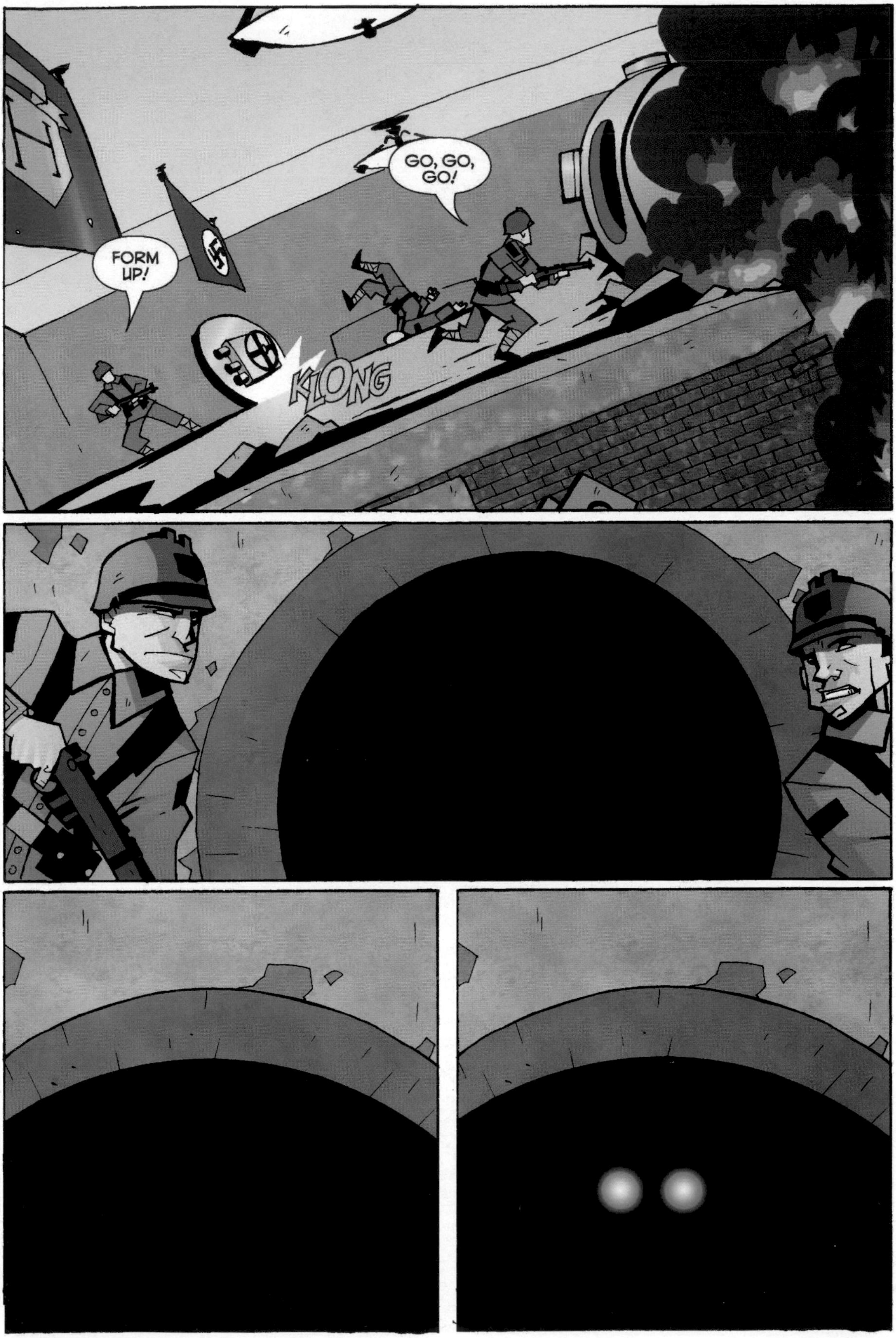
GO, GO, GO!
FORM UP!
KLONG

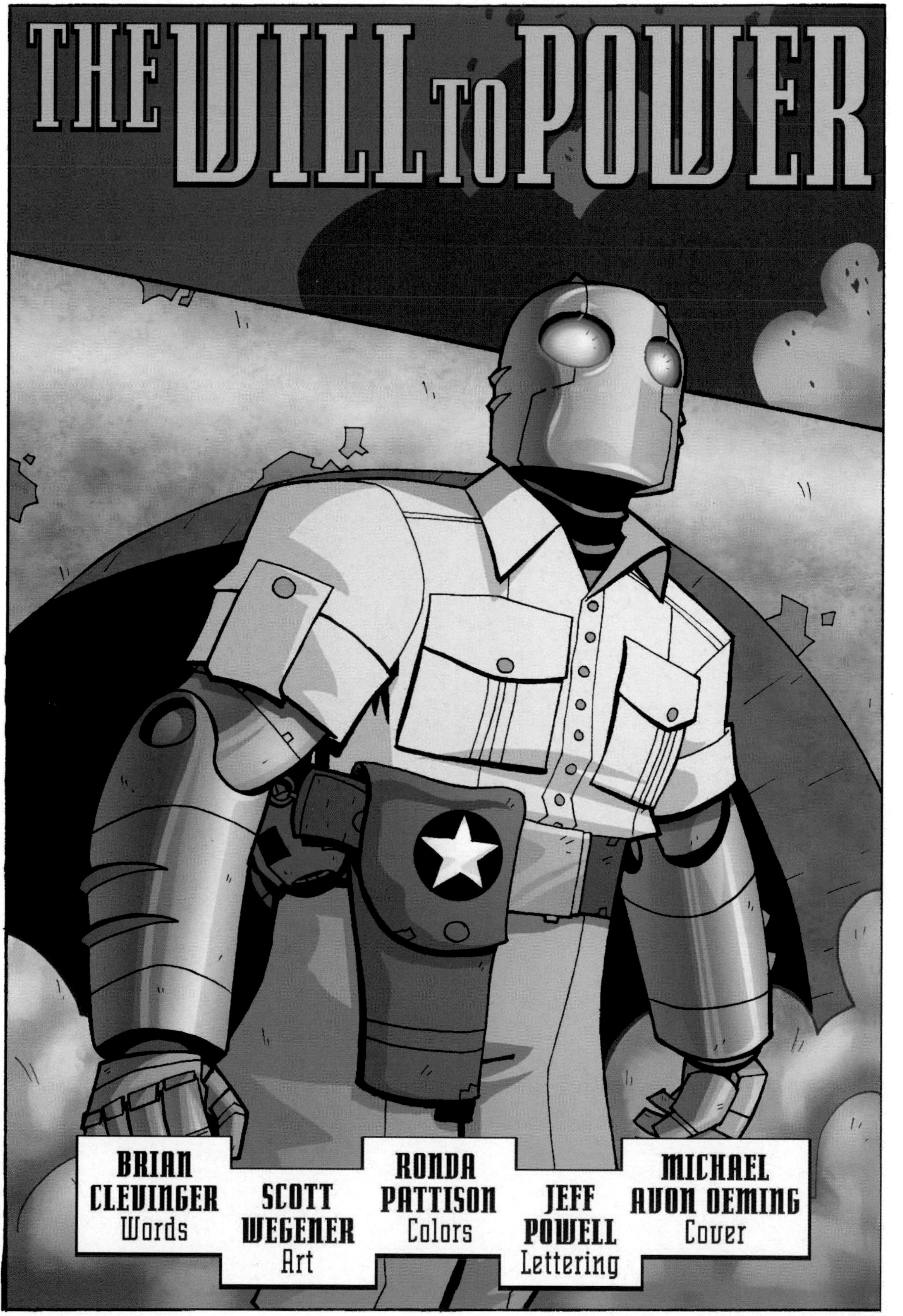
THE WILL TO POWER
BRIAN CLEVINGER Words
SCOTT WEGENER Art
RONDA PATTISON Colors
JEFF POWELL Lettering
MICHAEL AVON OEMING Cover

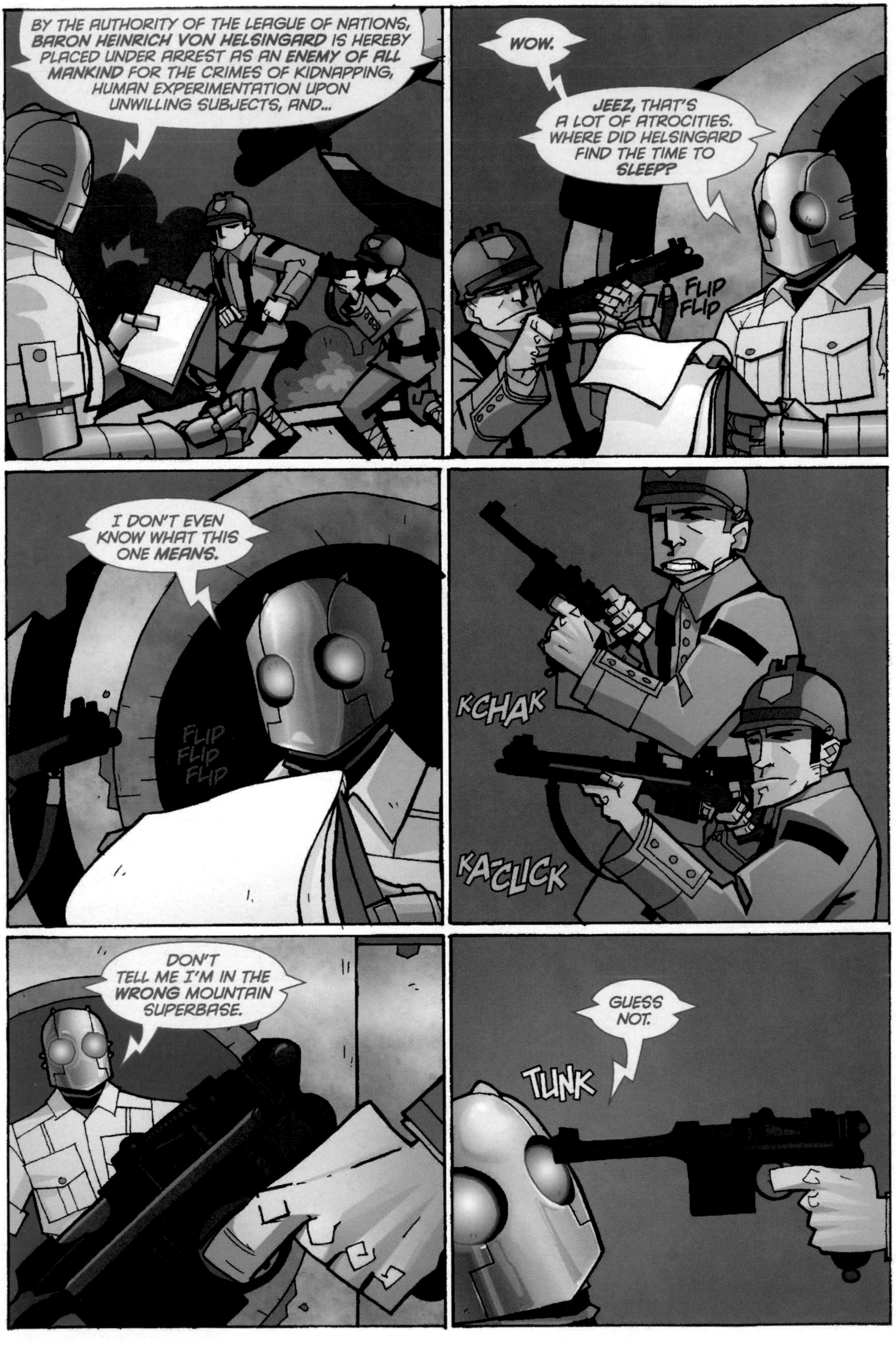
BY THE AUTHORITY OF THE LEAGUE OF NATIONS, BARON HEINRICH VON HELSINGARD IS HEREBY PLACED UNDER ARREST AS AN ENEMY OF ALL MANKIND FOR THE CRIMES OF KIDNAPPING, HUMAN EXPERIMENTATION UPON UNWILLING SUBJECTS, AND...
WOW.
JEEZ, THAT'S A LOT OF ATROCITIES. WHERE DID HELSINGARD FIND THE TIME TO SLEEP?
FLIP FLIP
I DON'T EVEN KNOW WHAT THIS ONE MEANS.
FLIP FLIP FLIP
KCHAK
KA-CLICK
DON'T TELL ME I'M IN THE WRONG MOUNTAIN SUPERBASE.
GUESS NOT.
TUNK

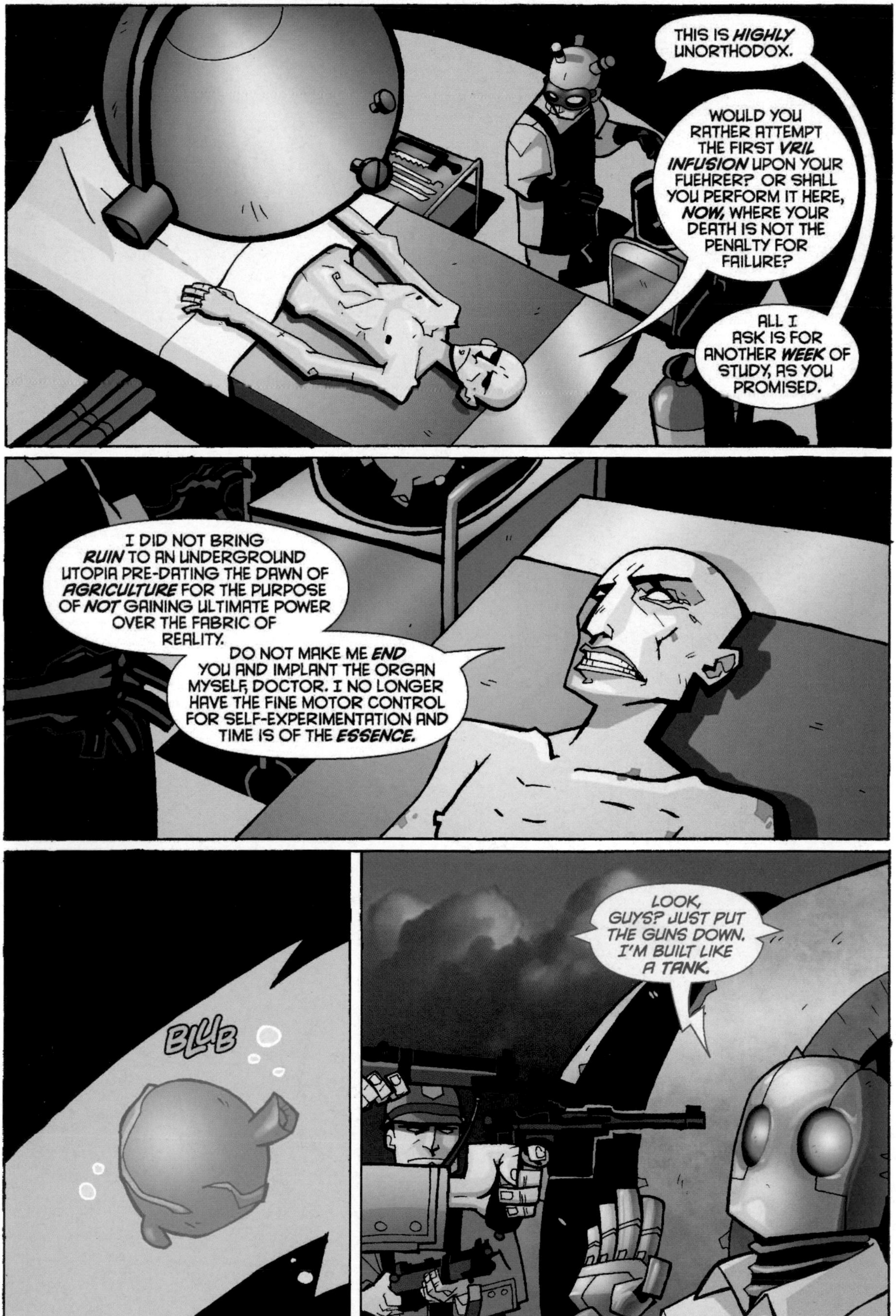
THIS IS HIGHLY UNORTHODOX.
WOULD YOU RATHER ATTEMPT THE FIRST VRIL INFUSION UPON YOUR FUEHRER? OR SHALL YOU PERFORM IT HERE, NOW, WHERE YOUR DEATH IS NOT THE PENALTY FOR FAILURE?
ALL I ASK IS FOR ANOTHER WEEK OF STUDY, AS YOU PROMISED.
I DID NOT BRING RUIN TO AN UNDERGROUND UTOPIA PRE-DATING THE DAWN OF AGRICULTURE FOR THE PURPOSE OF NOT GAINING ULTIMATE POWER OVER THE FABRIC OF REALITY.
DO NOT MAKE ME END YOU AND IMPLANT THE ORGAN MYSELF, DOCTOR. I NO LONGER HAVE THE FINE MOTOR CONTROL FOR SELF-EXPERIMENTATION AND TIME IS OF THE ESSENCE.
BLUB
LOOK, GUYS? JUST PUT THE GUNS DOWN. I'M BUILT LIKE A TANK.

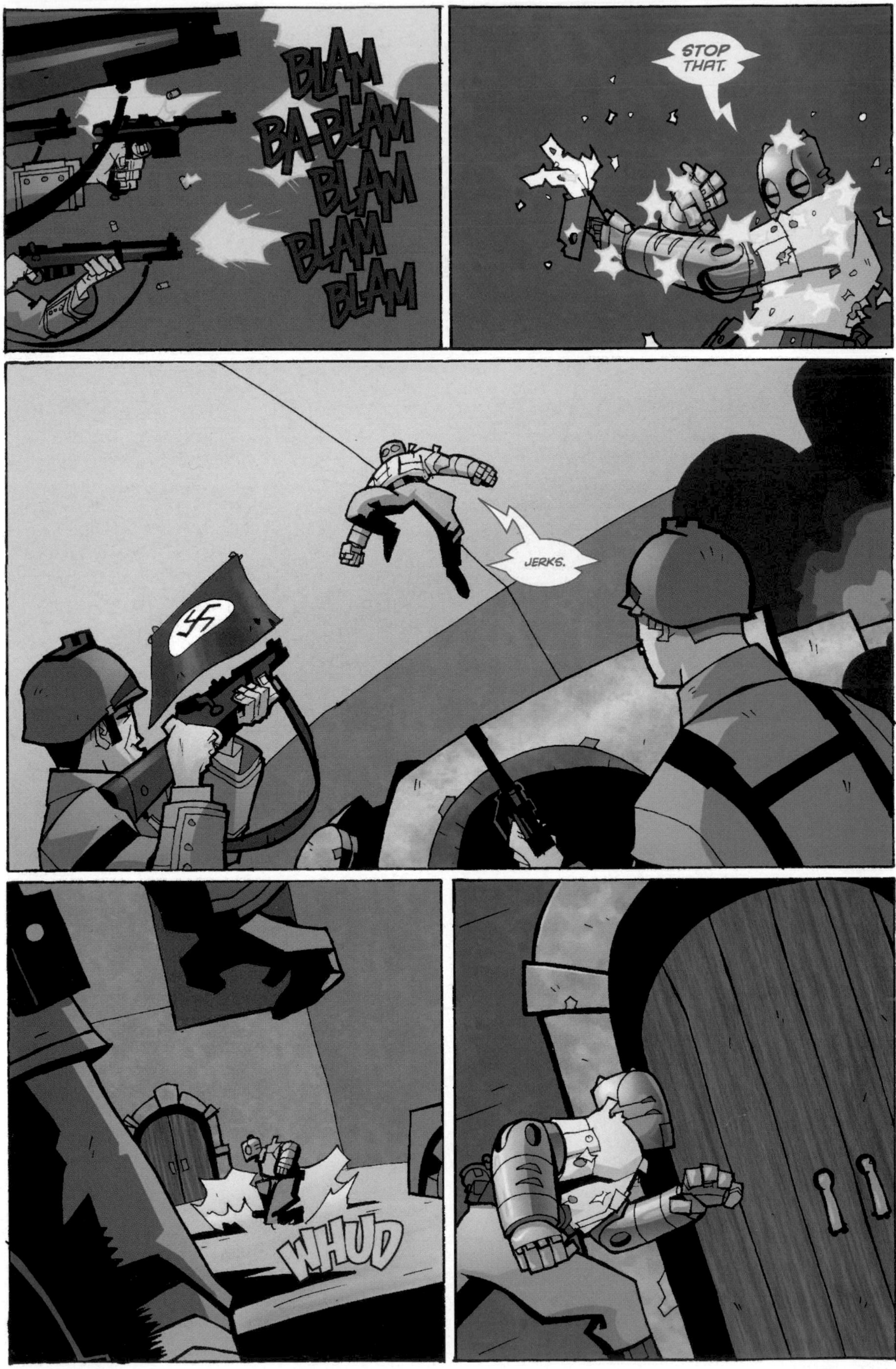
BLAM
BA-BLAM
BLAM
BLAM
BLAM
STOP THAT.
JERKS.
WHUD

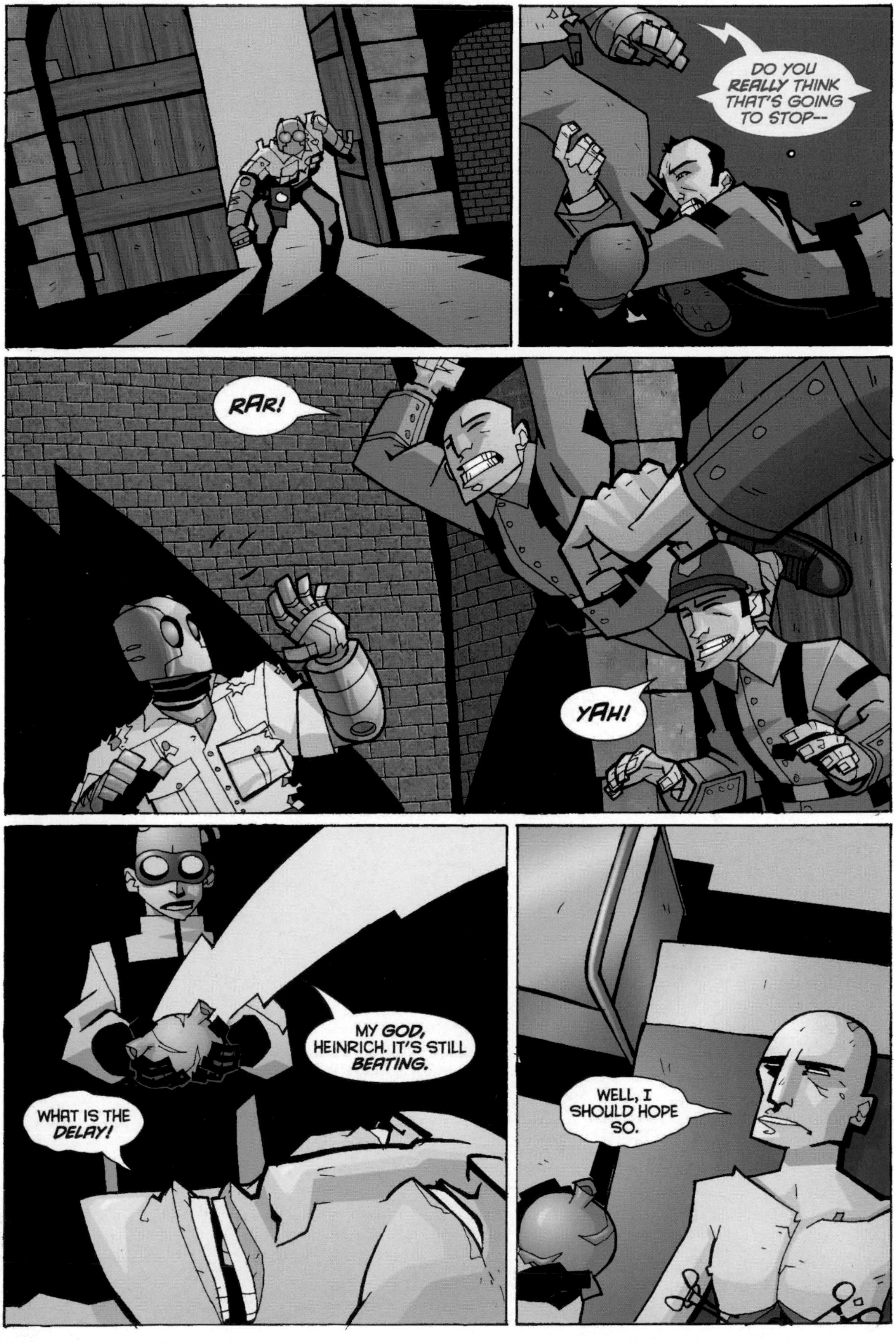
DO YOU REALLY THINK THAT'S GOING TO STOP--
RAR!
YAH!
MY GOD, HEINRICH. IT'S STILL BEATING.
WHAT IS THE DELAY!
WELL, I SHOULD HOPE SO.

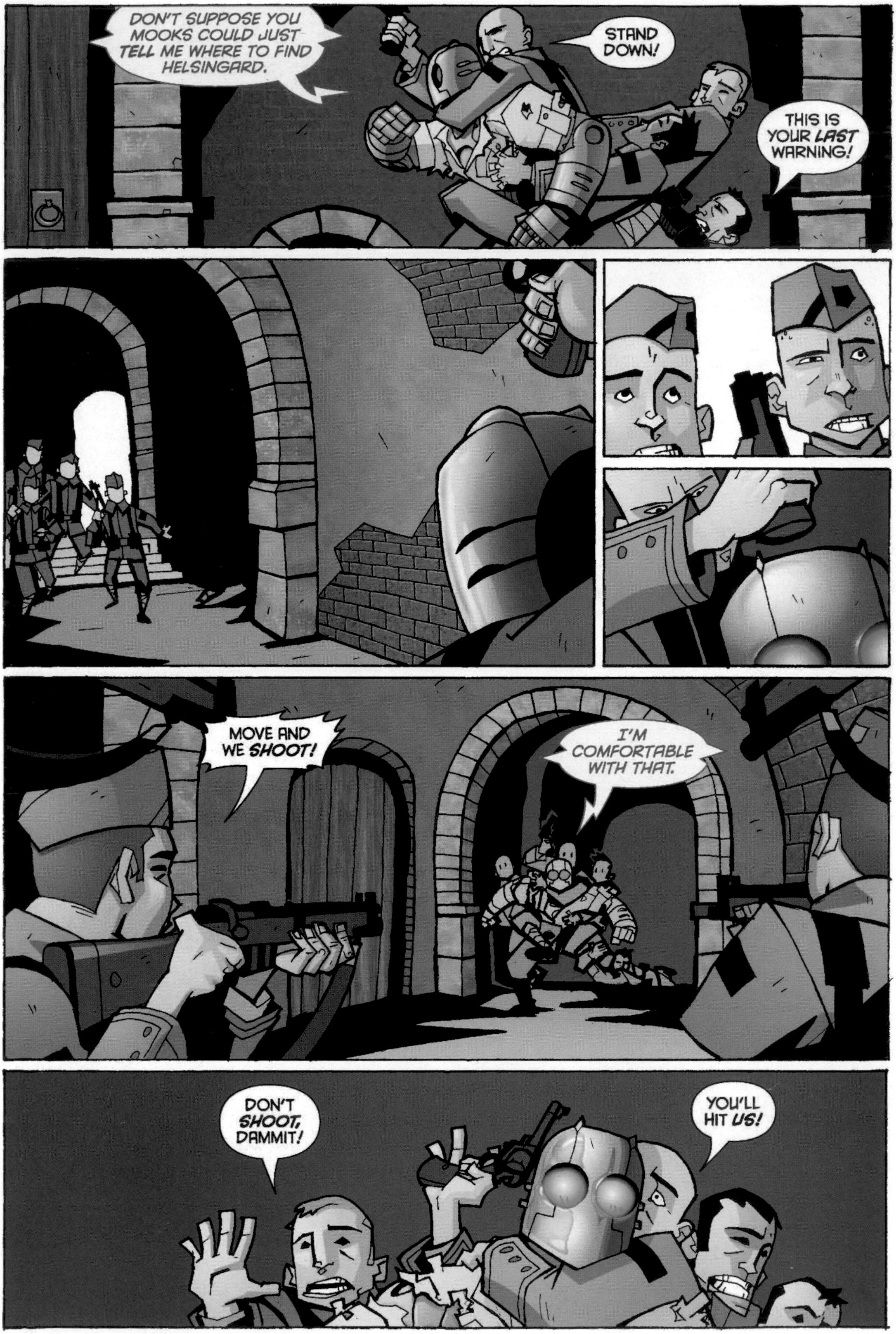
DON'T SUPPOSE YOU MOOKS COULD JUST TELL ME WHERE TO FIND HELSINGARD.
STAND DOWN!
THIS IS YOUR LAST WARNING!
MOVE AND WE SHOOT!
I'M COMFORTABLE WITH THAT.
DON'T SHOOT, DAMMIT!
YOU'LL HIT US!

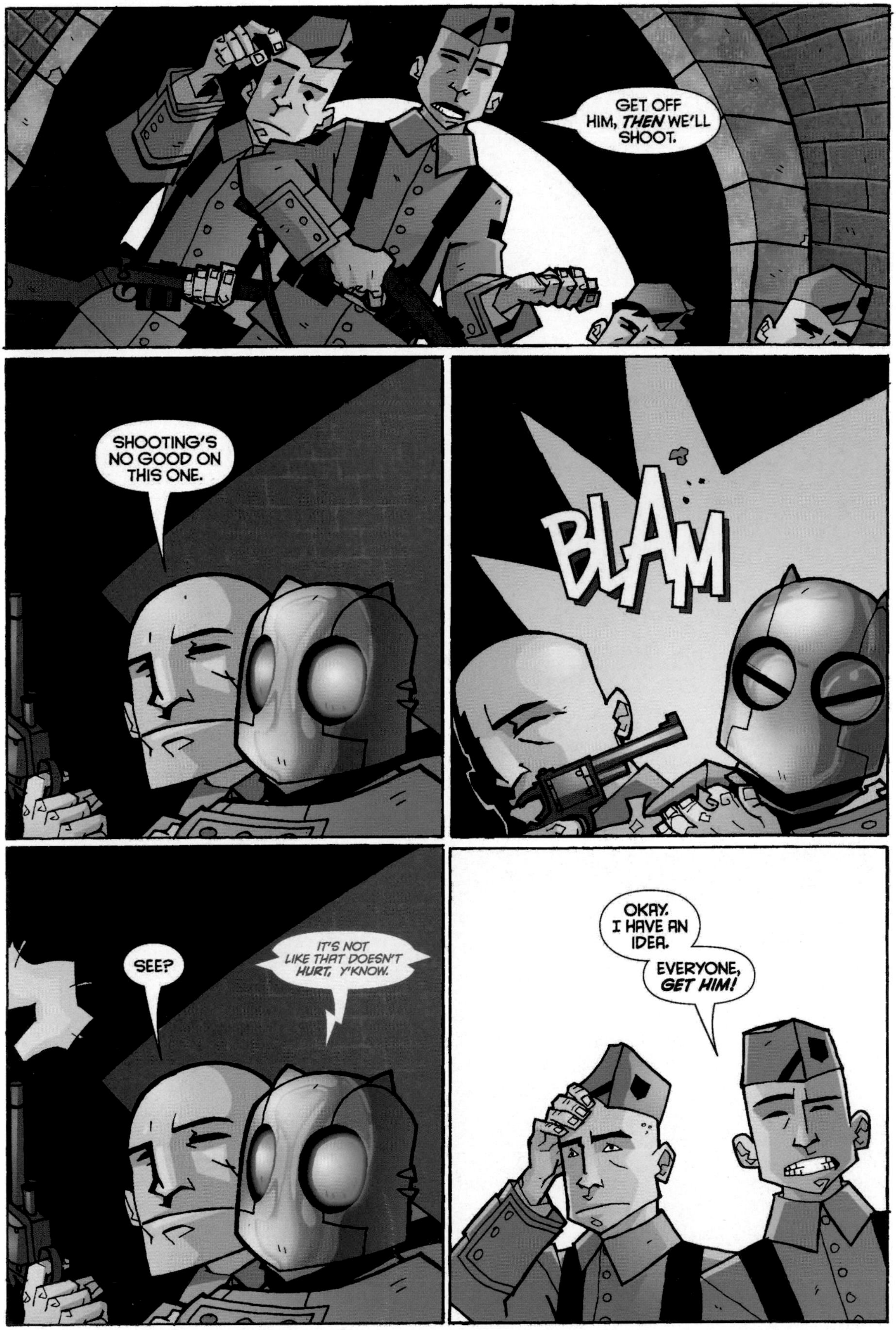
GET OFF HIM, *THEN* WE'LL SHOOT.
SHOOTING'S NO GOOD ON THIS ONE.
BLAM
SEE?
IT'S NOT LIKE THAT DOESN'T *HURT*, Y'KNOW.
OKAY. I HAVE AN IDEA.
EVERYONE, *GET HIM!*

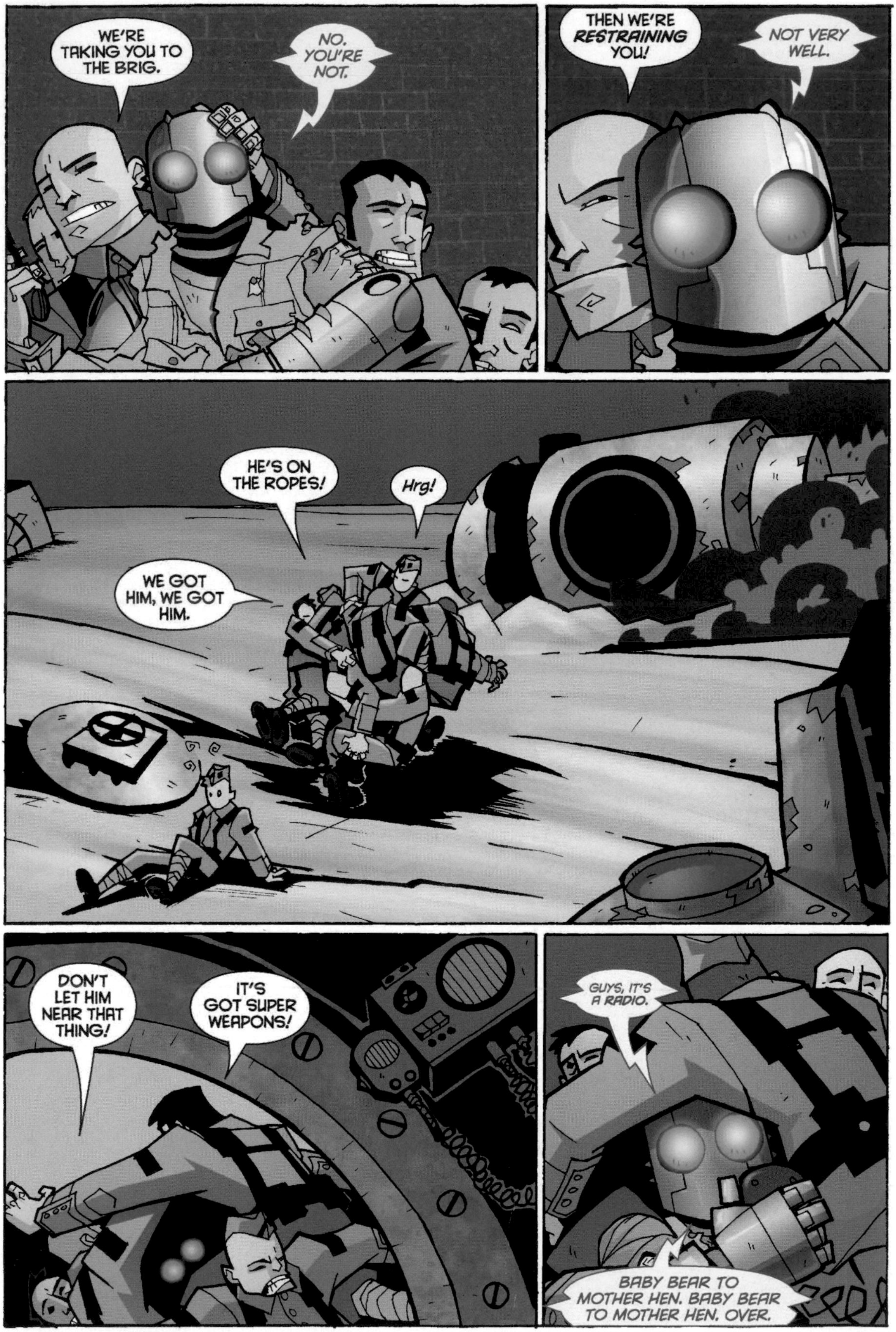
WE'RE TAKING YOU TO THE BRIG.
NO. YOU'RE NOT.
THEN WE'RE RESTRAINING YOU!
NOT VERY WELL.
HE'S ON THE ROPES!
Hrg!
WE GOT HIM, WE GOT HIM.
DON'T LET HIM NEAR THAT THING!
IT'S GOT SUPER WEAPONS!
GUYS, IT'S A RADIO.
BABY BEAR TO MOTHER HEN. BABY BEAR TO MOTHER HEN. OVER.

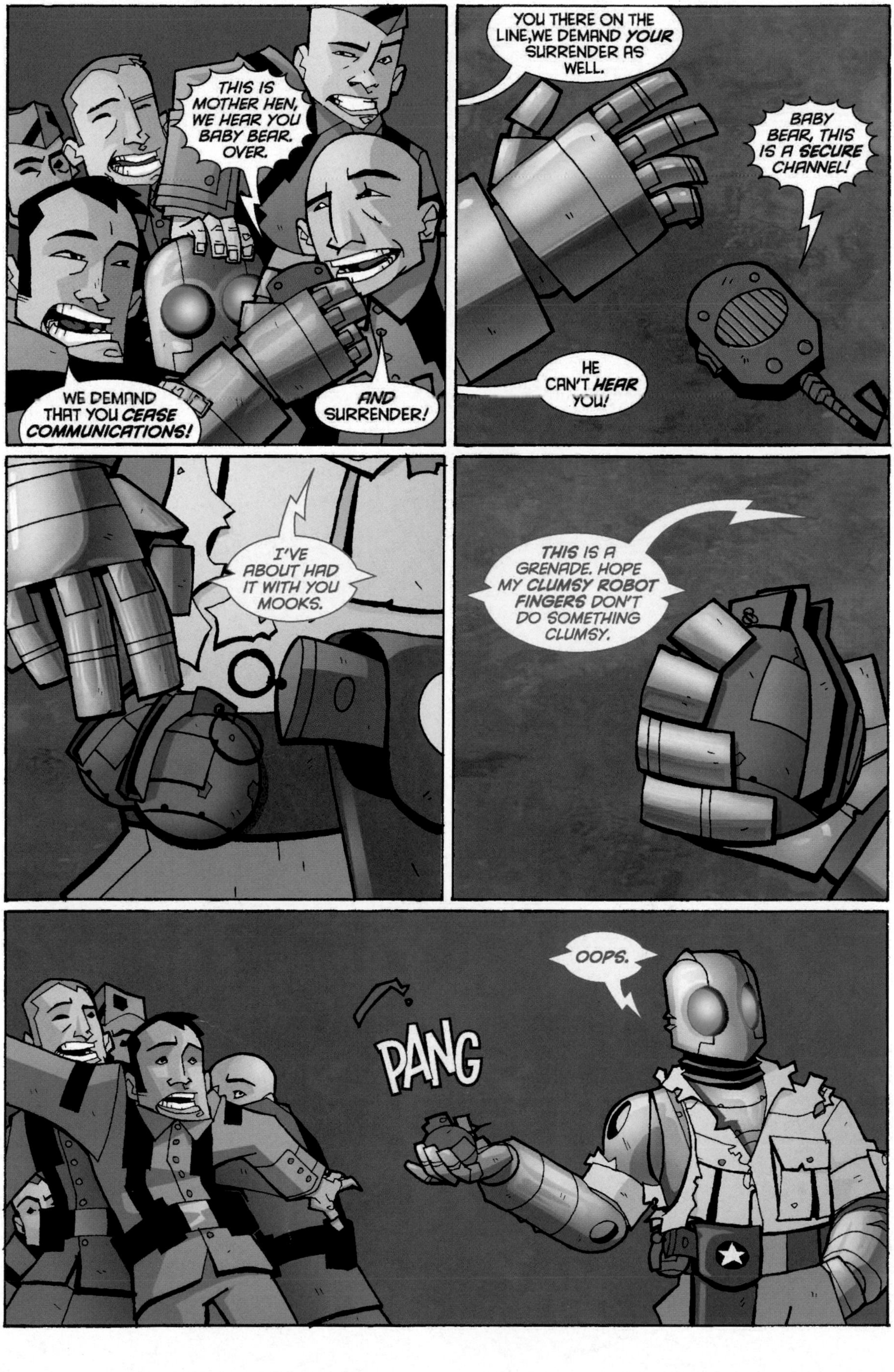
THIS IS MOTHER HEN, WE HEAR YOU BABY BEAR. OVER.
WE DEMAND THAT YOU CEASE COMMUNICATIONS!
AND SURRENDER!
YOU THERE ON THE LINE,WE DEMAND YOUR SURRENDER AS WELL.
BABY BEAR, THIS IS A SECURE CHANNEL!
HE CAN'T HEAR YOU!
I'VE ABOUT HAD IT WITH YOU MOOKS.
THIS IS A GRENADE. HOPE MY CLUMSY ROBOT FINGERS DON'T DO SOMETHING CLUMSY.
OOPS.
PANG

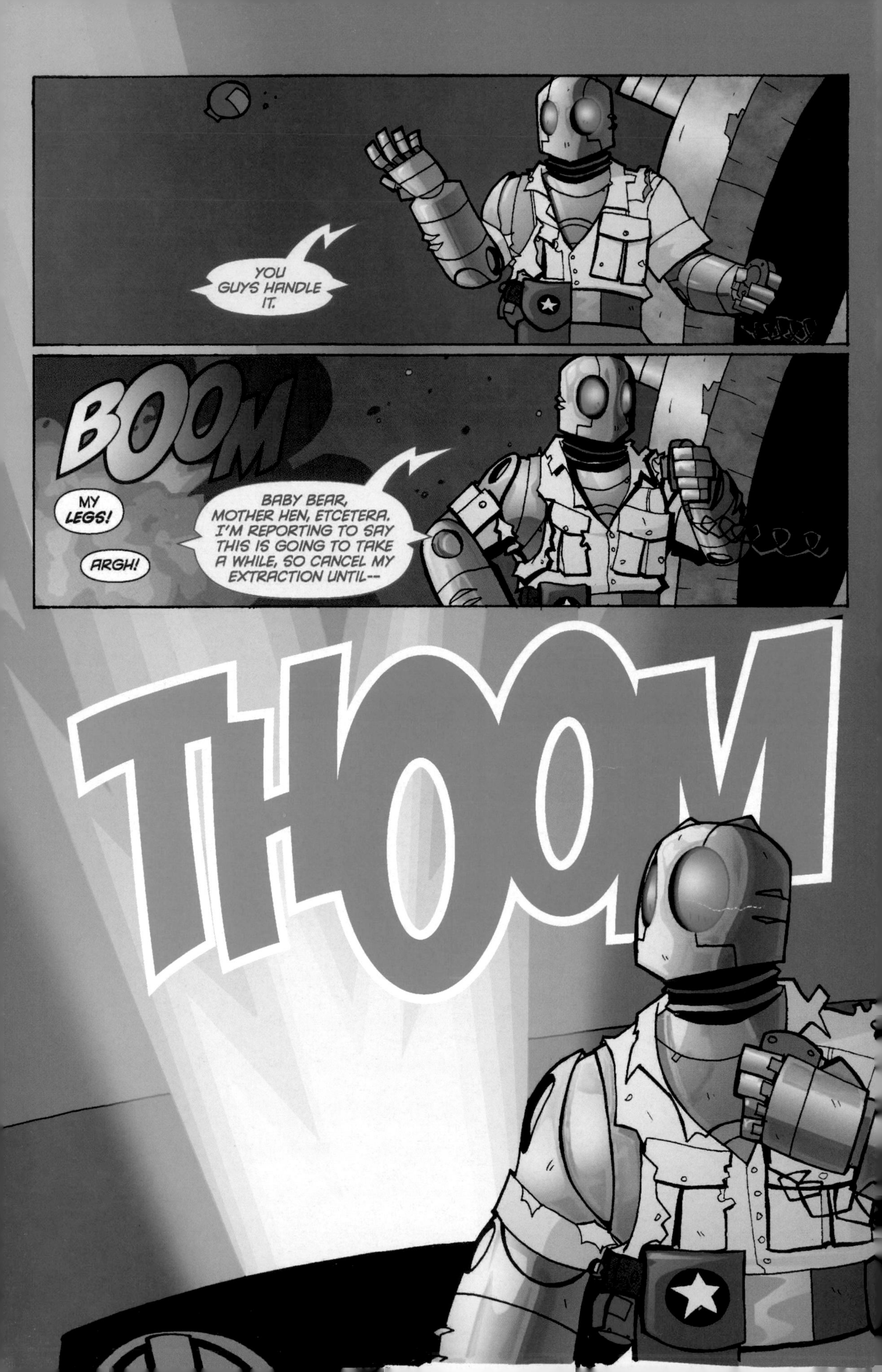
YOU GUYS HANDLE IT.
BOOM
MY LEGS!
ARGH!
BABY BEAR, MOTHER HEN, ETCETERA. I'M REPORTING TO SAY THIS IS GOING TO TAKE A WHILE, SO CANCEL MY EXTRACTION UNTIL--
THOOM

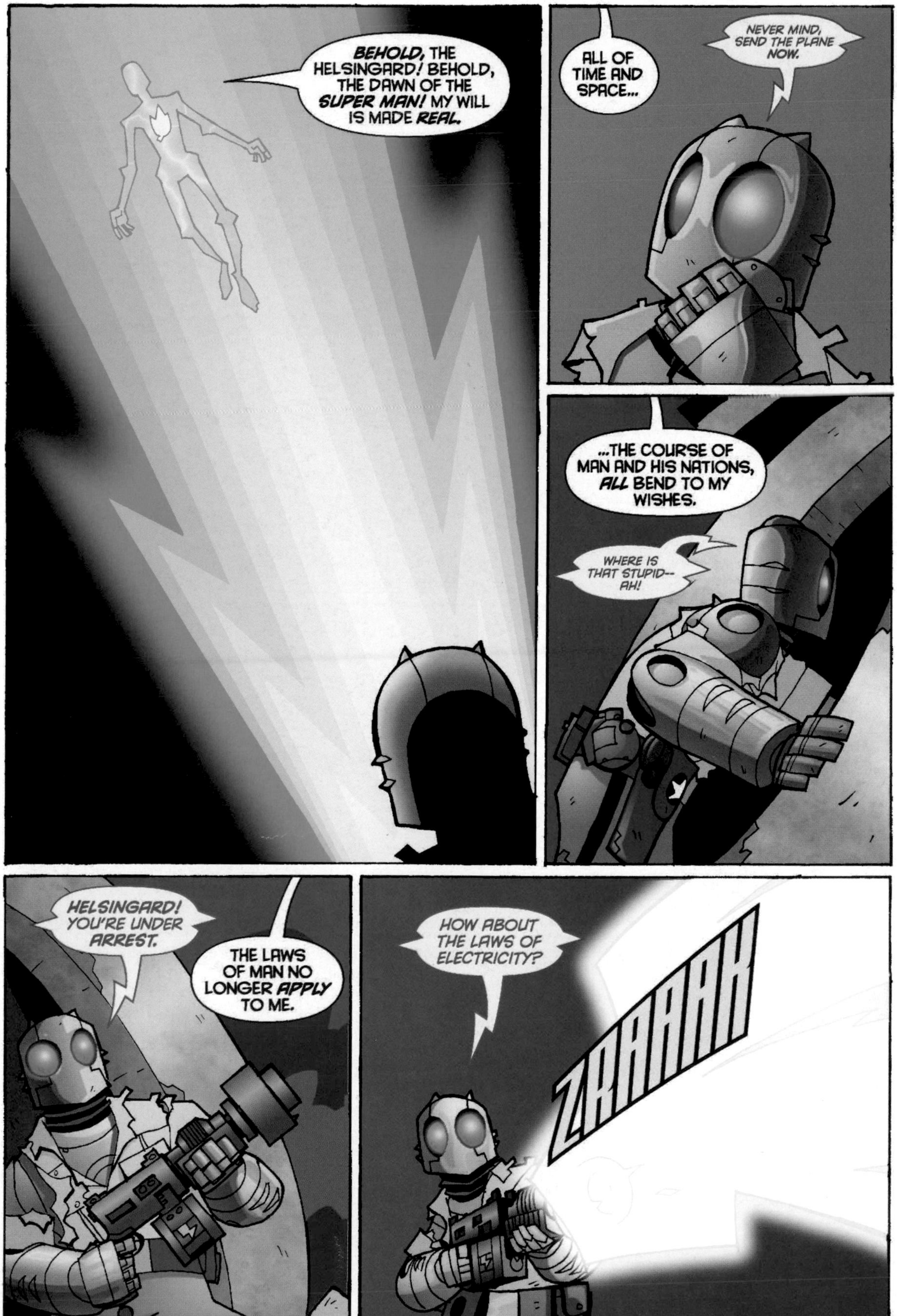
BEHOLD, THE HELSINGARD! BEHOLD, THE DAWN OF THE SUPER MAN! MY WILL IS MADE REAL.
ALL OF TIME AND SPACE...
NEVER MIND, SEND THE PLANE NOW.
...THE COURSE OF MAN AND HIS NATIONS, ALL BEND TO MY WISHES.
WHERE IS THAT STUPID-- AH!
HELSINGARD! YOU'RE UNDER ARREST.
THE LAWS OF MAN NO LONGER APPLY TO ME.
HOW ABOUT THE LAWS OF ELECTRICITY?
ZRAAAK

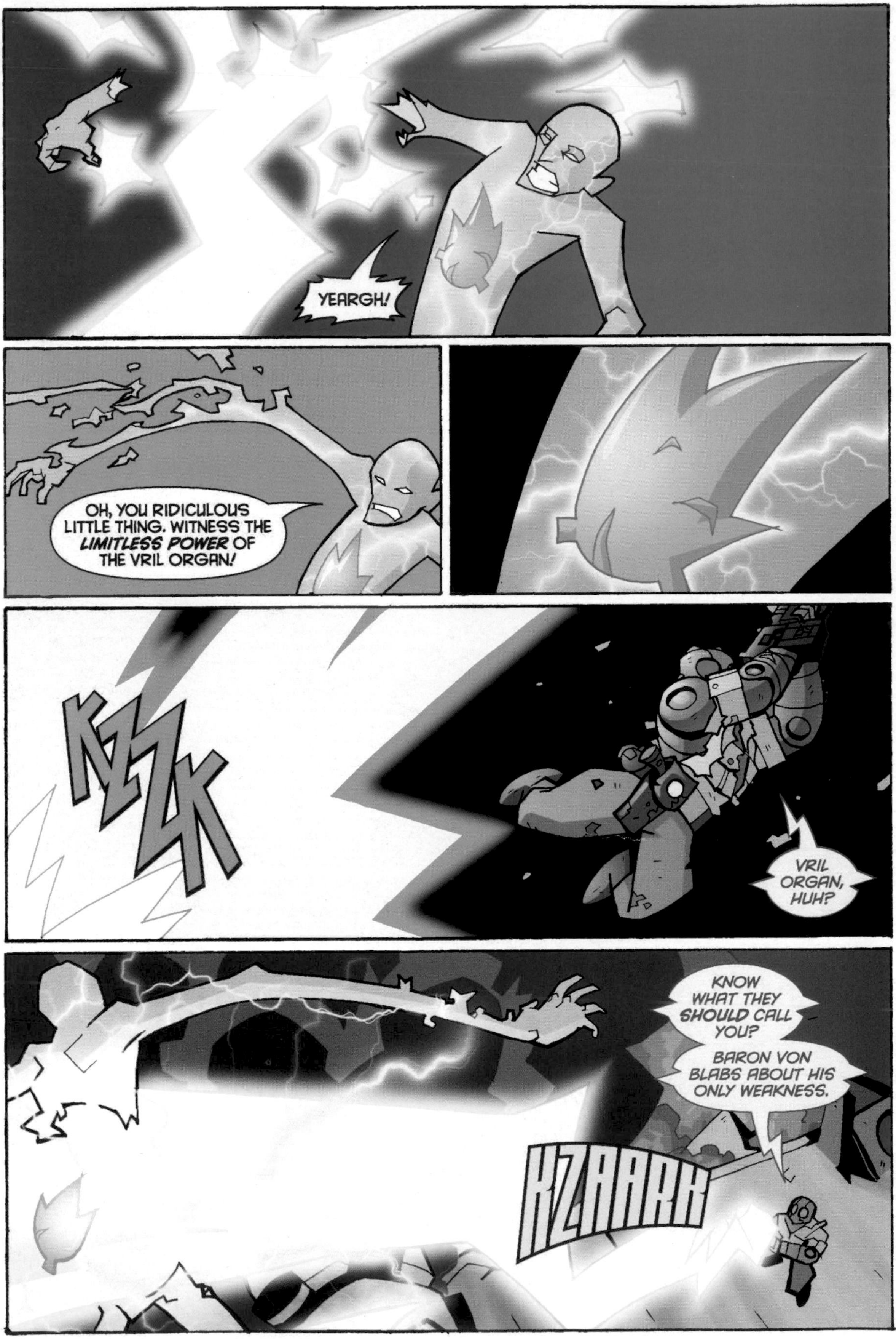
YEARGH!
OH, YOU RIDICULOUS LITTLE THING. WITNESS THE LIMITLESS POWER OF THE VRIL ORGAN!
KZZZK
VRIL ORGAN, HUH?
KNOW WHAT THEY SHOULD CALL YOU?
BARON VON BLABS ABOUT HIS ONLY WEAKNESS.
KZAARK

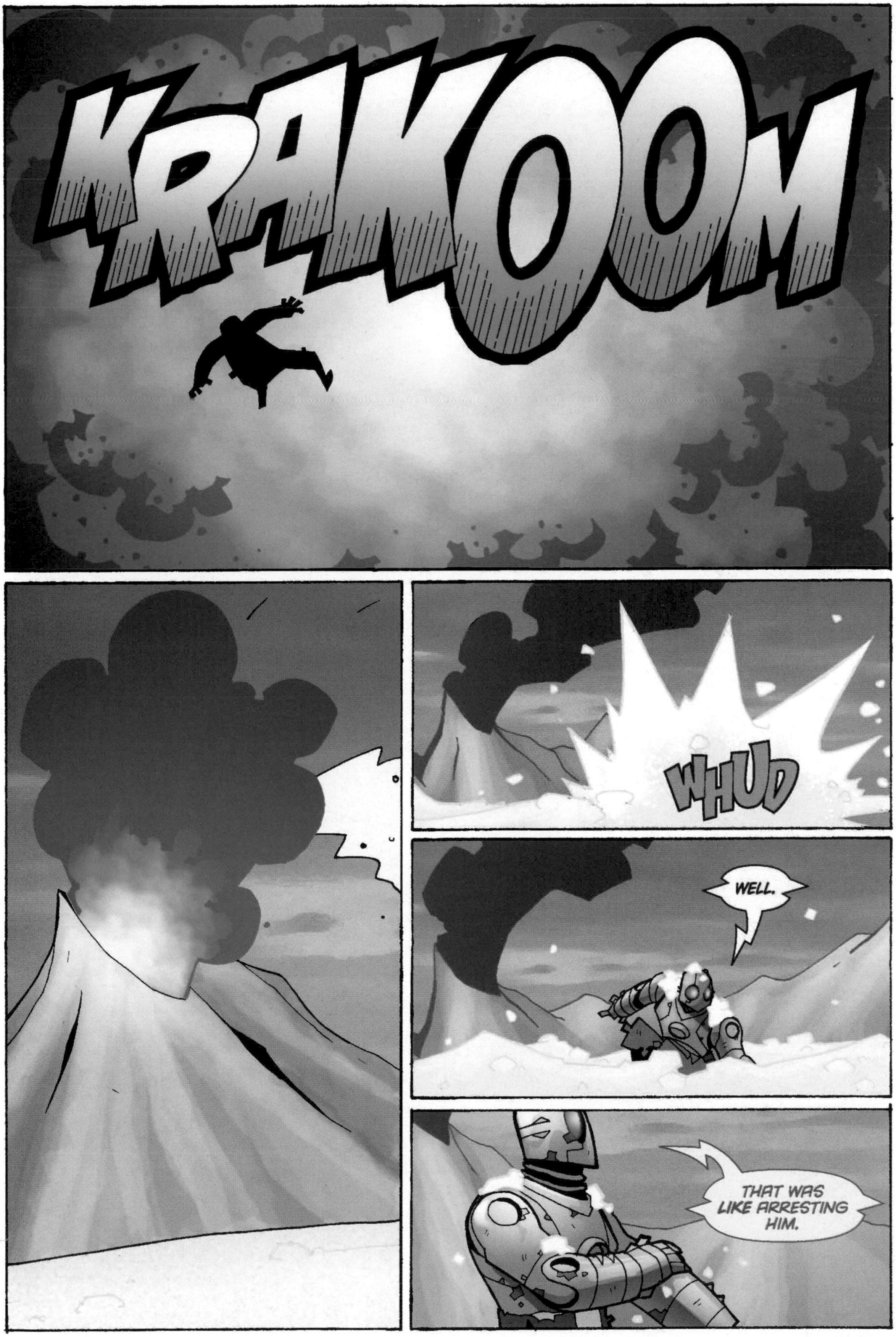
KRAKOOM
WHUD
WELL.
THAT WAS LIKE ARRESTING HIM.

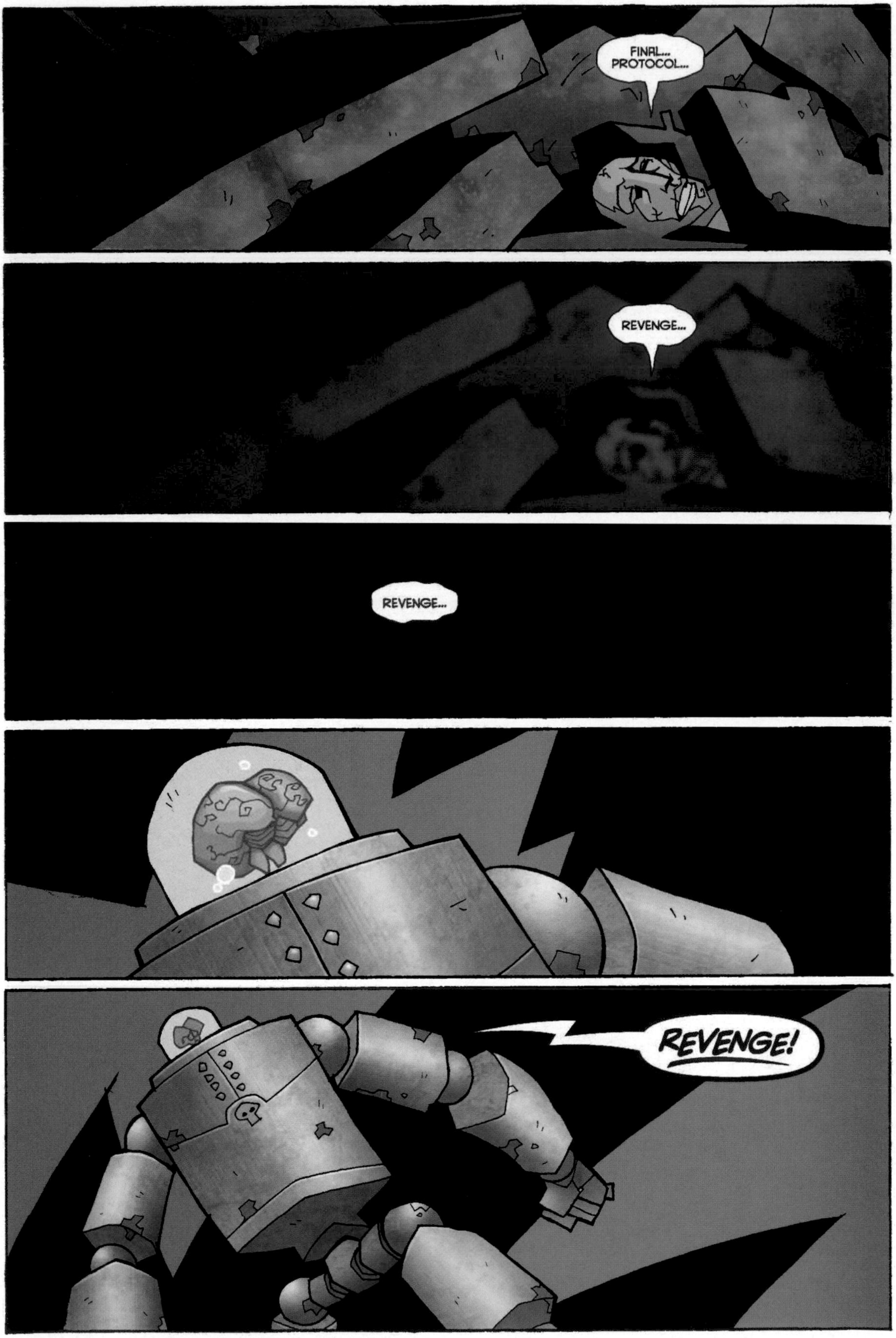
FINAL... PROTOCOL...
REVENGE...
REVENGE...
REVENGE!

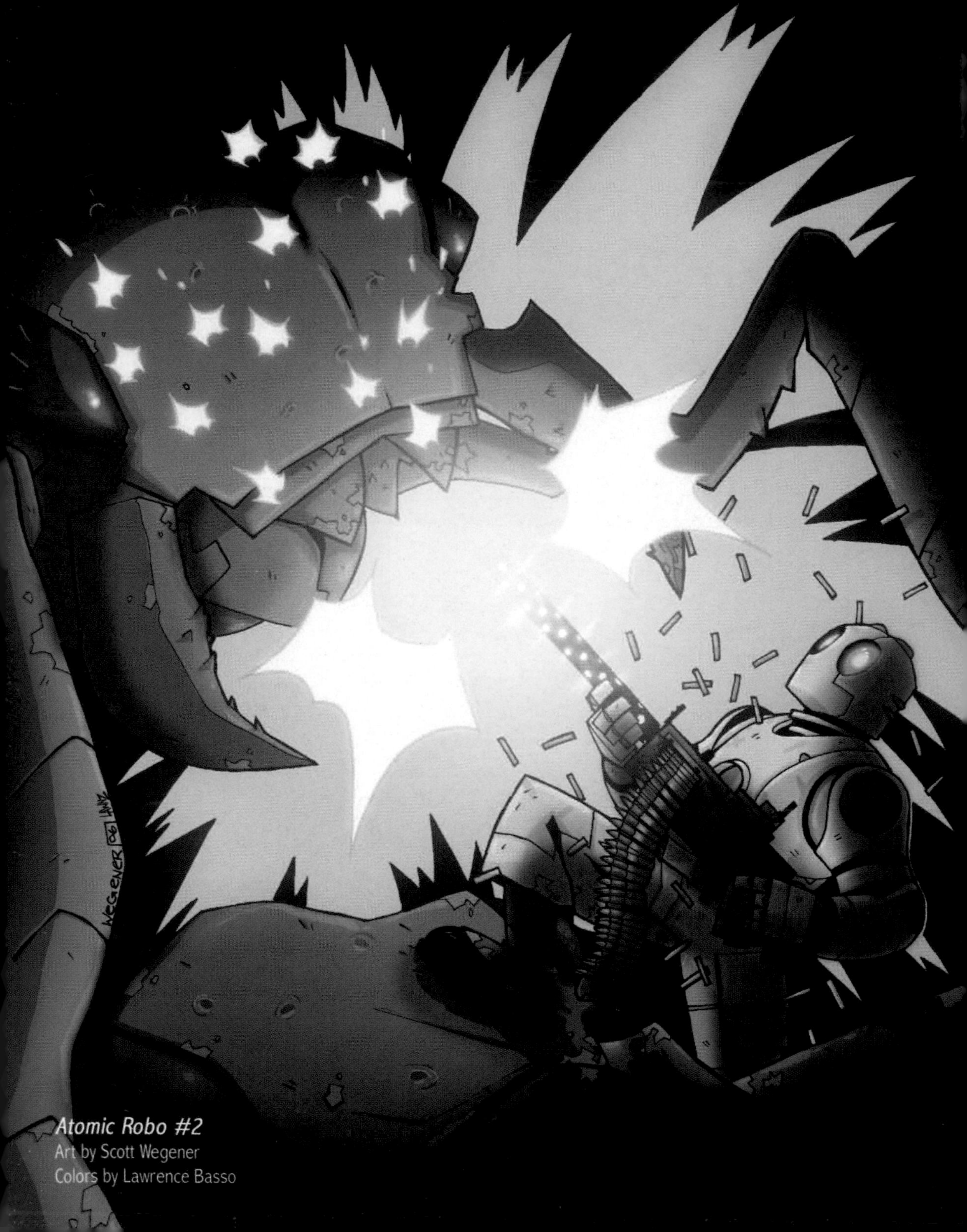

Atomic Robo #2
Art by Scott Wegener
Colors by Lawrence Basso

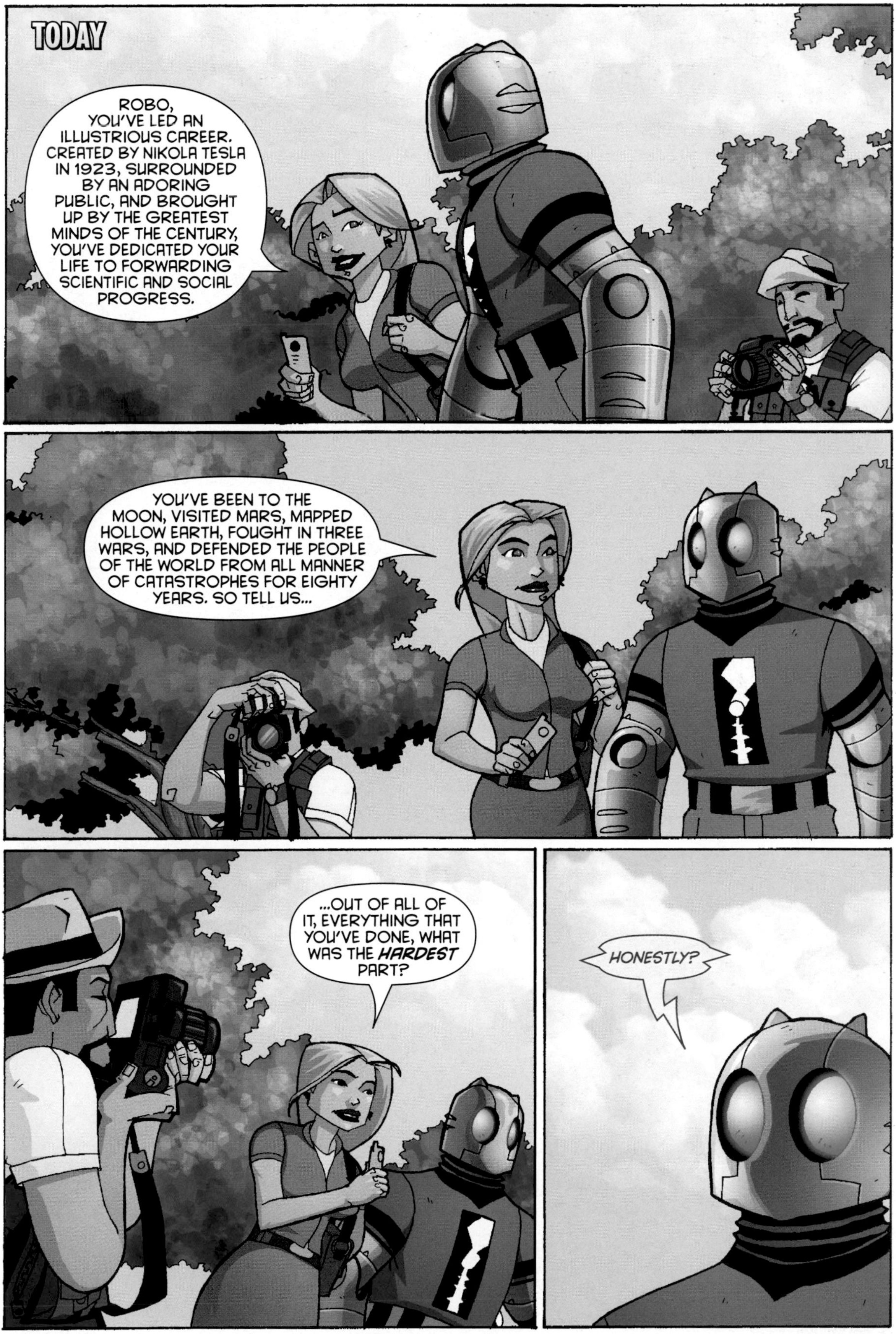
TODAY
ROBO, YOU'VE LED AN ILLUSTRIOUS CAREER. CREATED BY NIKOLA TESLA IN 1923, SURROUNDED BY AN ADORING PUBLIC, AND BROUGHT UP BY THE GREATEST MINDS OF THE CENTURY, YOU'VE DEDICATED YOUR LIFE TO FORWARDING SCIENTIFIC AND SOCIAL PROGRESS.
YOU'VE BEEN TO THE MOON, VISITED MARS, MAPPED HOLLOW EARTH, FOUGHT IN THREE WARS, AND DEFENDED THE PEOPLE OF THE WORLD FROM ALL MANNER OF CATASTROPHES FOR EIGHTY YEARS. SO TELL US...
...OUT OF ALL OF IT, EVERYTHING THAT YOU'VE DONE, WHAT WAS THE *HARDEST* PART?
HONESTLY?

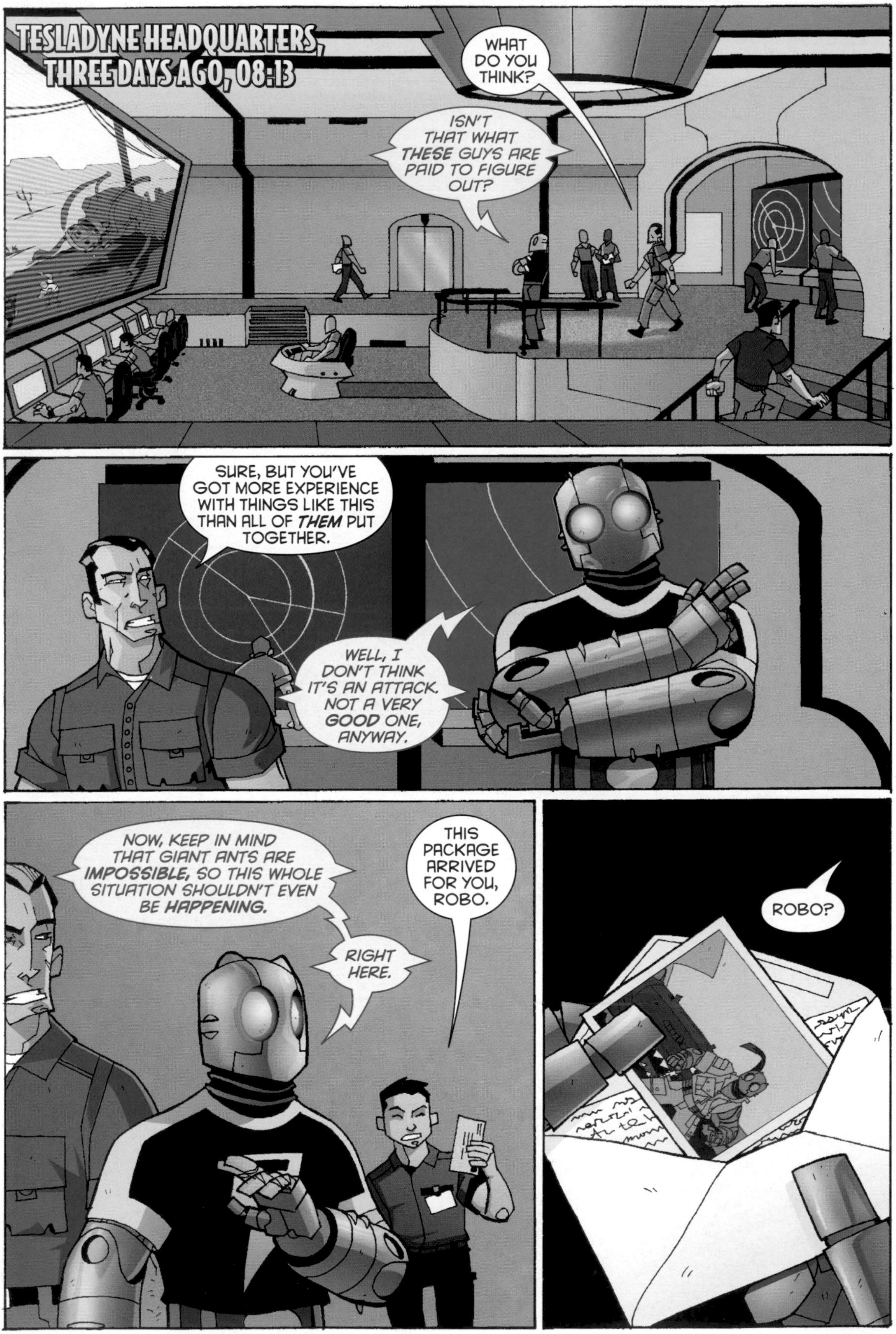
TESLADYNE HEADQUARTERS, THREE DAYS AGO, 08:13
WHAT DO YOU THINK?
ISN'T THAT WHAT *THESE* GUYS ARE PAID TO FIGURE OUT?
SURE, BUT YOU'VE GOT MORE EXPERIENCE WITH THINGS LIKE THIS THAN ALL OF *THEM* PUT TOGETHER.
WELL, I DON'T THINK IT'S AN ATTACK. NOT A VERY *GOOD* ONE, ANYWAY.
NOW, KEEP IN MIND THAT GIANT ANTS ARE *IMPOSSIBLE*, SO THIS WHOLE SITUATION SHOULDN'T EVEN BE *HAPPENING*.
RIGHT HERE.
THIS PACKAGE ARRIVED FOR YOU, ROBO.
ROBO?

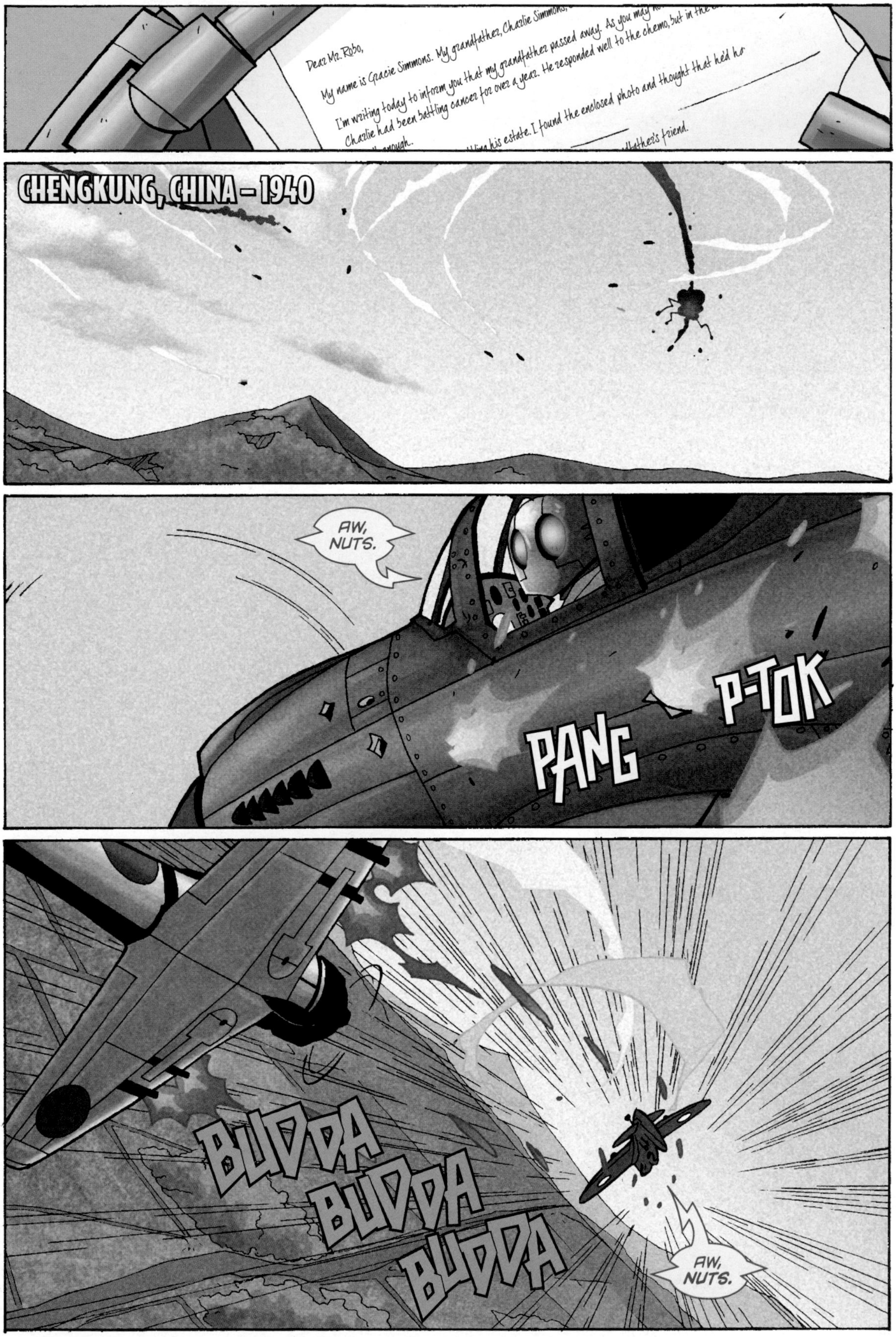
Dear Mr. Robo,
My name is Gracie Simmons. My grandfather, Charlie Simmons,
I'm writing today to inform you that my grandfather passed away. As you may
Charlie had been battling cancer for over a year. He responded well to the chemo, but in the
enough.
his estate. I found the enclosed photo and thought that he'd
father's friend.
CHENGKUNG, CHINA – 1940
AW, NUTS.
PANG
P-TOK
BUDDA
BUDDA
BUDDA
AW, NUTS.

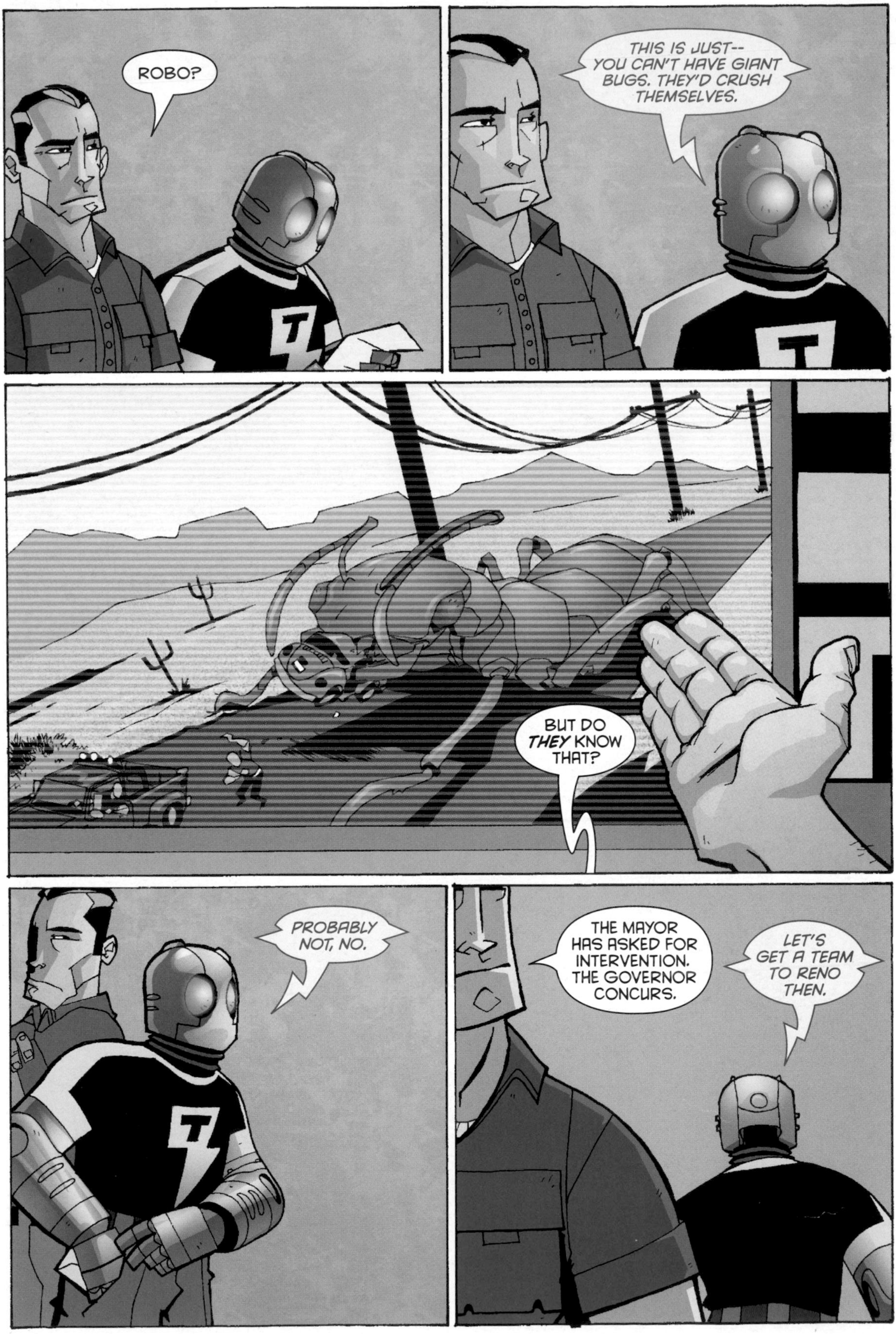
ROBO?
THIS IS JUST-- YOU CAN'T HAVE GIANT BUGS. THEY'D CRUSH THEMSELVES.
BUT DO *THEY* KNOW THAT?
PROBABLY NOT, NO.
THE MAYOR HAS ASKED FOR INTERVENTION. THE GOVERNOR CONCURS.
LET'S GET A TEAM TO RENO THEN.

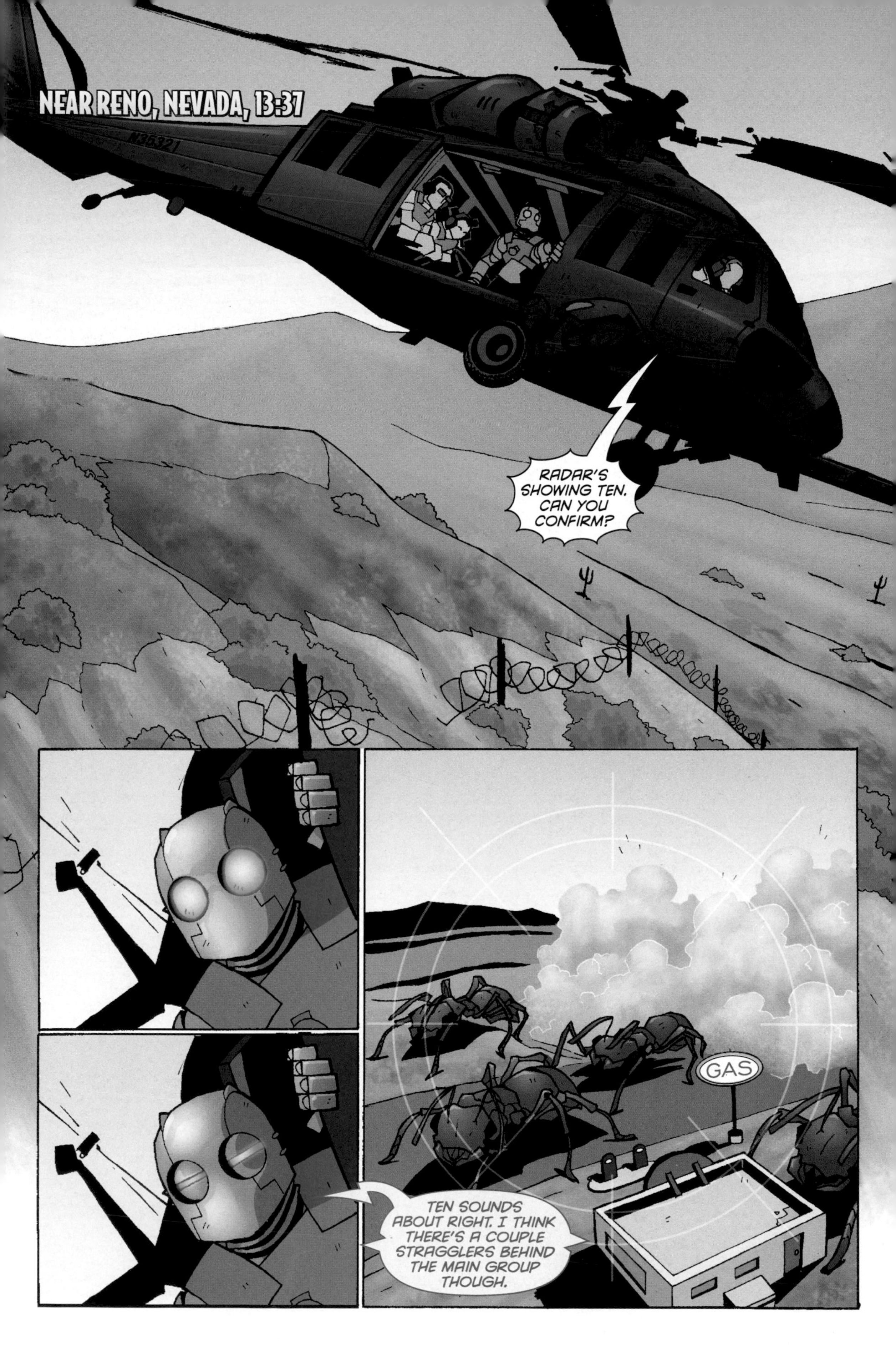
NEAR RENO, NEVADA, 13:37
N35321
RADAR'S SHOWING TEN. CAN YOU CONFIRM?
GAS
TEN SOUNDS ABOUT RIGHT. I THINK THERE'S A COUPLE STRAGGLERS BEHIND THE MAIN GROUP THOUGH.

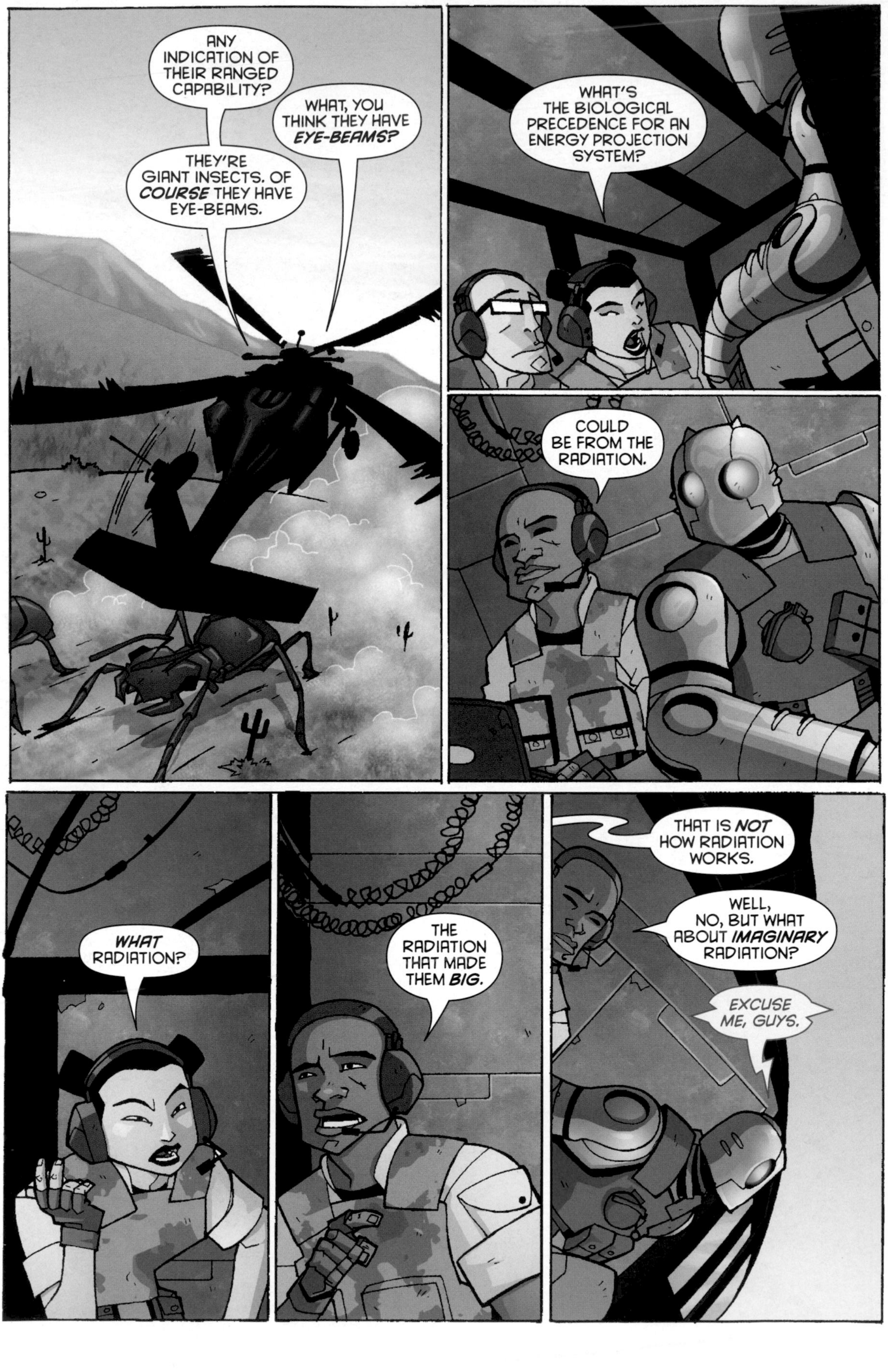
ANY INDICATION OF THEIR RANGED CAPABILITY?
THEY'RE GIANT INSECTS. OF *COURSE* THEY HAVE EYE-BEAMS.
WHAT, YOU THINK THEY HAVE *EYE-BEAMS?*
WHAT'S THE BIOLOGICAL PRECEDENCE FOR AN ENERGY PROJECTION SYSTEM?
COULD BE FROM THE RADIATION.
WHAT RADIATION?
THE RADIATION THAT MADE THEM *BIG*.
THAT IS *NOT* HOW RADIATION WORKS.
WELL, NO, BUT WHAT ABOUT *IMAGINARY* RADIATION?
EXCUSE ME, GUYS.

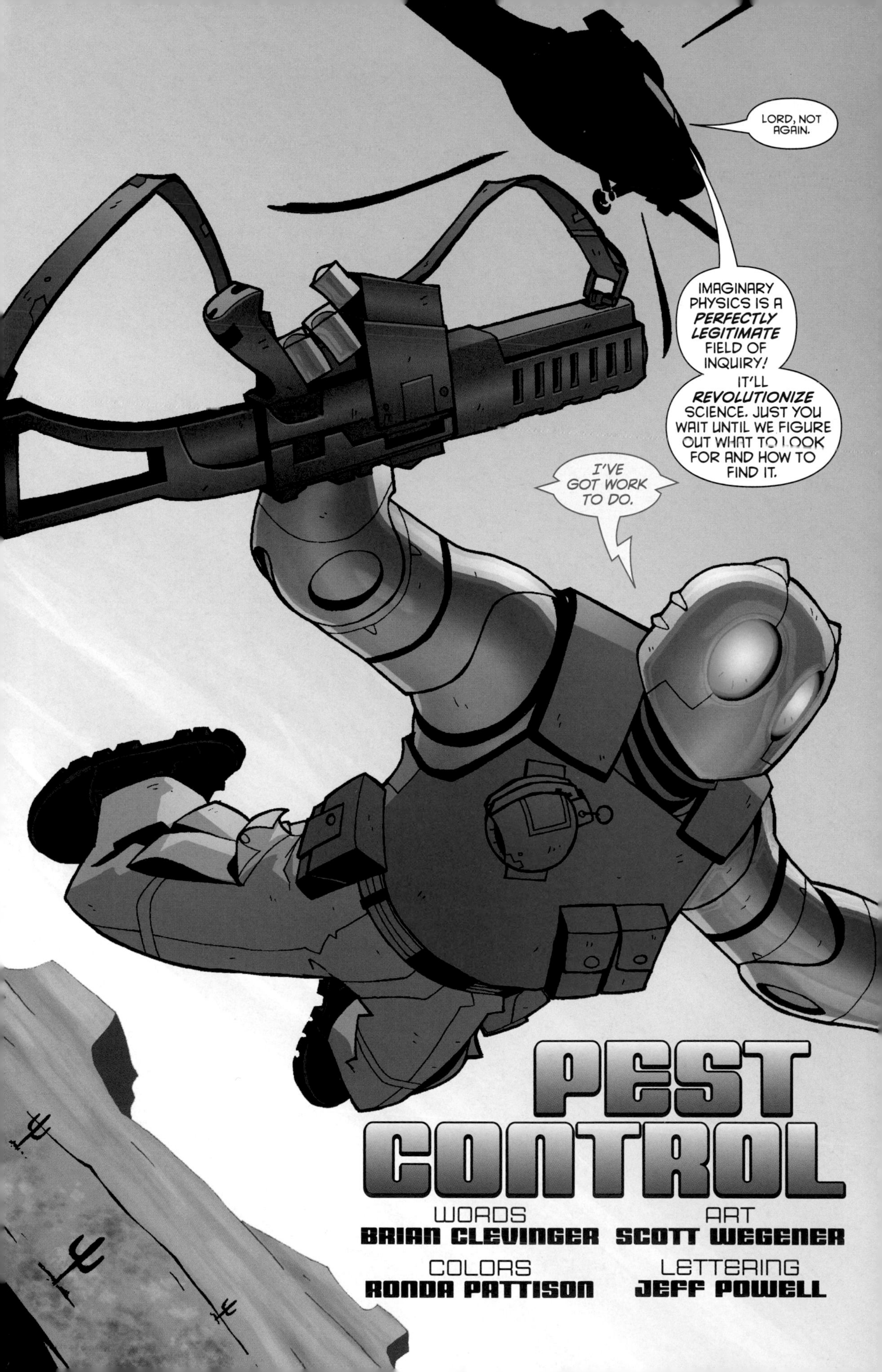

LORD, NOT AGAIN.
IMAGINARY PHYSICS IS A *PERFECTLY LEGITIMATE* FIELD OF INQUIRY!
IT'LL *REVOLUTIONIZE* SCIENCE. JUST YOU WAIT UNTIL WE FIGURE OUT WHAT TO LOOK FOR AND HOW TO FIND IT.
I'VE GOT WORK TO DO.
PEST CONTROL
WORDS
BRIAN CLEVINGER
ART
SCOTT WEGENER
COLORS
RONDA PATTISON
LETTERING
JEFF POWELL

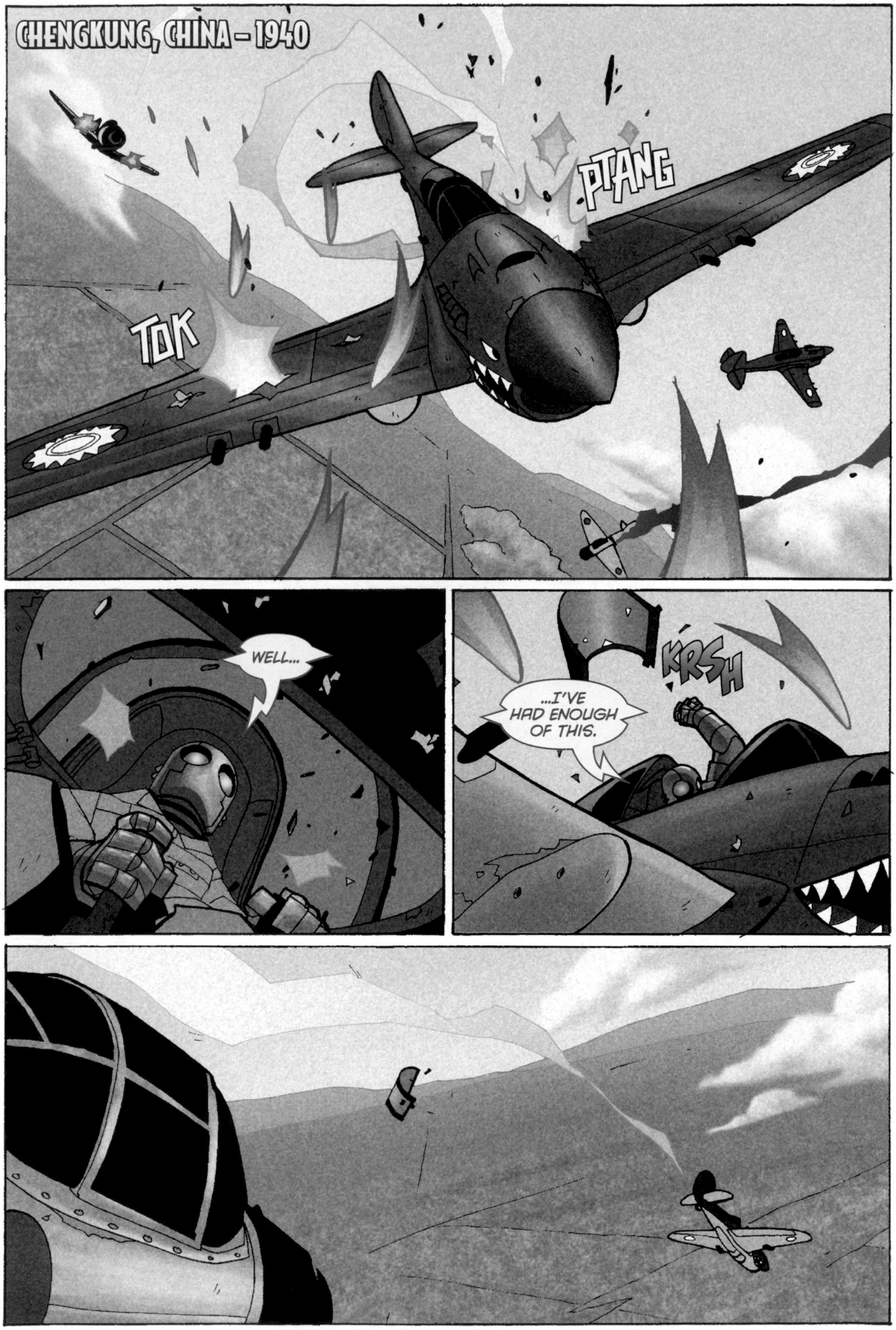
CHENGKUNG, CHINA – 1940
PTANG
TOK
WELL...
KRSH
...I'VE HAD ENOUGH OF THIS.

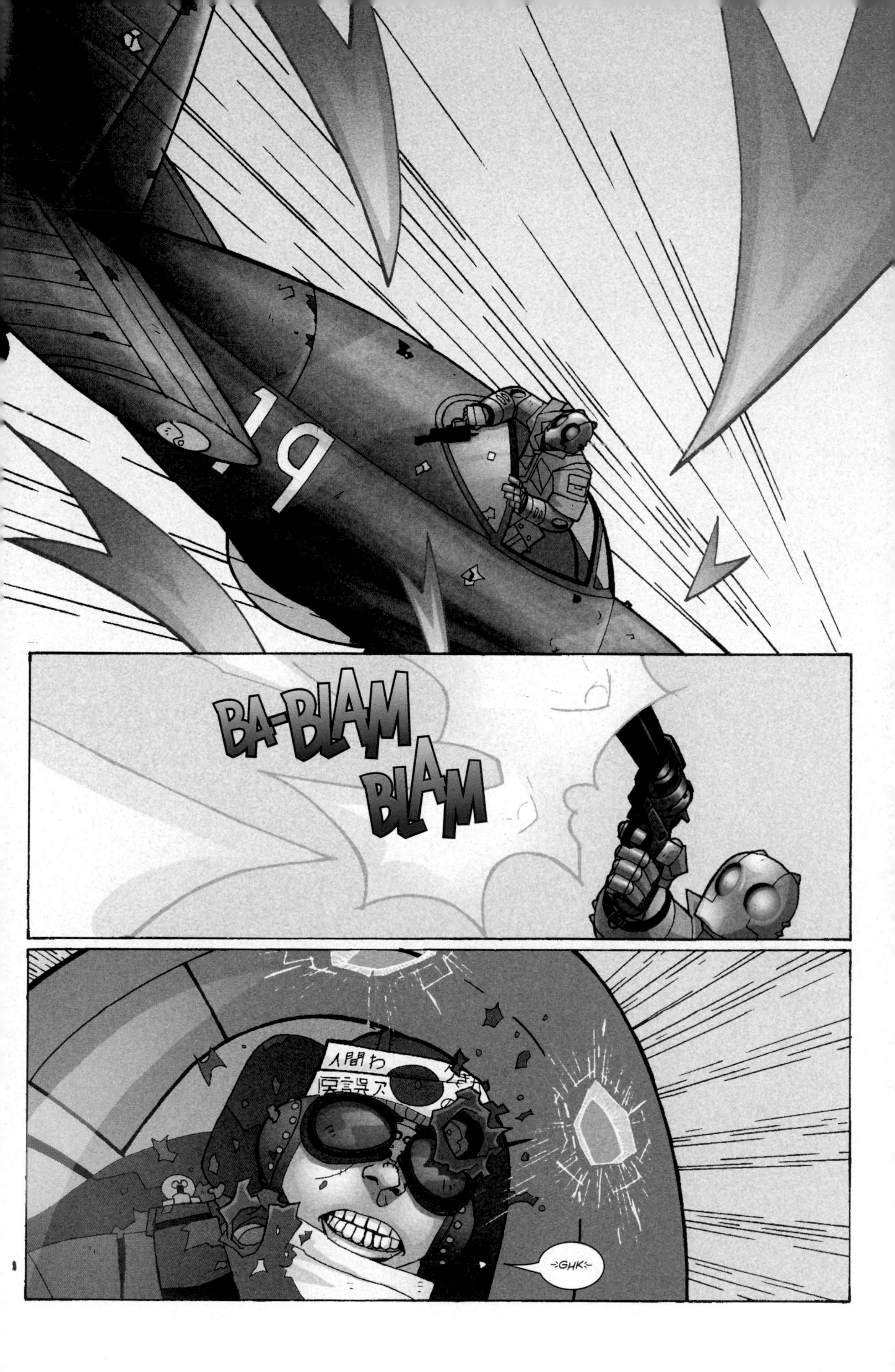
19
BA-BLAM
BLAM
GHK

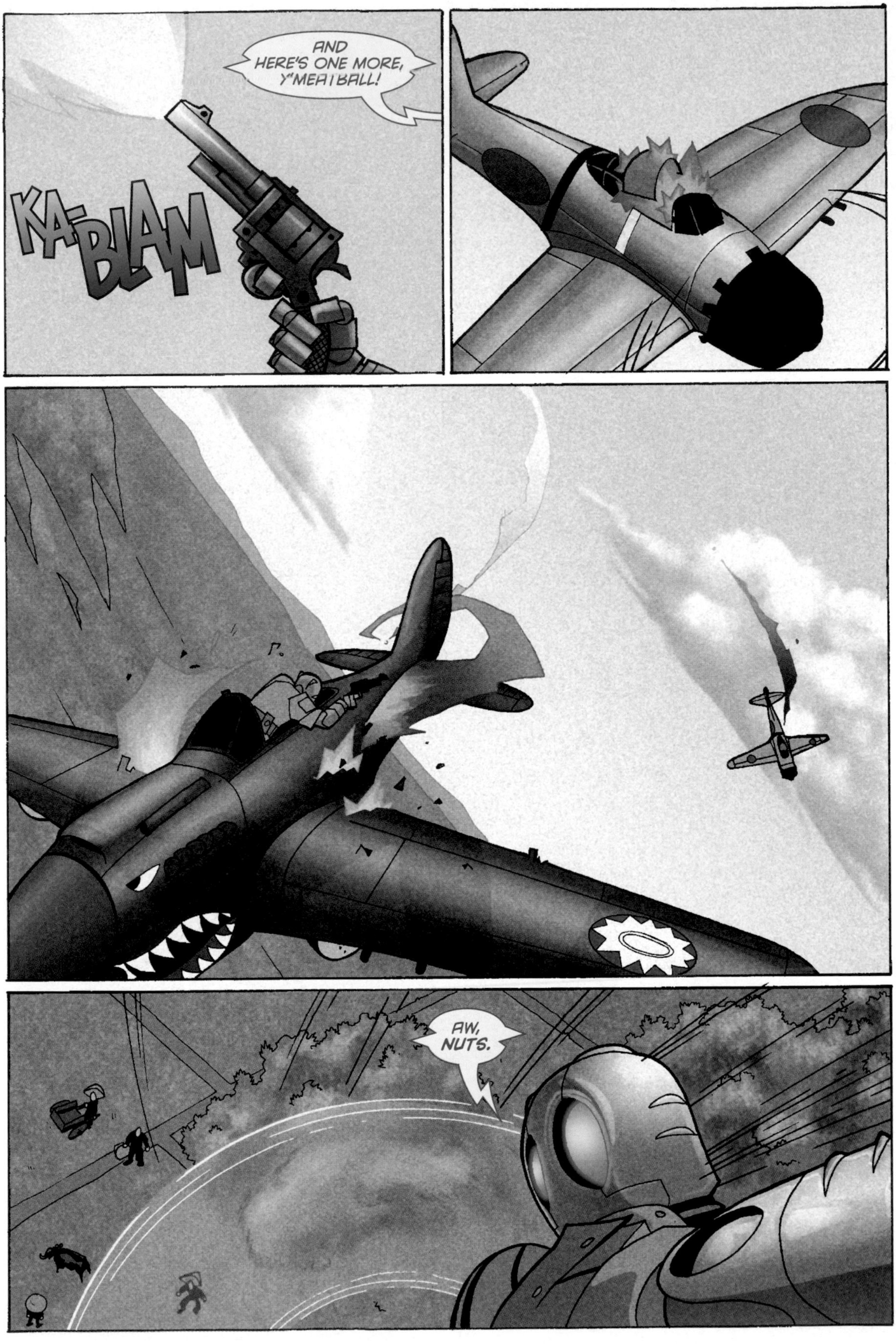
AND HERE'S ONE MORE, Y'MEATBALL!
KA-BLAM
AW, NUTS.

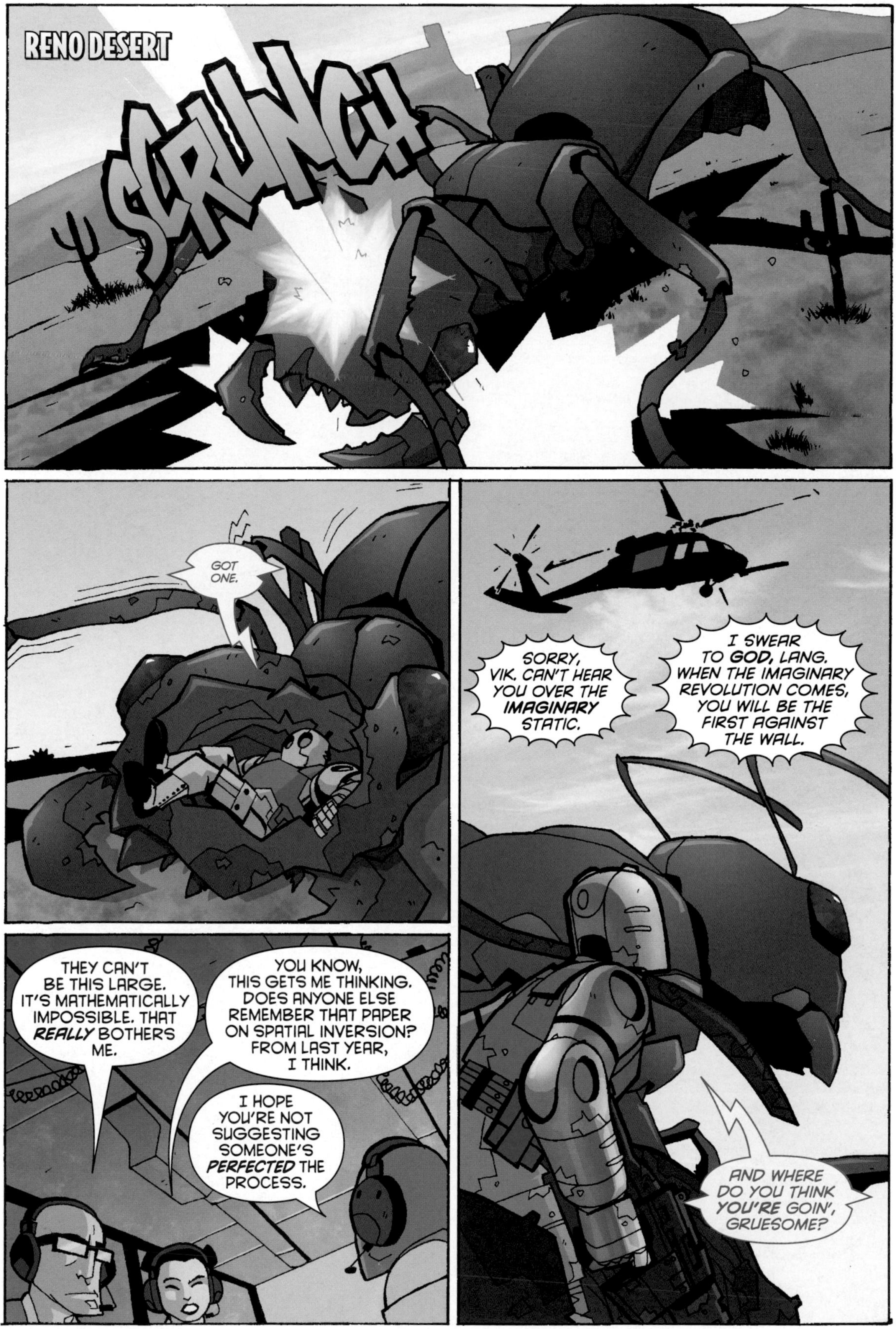
RENO DESERT
SCRUNCH
GOT ONE.
SORRY, VIK. CAN'T HEAR YOU OVER THE *IMAGINARY* STATIC.
I SWEAR TO **GOD,** LANG. WHEN THE IMAGINARY REVOLUTION COMES, YOU WILL BE THE FIRST AGAINST THE WALL.
THEY CAN'T BE THIS LARGE. IT'S MATHEMATICALLY IMPOSSIBLE. THAT *REALLY* BOTHERS ME.
YOU KNOW, THIS GETS ME THINKING. DOES ANYONE ELSE REMEMBER THAT PAPER ON SPATIAL INVERSION? FROM LAST YEAR, I THINK.
I HOPE YOU'RE NOT SUGGESTING SOMEONE'S *PERFECTED* THE PROCESS.
AND WHERE DO YOU THINK *YOU'RE* GOIN', GRUESOME?

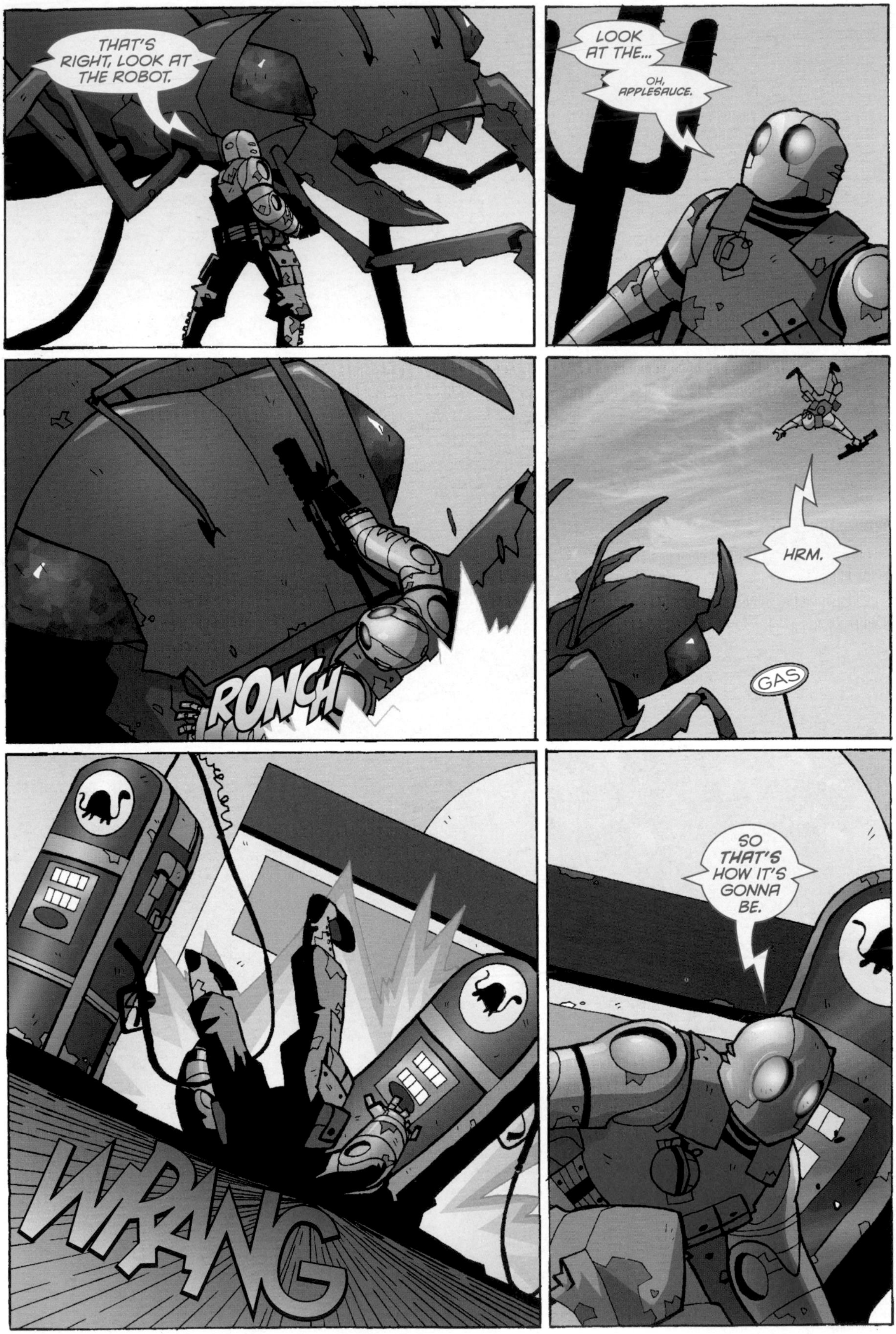
THAT'S RIGHT, LOOK AT THE ROBOT.
LOOK AT THE...
OH, APPLESAUCE.
RONCH
HRM.
GAS
WRANG
SO THAT'S HOW IT'S GONNA BE.

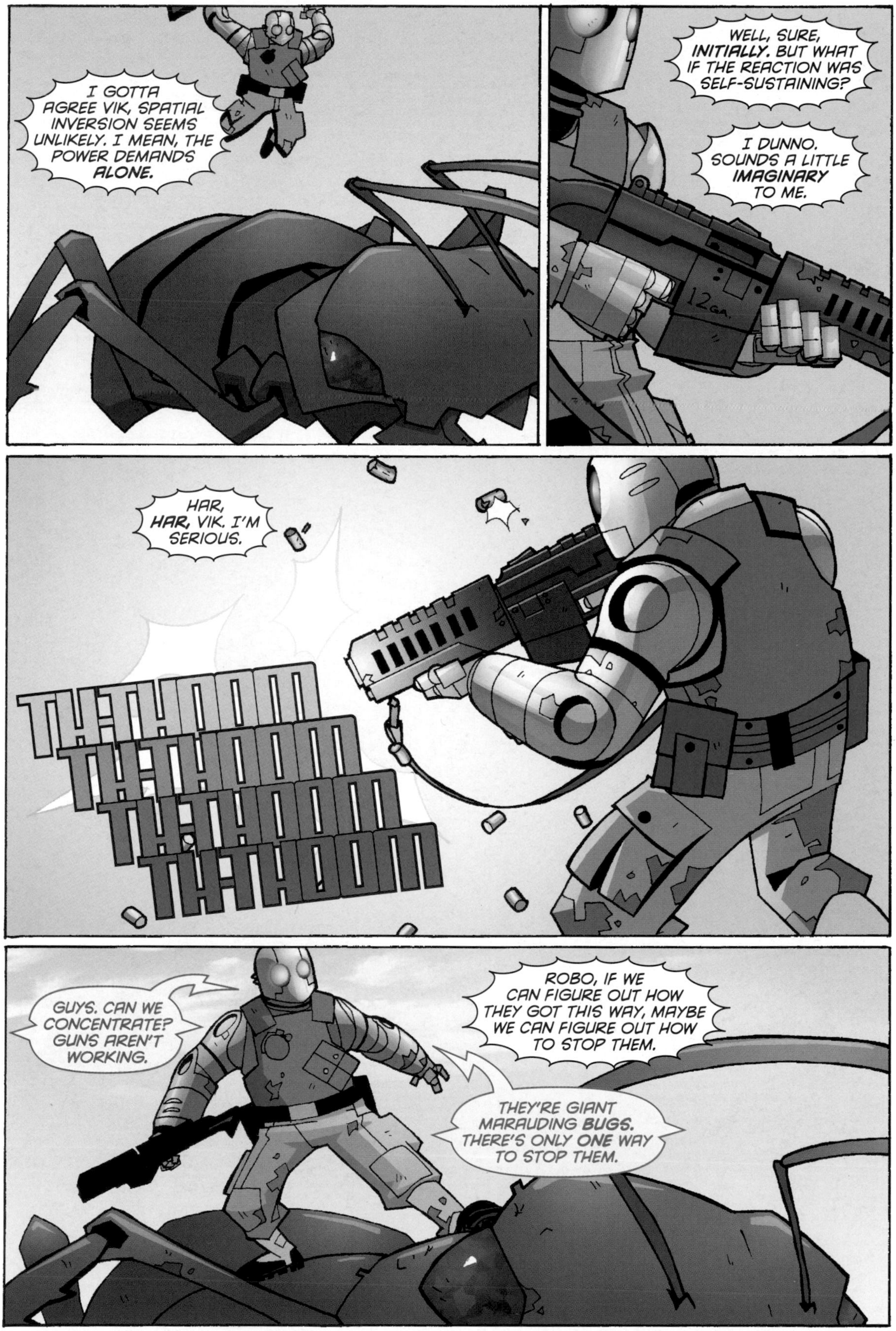
I GOTTA AGREE VIK, SPATIAL INVERSION SEEMS UNLIKELY. I MEAN, THE POWER DEMANDS ALONE.
WELL, SURE, INITIALLY. BUT WHAT IF THE REACTION WAS SELF-SUSTAINING?
I DUNNO. SOUNDS A LITTLE IMAGINARY TO ME.
12GA.
HAR, HAR, VIK. I'M SERIOUS.
TH-THOOM
TH-THOOM
TH-THOOM
TH-THOOM
GUYS. CAN WE CONCENTRATE? GUNS AREN'T WORKING.
ROBO, IF WE CAN FIGURE OUT HOW THEY GOT THIS WAY, MAYBE WE CAN FIGURE OUT HOW TO STOP THEM.
THEY'RE GIANT MARAUDING BUGS. THERE'S ONLY ONE WAY TO STOP THEM.

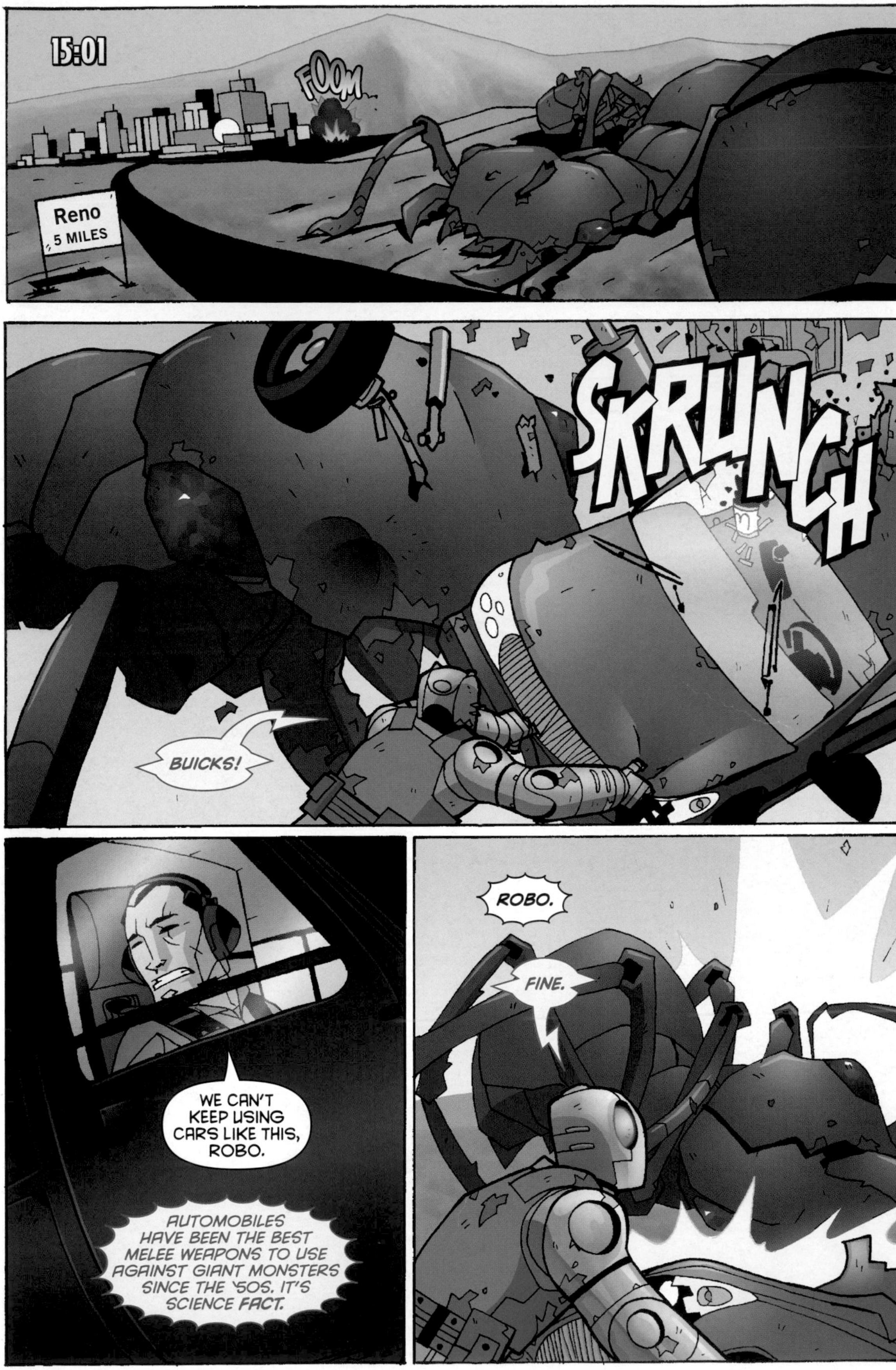
15:01
Reno
5 MILES
FOOM
SKRUNCH
BUICKS!
WE CAN'T KEEP USING CARS LIKE THIS, ROBO.
AUTOMOBILES HAVE BEEN THE BEST MELEE WEAPONS TO USE AGAINST GIANT MONSTERS SINCE THE '50S. IT'S SCIENCE FACT.
ROBO.
FINE.

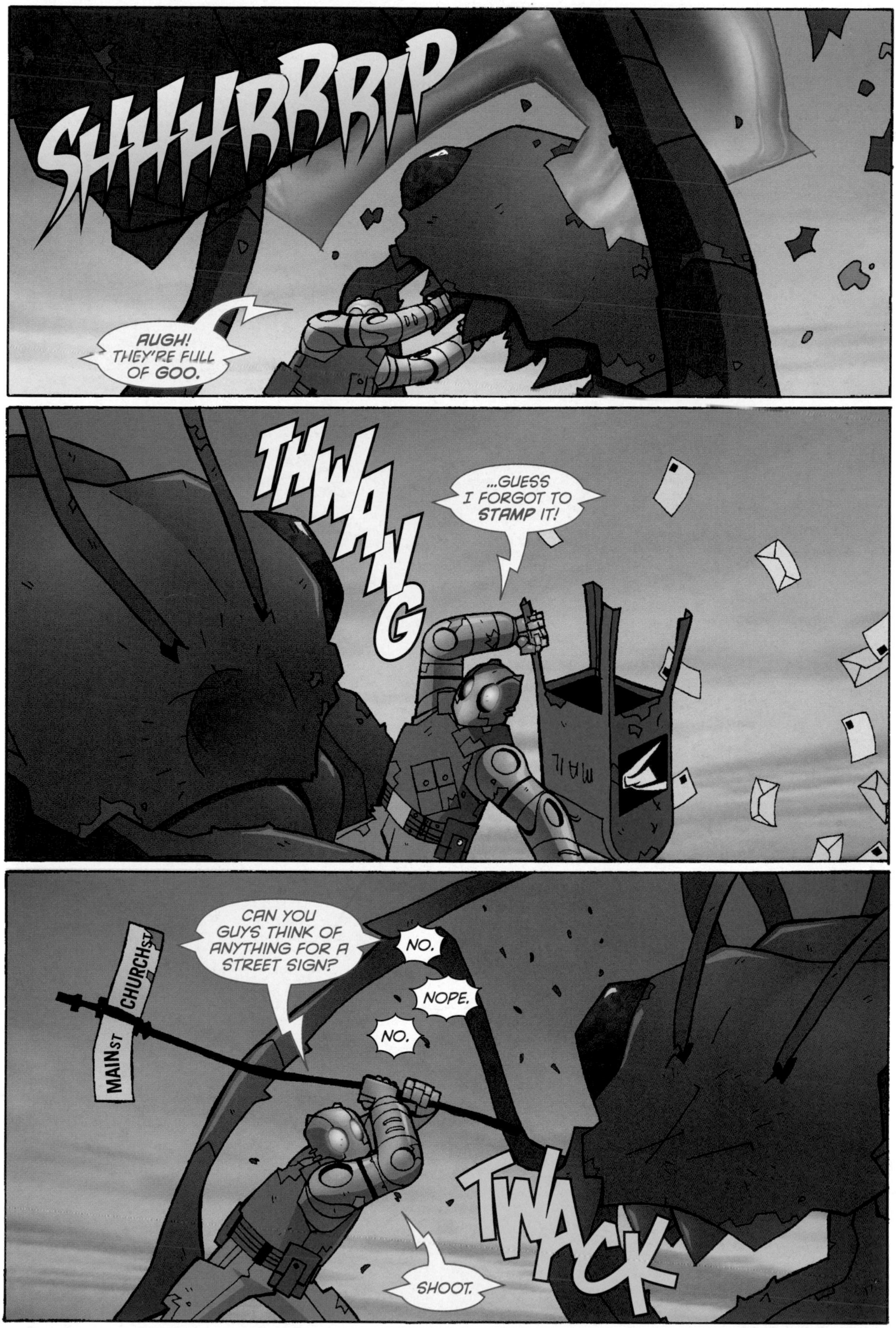
SHHHRRRIP
AUGH! THEY'RE FULL OF GOO.
THWANG
...GUESS I FORGOT TO STAMP IT!
MAIL
CAN YOU GUYS THINK OF ANYTHING FOR A STREET SIGN?
NO.
NOPE.
NO.
CHURCH ST
MAIN ST
TWACK
SHOOT.

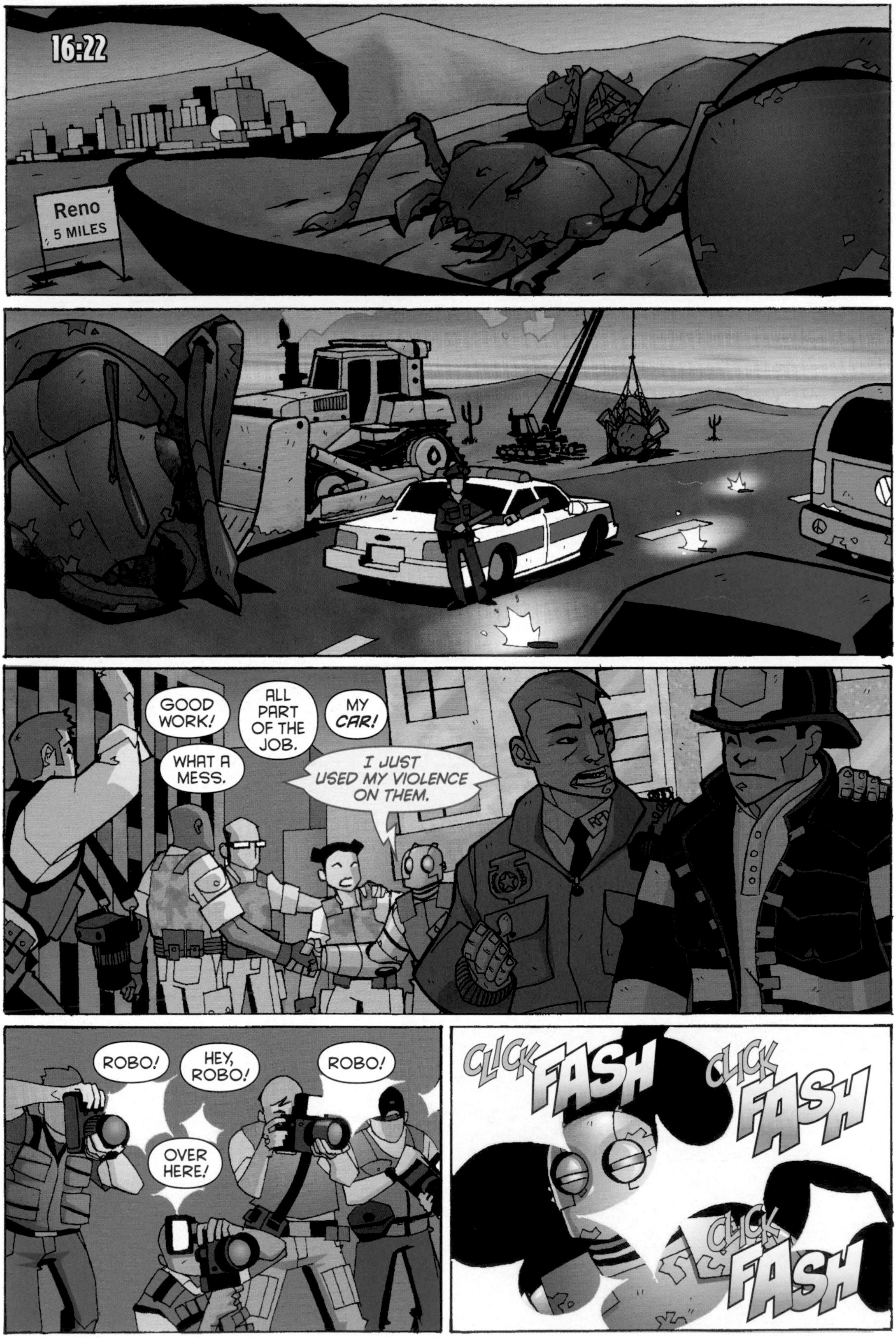
16:22
Reno
5 MILES
GOOD WORK!
ALL PART OF THE JOB.
MY CAR!
WHAT A MESS.
I JUST USED MY VIOLENCE ON THEM.
ROBO!
HEY, ROBO!
ROBO!
OVER HERE!
CLICK
FASH
CLICK
FASH
CLICK
FASH

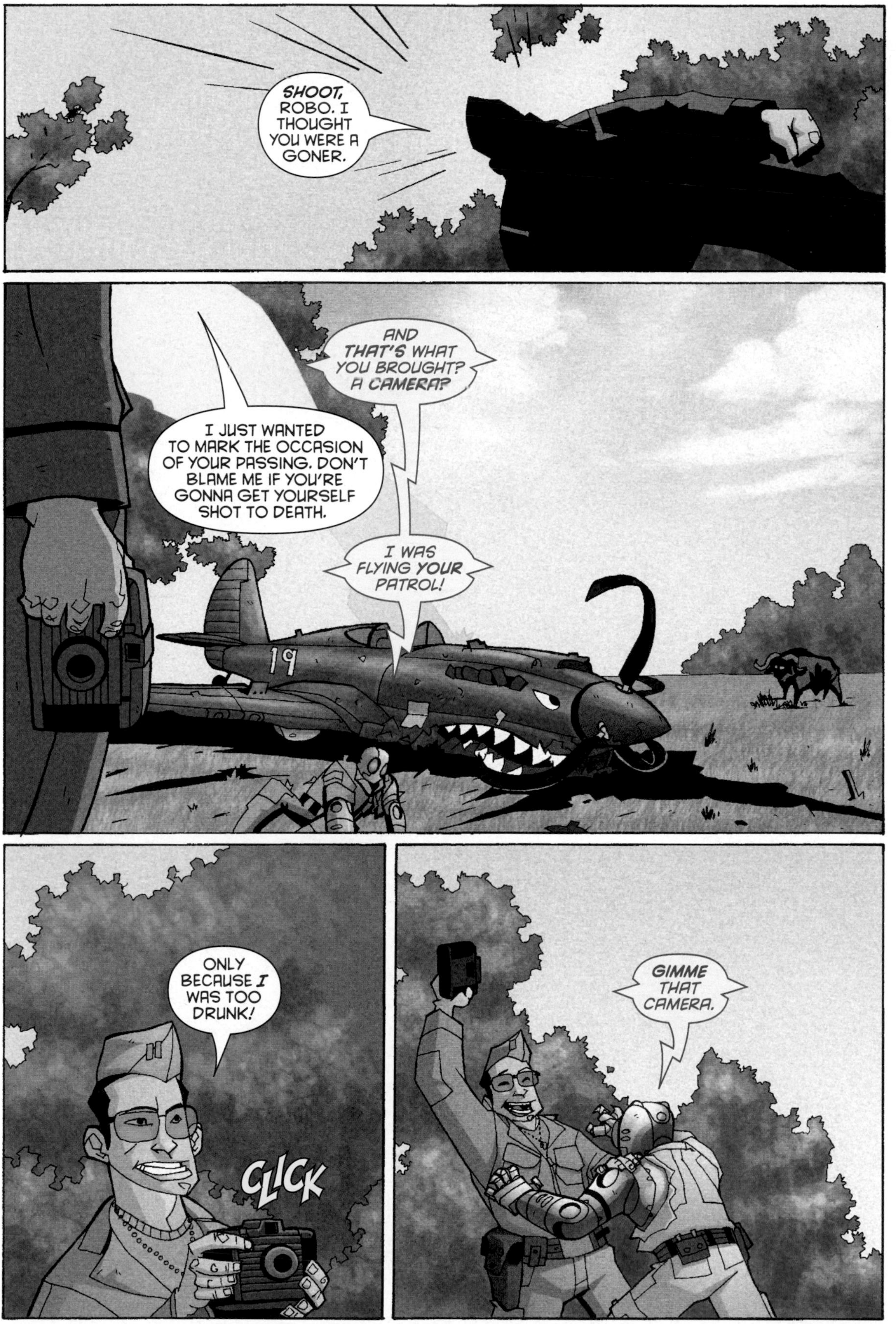
SHOOT, ROBO. I THOUGHT YOU WERE A GONER.
AND THAT'S WHAT YOU BROUGHT? A CAMERA?
I JUST WANTED TO MARK THE OCCASION OF YOUR PASSING. DON'T BLAME ME IF YOU'RE GONNA GET YOURSELF SHOT TO DEATH.
I WAS FLYING YOUR PATROL!
19
ONLY BECAUSE I WAS TOO DRUNK!
CLICK
GIMME THAT CAMERA.

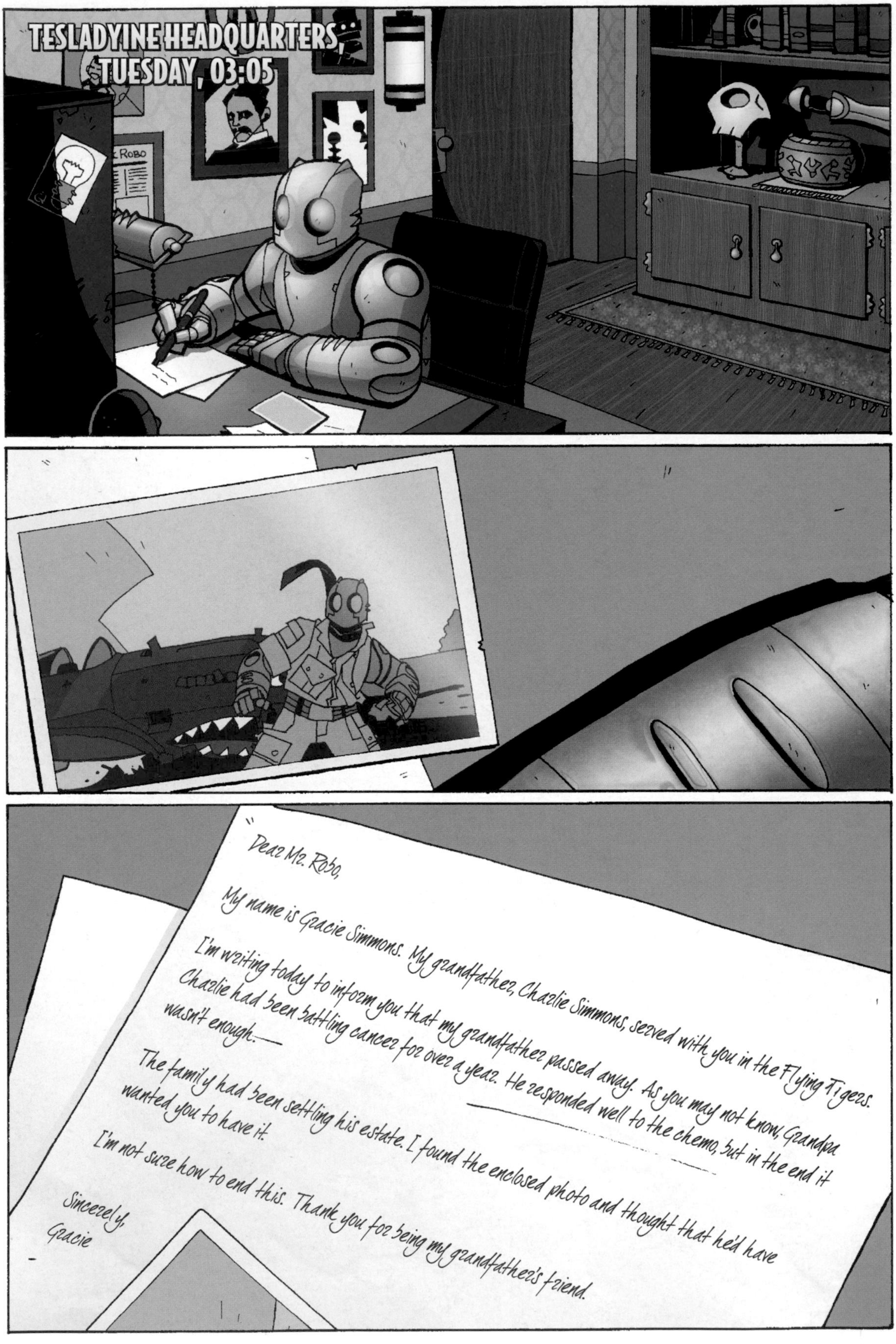
TESLADYINE HEADQUARTERS, TUESDAY, 03:05
Dear Mr. Robo,
My name is Gracie Simmons. My grandfather, Charlie Simmons, served with you in the Flying Tigers.
I'm writing today to inform you that my grandfather passed away. As you may not know, Grandpa Charlie had been battling cancer for over a year. He responded well to the chemo, but in the end it wasn't enough.
The family had been settling his estate. I found the enclosed photo and thought that he'd have wanted you to have it.
I'm not sure how to end this. Thank you for being my grandfather's friend.
Sincerely,
Gracie

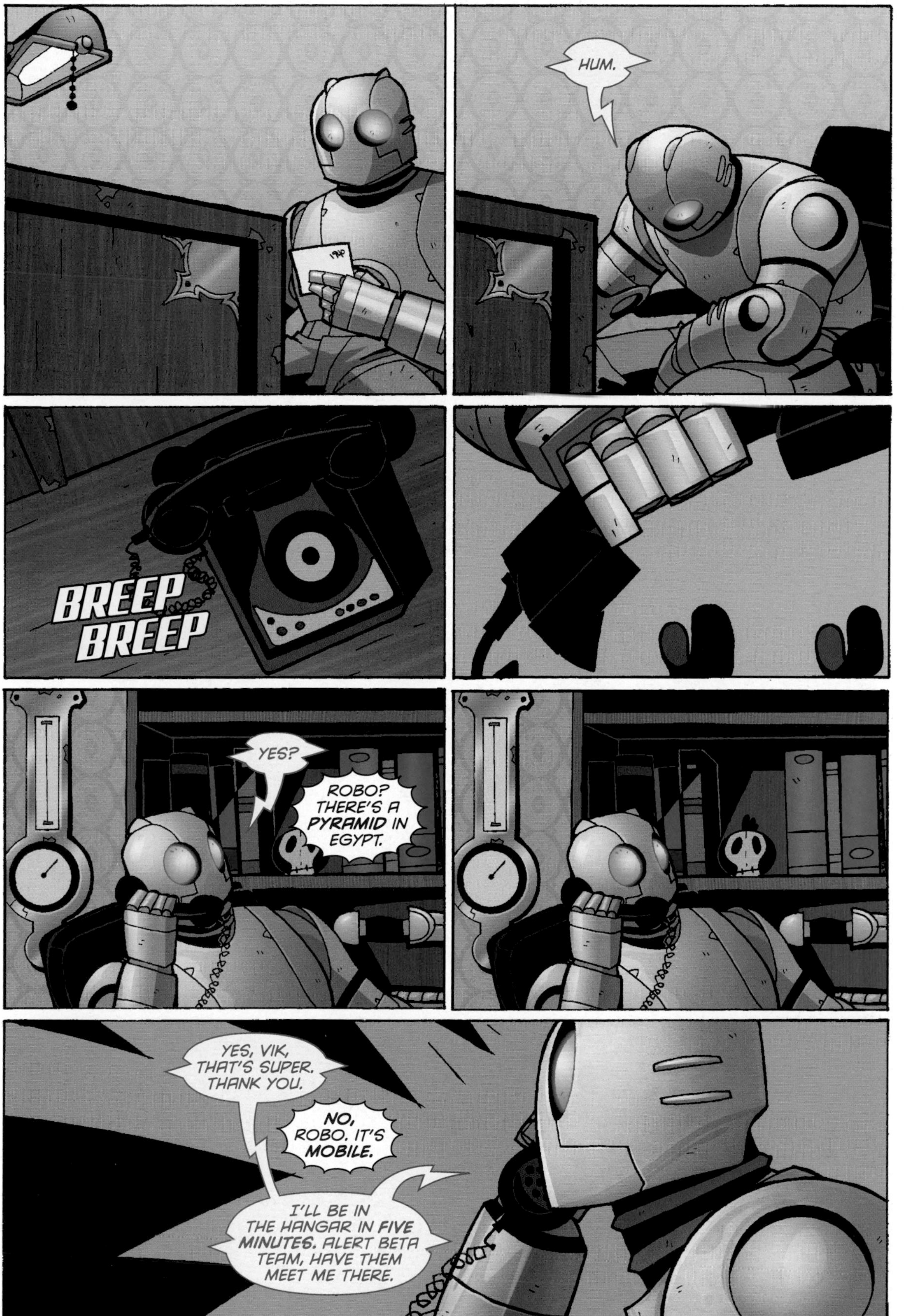
HUM.
BREEP
BREEP
YES?
ROBO? THERE'S A PYRAMID IN EGYPT.
YES, VIK, THAT'S SUPER. THANK YOU.
NO, ROBO. IT'S MOBILE.
I'LL BE IN THE HANGAR IN FIVE MINUTES. ALERT BETA TEAM, HAVE THEM MEET ME THERE.

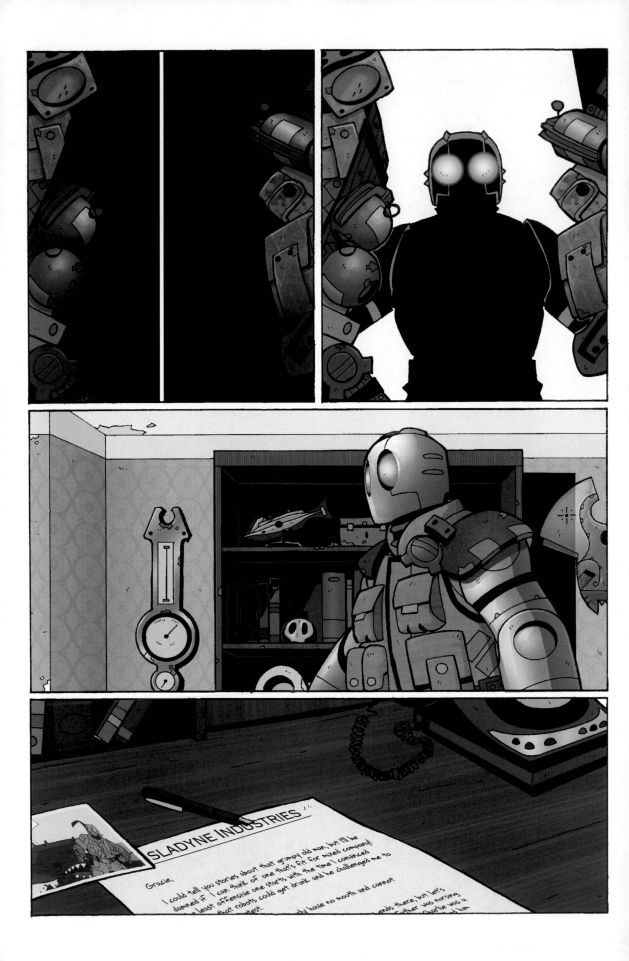

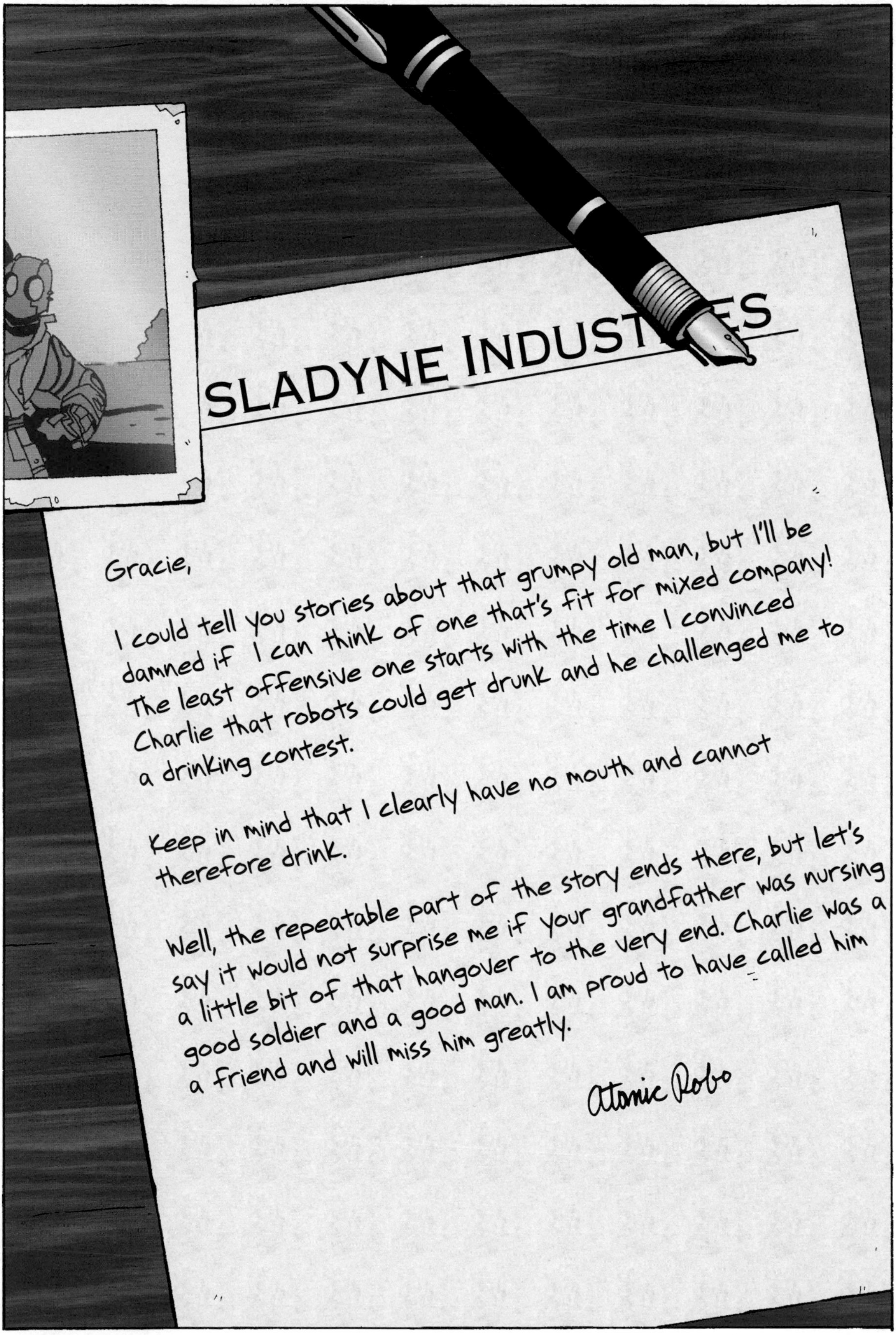
SLADYNE INDUSTRIES
Gracie,
I could tell you stories about that grumpy old man, but I'll be damned if I can think of one that's fit for mixed company! The least offensive one starts with the time I convinced Charlie that robots could get drunk and he challenged me to a drinking contest.
Keep in mind that I clearly have no mouth and cannot therefore drink.
Well, the repeatable part of the story ends there, but let's say it would not surprise me if your grandfather was nursing a little bit of that hangover to the very end. Charlie was a good soldier and a good man. I am proud to have called him a friend and will miss him greatly.
Atomic Robo

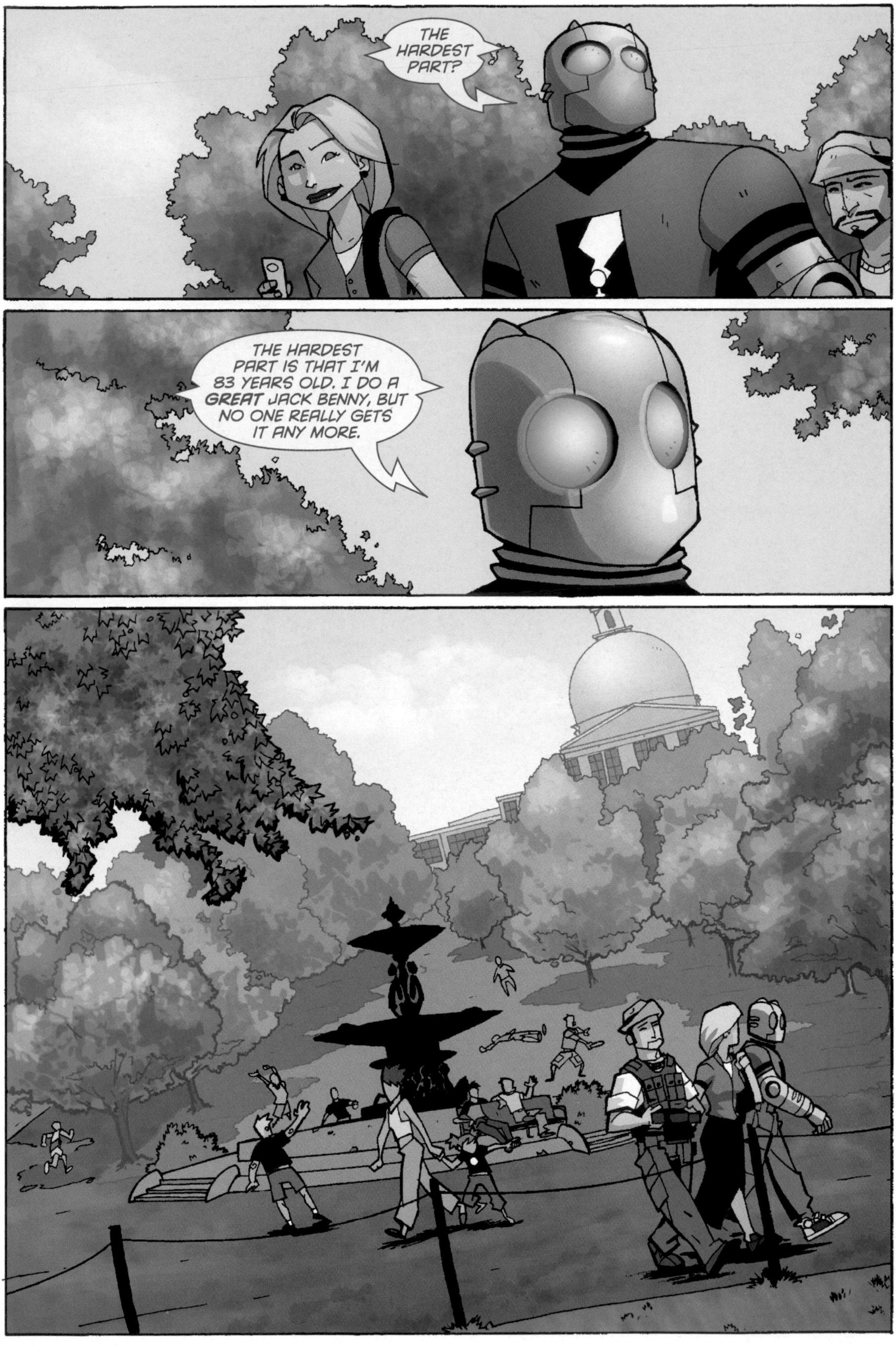
THE HARDEST PART?
THE HARDEST PART IS THAT I'M 83 YEARS OLD. I DO A GREAT JACK BENNY, BUT NO ONE REALLY GETS IT ANY MORE.

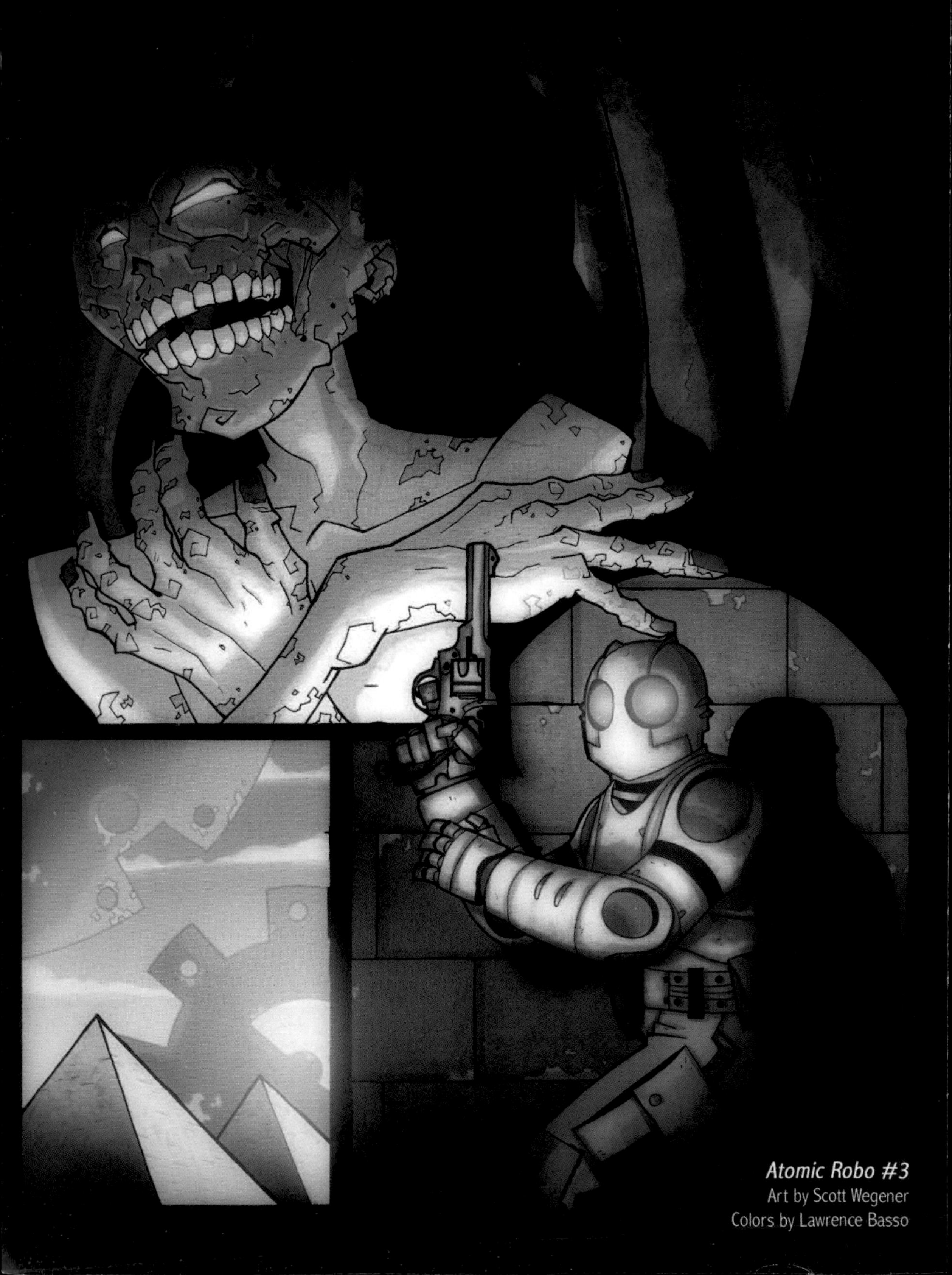

Atomic Robo #3
Art by Scott Wegener
Colors by Lawrence Basso

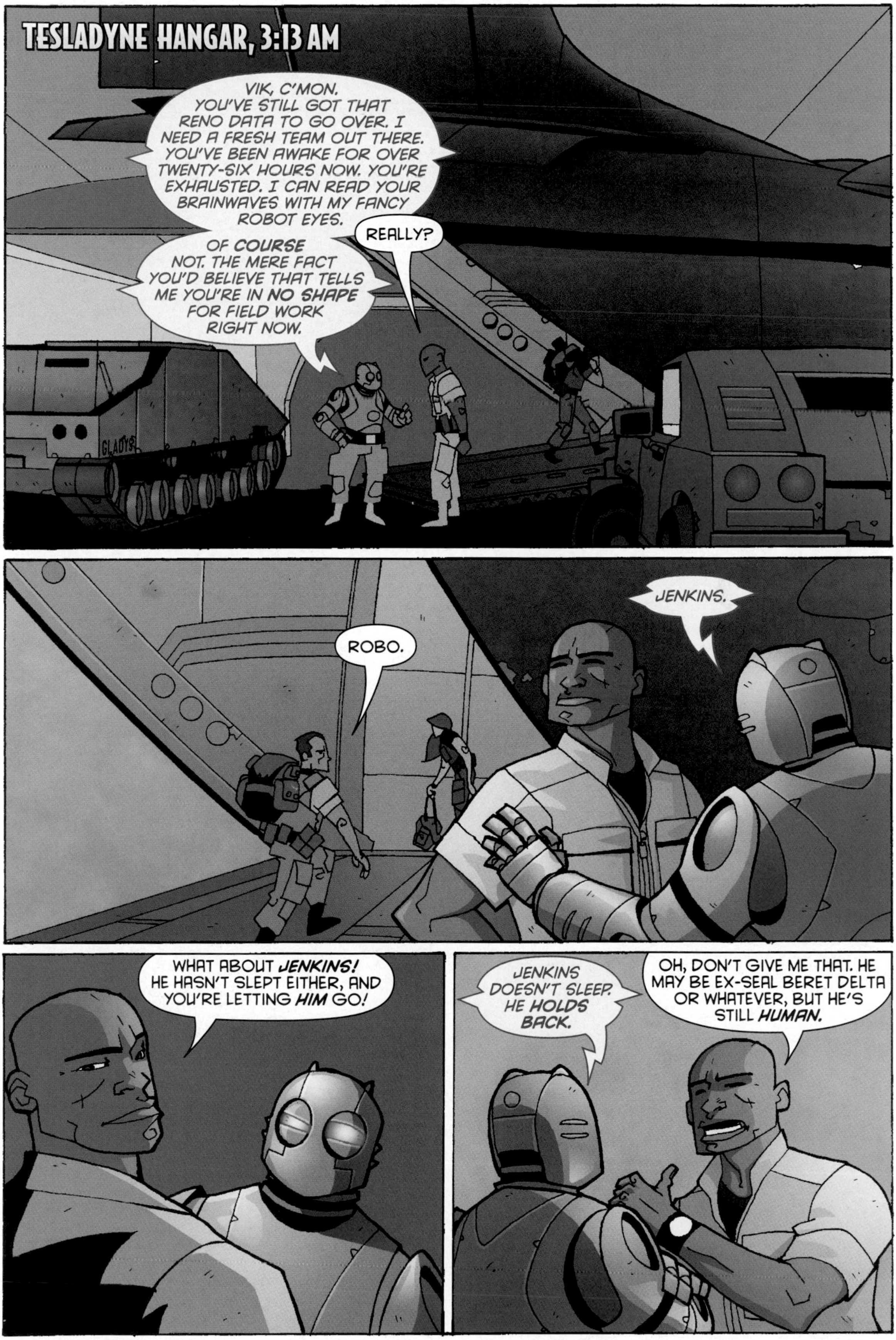
TESLADYNE HANGAR, 3:13 AM
VIK, C'MON. YOU'VE STILL GOT THAT RENO DATA TO GO OVER. I NEED A FRESH TEAM OUT THERE. YOU'VE BEEN AWAKE FOR OVER TWENTY-SIX HOURS NOW. YOU'RE EXHAUSTED. I CAN READ YOUR BRAINWAVES WITH MY FANCY ROBOT EYES.
REALLY?
OF COURSE NOT. THE MERE FACT YOU'D BELIEVE THAT TELLS ME YOU'RE IN NO SHAPE FOR FIELD WORK RIGHT NOW.
GLADYS
JENKINS.
ROBO.
WHAT ABOUT JENKINS! HE HASN'T SLEPT EITHER, AND YOU'RE LETTING HIM GO!
OH, DON'T GIVE ME THAT. HE MAY BE EX-SEAL BERET DELTA OR WHATEVER, BUT HE'S STILL HUMAN.
JENKINS DOESN'T SLEEP. HE HOLDS BACK.

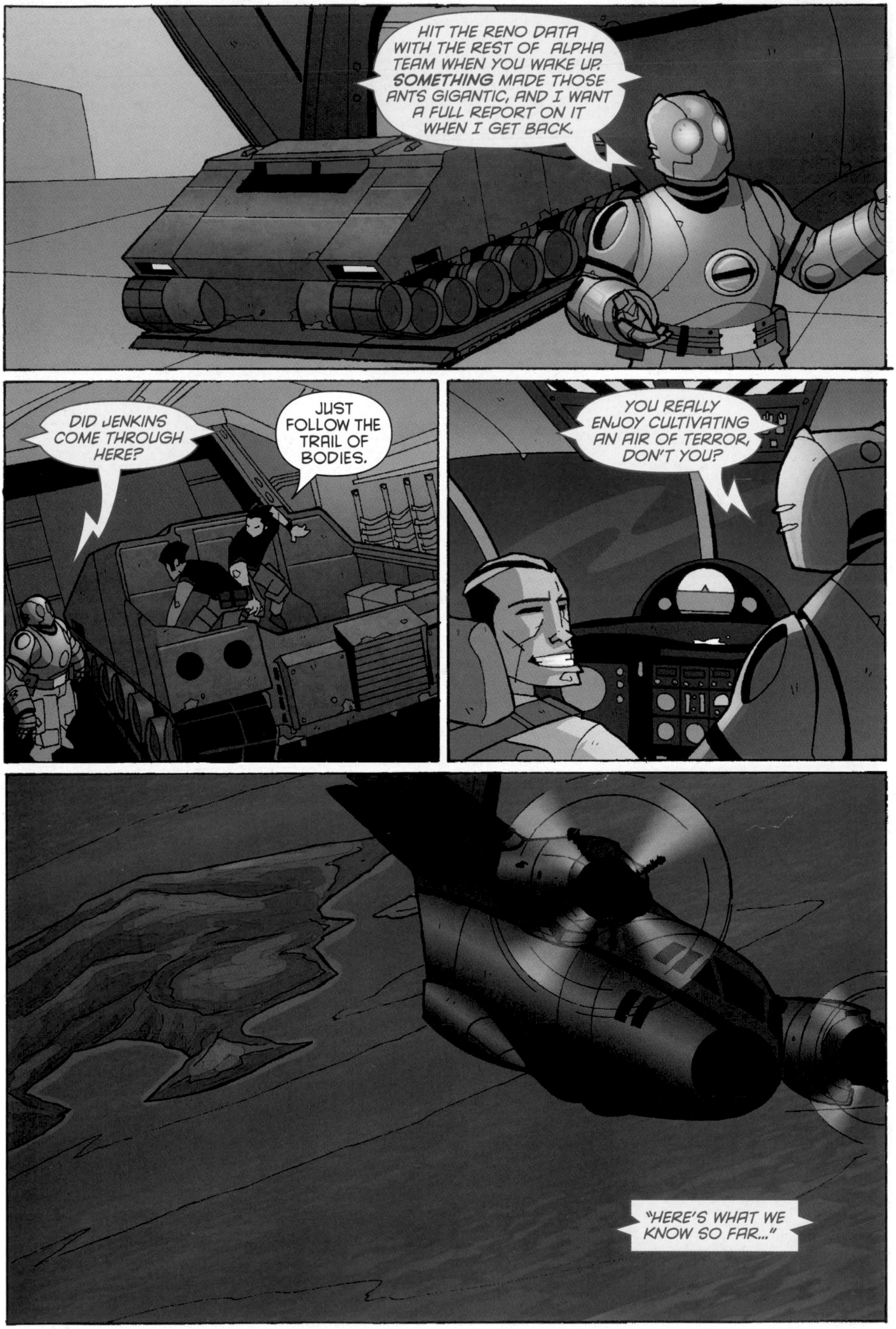
HIT THE RENO DATA WITH THE REST OF ALPHA TEAM WHEN YOU WAKE UP. SOMETHING MADE THOSE ANTS GIGANTIC, AND I WANT A FULL REPORT ON IT WHEN I GET BACK.
DID JENKINS COME THROUGH HERE?
JUST FOLLOW THE TRAIL OF BODIES.
YOU REALLY ENJOY CULTIVATING AN AIR OF TERROR, DON'T YOU?
"HERE'S WHAT WE KNOW SO FAR..."

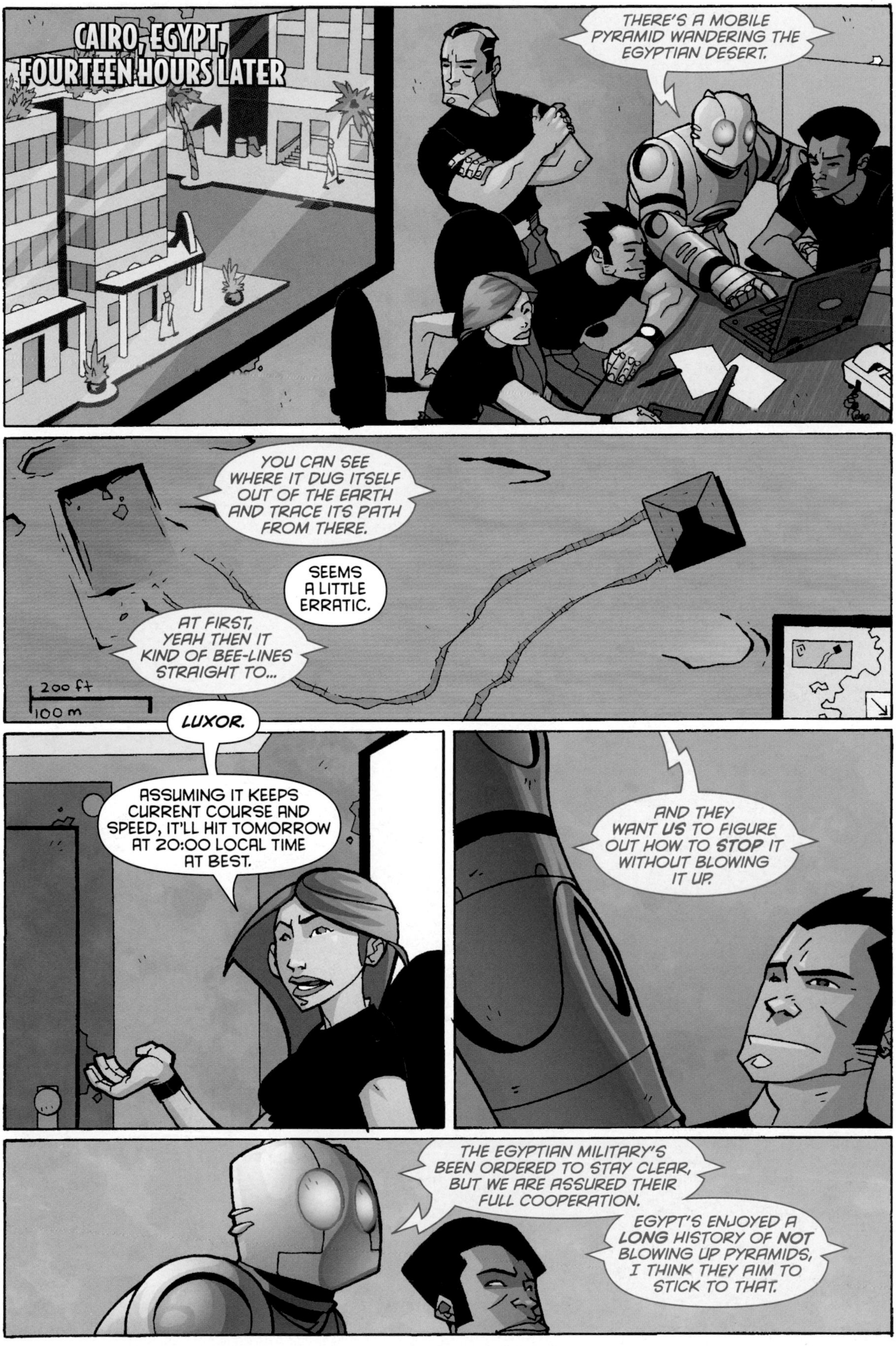
CAIRO, EGYPT, FOURTEEN HOURS LATER
THERE'S A MOBILE PYRAMID WANDERING THE EGYPTIAN DESERT.
YOU CAN SEE WHERE IT DUG ITSELF OUT OF THE EARTH AND TRACE ITS PATH FROM THERE.
SEEMS A LITTLE ERRATIC.
AT FIRST, YEAH THEN IT KIND OF BEE-LINES STRAIGHT TO...
200 ft
100 m
LUXOR.
ASSUMING IT KEEPS CURRENT COURSE AND SPEED, IT'LL HIT TOMORROW AT 20:00 LOCAL TIME AT BEST.
AND THEY WANT US TO FIGURE OUT HOW TO STOP IT WITHOUT BLOWING IT UP.
THE EGYPTIAN MILITARY'S BEEN ORDERED TO STAY CLEAR, BUT WE ARE ASSURED THEIR FULL COOPERATION.
EGYPT'S ENJOYED A LONG HISTORY OF NOT BLOWING UP PYRAMIDS, I THINK THEY AIM TO STICK TO THAT.

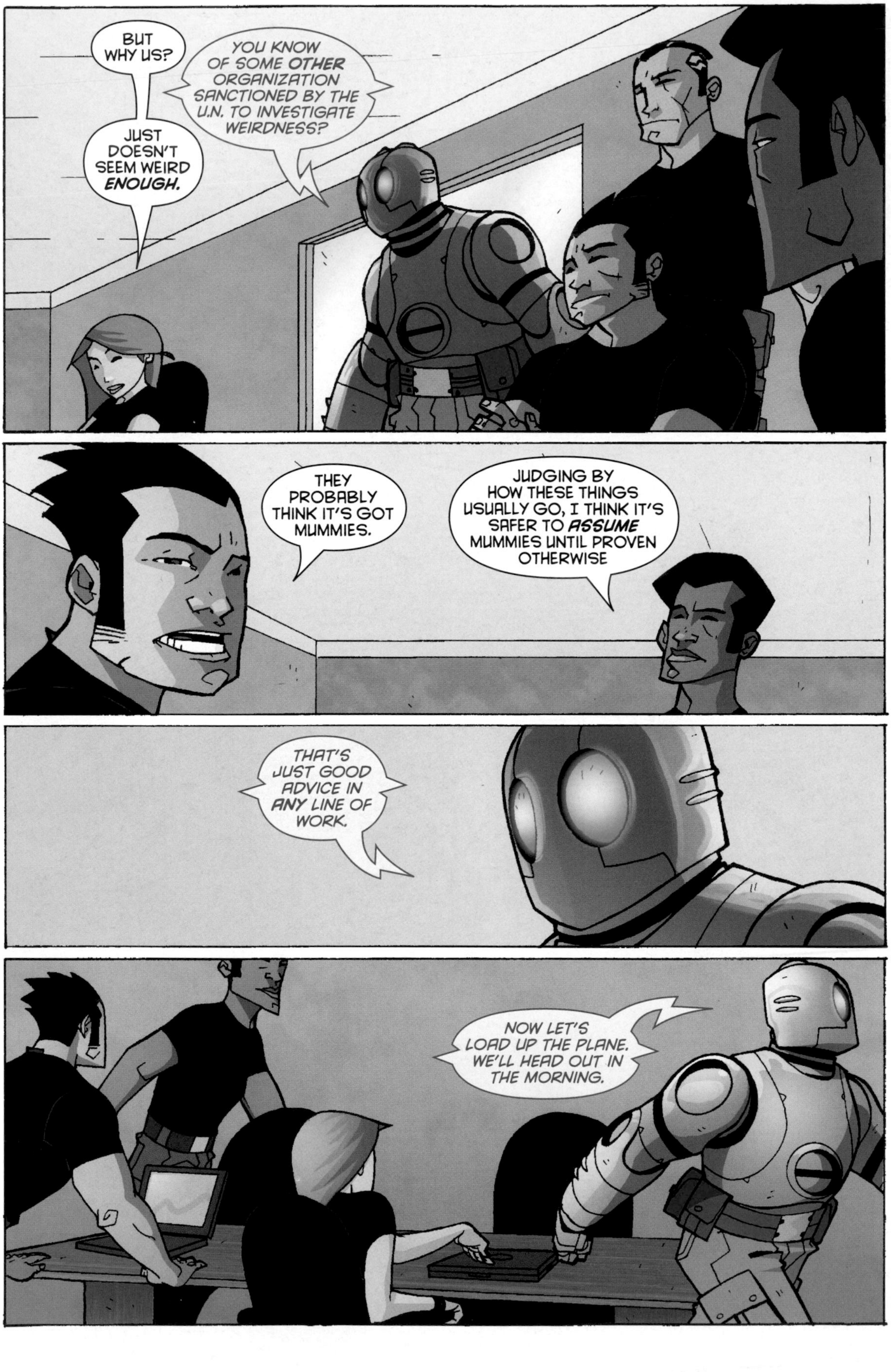

BUT WHY US?
YOU KNOW OF SOME *OTHER* ORGANIZATION SANCTIONED BY THE U.N. TO INVESTIGATE WEIRDNESS?
JUST DOESN'T SEEM WEIRD *ENOUGH.*
THEY PROBABLY THINK IT'S GOT MUMMIES.
JUDGING BY HOW THESE THINGS USUALLY GO, I THINK IT'S SAFER TO *ASSUME* MUMMIES UNTIL PROVEN OTHERWISE
THAT'S JUST GOOD ADVICE IN *ANY* LINE OF WORK.
NOW LET'S LOAD UP THE PLANE. WE'LL HEAD OUT IN THE MORNING.

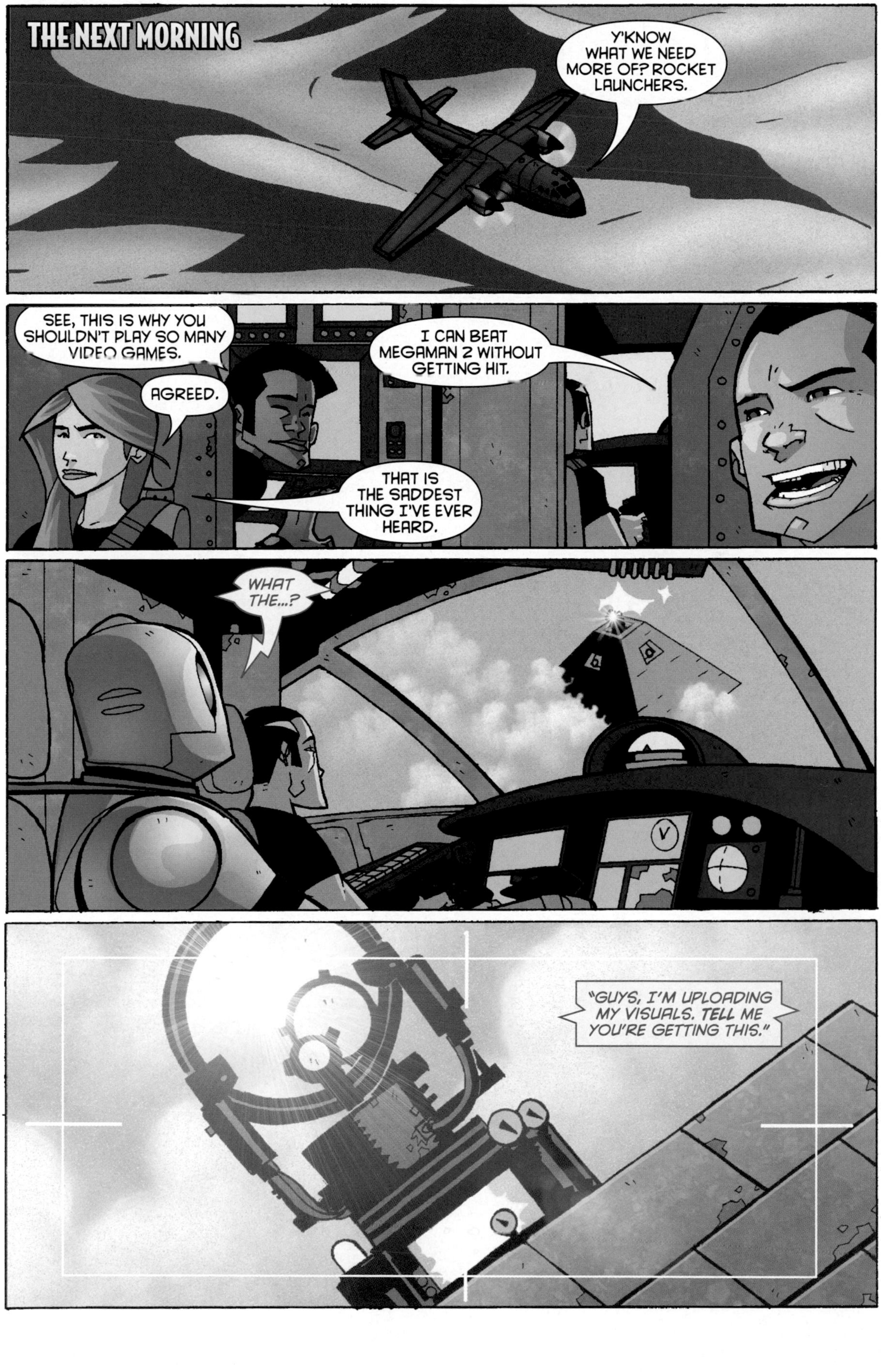
THE NEXT MORNING
Y'KNOW WHAT WE NEED MORE OF? ROCKET LAUNCHERS.
SEE, THIS IS WHY YOU SHOULDN'T PLAY SO MANY VIDEO GAMES.
AGREED.
I CAN BEAT MEGAMAN 2 WITHOUT GETTING HIT.
THAT IS THE SADDEST THING I'VE EVER HEARD.
WHAT THE...?
"GUYS, I'M UPLOADING MY VISUALS. TELL ME YOU'RE GETTING THIS."

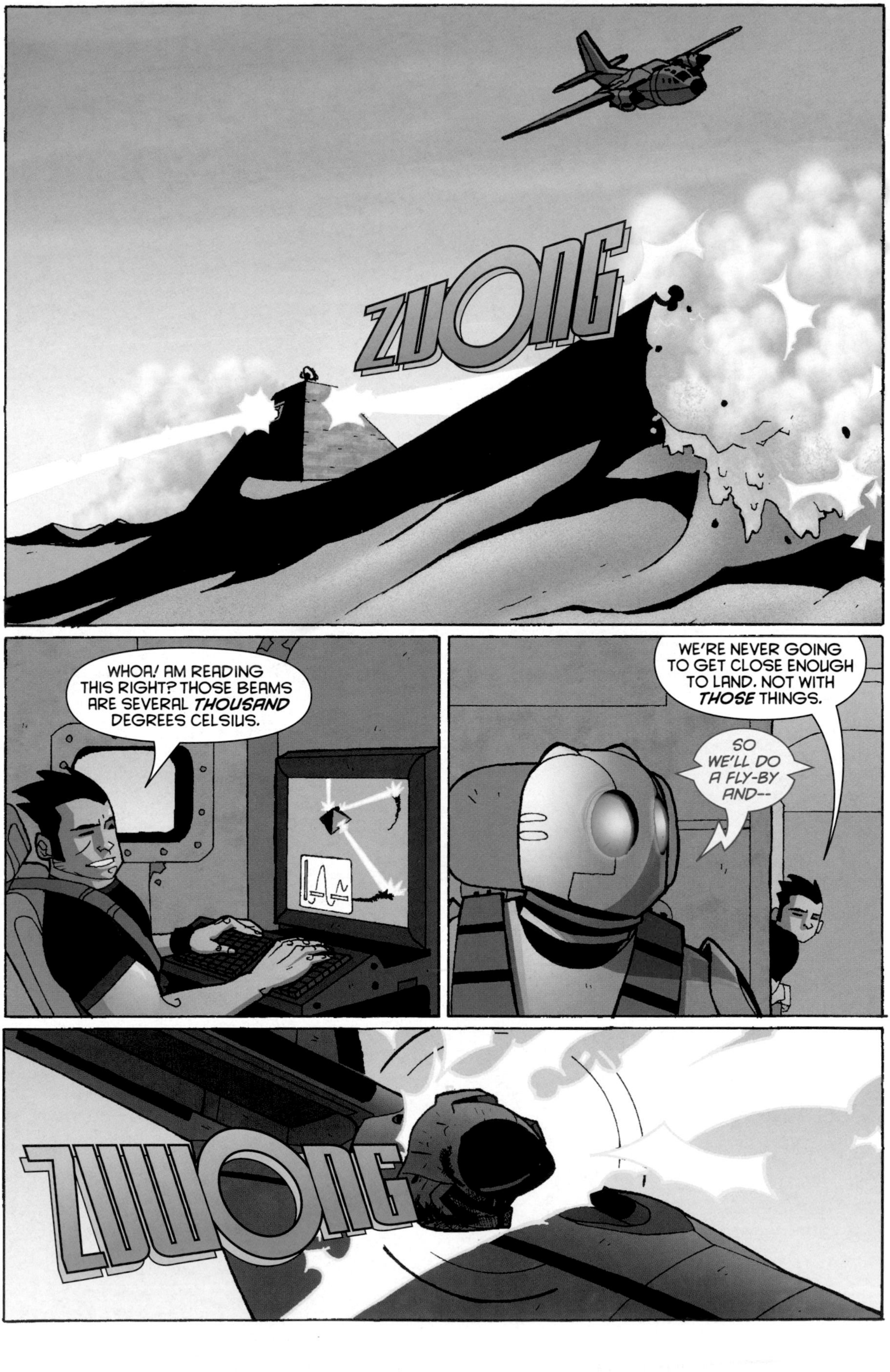
ZWONG
WHOA! AM READING THIS RIGHT? THOSE BEAMS ARE SEVERAL *THOUSAND* DEGREES CELSIUS.
WE'RE NEVER GOING TO GET CLOSE ENOUGH TO LAND. NOT WITH *THOSE* THINGS.
SO WE'LL DO A FLY-BY AND--
ZWWONG

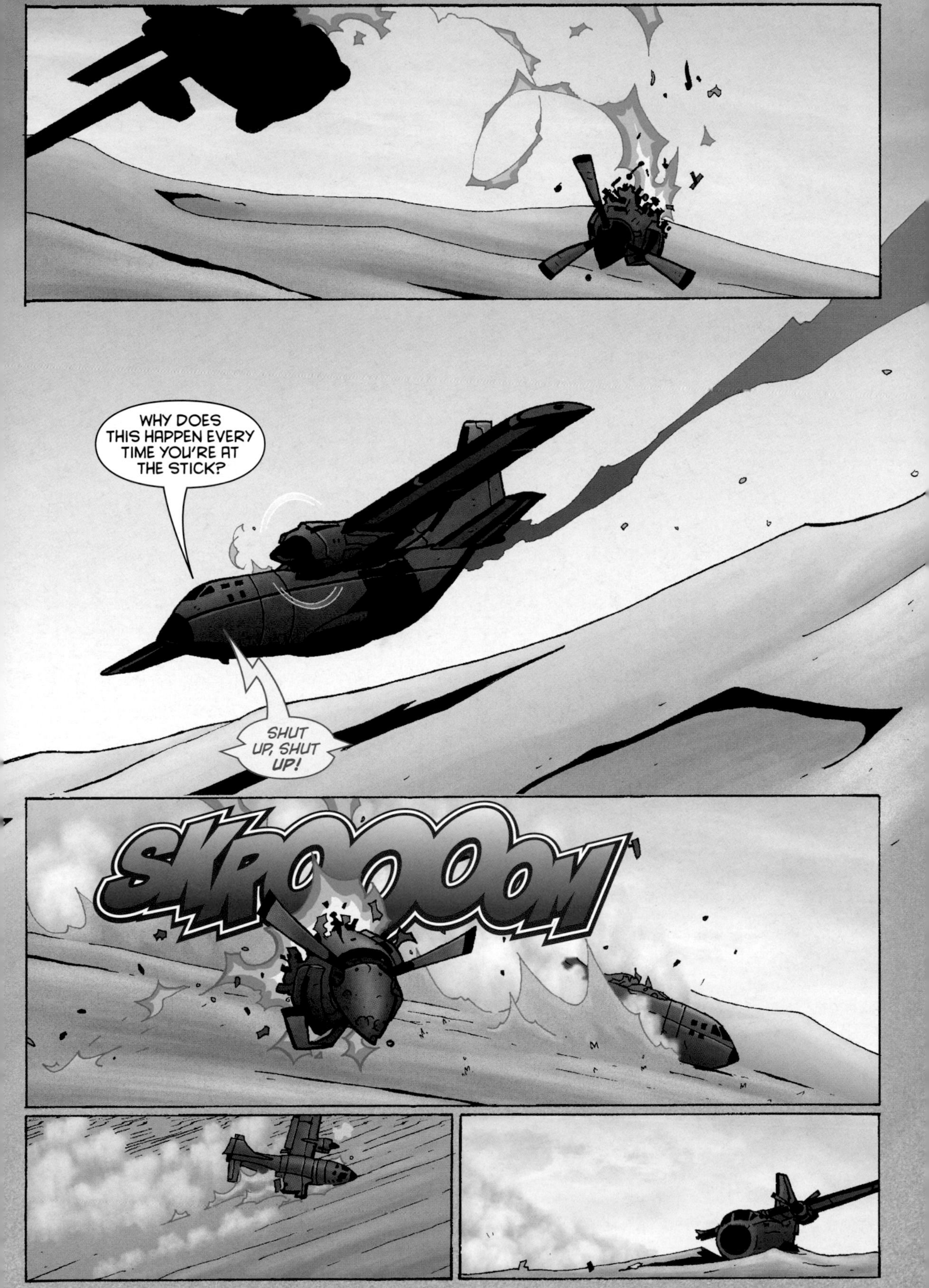
WHY DOES THIS HAPPEN EVERY TIME YOU'RE AT THE STICK?
SHUT UP, SHUT UP!
SKROOOOOM

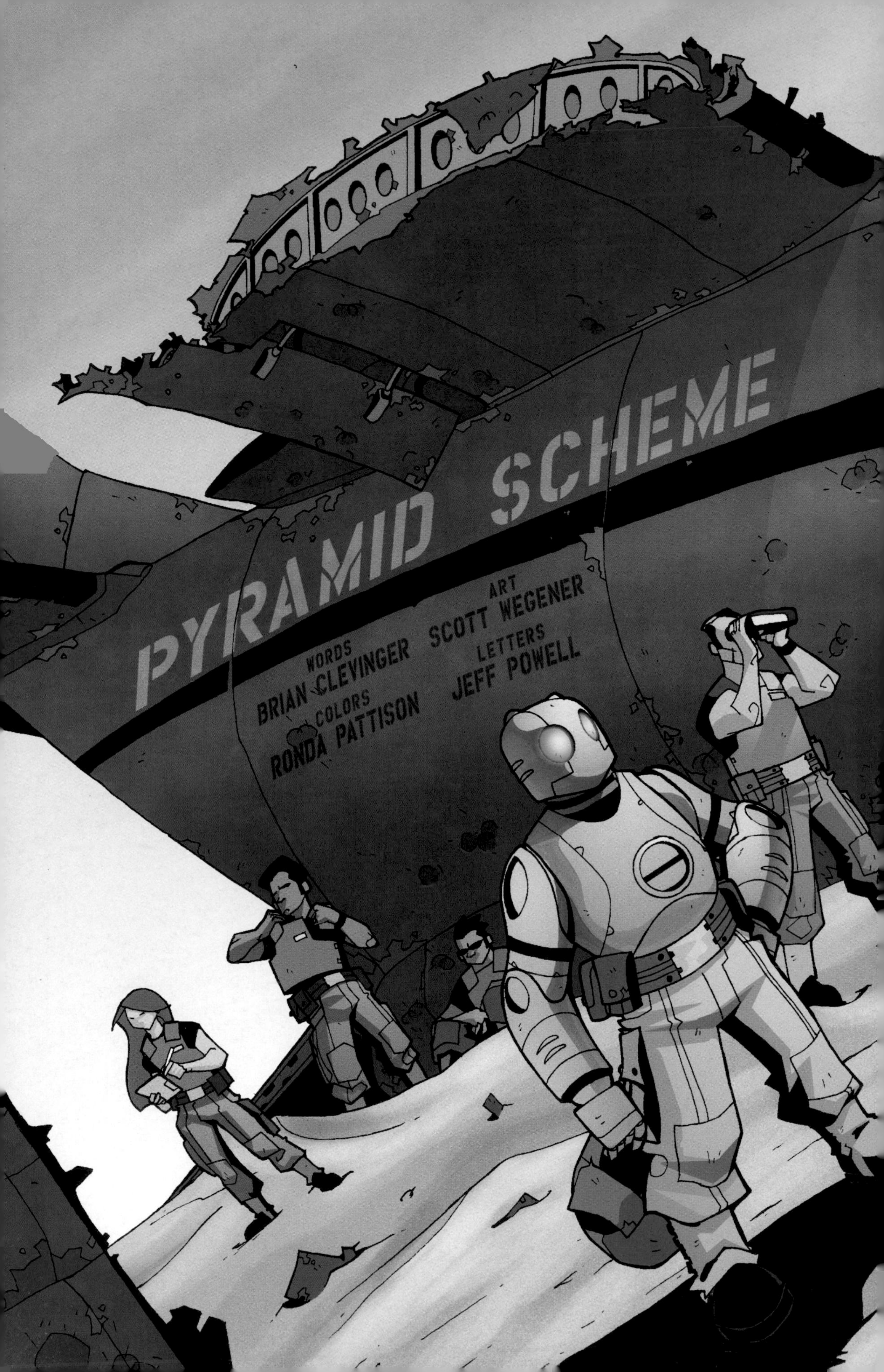
PYRAMID SCHEME
WORDS
BRIAN CLEVINGER
ART
SCOTT WEGENER
COLORS
RONDA PATTISON
LETTERS
JEFF POWELL

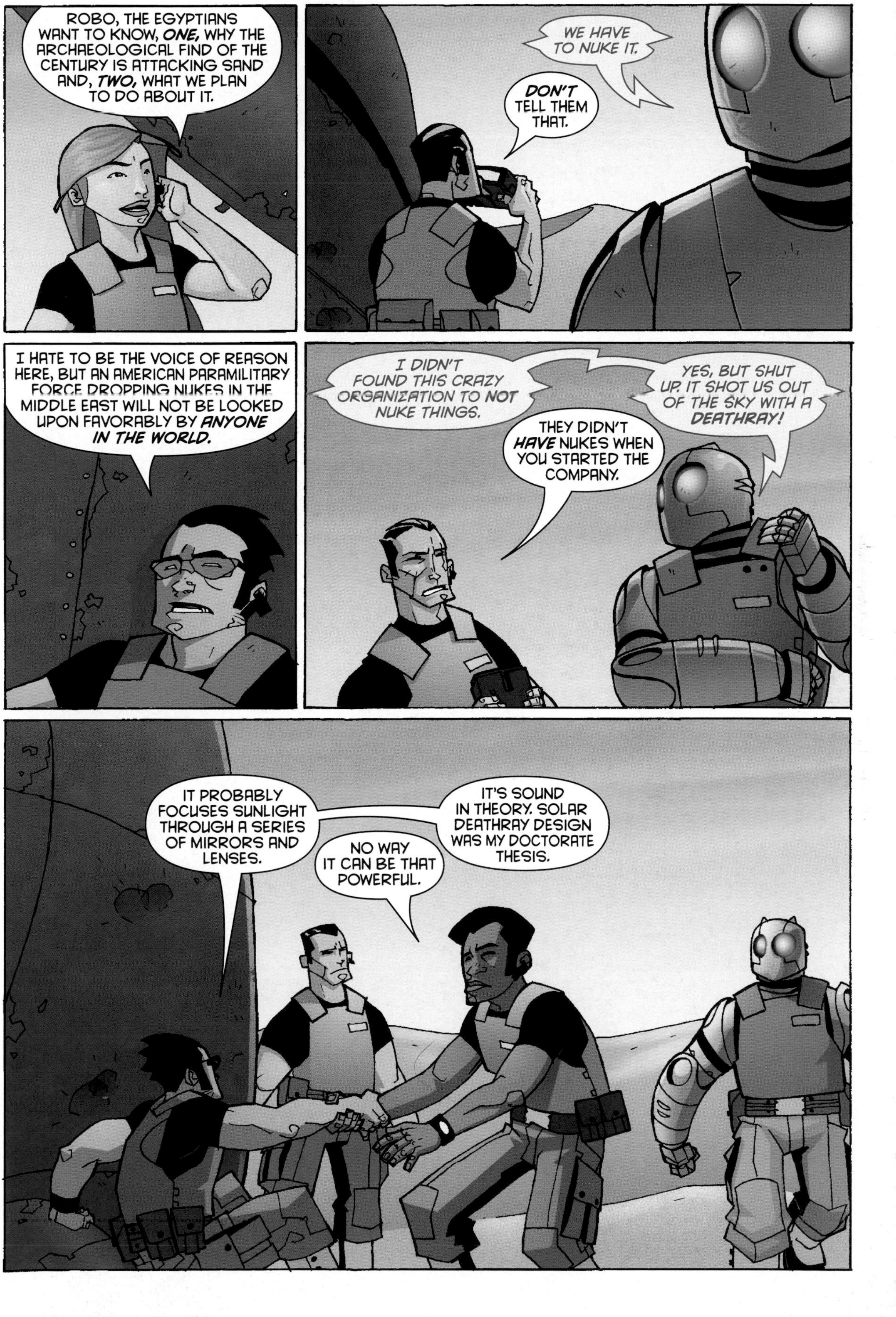
ROBO, THE EGYPTIANS WANT TO KNOW, ONE, WHY THE ARCHAEOLOGICAL FIND OF THE CENTURY IS ATTACKING SAND AND, TWO, WHAT WE PLAN TO DO ABOUT IT.
WE HAVE TO NUKE IT.
DON'T TELL THEM THAT.
I HATE TO BE THE VOICE OF REASON HERE, BUT AN AMERICAN PARAMILITARY FORCE DROPPING NUKES IN THE MIDDLE EAST WILL NOT BE LOOKED UPON FAVORABLY BY ANYONE IN THE WORLD.
I DIDN'T FOUND THIS CRAZY ORGANIZATION TO NOT NUKE THINGS.
THEY DIDN'T HAVE NUKES WHEN YOU STARTED THE COMPANY.
YES, BUT SHUT UP. IT SHOT US OUT OF THE SKY WITH A DEATHRAY!
IT PROBABLY FOCUSES SUNLIGHT THROUGH A SERIES OF MIRRORS AND LENSES.
NO WAY IT CAN BE THAT POWERFUL.
IT'S SOUND IN THEORY. SOLAR DEATHRAY DESIGN WAS MY DOCTORATE THESIS.

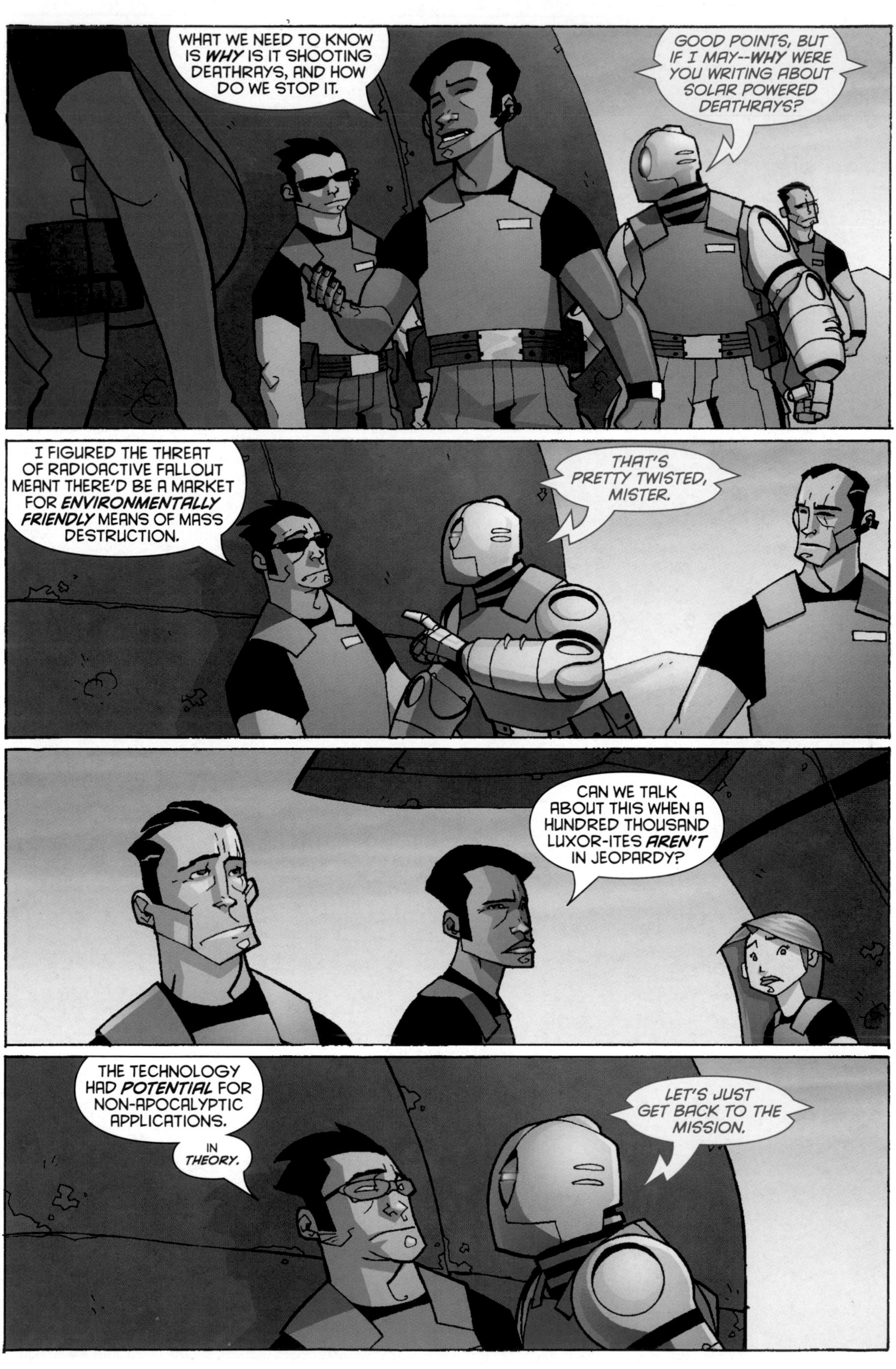
WHAT WE NEED TO KNOW IS WHY IS IT SHOOTING DEATHRAYS, AND HOW DO WE STOP IT.
GOOD POINTS, BUT IF I MAY--WHY WERE YOU WRITING ABOUT SOLAR POWERED DEATHRAYS?
I FIGURED THE THREAT OF RADIOACTIVE FALLOUT MEANT THERE'D BE A MARKET FOR ENVIRONMENTALLY FRIENDLY MEANS OF MASS DESTRUCTION.
THAT'S PRETTY TWISTED, MISTER.
CAN WE TALK ABOUT THIS WHEN A HUNDRED THOUSAND LUXOR-ITES AREN'T IN JEOPARDY?
THE TECHNOLOGY HAD POTENTIAL FOR NON-APOCALYPTIC APPLICATIONS.
IN THEORY.
LET'S JUST GET BACK TO THE MISSION.

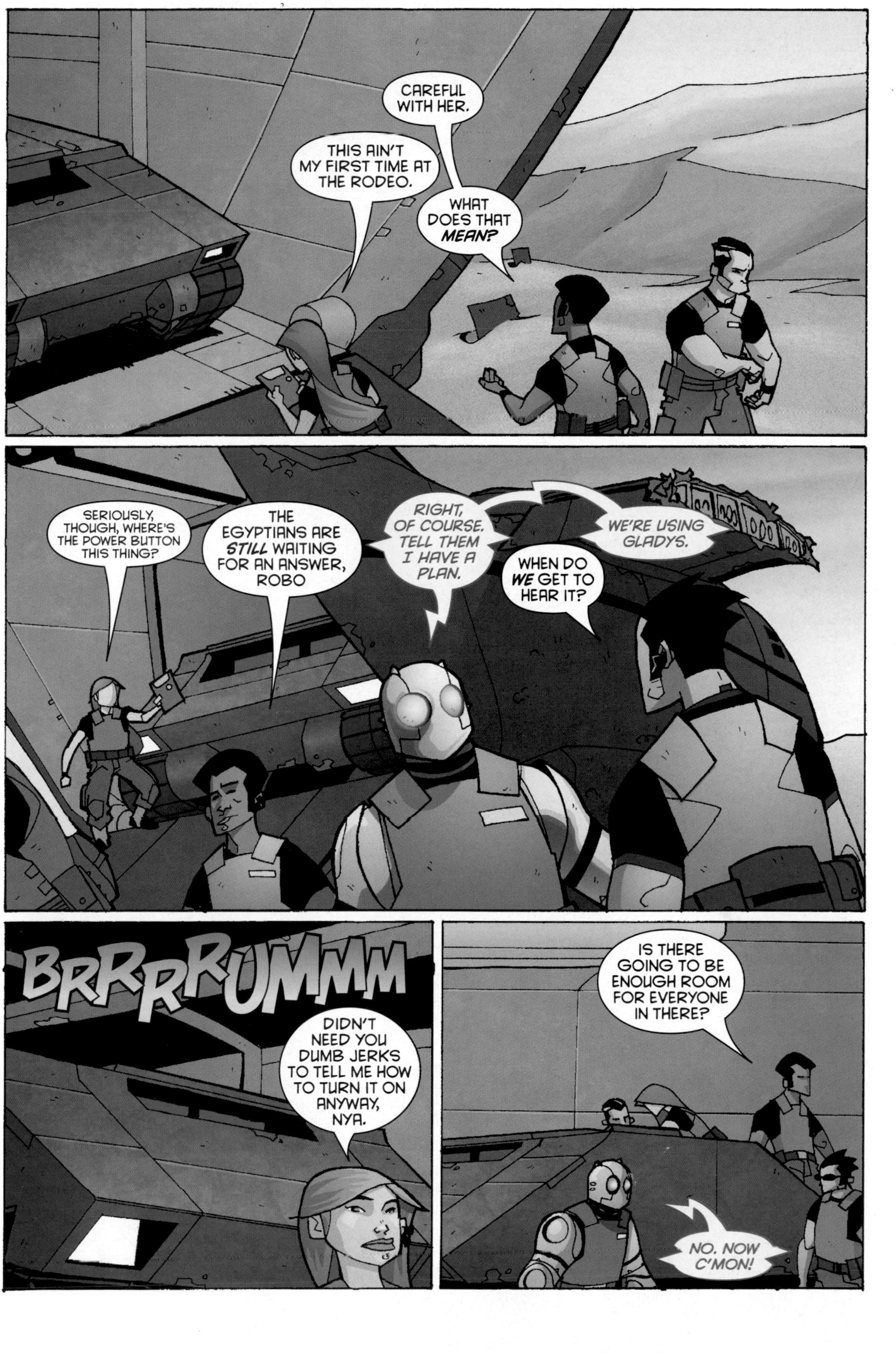
CAREFUL WITH HER.
THIS AIN'T MY FIRST TIME AT THE RODEO.
WHAT DOES THAT MEAN?
SERIOUSLY, THOUGH, WHERE'S THE POWER BUTTON THIS THING?
THE EGYPTIANS ARE STILL WAITING FOR AN ANSWER, ROBO
RIGHT, OF COURSE. TELL THEM I HAVE A PLAN.
WE'RE USING GLADYS.
WHEN DO WE GET TO HEAR IT?
BRRRRUMMM
DIDN'T NEED YOU DUMB JERKS TO TELL ME HOW TO TURN IT ON ANYWAY, NYA.
IS THERE GOING TO BE ENOUGH ROOM FOR EVERYONE IN THERE?
NO. NOW C'MON!

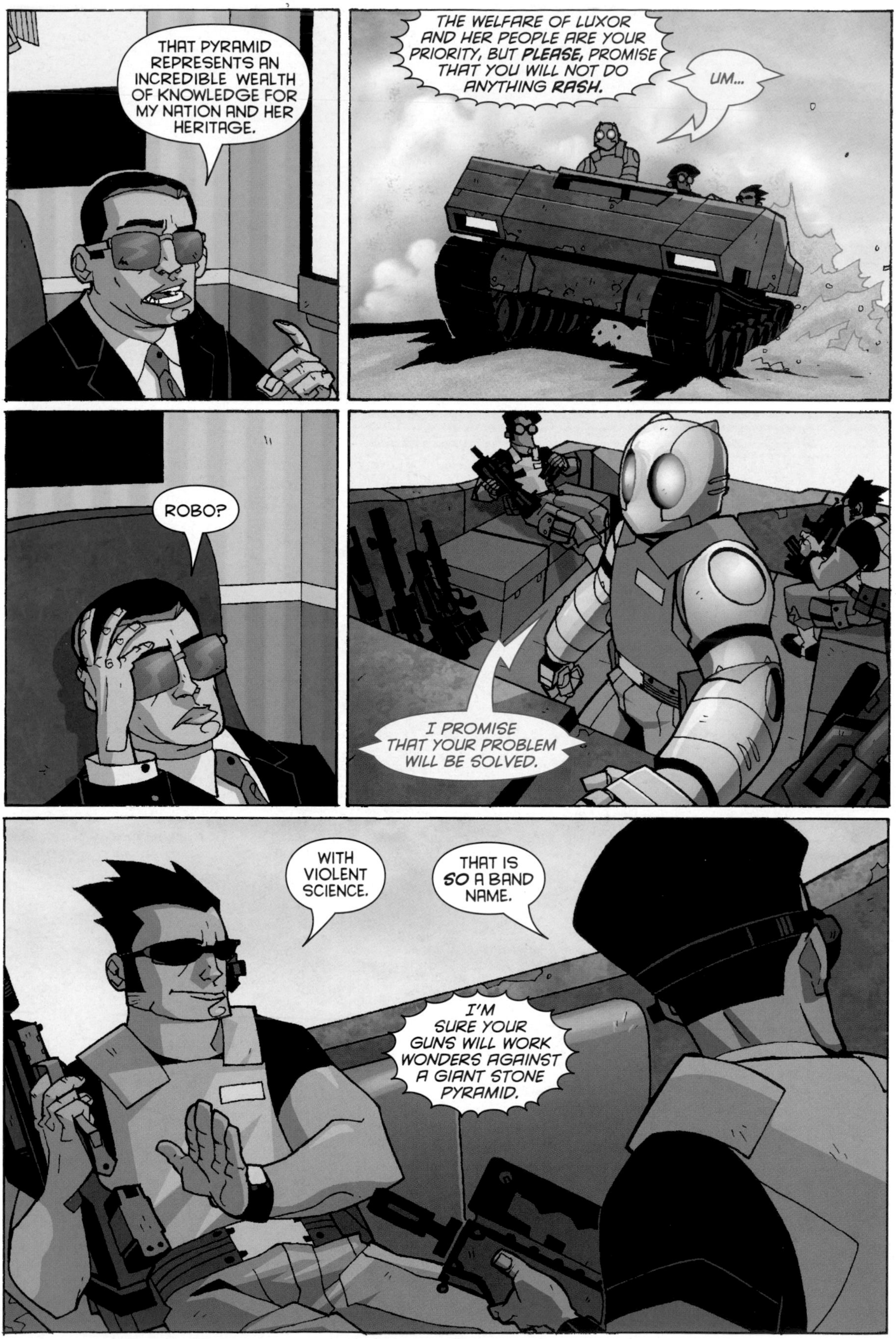
THAT PYRAMID REPRESENTS AN INCREDIBLE WEALTH OF KNOWLEDGE FOR MY NATION AND HER HERITAGE.
THE WELFARE OF LUXOR AND HER PEOPLE ARE YOUR PRIORITY, BUT PLEASE, PROMISE THAT YOU WILL NOT DO ANYTHING RASH.
UM...
ROBO?
I PROMISE THAT YOUR PROBLEM WILL BE SOLVED.
WITH VIOLENT SCIENCE.
THAT IS SO A BAND NAME.
I'M SURE YOUR GUNS WILL WORK WONDERS AGAINST A GIANT STONE PYRAMID.

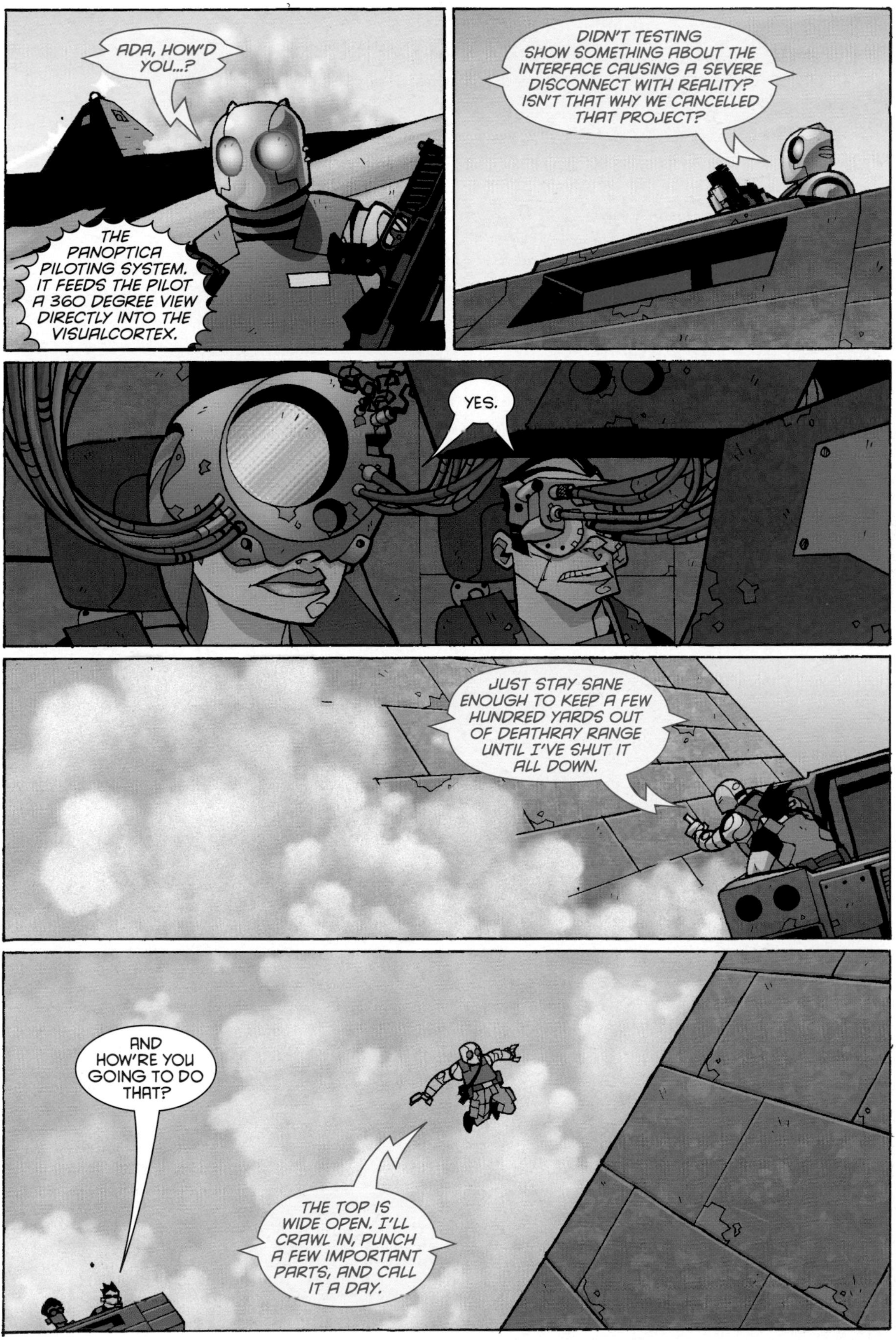
ADA, HOW'D YOU...?
THE PANOPTICA PILOTING SYSTEM. IT FEEDS THE PILOT A 360 DEGREE VIEW DIRECTLY INTO THE VISUALCORTEX.
DIDN'T TESTING SHOW SOMETHING ABOUT THE INTERFACE CAUSING A SEVERE DISCONNECT WITH REALITY? ISN'T THAT WHY WE CANCELLED THAT PROJECT?
YES.
JUST STAY SANE ENOUGH TO KEEP A FEW HUNDRED YARDS OUT OF DEATHRAY RANGE UNTIL I'VE SHUT IT ALL DOWN.
AND HOW'RE YOU GOING TO DO THAT?
THE TOP IS WIDE OPEN. I'LL CRAWL IN, PUNCH A FEW IMPORTANT PARTS, AND CALL IT A DAY.

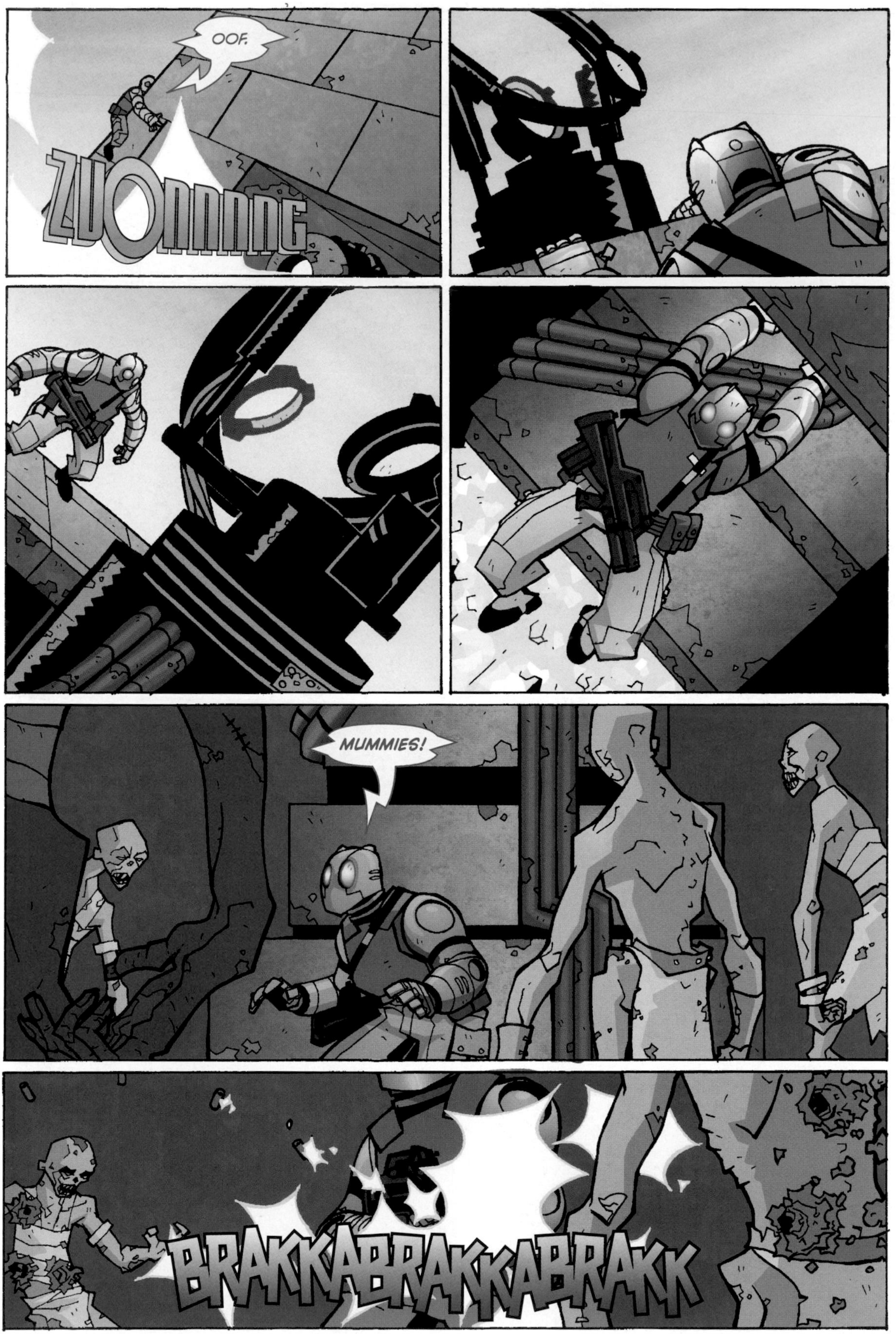
OOF.
ZUONNNNG
MUMMIES!
BRAKKABRAKKABRAKK

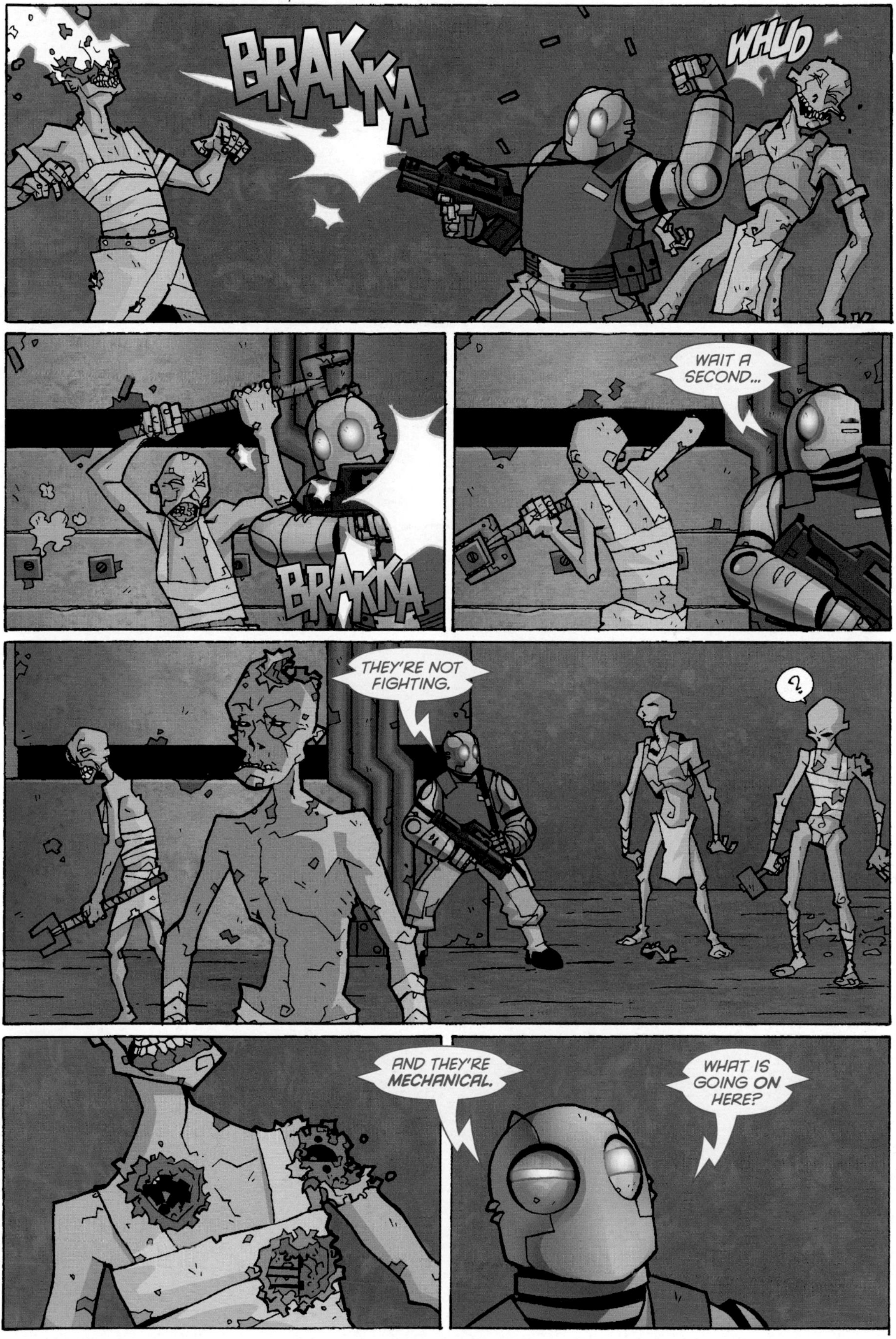
BRAKKA
WHUD
BRAKKA
WAIT A SECOND...
THEY'RE NOT FIGHTING.
?
AND THEY'RE MECHANICAL.
WHAT IS GOING ON HERE?

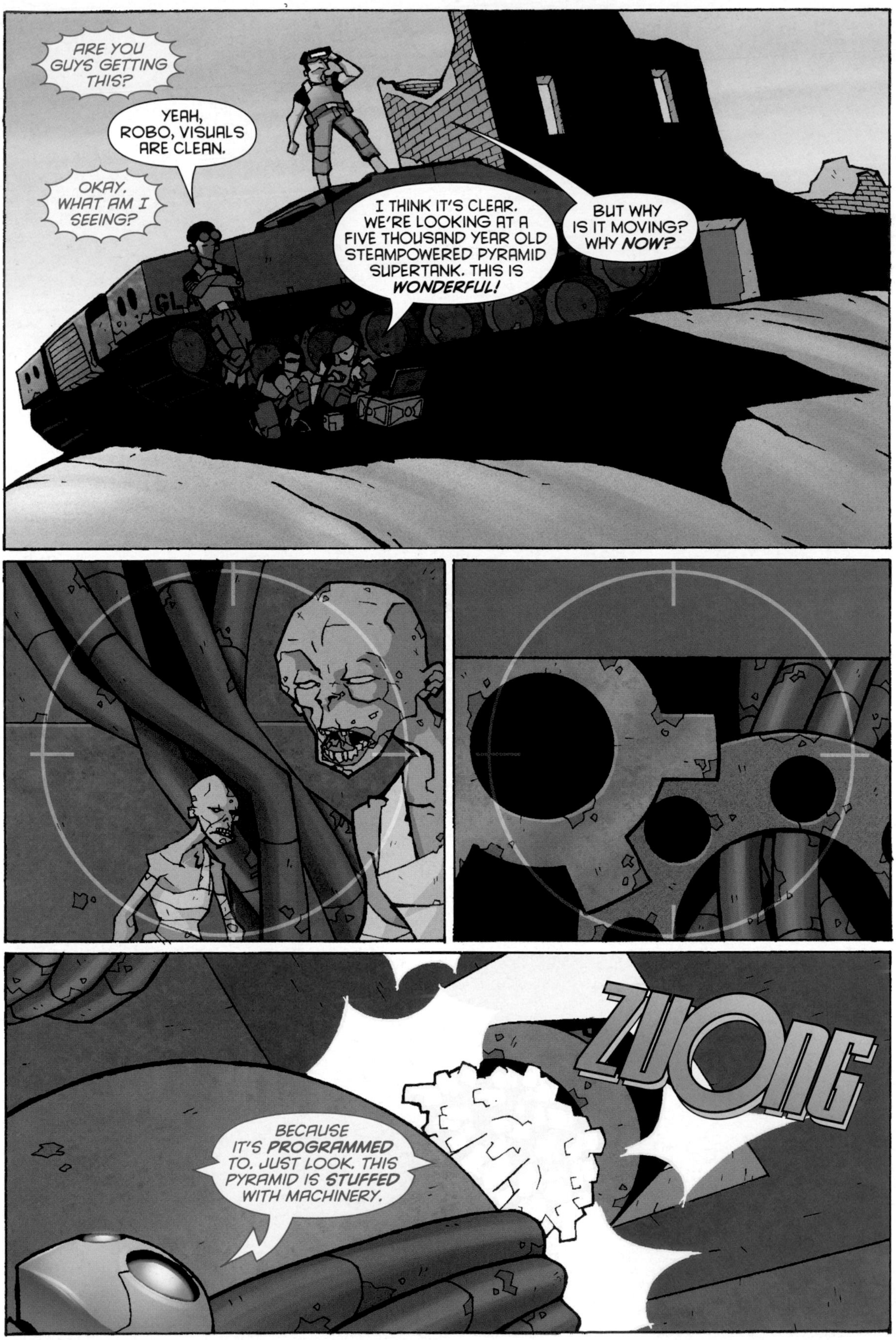
ARE YOU GUYS GETTING THIS?
YEAH, ROBO, VISUALS ARE CLEAN.
OKAY. WHAT AM I SEEING?
I THINK IT'S CLEAR. WE'RE LOOKING AT A FIVE THOUSAND YEAR OLD STEAMPOWERED PYRAMID SUPERTANK. THIS IS WONDERFUL!
BUT WHY IS IT MOVING? WHY NOW?
ZWONG
BECAUSE IT'S PROGRAMMED TO. JUST LOOK. THIS PYRAMID IS STUFFED WITH MACHINERY.

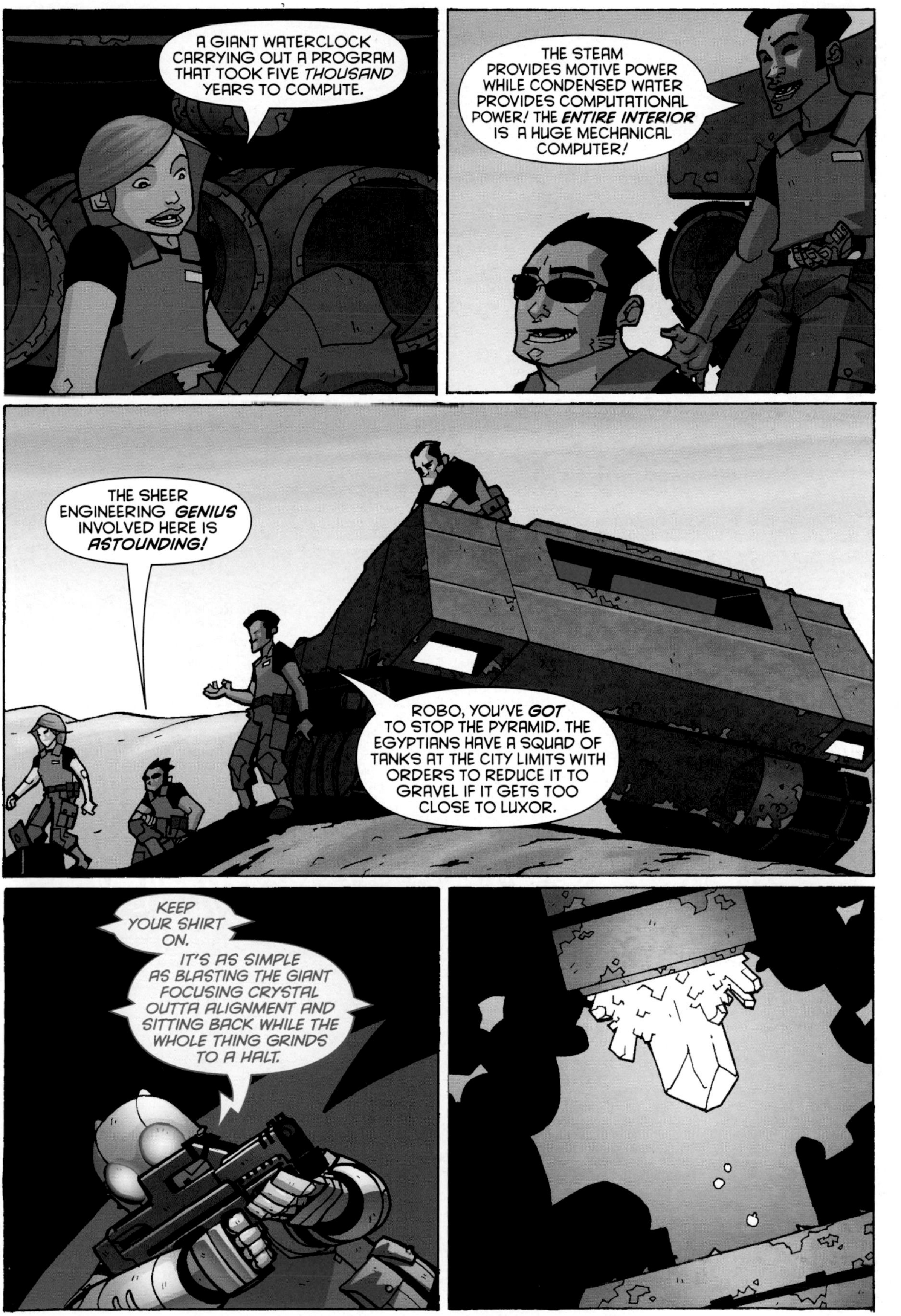
A GIANT WATERCLOCK CARRYING OUT A PROGRAM THAT TOOK FIVE *THOUSAND* YEARS TO COMPUTE.
THE STEAM PROVIDES MOTIVE POWER WHILE CONDENSED WATER PROVIDES COMPUTATIONAL POWER! THE **ENTIRE INTERIOR** IS A HUGE MECHANICAL COMPUTER!
THE SHEER ENGINEERING ***GENIUS*** INVOLVED HERE IS ***ASTOUNDING!***
ROBO, YOU'VE ***GOT*** TO STOP THE PYRAMID. THE EGYPTIANS HAVE A SQUAD OF TANKS AT THE CITY LIMITS WITH ORDERS TO REDUCE IT TO GRAVEL IF IT GETS TOO CLOSE TO LUXOR.
KEEP YOUR SHIRT ON.
IT'S AS SIMPLE AS BLASTING THE GIANT FOCUSING CRYSTAL OUTTA ALIGNMENT AND SITTING BACK WHILE THE WHOLE THING GRINDS TO A HALT.

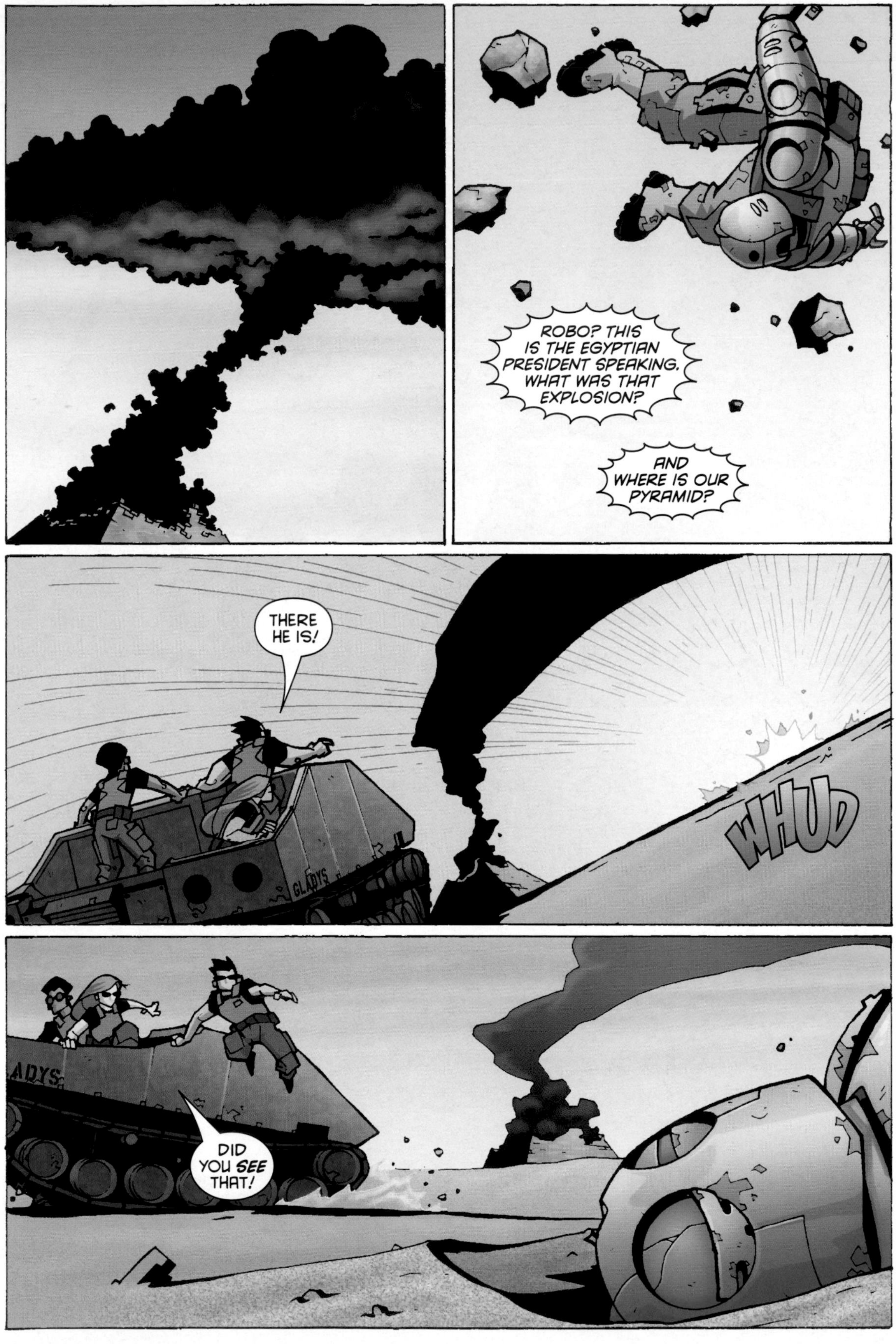
ROBO? THIS IS THE EGYPTIAN PRESIDENT SPEAKING. WHAT WAS THAT EXPLOSION?
AND WHERE IS OUR PYRAMID?
THERE HE IS!
WHUD
GLADYS
DID YOU SEE THAT!

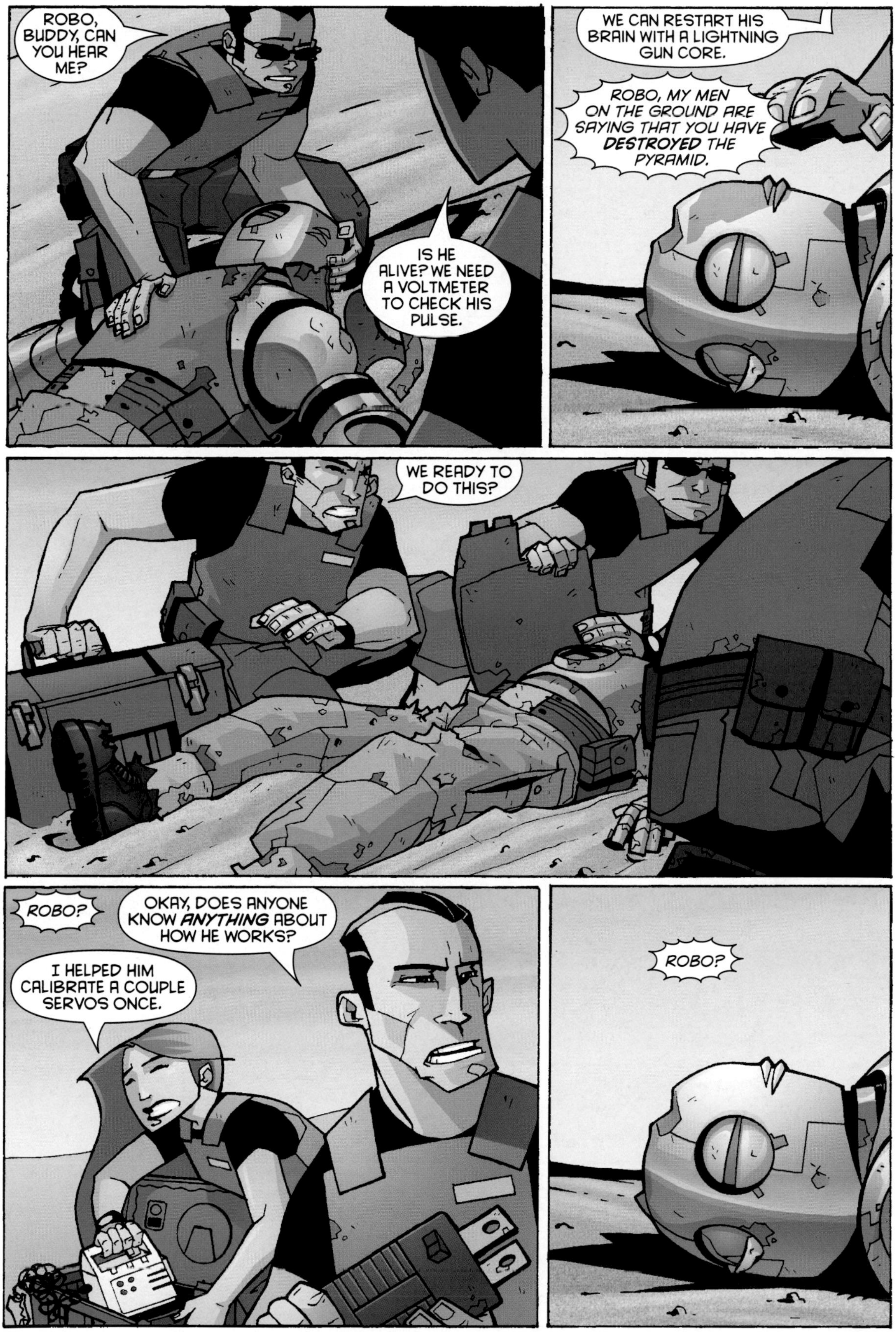
ROBO, BUDDY, CAN YOU HEAR ME?
IS HE ALIVE? WE NEED A VOLTMETER TO CHECK HIS PULSE.
WE CAN RESTART HIS BRAIN WITH A LIGHTNING GUN CORE.
ROBO, MY MEN ON THE GROUND ARE SAYING THAT YOU HAVE DESTROYED THE PYRAMID.
WE READY TO DO THIS?
ROBO?
OKAY, DOES ANYONE KNOW ANYTHING ABOUT HOW HE WORKS?
I HELPED HIM CALIBRATE A COUPLE SERVOS ONCE.
ROBO?

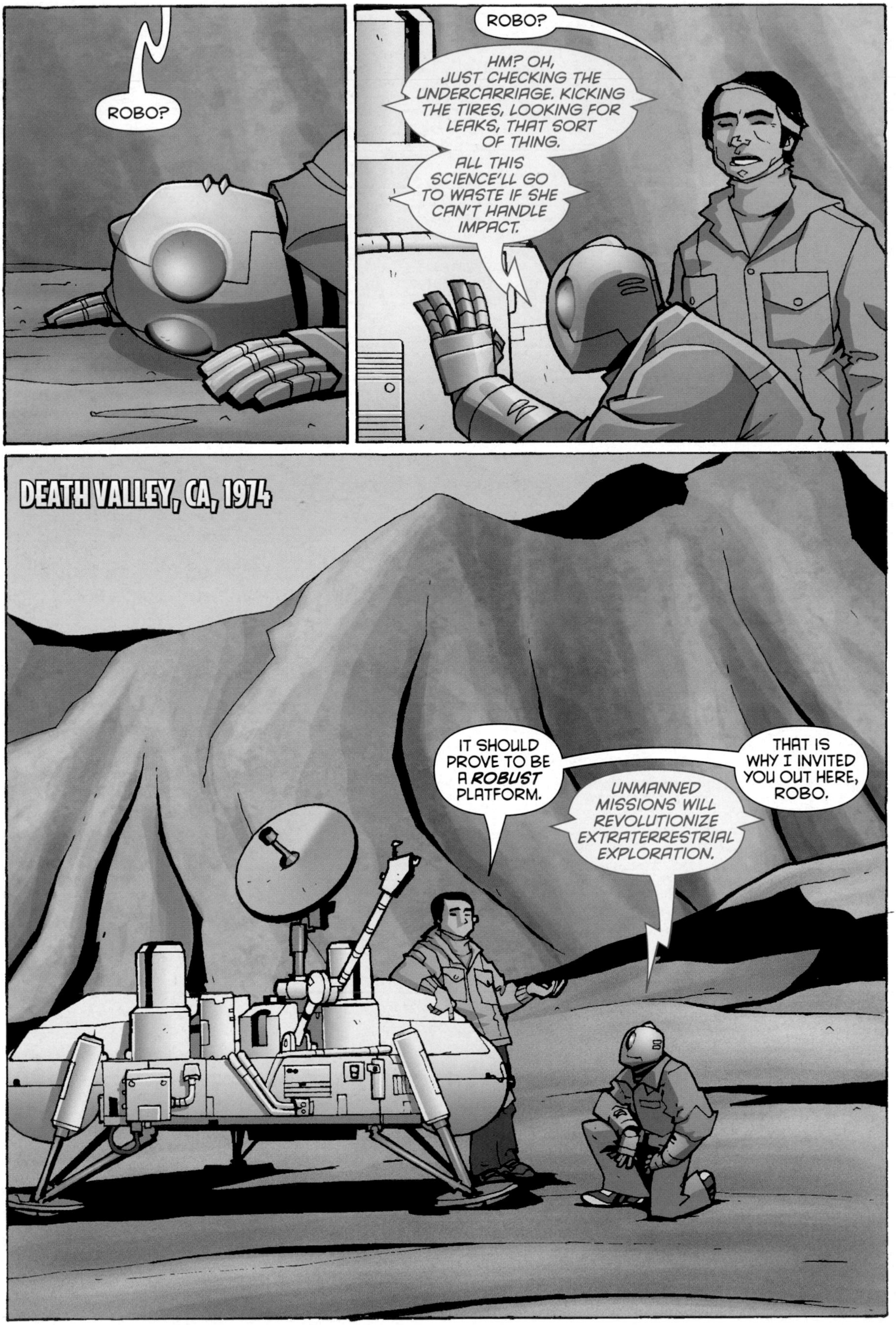
ROBO?
ROBO?
HM? OH, JUST CHECKING THE UNDERCARRIAGE. KICKING THE TIRES, LOOKING FOR LEAKS, THAT SORT OF THING.
ALL THIS SCIENCE'LL GO TO WASTE IF SHE CAN'T HANDLE IMPACT.
DEATH VALLEY, CA, 1974
IT SHOULD PROVE TO BE A ROBUST PLATFORM.
THAT IS WHY I INVITED YOU OUT HERE, ROBO.
UNMANNED MISSIONS WILL REVOLUTIONIZE EXTRATERRESTRIAL EXPLORATION.

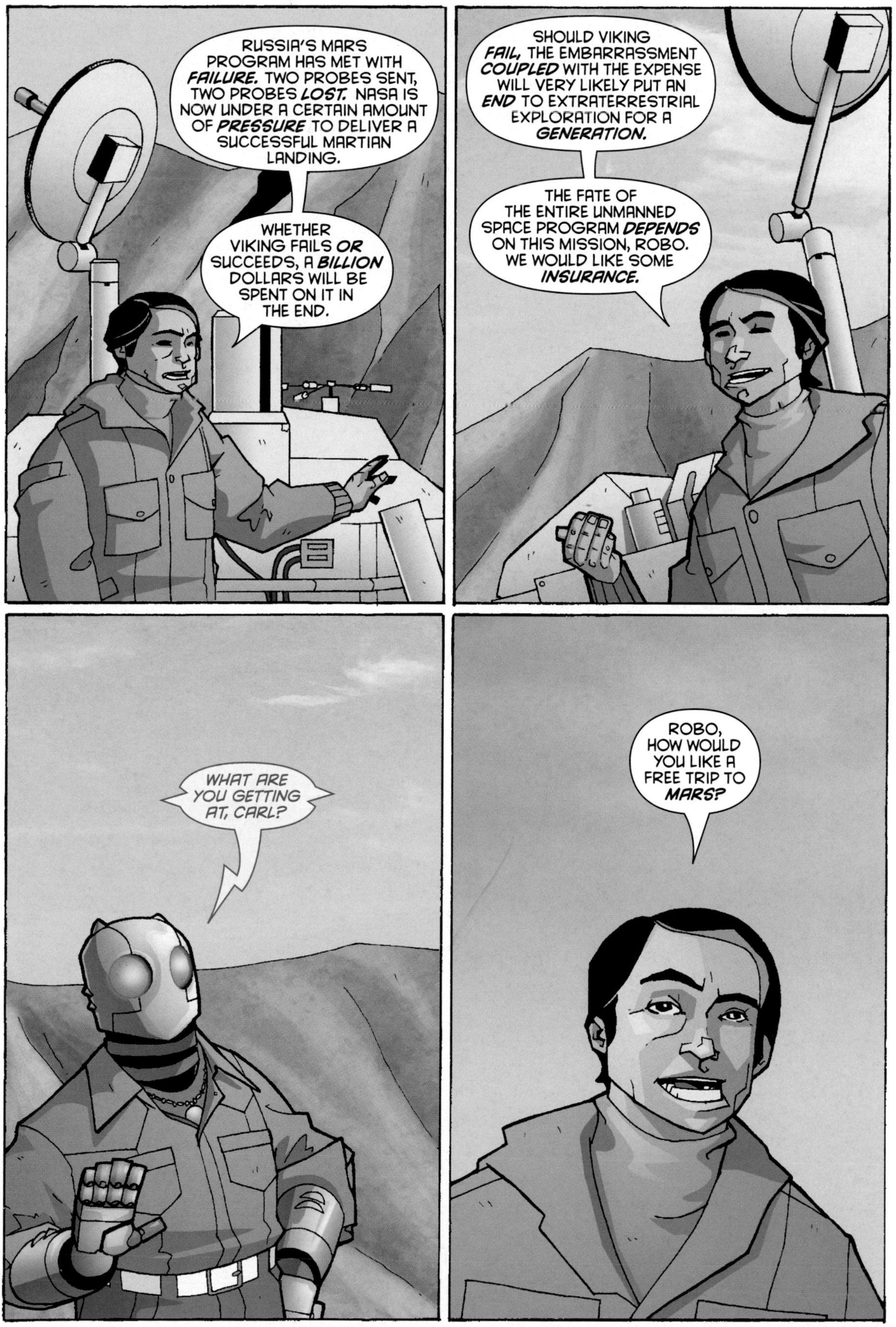
RUSSIA'S MARS PROGRAM HAS MET WITH *FAILURE.* TWO PROBES SENT, TWO PROBES *LOST.* NASA IS NOW UNDER A CERTAIN AMOUNT OF *PRESSURE* TO DELIVER A SUCCESSFUL MARTIAN LANDING.
WHETHER VIKING FAILS *OR* SUCCEEDS, A *BILLION* DOLLARS WILL BE SPENT ON IT IN THE END.
SHOULD VIKING *FAIL,* THE EMBARRASSMENT *COUPLED* WITH THE EXPENSE WILL VERY LIKELY PUT AN *END* TO EXTRATERRESTRIAL EXPLORATION FOR A *GENERATION.*
THE FATE OF THE ENTIRE UNMANNED SPACE PROGRAM *DEPENDS* ON THIS MISSION, ROBO. WE WOULD LIKE SOME *INSURANCE.*
WHAT ARE YOU GETTING AT, CARL?
ROBO, HOW WOULD YOU LIKE A FREE TRIP TO *MARS?*

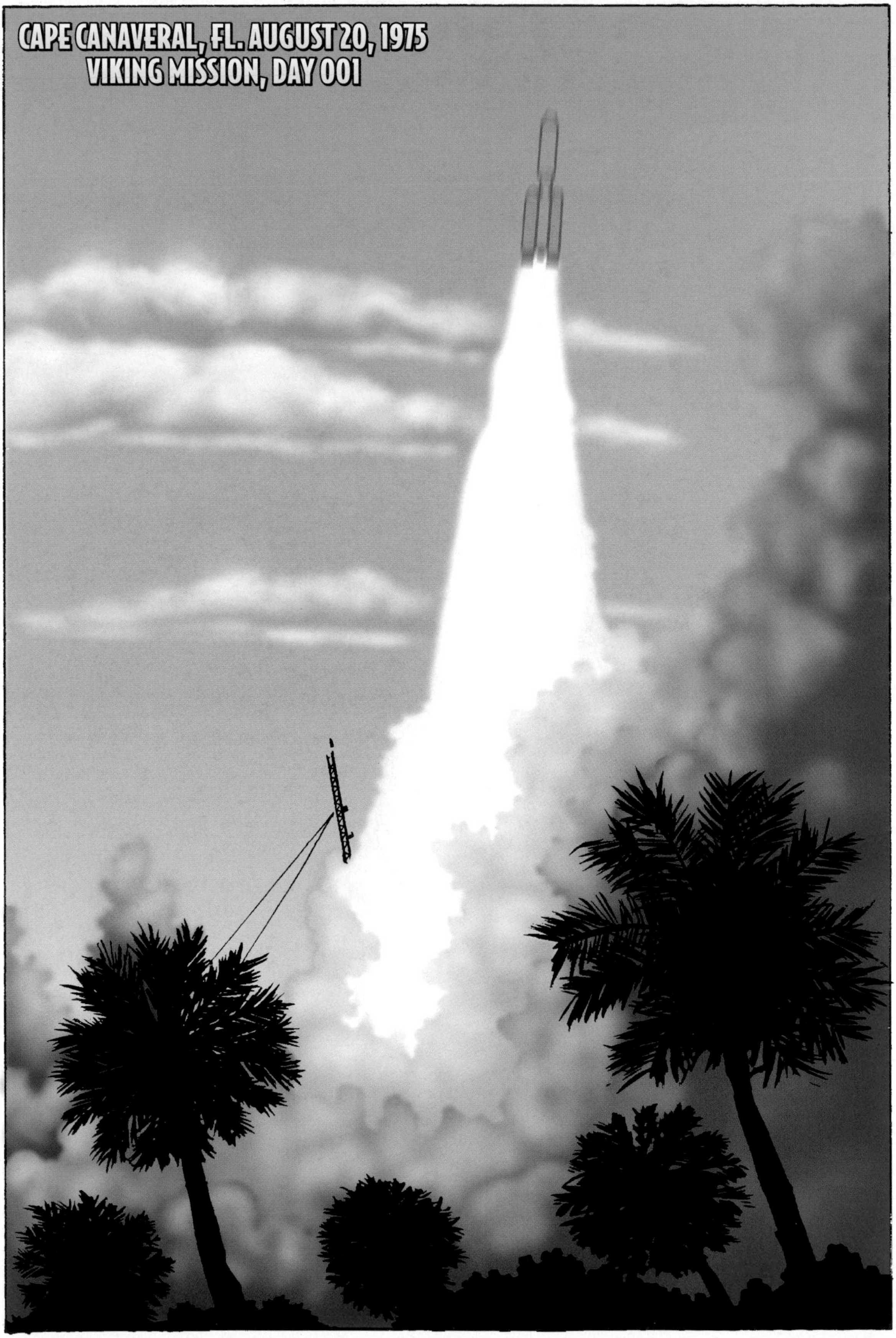
CAPE CANAVERAL, FL. AUGUST 20, 1975
VIKING MISSION, DAY 001

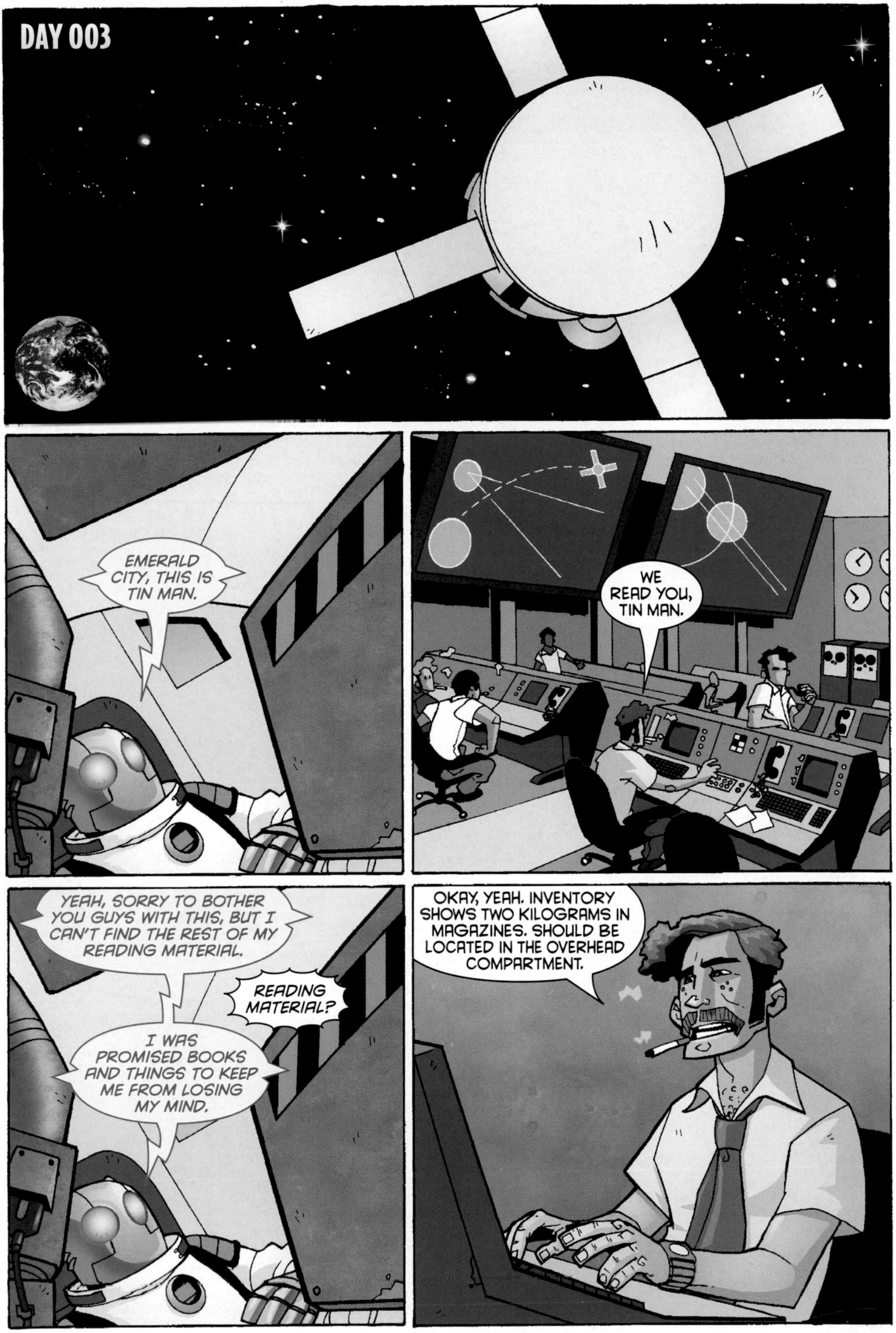
DAY 003
EMERALD CITY, THIS IS TIN MAN.
WE READ YOU, TIN MAN.
YEAH, SORRY TO BOTHER YOU GUYS WITH THIS, BUT I CAN'T FIND THE REST OF MY READING MATERIAL.
READING MATERIAL?
I WAS PROMISED BOOKS AND THINGS TO KEEP ME FROM LOSING MY MIND.
OKAY, YEAH. INVENTORY SHOWS TWO KILOGRAMS IN MAGAZINES. SHOULD BE LOCATED IN THE OVERHEAD COMPARTMENT.

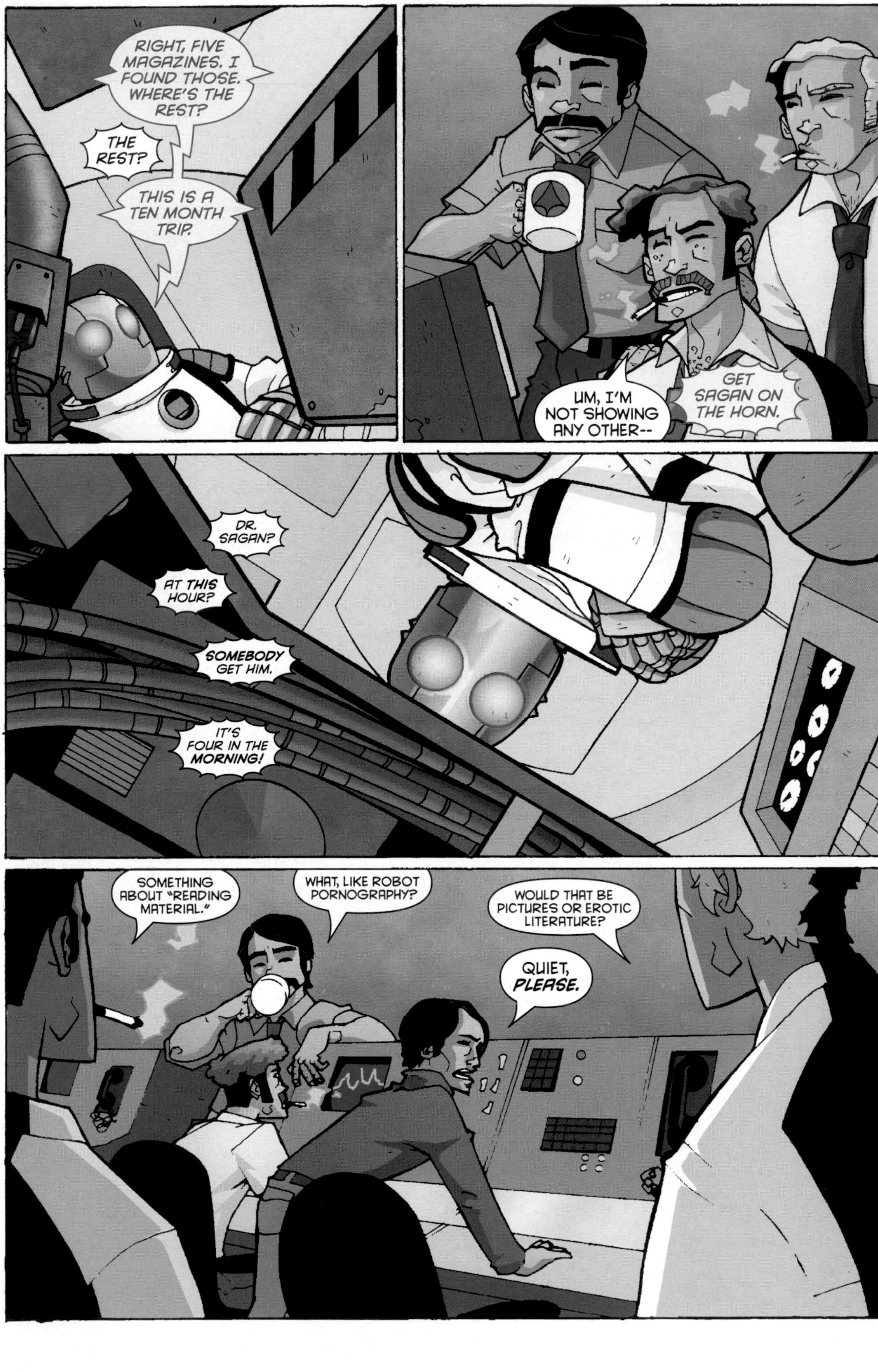
RIGHT, FIVE MAGAZINES. I FOUND THOSE. WHERE'S THE REST?
THE REST?
THIS IS A TEN MONTH TRIP.
UM, I'M NOT SHOWING ANY OTHER--
GET SAGAN ON THE HORN.
DR. SAGAN?
AT THIS HOUR?
SOMEBODY GET HIM.
IT'S FOUR IN THE MORNING!
SOMETHING ABOUT "READING MATERIAL."
WHAT, LIKE ROBOT PORNOGRAPHY?
WOULD THAT BE PICTURES OR EROTIC LITERATURE?
QUIET, PLEASE.

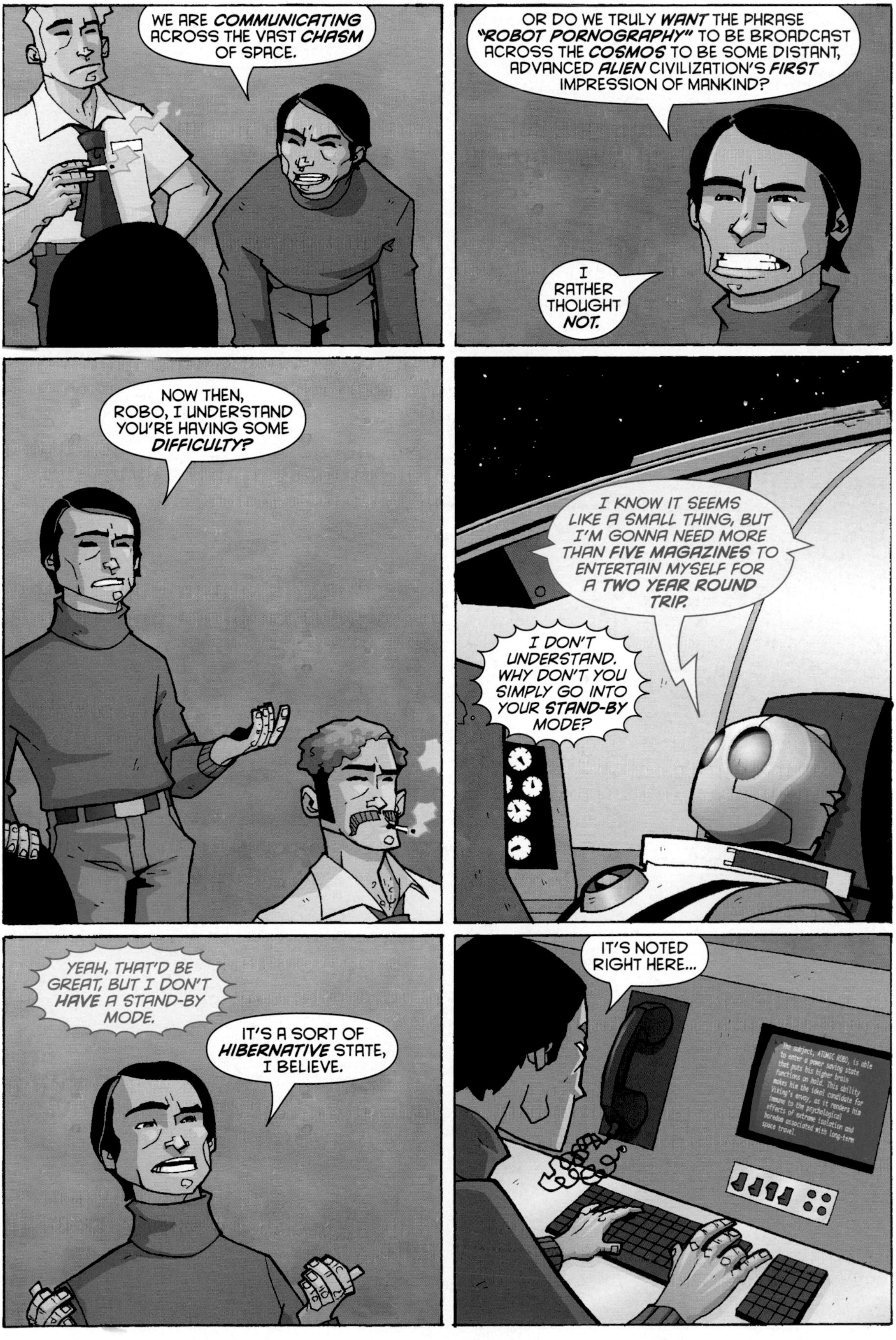
WE ARE COMMUNICATING ACROSS THE VAST CHASM OF SPACE.
OR DO WE TRULY WANT THE PHRASE "ROBOT PORNOGRAPHY" TO BE BROADCAST ACROSS THE COSMOS TO BE SOME DISTANT, ADVANCED ALIEN CIVILIZATION'S FIRST IMPRESSION OF MANKIND?
I RATHER THOUGHT NOT.
NOW THEN, ROBO, I UNDERSTAND YOU'RE HAVING SOME DIFFICULTY?
I KNOW IT SEEMS LIKE A SMALL THING, BUT I'M GONNA NEED MORE THAN FIVE MAGAZINES TO ENTERTAIN MYSELF FOR A TWO YEAR ROUND TRIP.
I DON'T UNDERSTAND. WHY DON'T YOU SIMPLY GO INTO YOUR STAND-BY MODE?
YEAH, THAT'D BE GREAT, BUT I DON'T HAVE A STAND-BY MODE.
IT'S A SORT OF HIBERNATIVE STATE, I BELIEVE.
IT'S NOTED RIGHT HERE...
The subject, ATOMIC ROBO, is able to enter a power saving state that puts his higher brain functions on hold. This ability makes him the ideal candidate for Viking's envoy, as it renders him immune to the psychological effects of extreme isolation and boredom associated with long-term space travel.

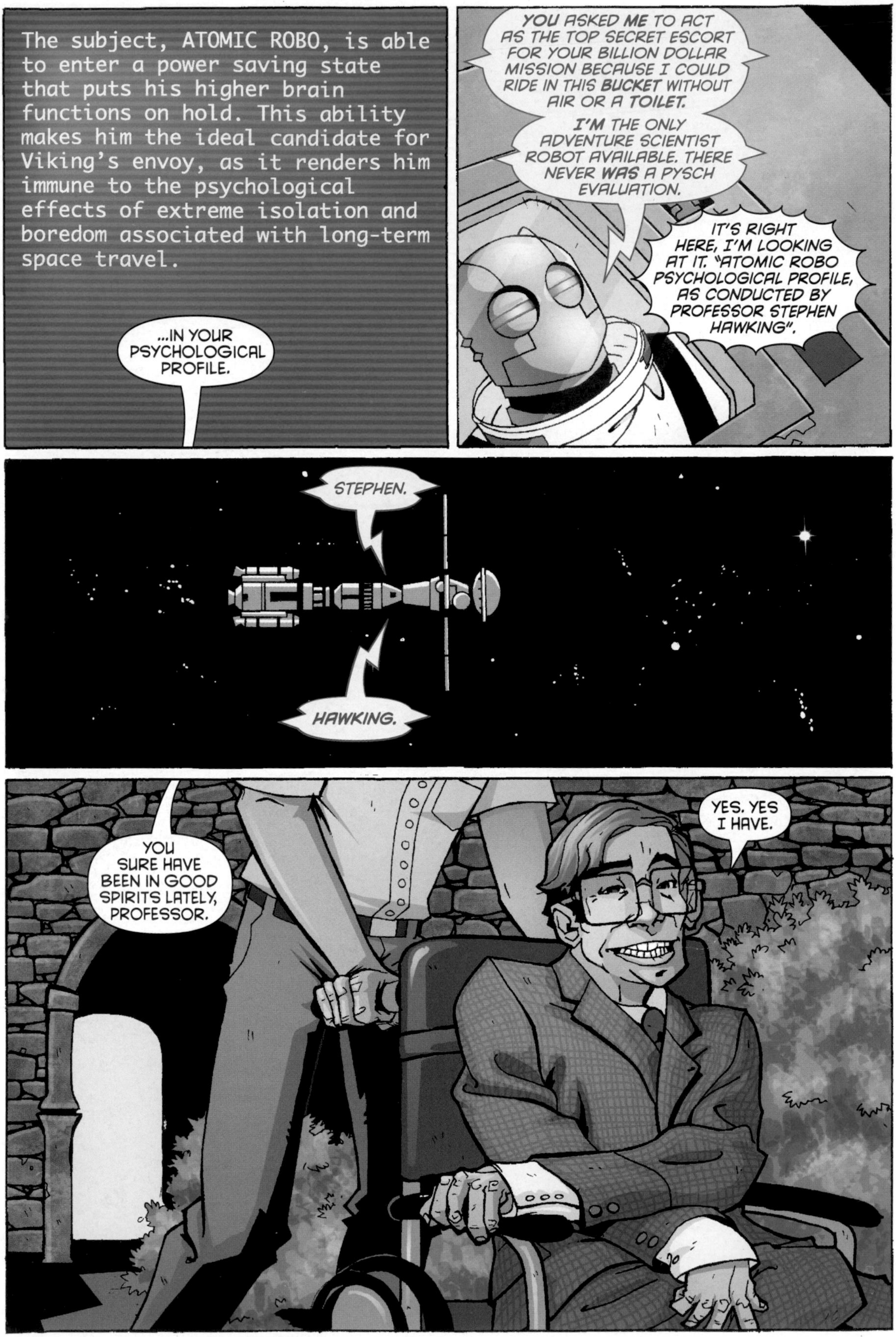
The subject, ATOMIC ROBO, is able to enter a power saving state that puts his higher brain functions on hold. This ability makes him the ideal candidate for Viking's envoy, as it renders him immune to the psychological effects of extreme isolation and boredom associated with long-term space travel.
...IN YOUR PSYCHOLOGICAL PROFILE.
YOU ASKED ME TO ACT AS THE TOP SECRET ESCORT FOR YOUR BILLION DOLLAR MISSION BECAUSE I COULD RIDE IN THIS BUCKET WITHOUT AIR OR A TOILET.
I'M THE ONLY ADVENTURE SCIENTIST ROBOT AVAILABLE. THERE NEVER WAS A PYSCH EVALUATION.
IT'S RIGHT HERE, I'M LOOKING AT IT. "ATOMIC ROBO PSYCHOLOGICAL PROFILE, AS CONDUCTED BY PROFESSOR STEPHEN HAWKING".
STEPHEN.
HAWKING.
YOU SURE HAVE BEEN IN GOOD SPIRITS LATELY, PROFESSOR.
YES. YES I HAVE.

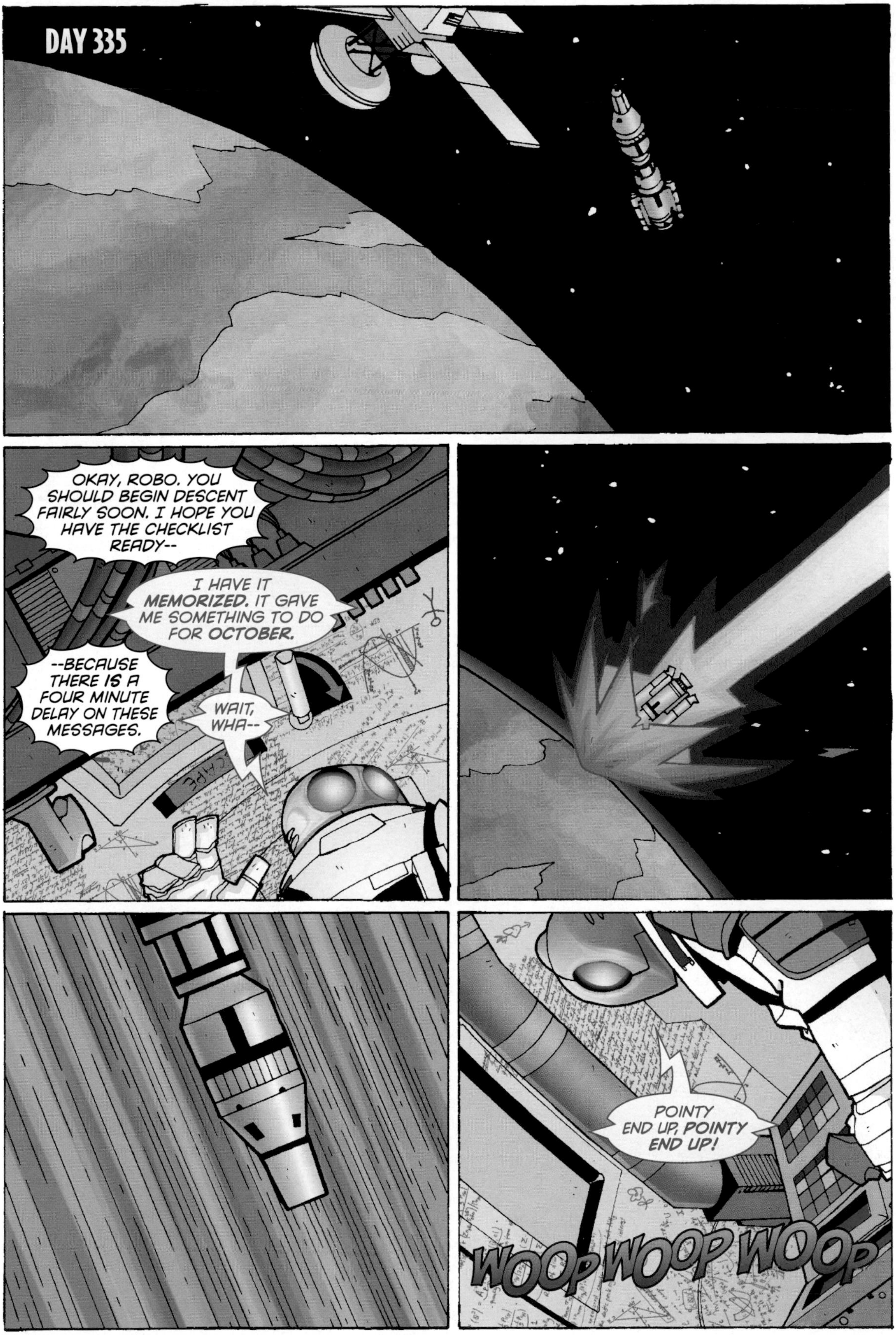
DAY 335
OKAY, ROBO. YOU SHOULD BEGIN DESCENT FAIRLY SOON. I HOPE YOU HAVE THE CHECKLIST READY--
I HAVE IT MEMORIZED. IT GAVE ME SOMETHING TO DO FOR OCTOBER.
--BECAUSE THERE IS A FOUR MINUTE DELAY ON THESE MESSAGES.
WAIT, WHA--
POINTY END UP, POINTY END UP!
WOOp WOOP WOOp

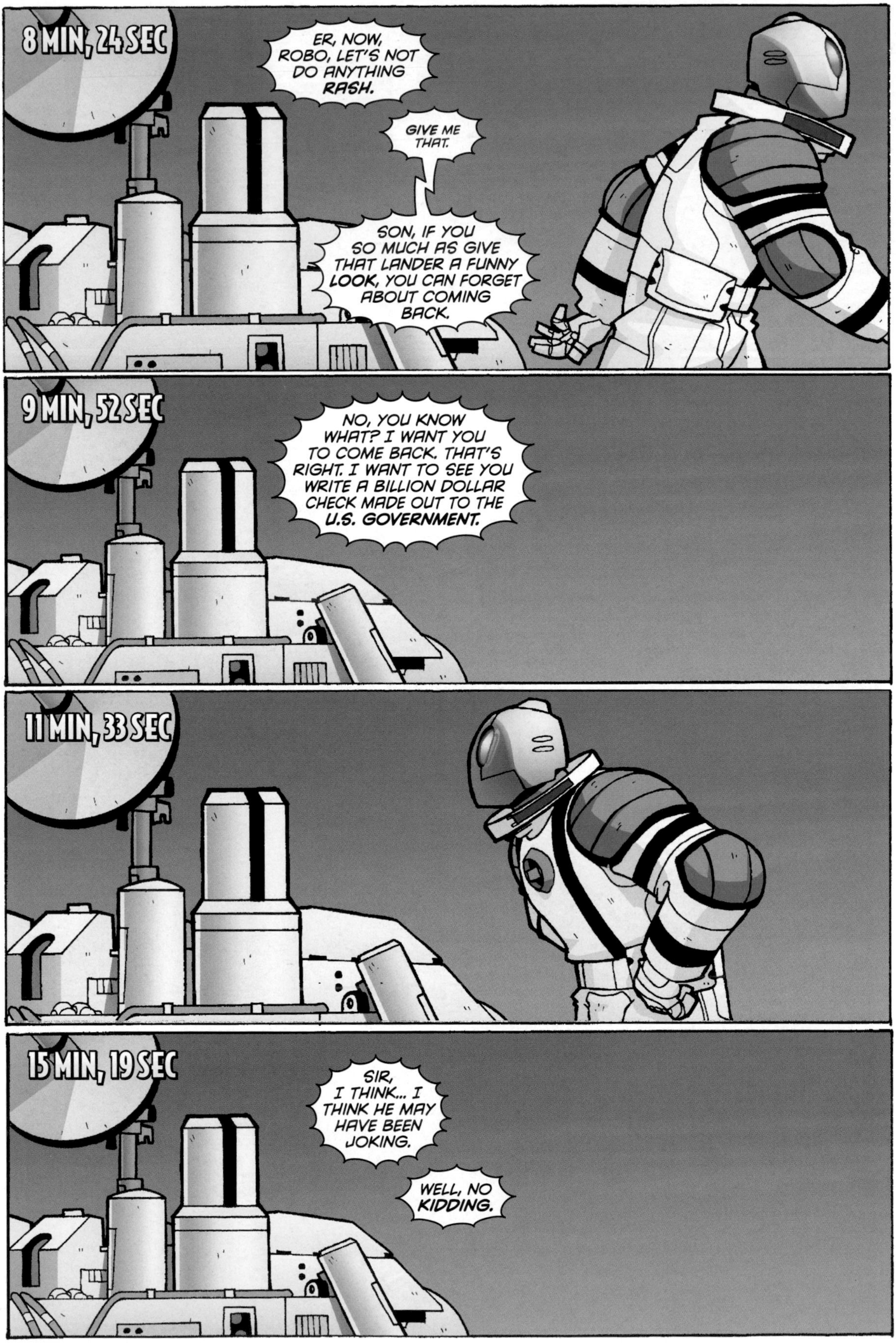
8 MIN, 24 SEC
ER, NOW, ROBO, LET'S NOT DO ANYTHING RASH.
GIVE ME THAT.
SON, IF YOU SO MUCH AS GIVE THAT LANDER A FUNNY LOOK, YOU CAN FORGET ABOUT COMING BACK.
9 MIN, 52 SEC
NO, YOU KNOW WHAT? I WANT YOU TO COME BACK. THAT'S RIGHT. I WANT TO SEE YOU WRITE A BILLION DOLLAR CHECK MADE OUT TO THE U.S. GOVERNMENT.
11 MIN, 33 SEC
15 MIN, 19 SEC
SIR, I THINK... I THINK HE MAY HAVE BEEN JOKING.
WELL, NO KIDDING.

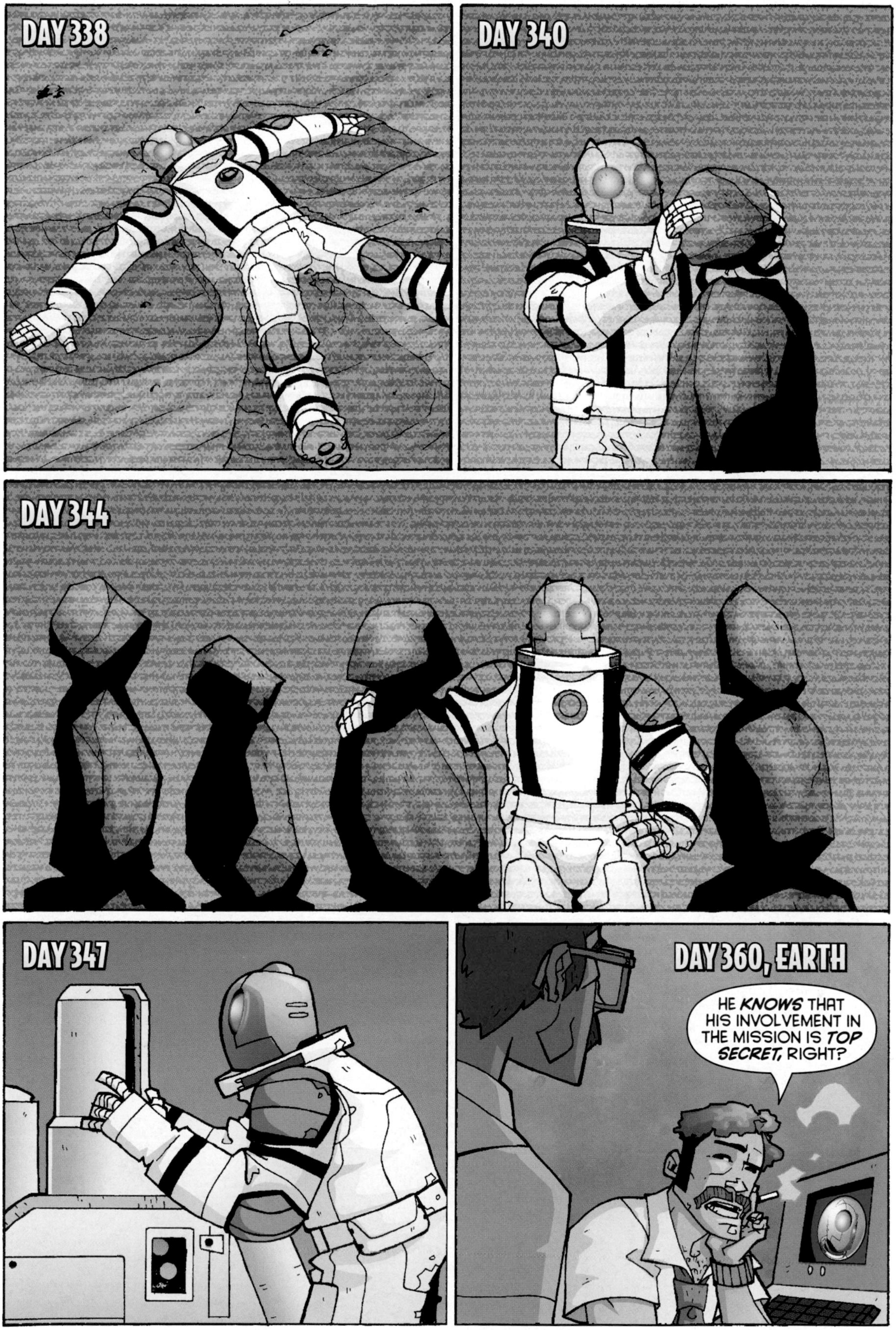
DAY 338
DAY 340
DAY 344
DAY 347
DAY 360, EARTH
HE KNOWS THAT HIS INVOLVEMENT IN THE MISSION IS TOP SECRET, RIGHT?

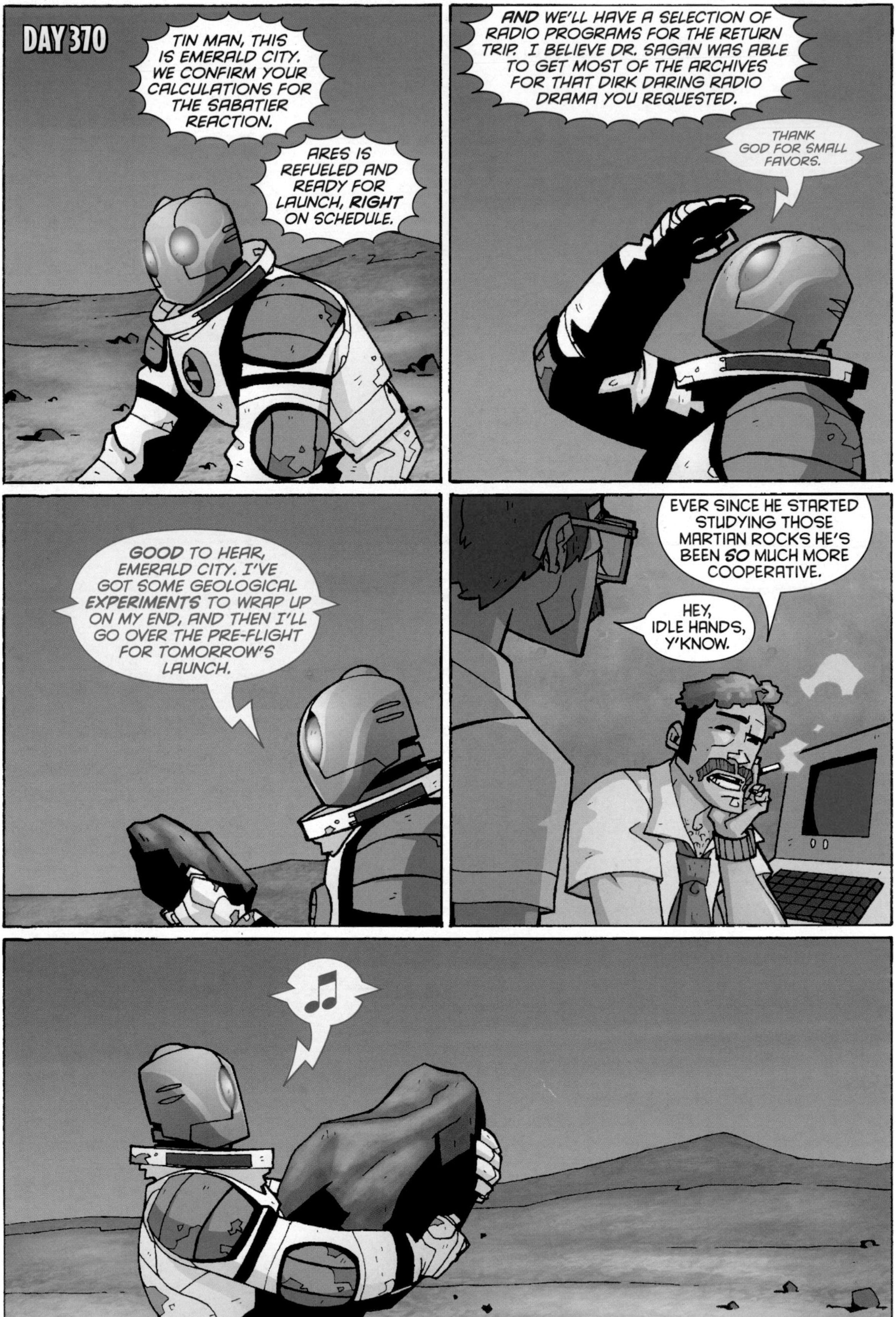
DAY 370
TIN MAN, THIS IS EMERALD CITY. WE CONFIRM YOUR CALCULATIONS FOR THE SABATIER REACTION.
ARES IS REFUELED AND READY FOR LAUNCH, RIGHT ON SCHEDULE.
AND WE'LL HAVE A SELECTION OF RADIO PROGRAMS FOR THE RETURN TRIP. I BELIEVE DR. SAGAN WAS ABLE TO GET MOST OF THE ARCHIVES FOR THAT DIRK DARING RADIO DRAMA YOU REQUESTED.
THANK GOD FOR SMALL FAVORS.
GOOD TO HEAR, EMERALD CITY. I'VE GOT SOME GEOLOGICAL EXPERIMENTS TO WRAP UP ON MY END, AND THEN I'LL GO OVER THE PRE-FLIGHT FOR TOMORROW'S LAUNCH.
EVER SINCE HE STARTED STUDYING THOSE MARTIAN ROCKS HE'S BEEN SO MUCH MORE COOPERATIVE.
HEY, IDLE HANDS, Y'KNOW.

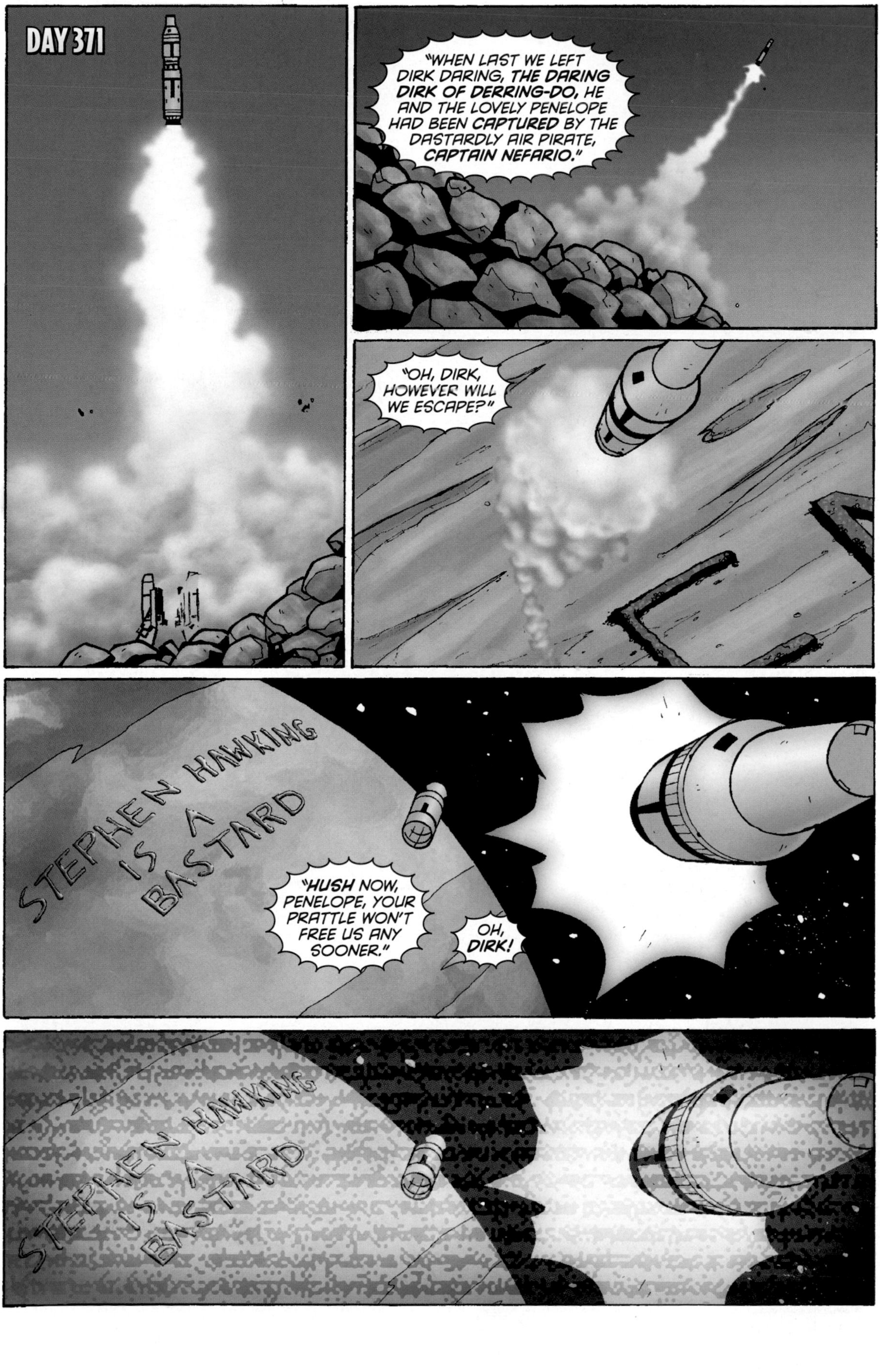
DAY 371
"WHEN LAST WE LEFT DIRK DARING, THE DARING DIRK OF DERRING-DO, HE AND THE LOVELY PENELOPE HAD BEEN CAPTURED BY THE DASTARDLY AIR PIRATE, CAPTAIN NEFARIO."
"OH, DIRK, HOWEVER WILL WE ESCAPE?"
STEPHEN HAWKING IS A BASTARD
"HUSH NOW, PENELOPE, YOUR PRATTLE WON'T FREE US ANY SOONER."
OH, DIRK!
STEPHEN HAWKING IS A BASTARD

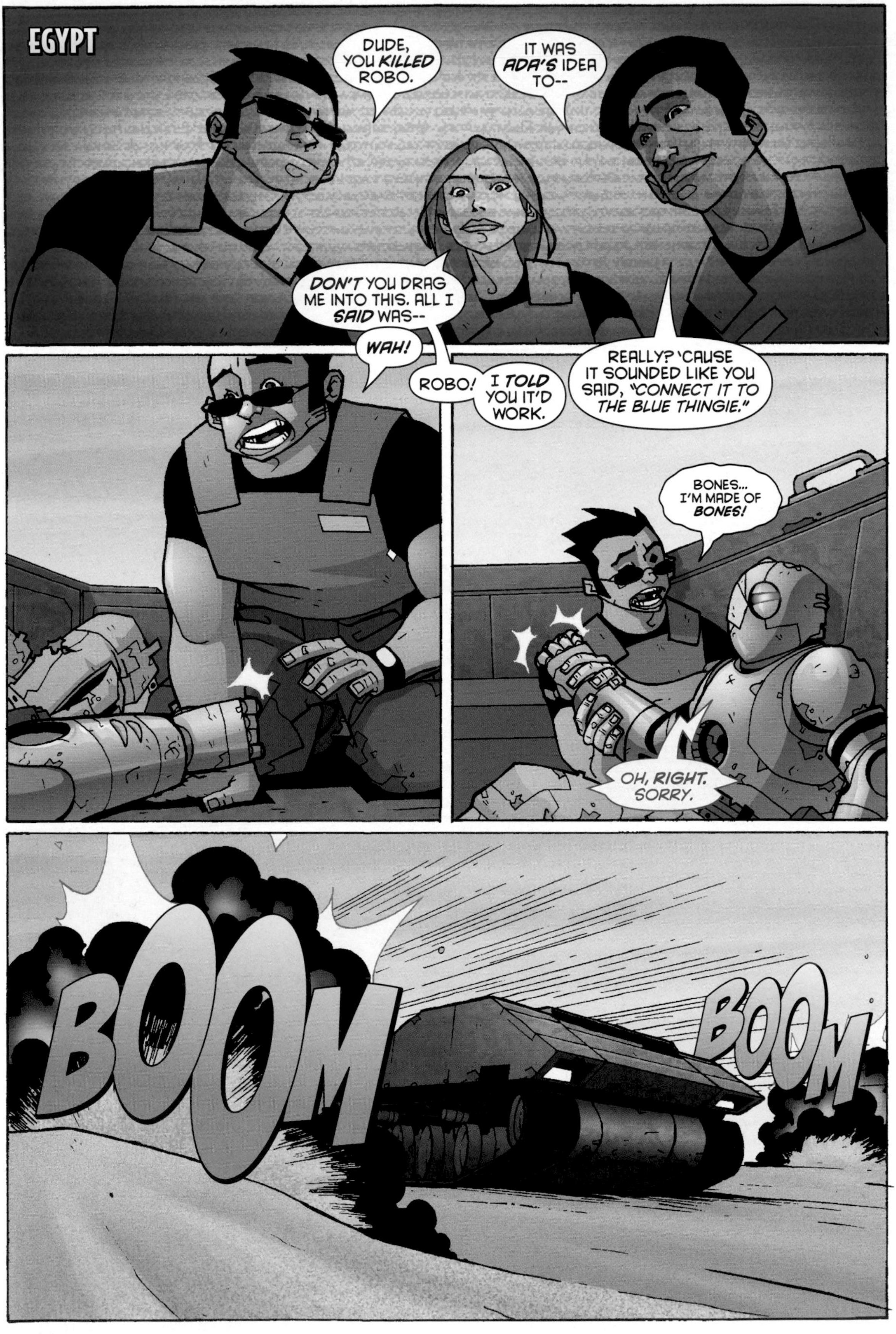
EGYPT
DUDE, YOU KILLED ROBO.
IT WAS ADA'S IDEA TO--
DON'T YOU DRAG ME INTO THIS. ALL I SAID WAS--
REALLY? 'CAUSE IT SOUNDED LIKE YOU SAID, "CONNECT IT TO THE BLUE THINGIE."
WAH!
ROBO!
I TOLD YOU IT'D WORK.
BONES... I'M MADE OF BONES!
OH, RIGHT. SORRY.
BOOM
BOOM

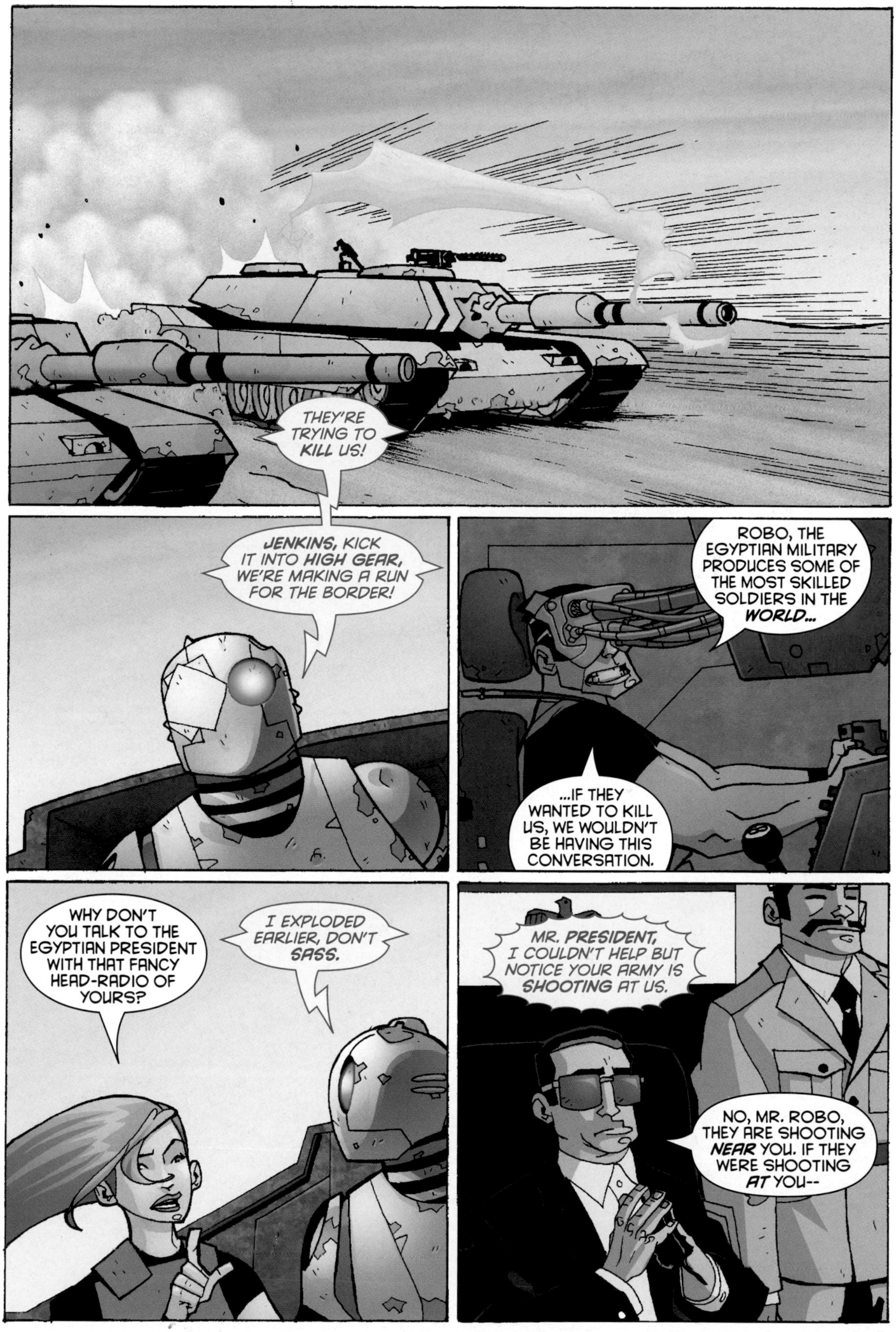
THEY'RE TRYING TO KILL US!
JENKINS, KICK IT INTO HIGH GEAR, WE'RE MAKING A RUN FOR THE BORDER!
ROBO, THE EGYPTIAN MILITARY PRODUCES SOME OF THE MOST SKILLED SOLDIERS IN THE WORLD...
...IF THEY WANTED TO KILL US, WE WOULDN'T BE HAVING THIS CONVERSATION.
WHY DON'T YOU TALK TO THE EGYPTIAN PRESIDENT WITH THAT FANCY HEAD-RADIO OF YOURS?
I EXPLODED EARLIER, DON'T SASS.
MR. PRESIDENT, I COULDN'T HELP BUT NOTICE YOUR ARMY IS SHOOTING AT US.
NO, MR. ROBO, THEY ARE SHOOTING NEAR YOU. IF THEY WERE SHOOTING AT YOU--

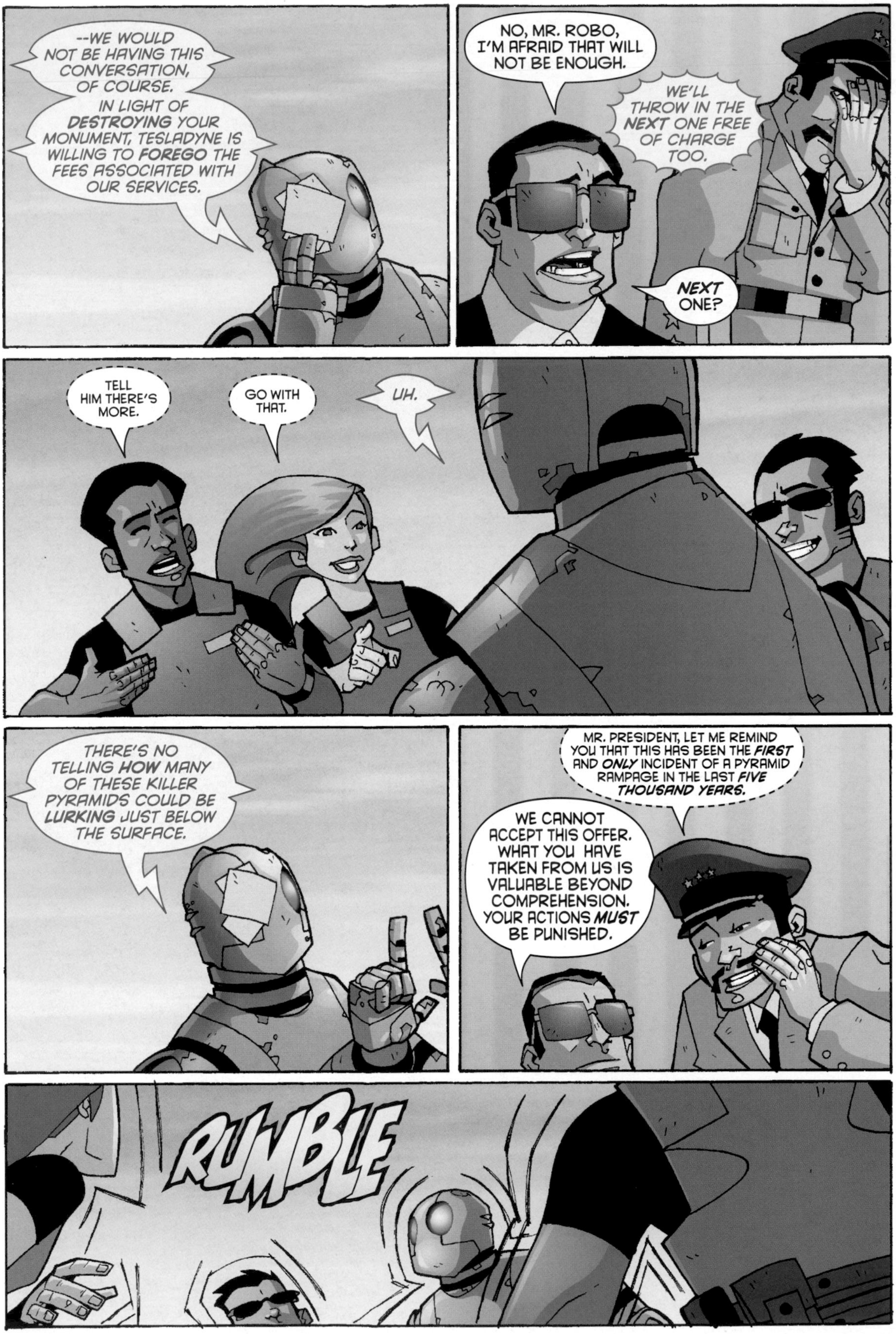
--WE WOULD NOT BE HAVING THIS CONVERSATION, OF COURSE.
IN LIGHT OF DESTROYING YOUR MONUMENT, TESLADYNE IS WILLING TO FOREGO THE FEES ASSOCIATED WITH OUR SERVICES.
NO, MR. ROBO, I'M AFRAID THAT WILL NOT BE ENOUGH.
WE'LL THROW IN THE NEXT ONE FREE OF CHARGE TOO.
NEXT ONE?
TELL HIM THERE'S MORE.
GO WITH THAT.
UH.
THERE'S NO TELLING HOW MANY OF THESE KILLER PYRAMIDS COULD BE LURKING JUST BELOW THE SURFACE.
MR. PRESIDENT, LET ME REMIND YOU THAT THIS HAS BEEN THE FIRST AND ONLY INCIDENT OF A PYRAMID RAMPAGE IN THE LAST FIVE THOUSAND YEARS.
WE CANNOT ACCEPT THIS OFFER. WHAT YOU HAVE TAKEN FROM US IS VALUABLE BEYOND COMPREHENSION. YOUR ACTIONS MUST BE PUNISHED.
RUMBLE

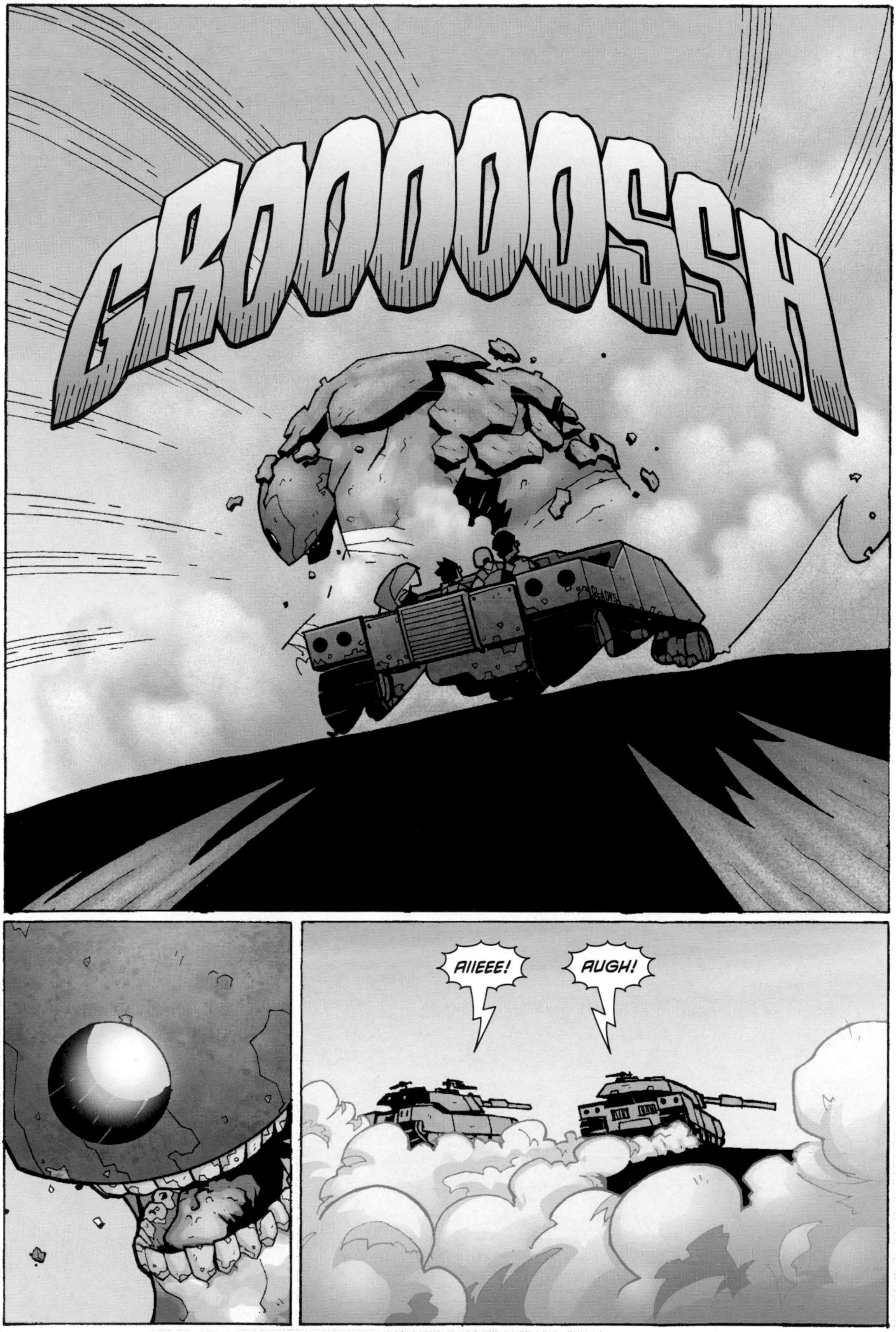
CROOOOOSSH
AIIEEE!
AUGH!

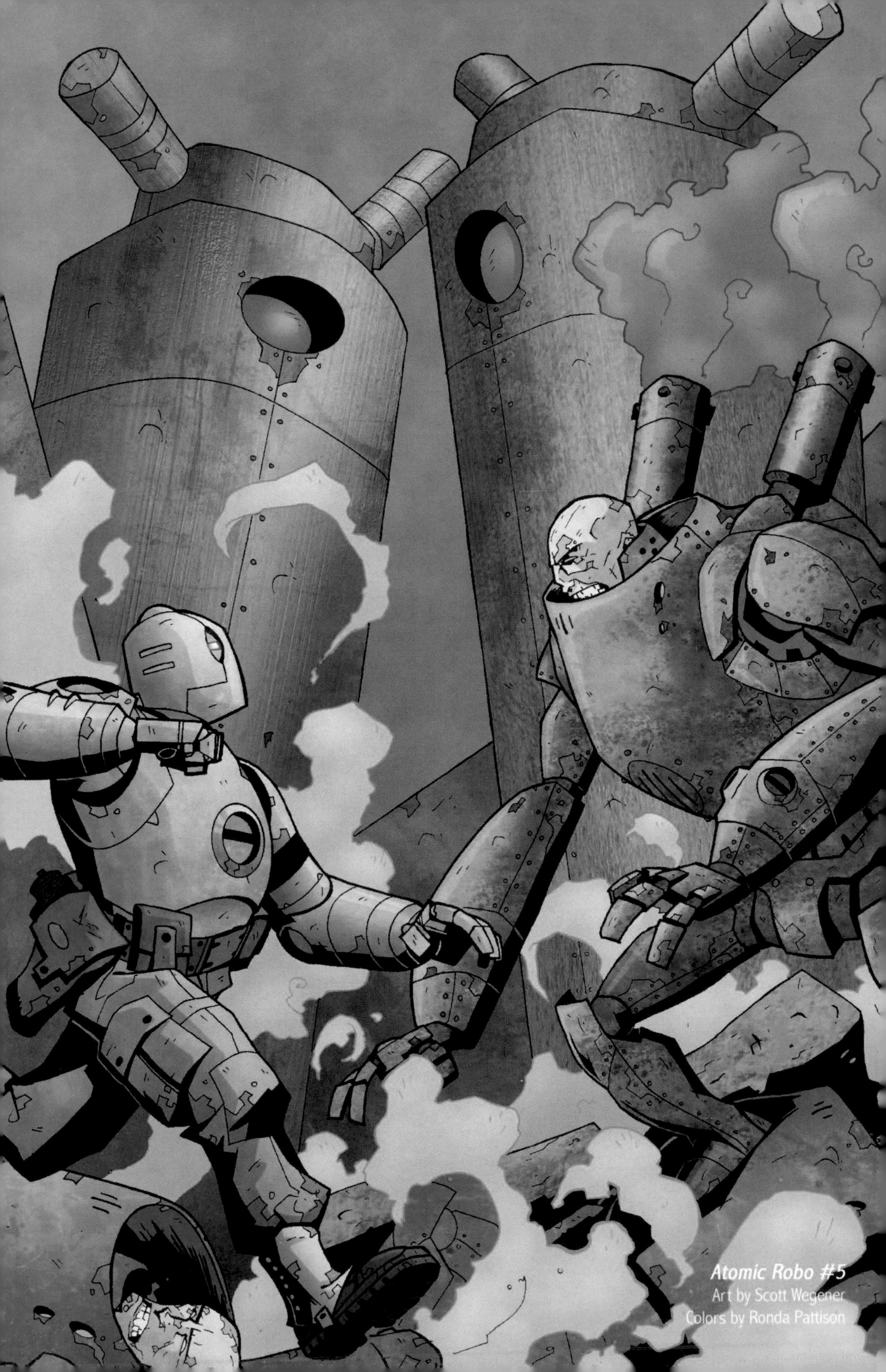

Atomic Robo #5
Art by Scott Wegener
Colors by Ronda Pattison

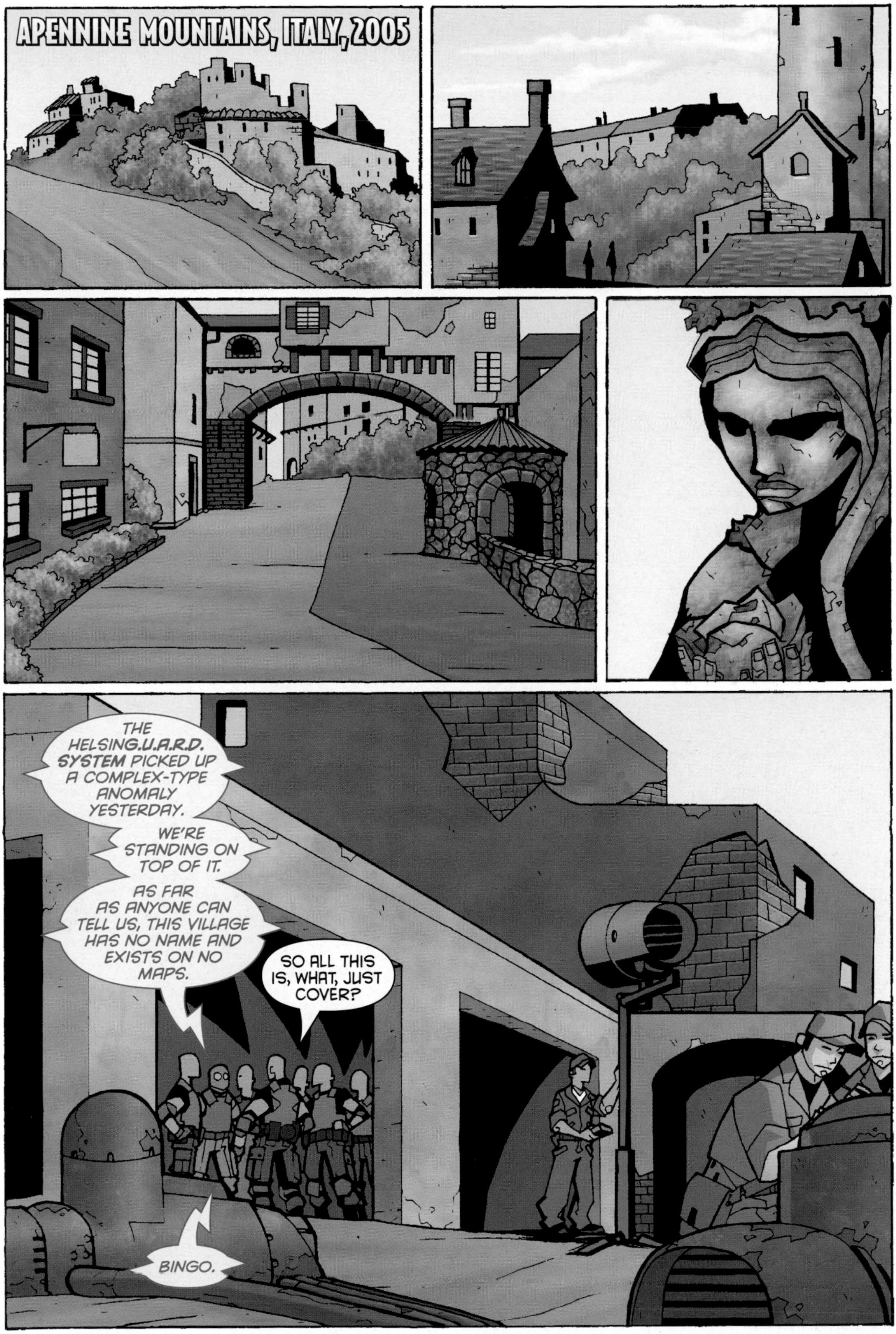
APENNINE MOUNTAINS, ITALY, 2005
THE HELSING.U.A.R.D. SYSTEM PICKED UP A COMPLEX-TYPE ANOMALY YESTERDAY.
WE'RE STANDING ON TOP OF IT.
AS FAR AS ANYONE CAN TELL US, THIS VILLAGE HAS NO NAME AND EXISTS ON NO MAPS.
SO ALL THIS IS, WHAT, JUST COVER?
BINGO.

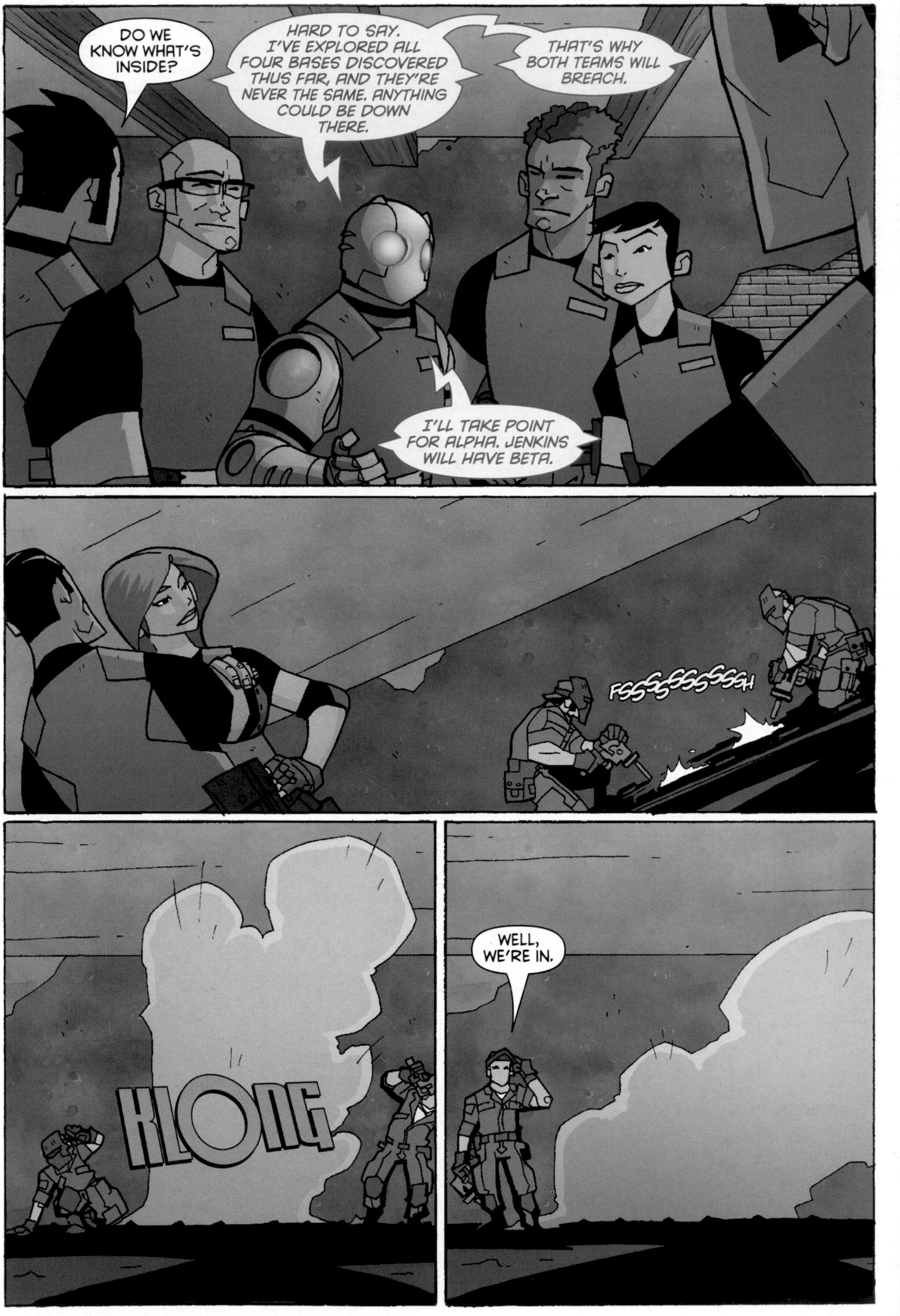
DO WE KNOW WHAT'S INSIDE?
HARD TO SAY. I'VE EXPLORED ALL FOUR BASES DISCOVERED THUS FAR, AND THEY'RE NEVER THE SAME. ANYTHING COULD BE DOWN THERE.
THAT'S WHY BOTH TEAMS WILL BREACH.
I'LL TAKE POINT FOR ALPHA. JENKINS WILL HAVE BETA.
FSSSSSSSSSSH
KLONG
WELL, WE'RE IN.

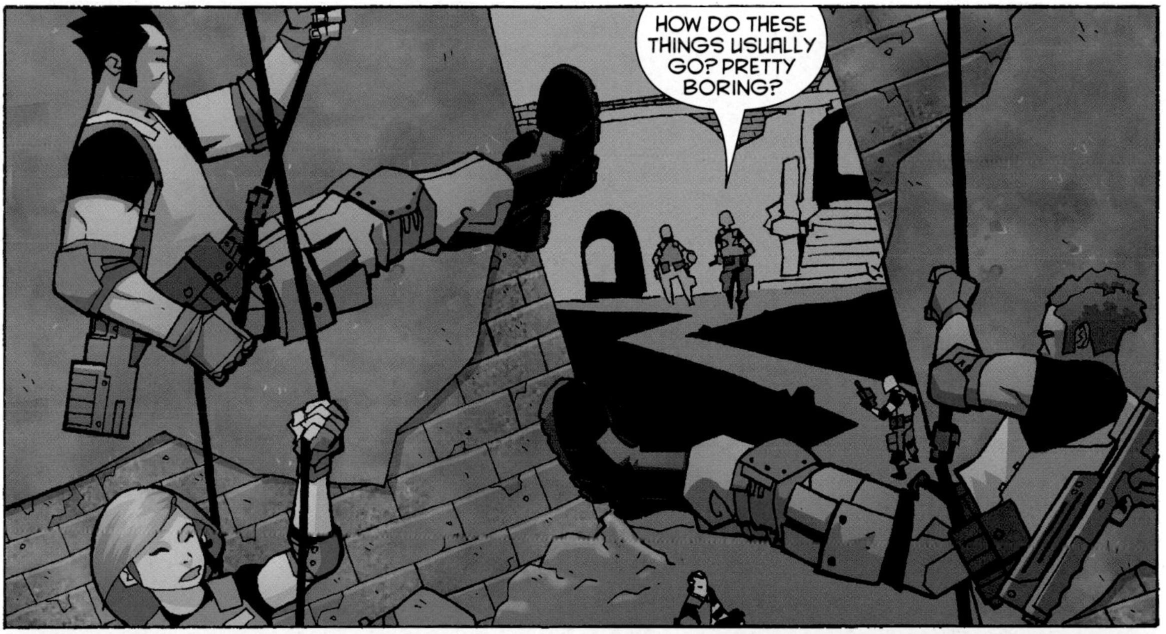
HOW DO THESE THINGS USUALLY GO? PRETTY BORING?

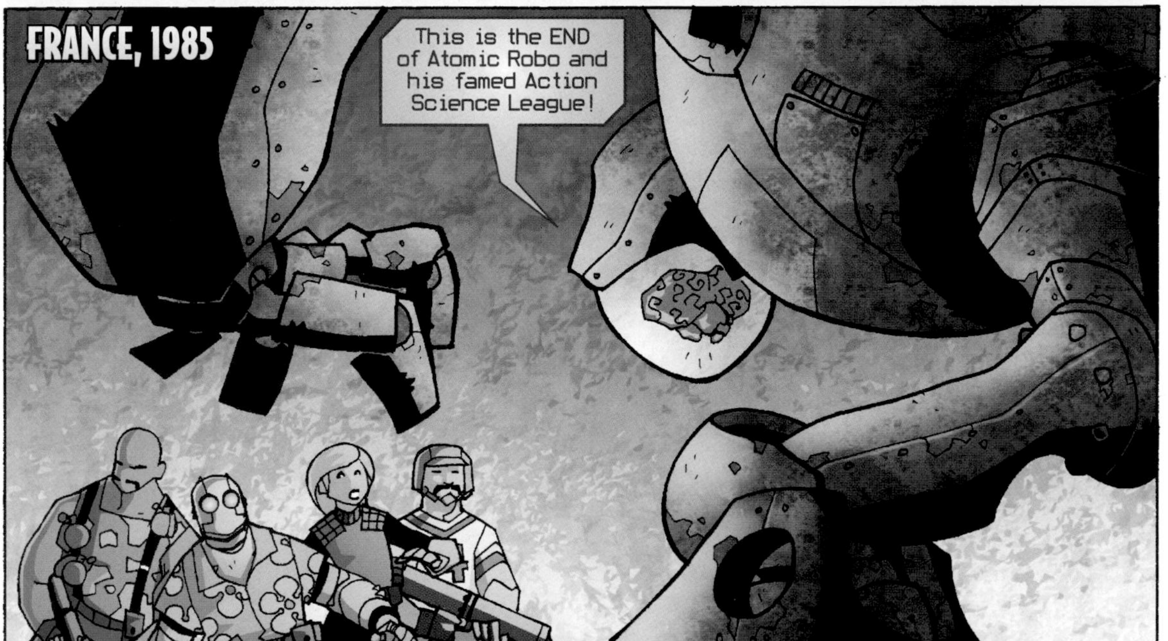
FRANCE, 1985
This is the END of Atomic Robo and his famed Action Science League!

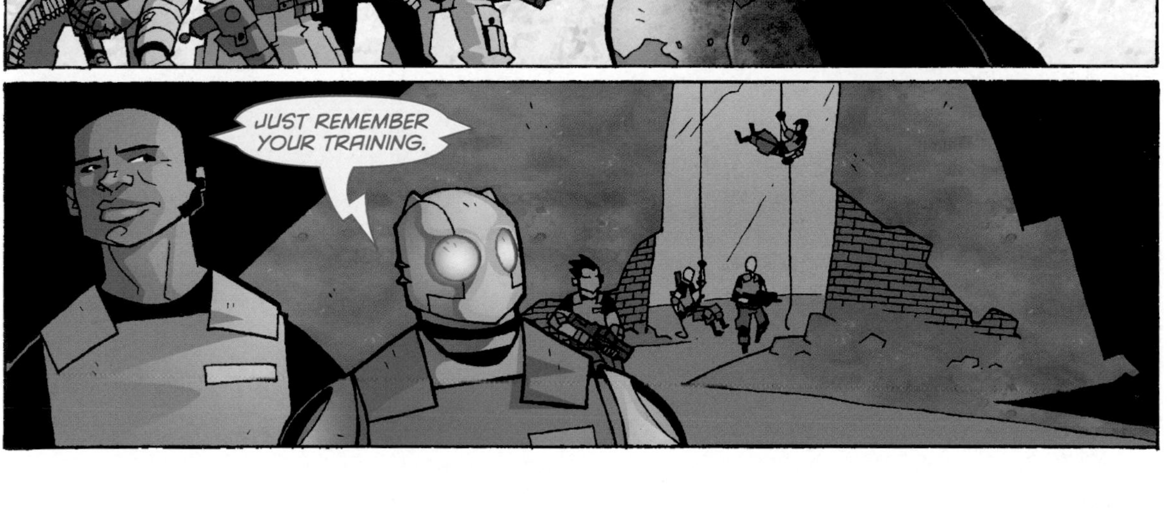
JUST REMEMBER YOUR TRAINING.

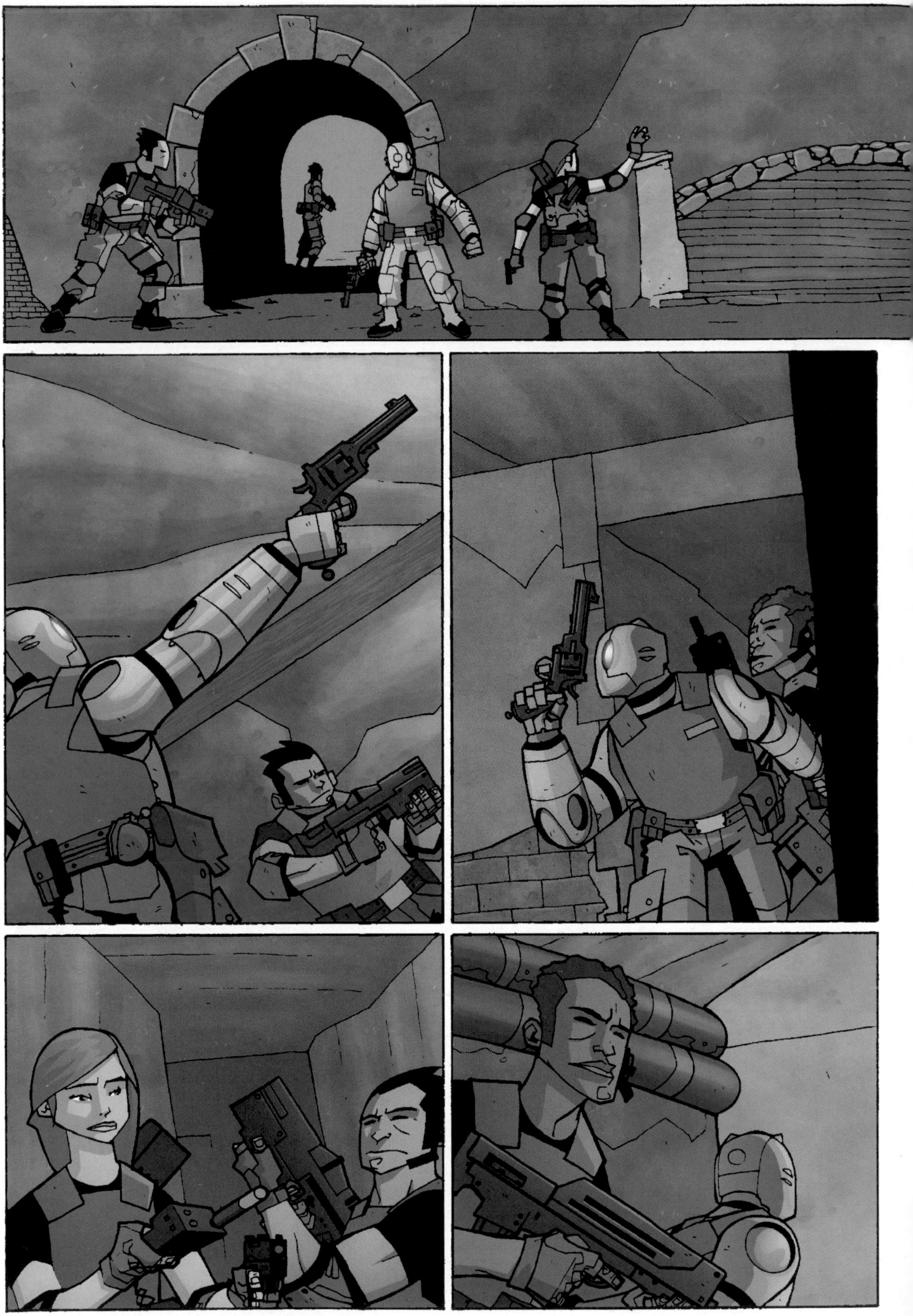

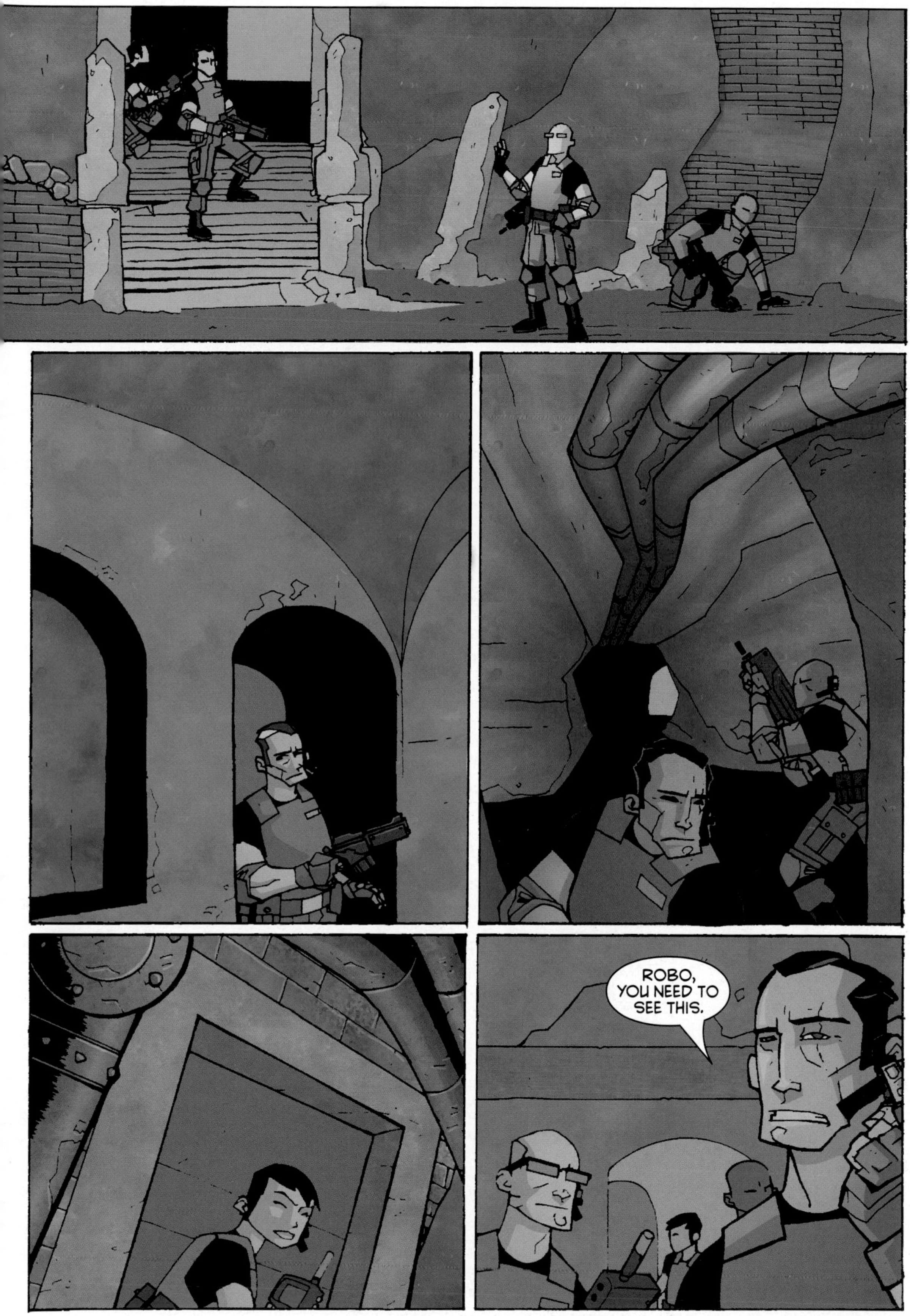
ROBO, YOU NEED TO SEE THIS.

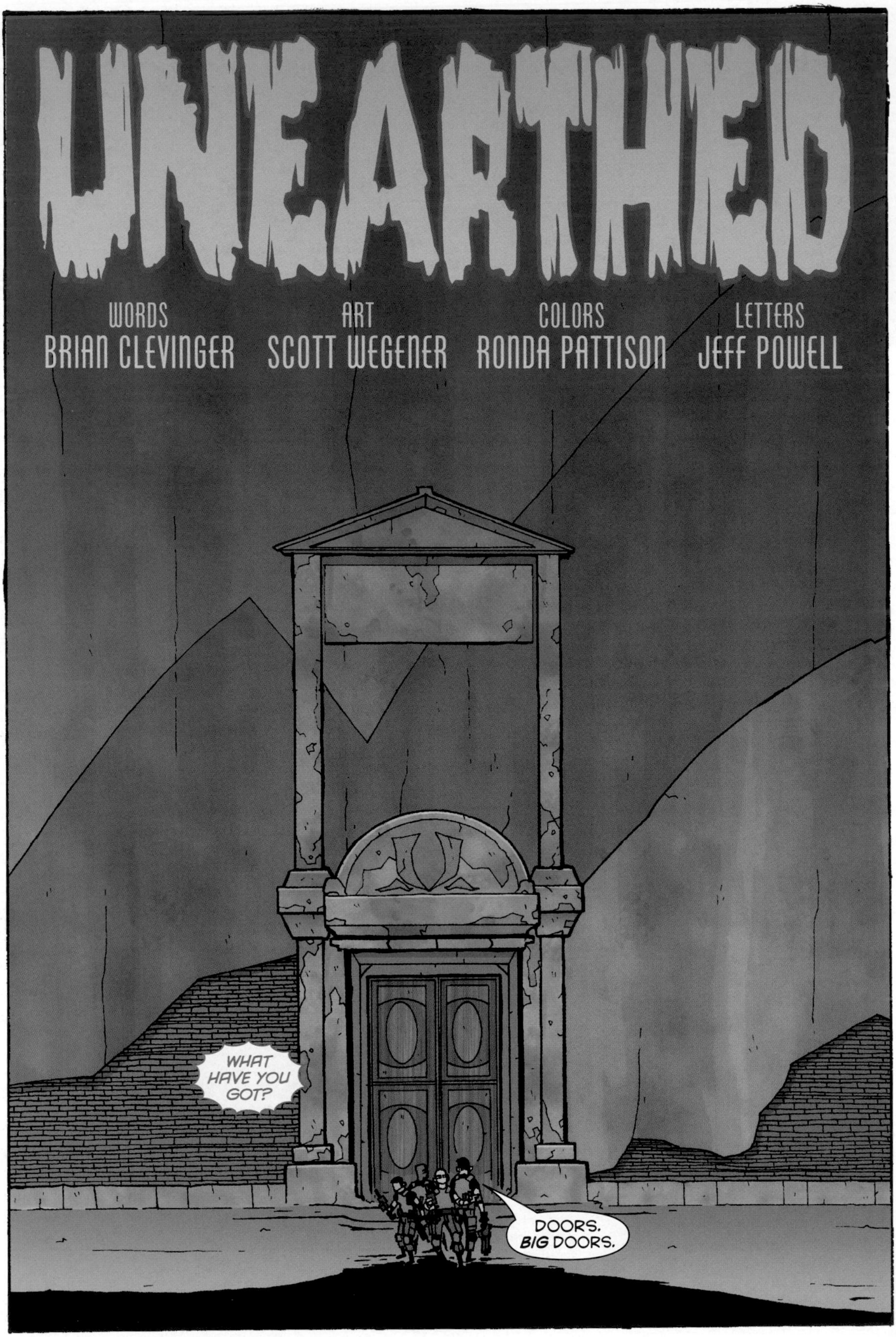
UNEARTHED
WORDS BRIAN CLEVINGER
ART SCOTT WEGENER
COLORS RONDA PATTISON
LETTERS JEFF POWELL
WHAT HAVE YOU GOT?
DOORS. BIG DOORS.

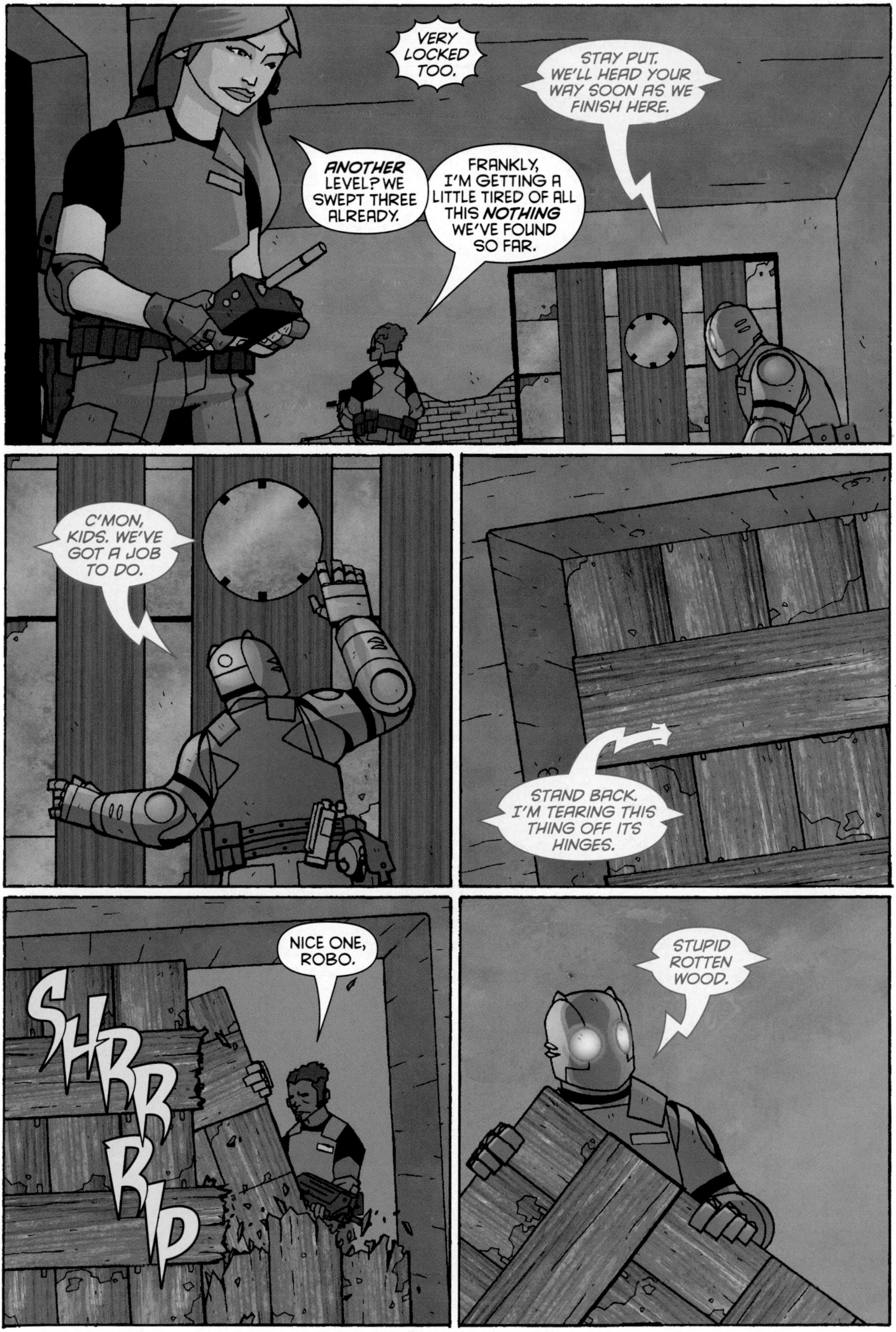
VERY LOCKED TOO.
STAY PUT. WE'LL HEAD YOUR WAY SOON AS WE FINISH HERE.
ANOTHER LEVEL? WE SWEPT THREE ALREADY.
FRANKLY, I'M GETTING A LITTLE TIRED OF ALL THIS NOTHING WE'VE FOUND SO FAR.
C'MON, KIDS. WE'VE GOT A JOB TO DO.
STAND BACK. I'M TEARING THIS THING OFF ITS HINGES.
SHRRRIP
NICE ONE, ROBO.
STUPID ROTTEN WOOD.

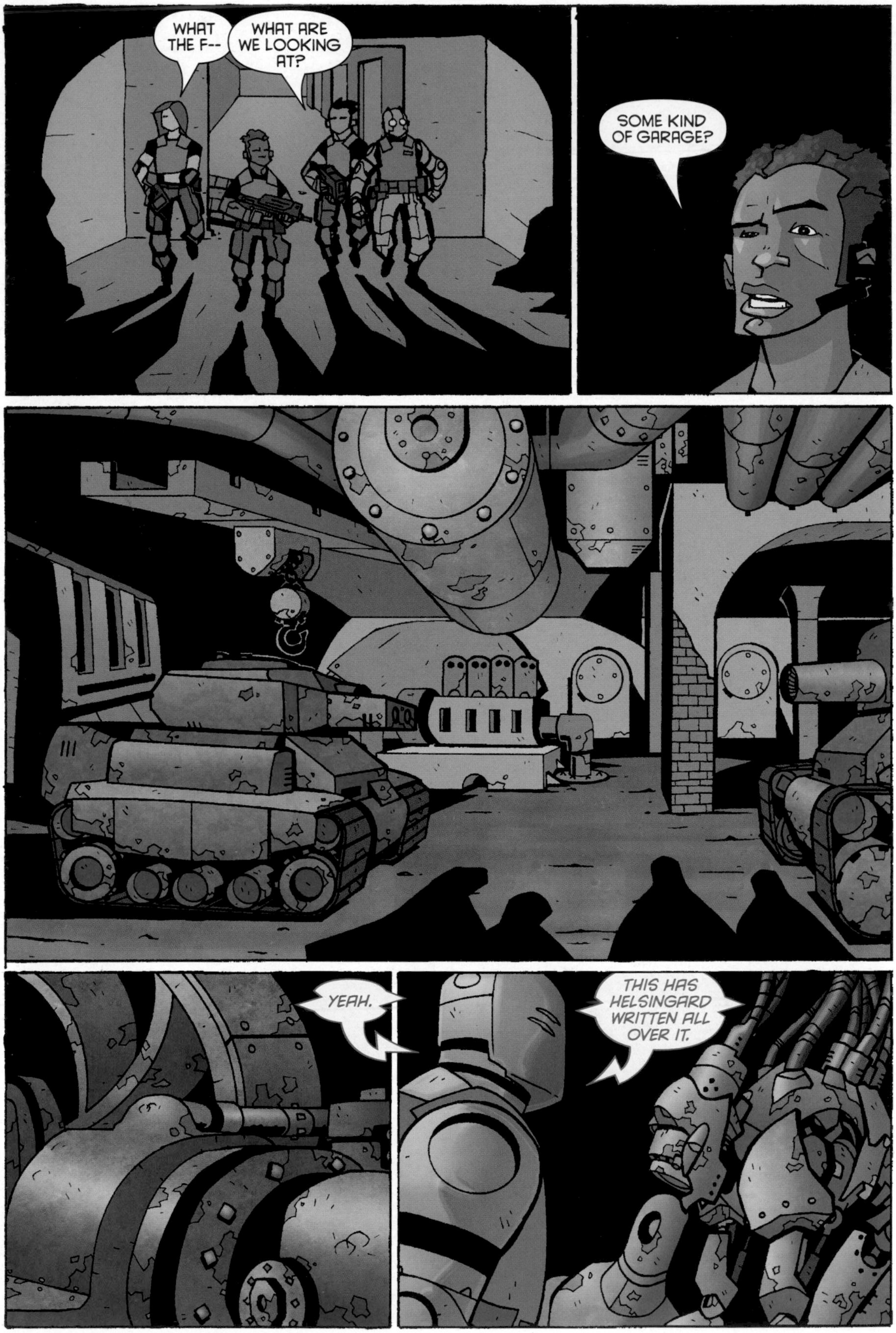
WHAT THE F--
WHAT ARE WE LOOKING AT?
SOME KIND OF GARAGE?
YEAH.
THIS HAS HELSINGARD WRITTEN ALL OVER IT.

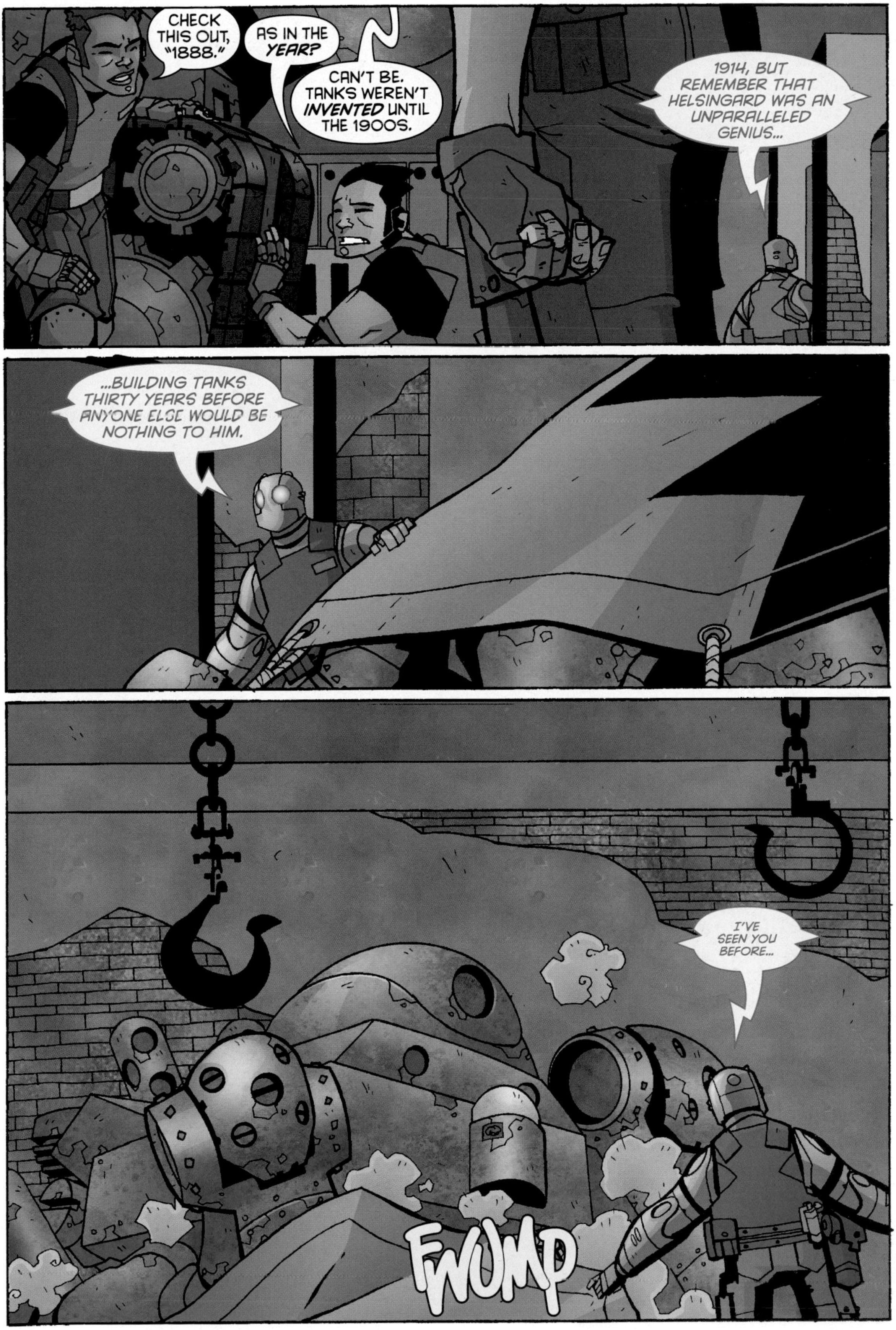
CHECK THIS OUT, "1888."
AS IN THE YEAR?
CAN'T BE. TANKS WEREN'T INVENTED UNTIL THE 1900S.
1914, BUT REMEMBER THAT HELSINGARD WAS AN UNPARALLELED GENIUS...
...BUILDING TANKS THIRTY YEARS BEFORE ANYONE ELSE WOULD BE NOTHING TO HIM.
I'VE SEEN YOU BEFORE...
FWUMP

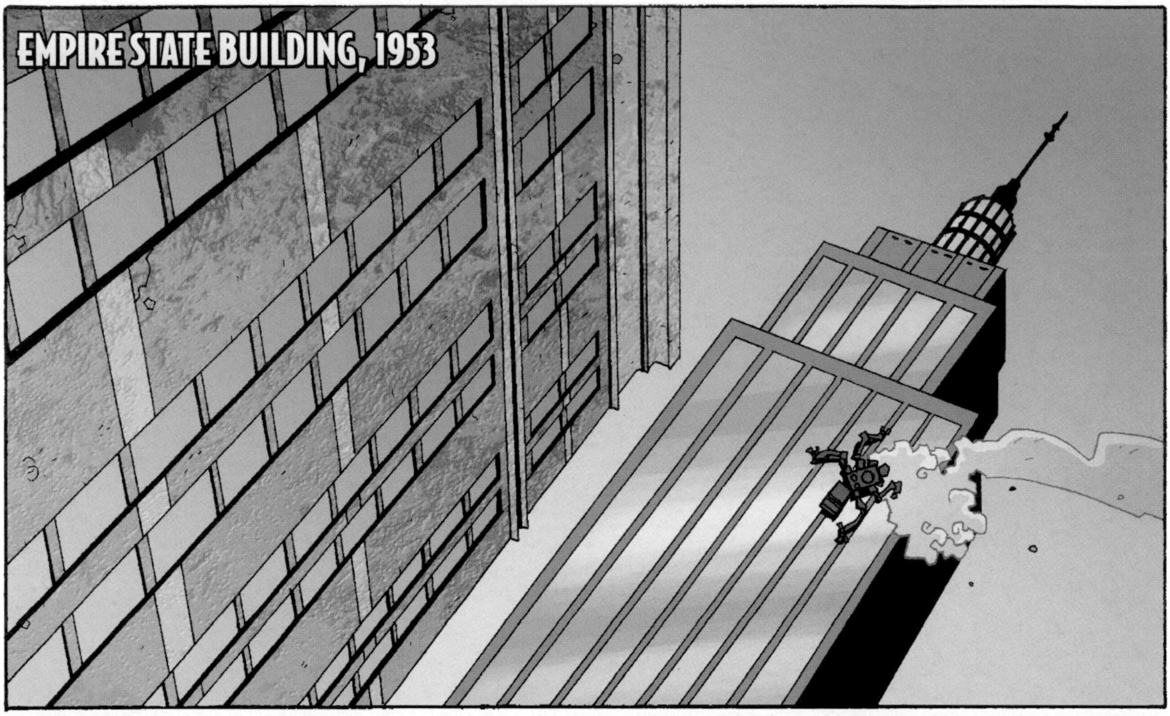
EMPIRE STATE BUILDING, 1953

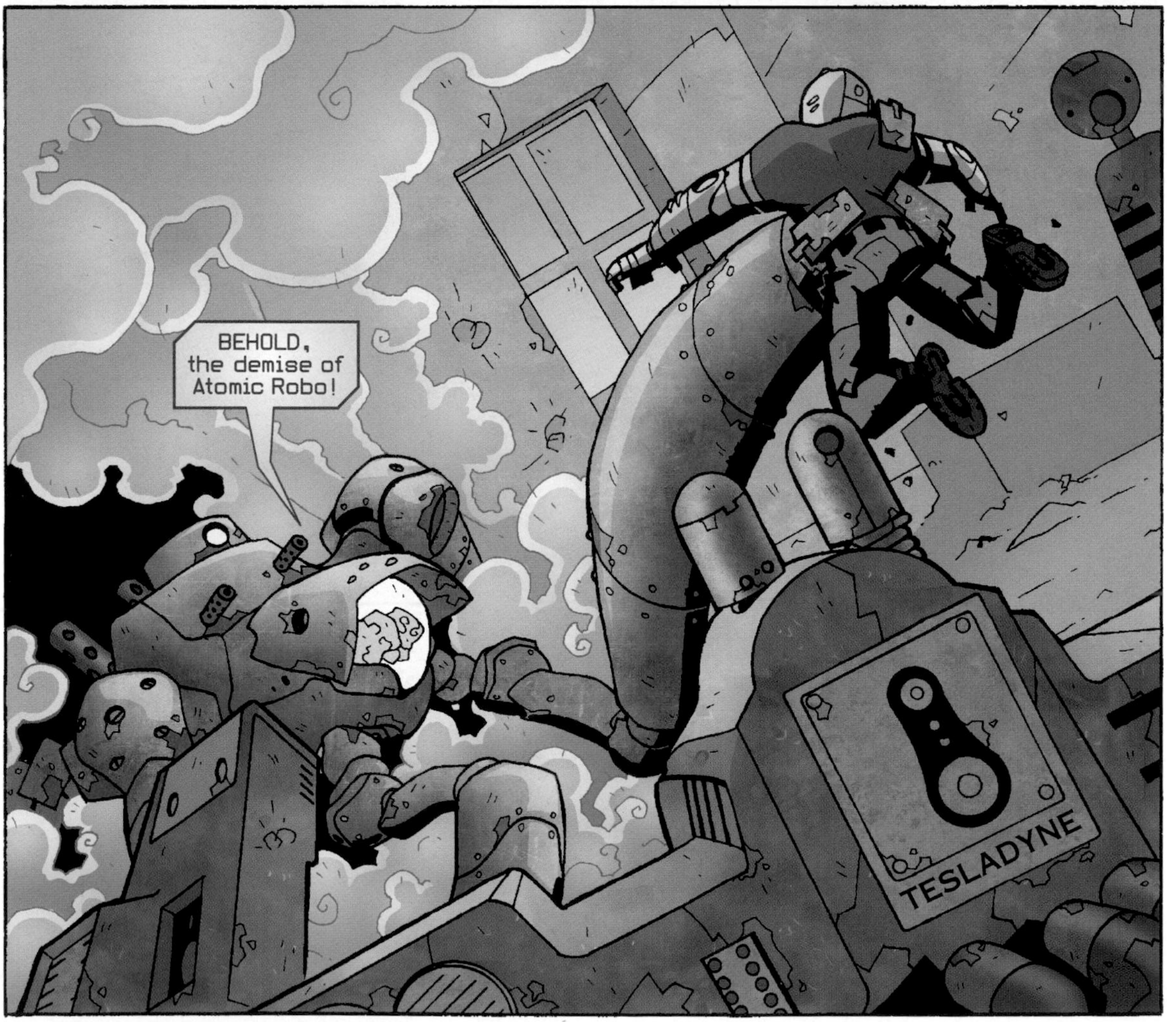
BEHOLD, the demise of Atomic Robo!
TESLADYNE

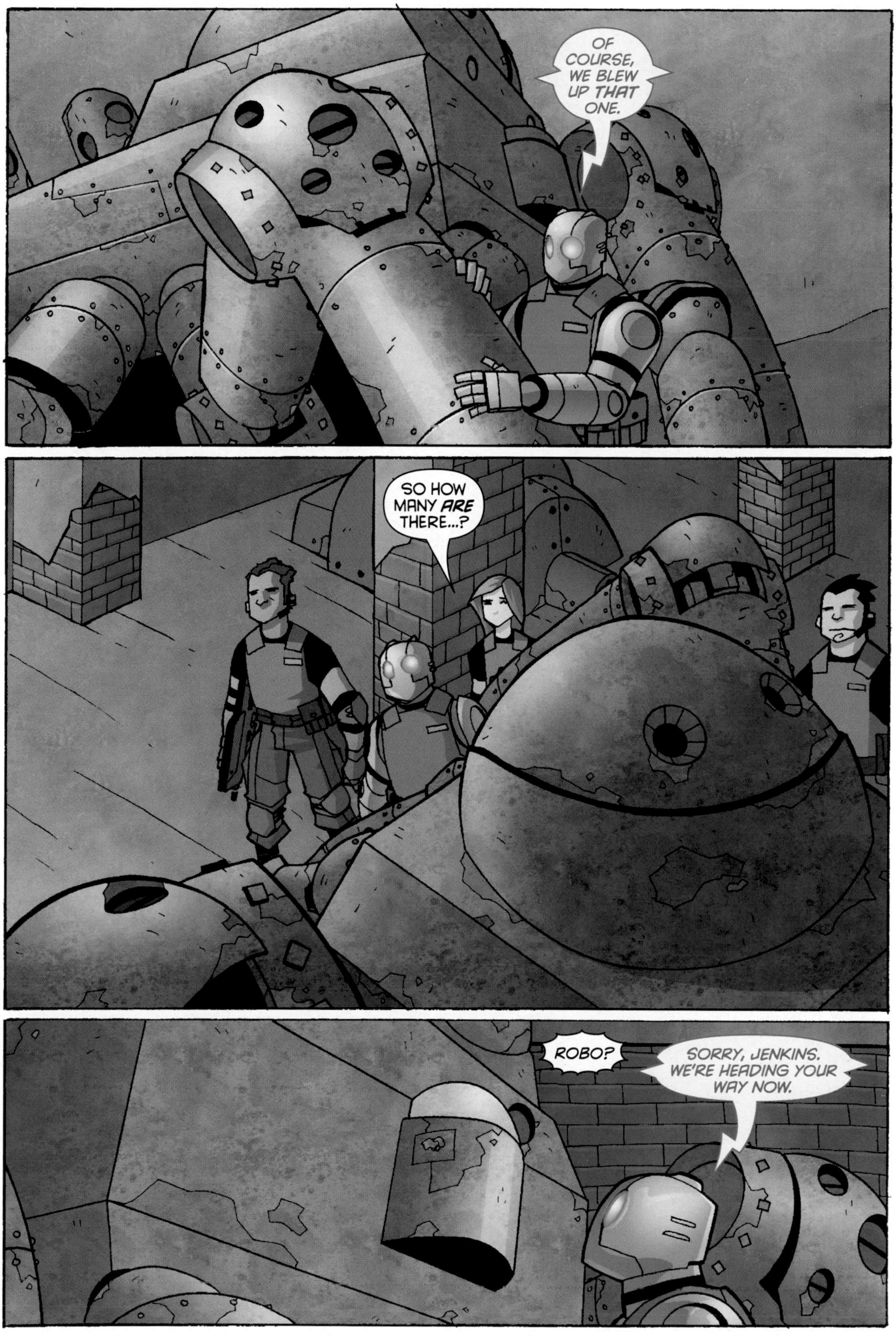
OF COURSE, WE BLEW UP THAT ONE.
SO HOW MANY ARE THERE...?
ROBO?
SORRY, JENKINS. WE'RE HEADING YOUR WAY NOW.

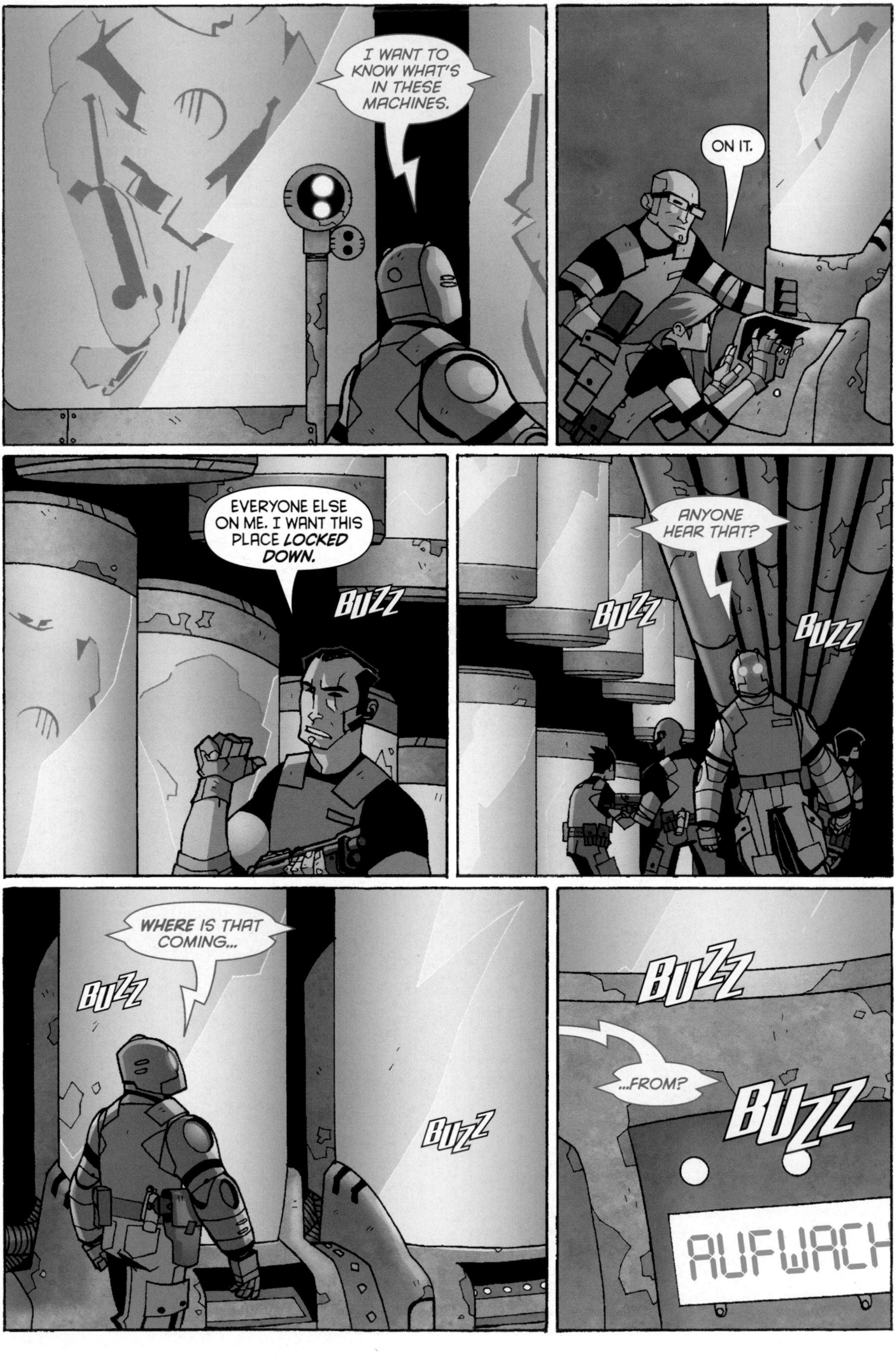
I WANT TO KNOW WHAT'S IN THESE MACHINES.
ON IT.
EVERYONE ELSE ON ME. I WANT THIS PLACE LOCKED DOWN.
BUZZ
ANYONE HEAR THAT?
BUZZ
BUZZ
WHERE IS THAT COMING...
BUZZ
BUZZ
BUZZ
...FROM?
BUZZ
AUFWACH

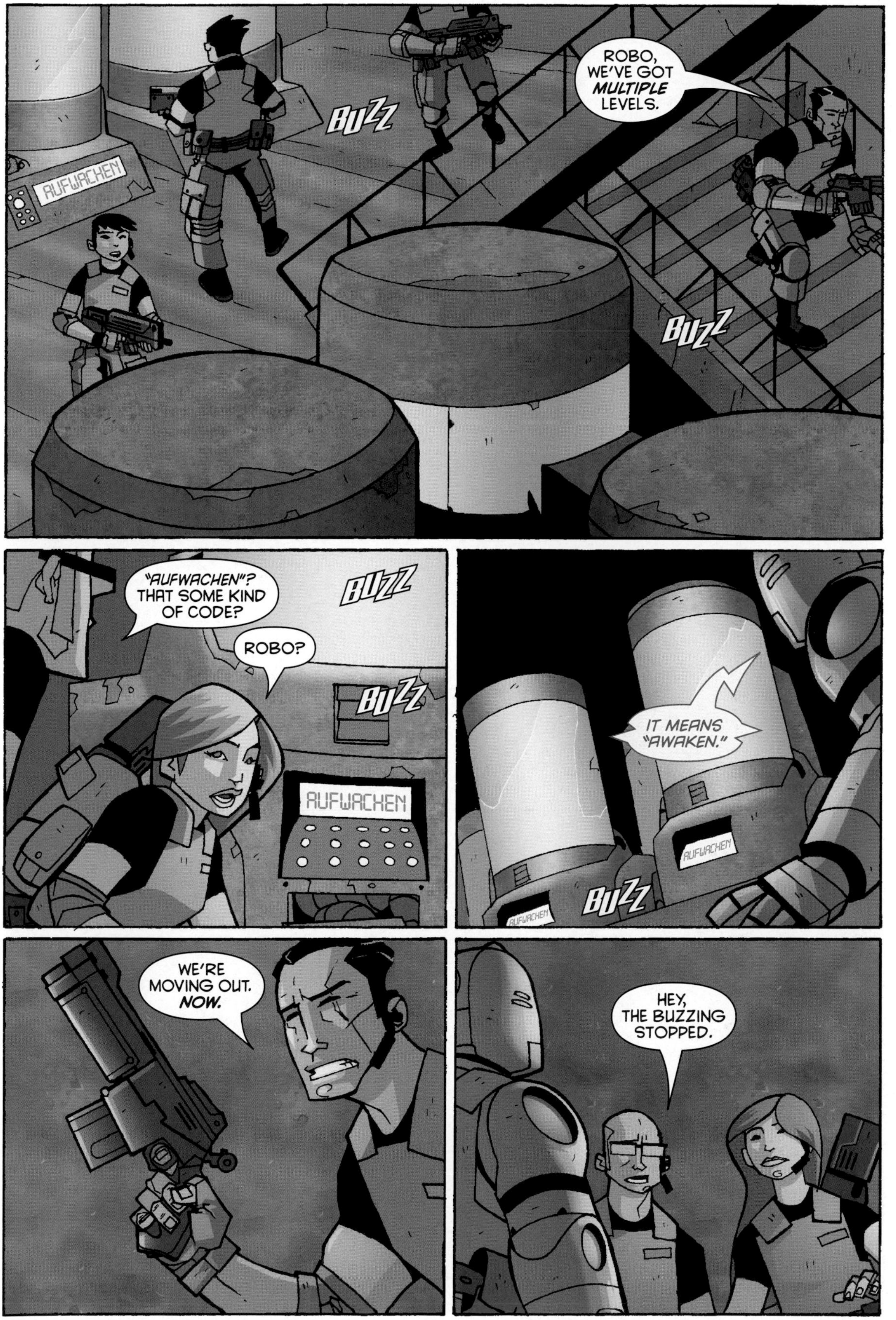
ROBO, WE'VE GOT MULTIPLE LEVELS.
BUZZ
AUFWACHEN
BUZZ
"AUFWACHEN"? THAT SOME KIND OF CODE?
ROBO?
BUZZ
BUZZ
AUFWACHEN
IT MEANS "AWAKEN."
AUFWACHEN
AUFWACHEN
BUZZ
WE'RE MOVING OUT. NOW.
HEY, THE BUZZING STOPPED.

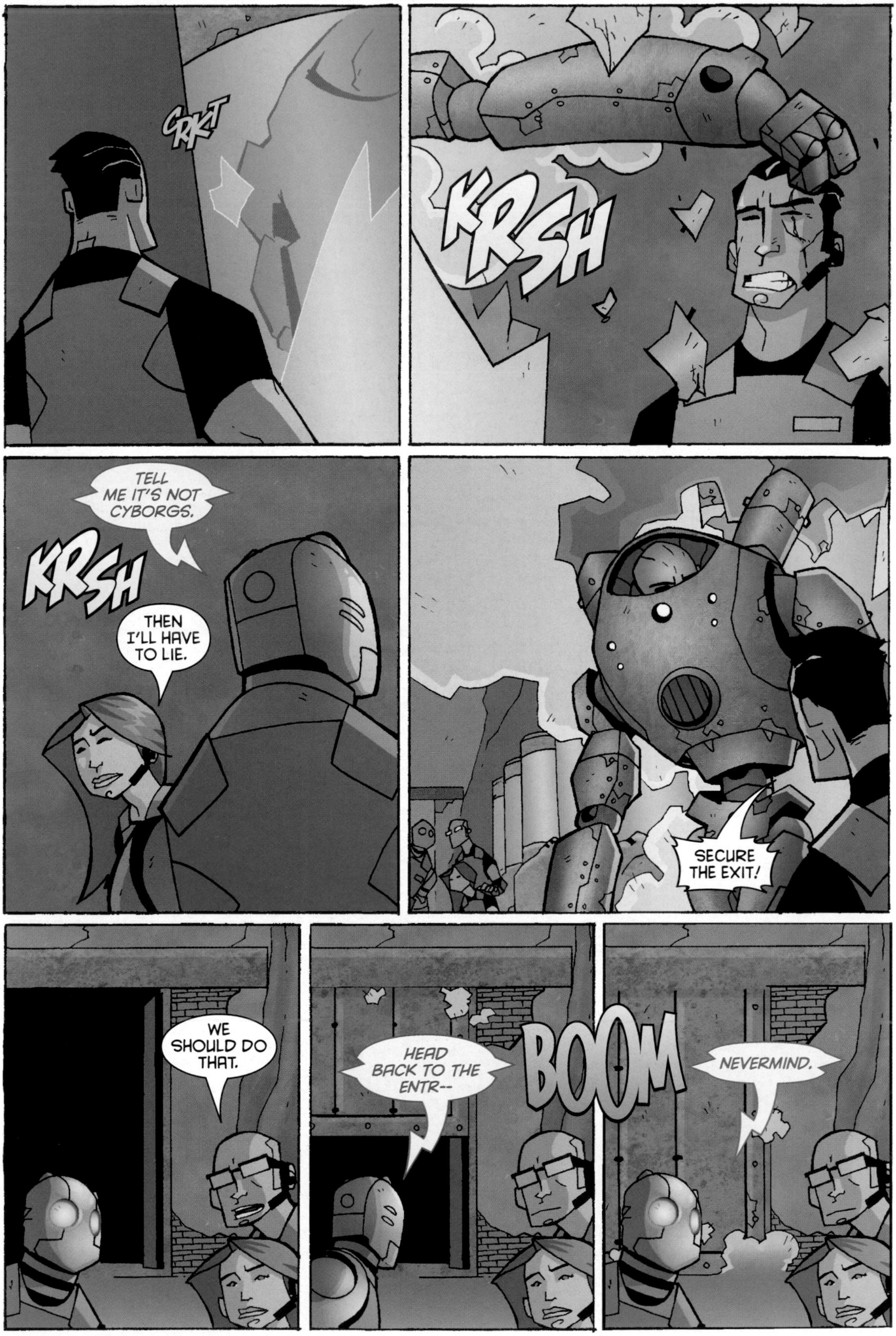
CRKT
KRSH
TELL ME IT'S NOT CYBORGS.
KRSH
THEN I'LL HAVE TO LIE.
SECURE THE EXIT!
WE SHOULD DO THAT.
HEAD BACK TO THE ENTR--
BOOM
NEVERMIND.

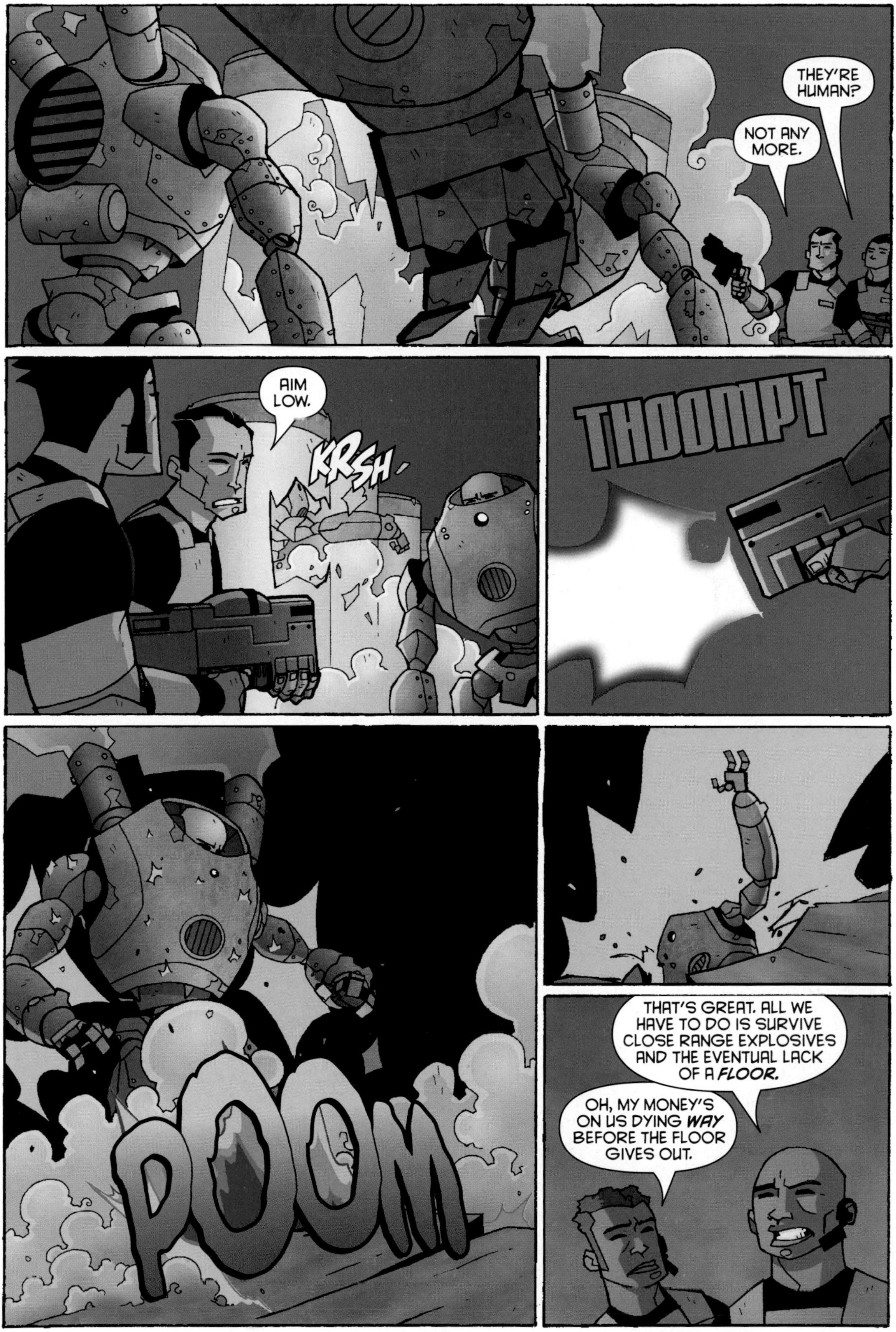
THEY'RE HUMAN?
NOT ANY MORE.
AIM LOW.
KRSH
THOOMPT
POOM
THAT'S GREAT. ALL WE HAVE TO DO IS SURVIVE CLOSE RANGE EXPLOSIVES AND THE EVENTUAL LACK OF A *FLOOR.*
OH, MY MONEY'S ON US DYING *WAY* BEFORE THE FLOOR GIVES OUT.

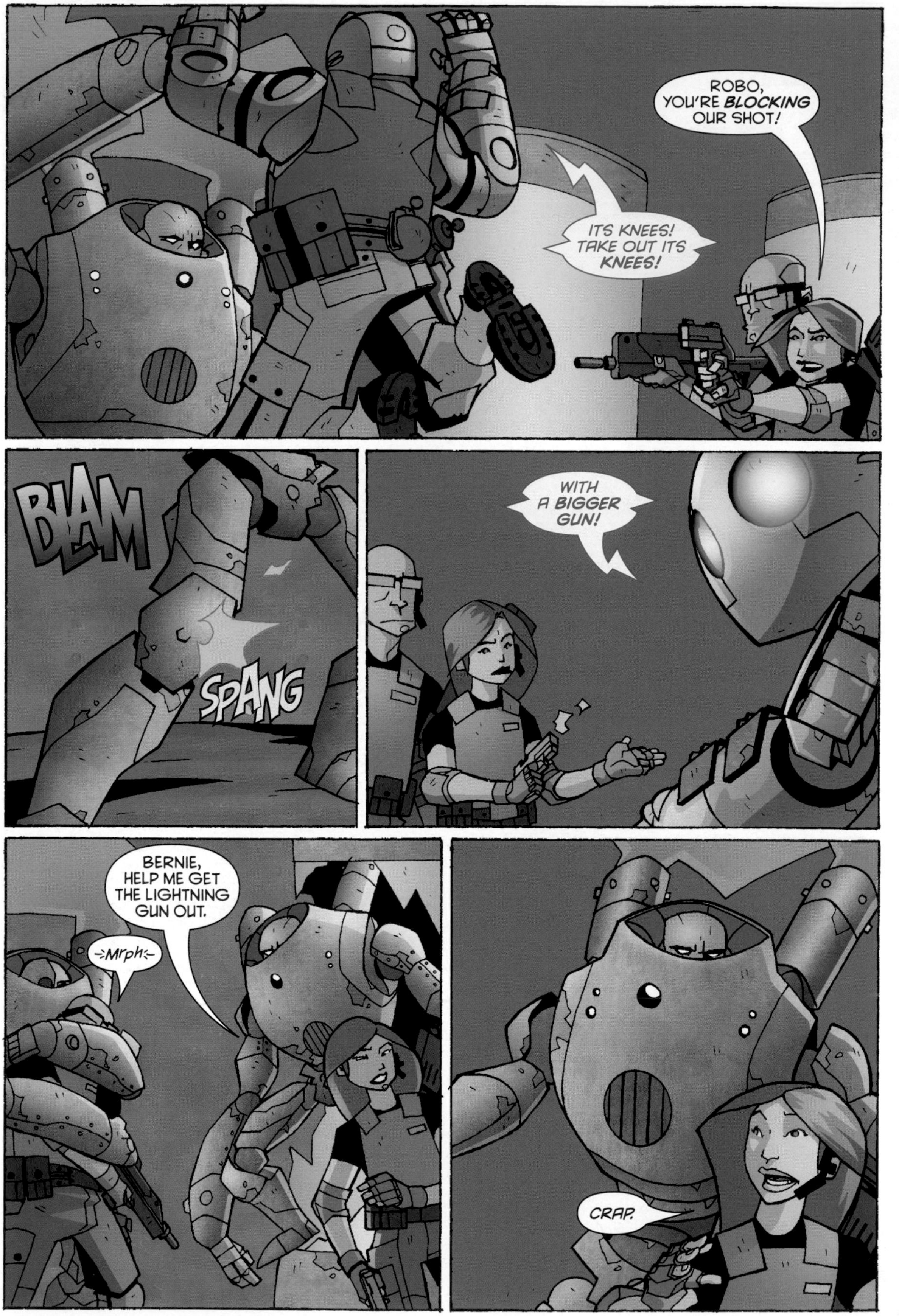
ROBO, YOU'RE BLOCKING OUR SHOT!
ITS KNEES! TAKE OUT ITS KNEES!
BLAM
SPANG
WITH A BIGGER GUN!
BERNIE, HELP ME GET THE LIGHTNING GUN OUT.
Mrph
CRAP.

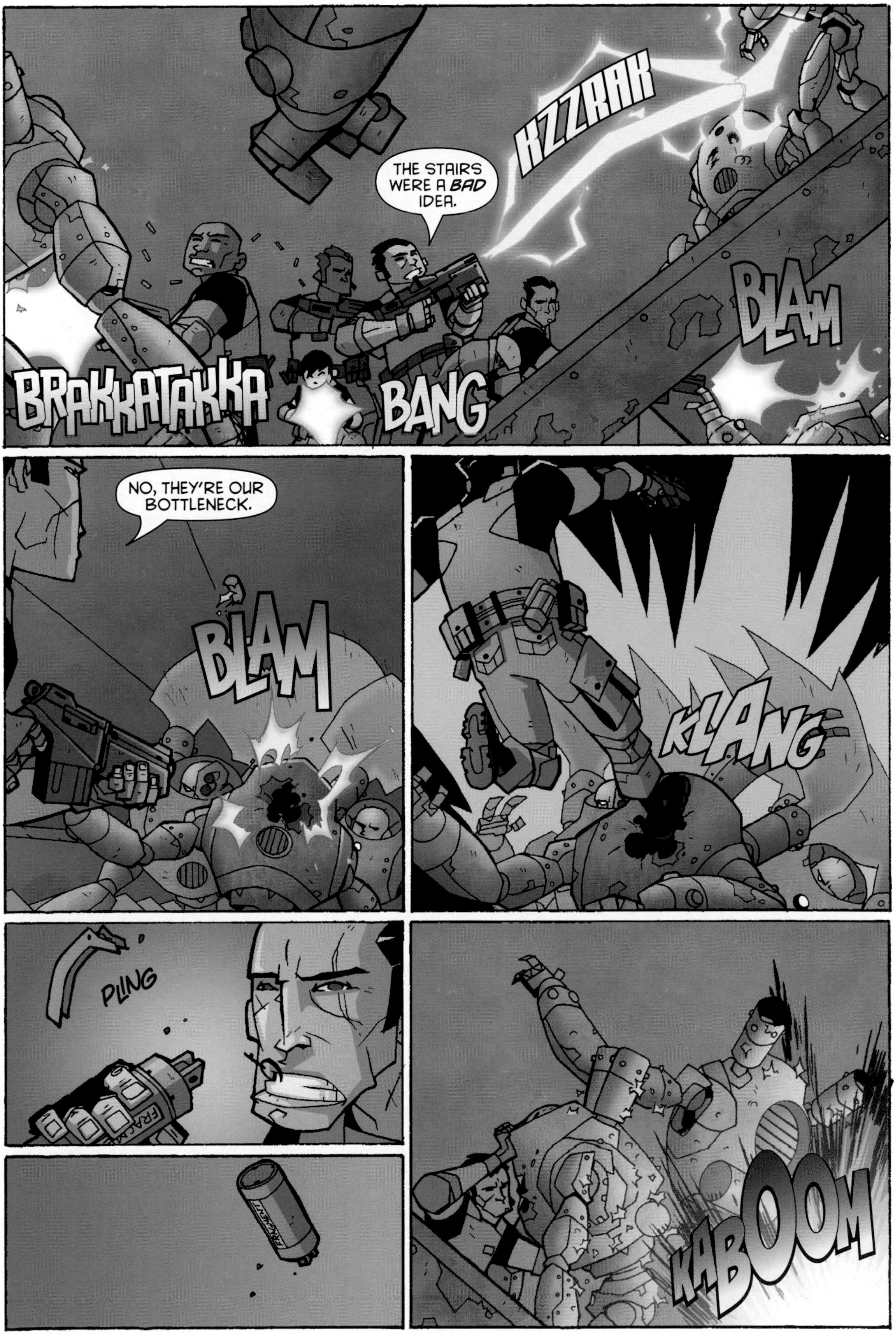
THE STAIRS WERE A *BAD* IDEA.
KZZRAK
BRAKKATAKKA
BANG
BLAM
NO, THEY'RE OUR BOTTLENECK.
BLAM
KLANG
PLING
KABOOM

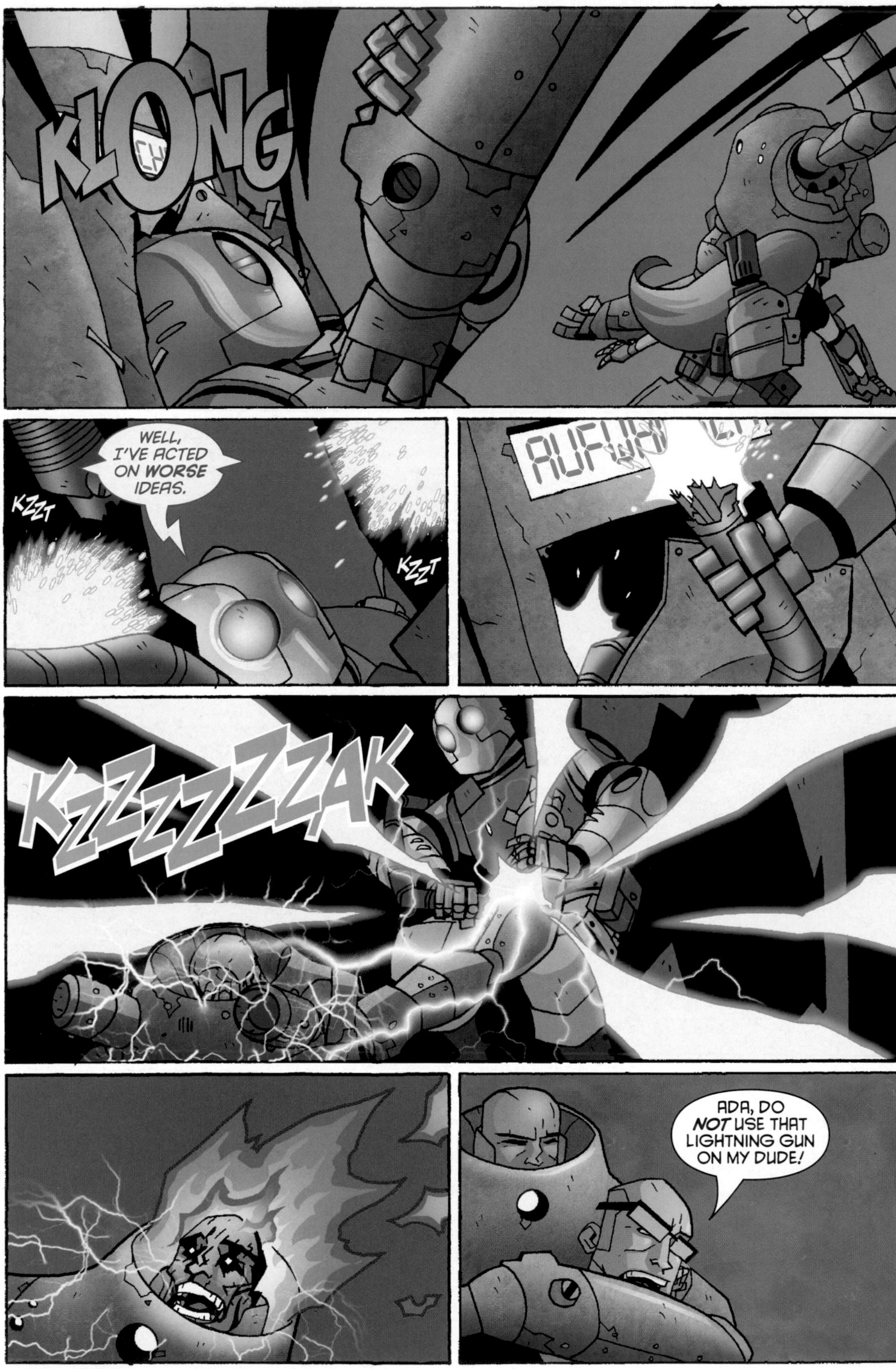
KLONG
WELL, I'VE ACTED ON WORSE IDEAS.
KZZZT
KZZZT
KZZZZZZAK
ADA, DO NOT USE THAT LIGHTNING GUN ON MY DUDE!

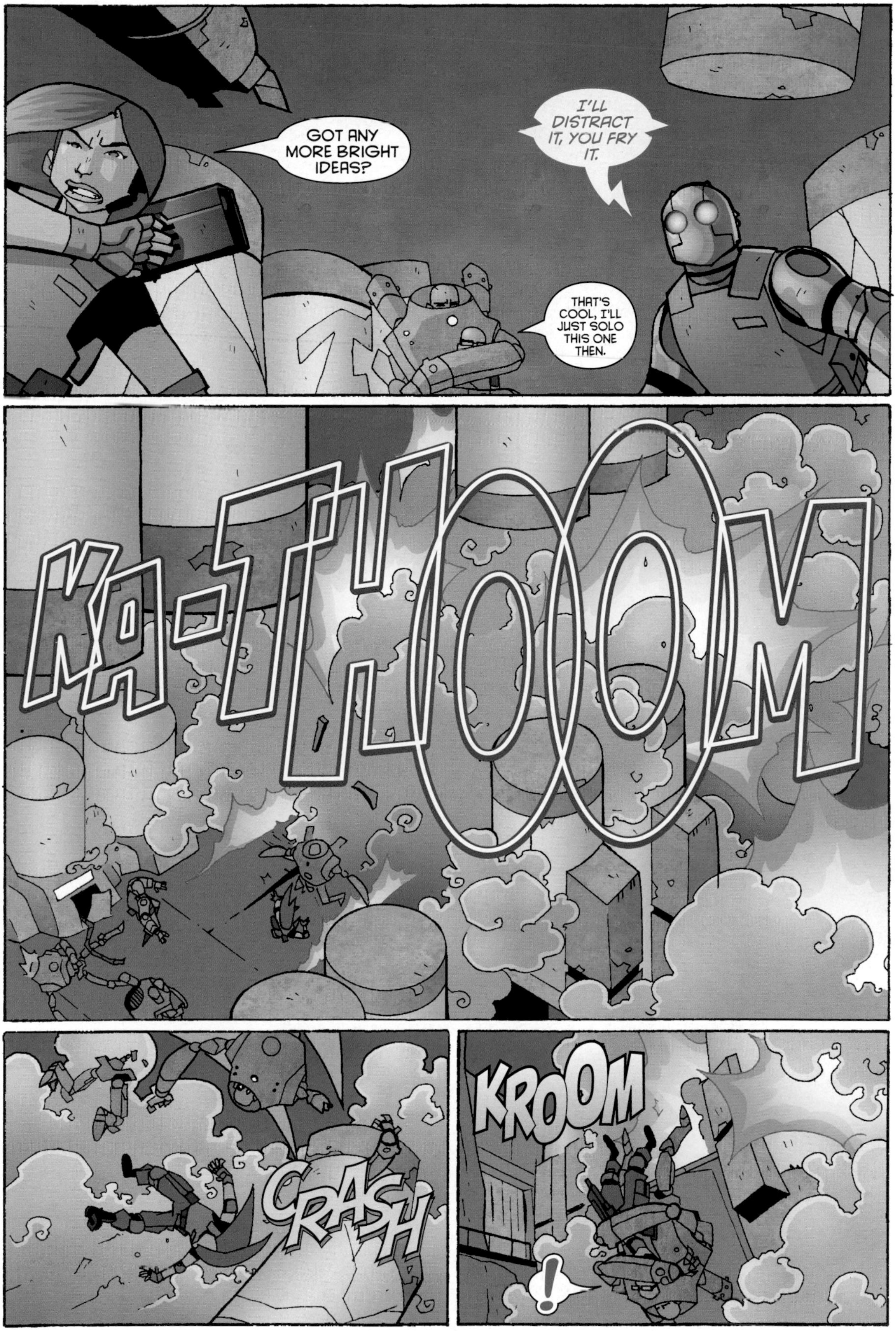
GOT ANY MORE BRIGHT IDEAS?
I'LL DISTRACT IT, YOU FRY IT.
THAT'S COOL, I'LL JUST SOLO THIS ONE THEN.
KA-THOOOM
CRASH
KROOM
!

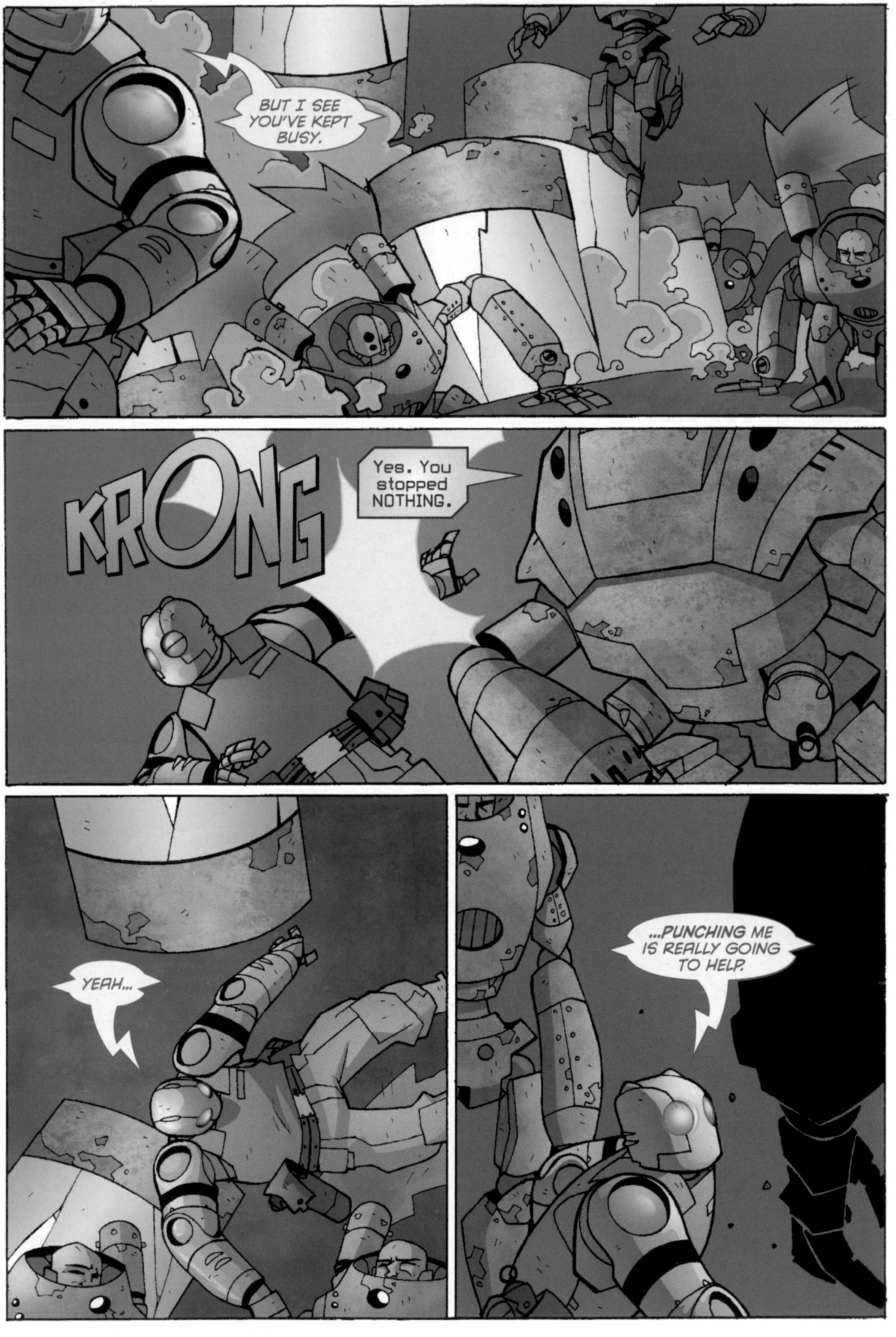
BUT I SEE YOU'VE KEPT BUSY.
KRONG
Yes. You stopped NOTHING.
YEAH...
...PUNCHING ME IS REALLY GOING TO HELP.

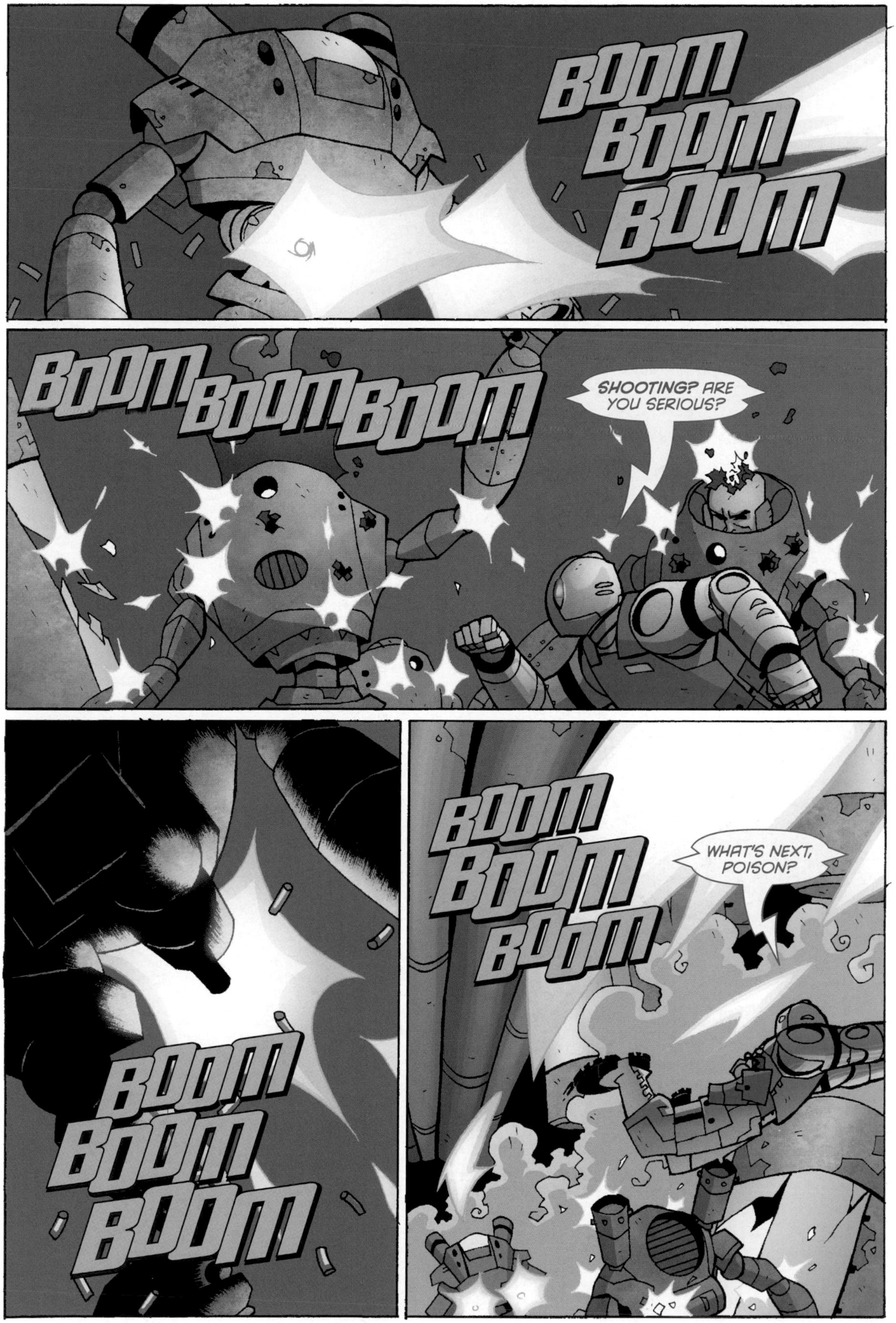
BOOM
BOOM
BOOM
BOOM BOOM BOOM
SHOOTING? ARE YOU SERIOUS?
BOOM
BOOM
BOOM
BOOM
BOOM
BOOM
WHAT'S NEXT, POISON?

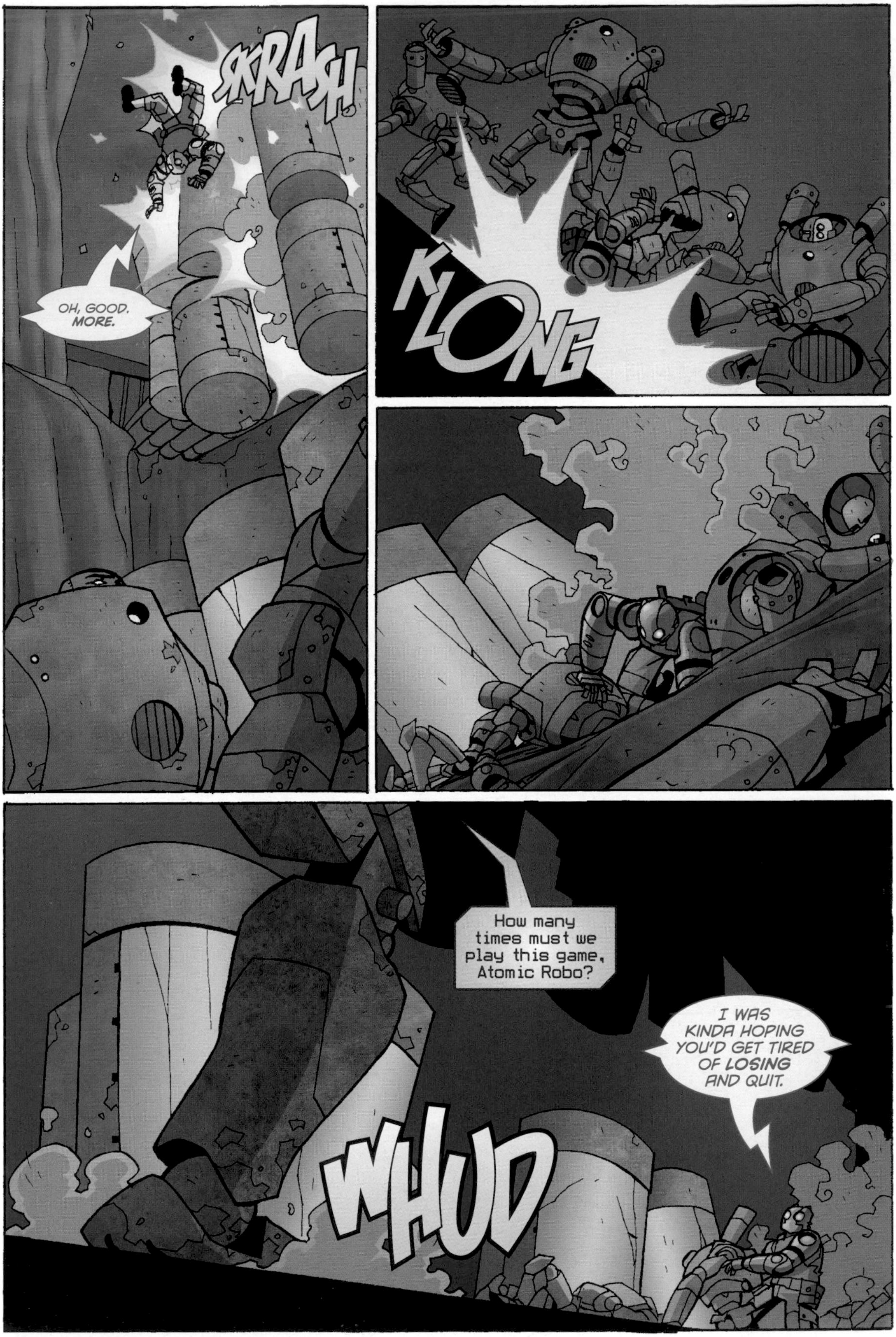
SKRASH
OH, GOOD. MORE.
KLONG
How many times must we play this game, Atomic Robo?
I WAS KINDA HOPING YOU'D GET TIRED OF LOSING AND QUIT.
WHUD

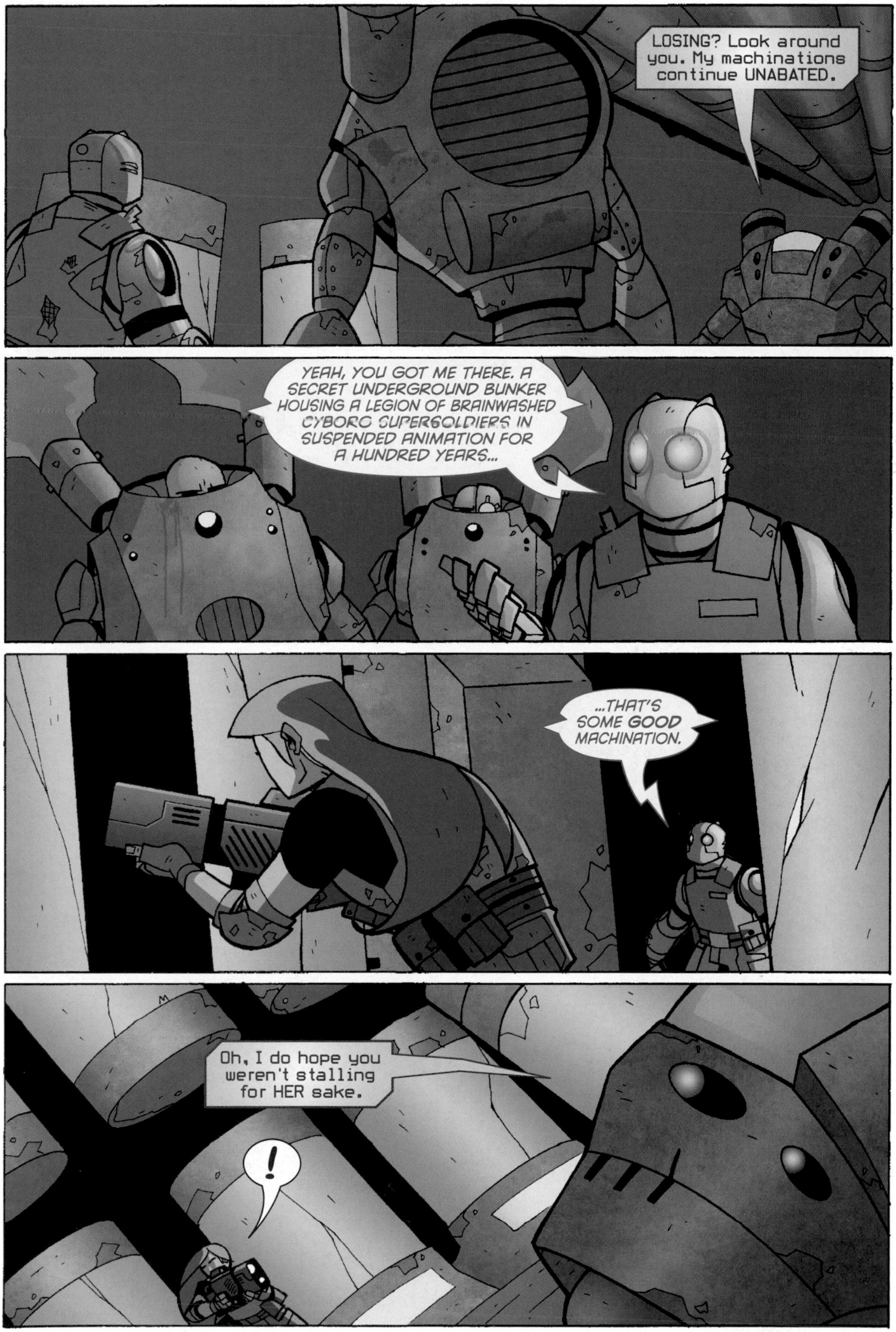
LOSING? Look around you. My machinations continue UNABATED.
YEAH, YOU GOT ME THERE. A SECRET UNDERGROUND BUNKER HOUSING A LEGION OF BRAINWASHED CYBORG SUPERSOLDIERS IN SUSPENDED ANIMATION FOR A HUNDRED YEARS...
...THAT'S SOME GOOD MACHINATION.
Oh, I do hope you weren't stalling for HER sake.
!

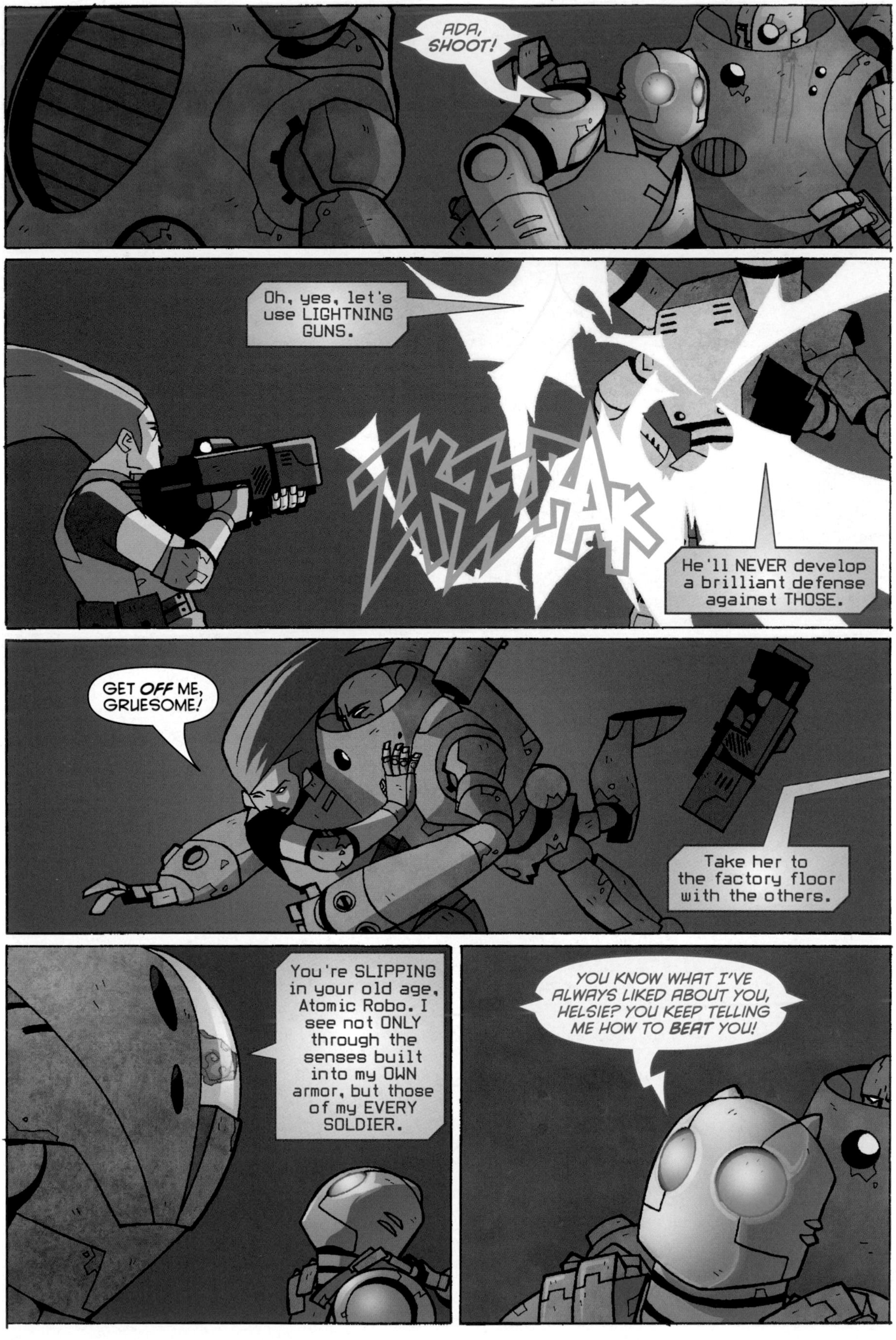
ADA, SHOOT!
Oh, yes, let's use LIGHTNING GUNS.
ZZKZZTAK
He'll NEVER develop a brilliant defense against THOSE.
GET OFF ME, GRUESOME!
Take her to the factory floor with the others.
You're SLIPPING in your old age, Atomic Robo. I see not ONLY through the senses built into my OWN armor, but those of my EVERY SOLDIER.
YOU KNOW WHAT I'VE ALWAYS LIKED ABOUT YOU, HELSIE? YOU KEEP TELLING ME HOW TO BEAT YOU!

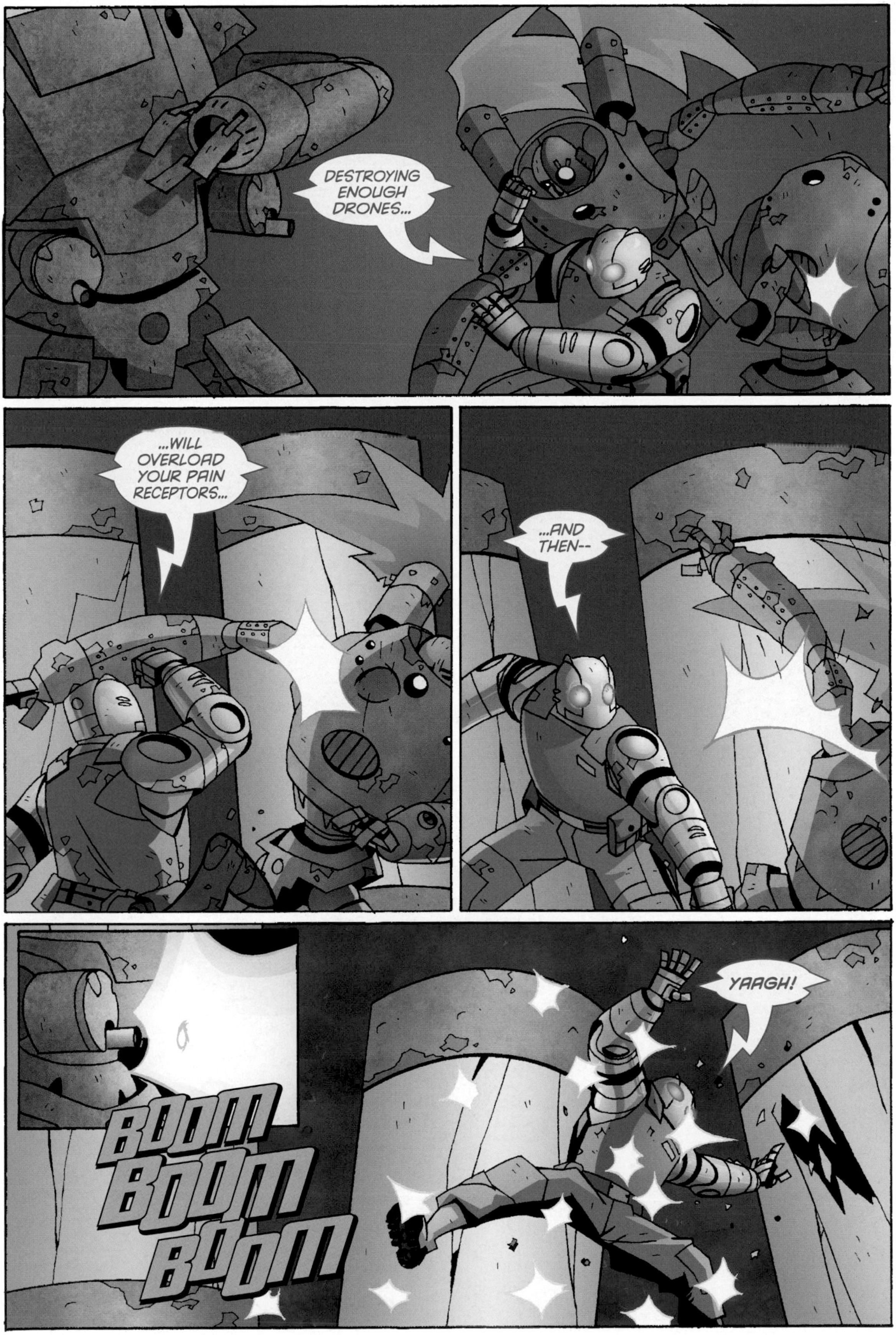
DESTROYING ENOUGH DRONES...
...WILL OVERLOAD YOUR PAIN RECEPTORS...
...AND THEN--
BOOM BOOM BOOM
YAAGH!

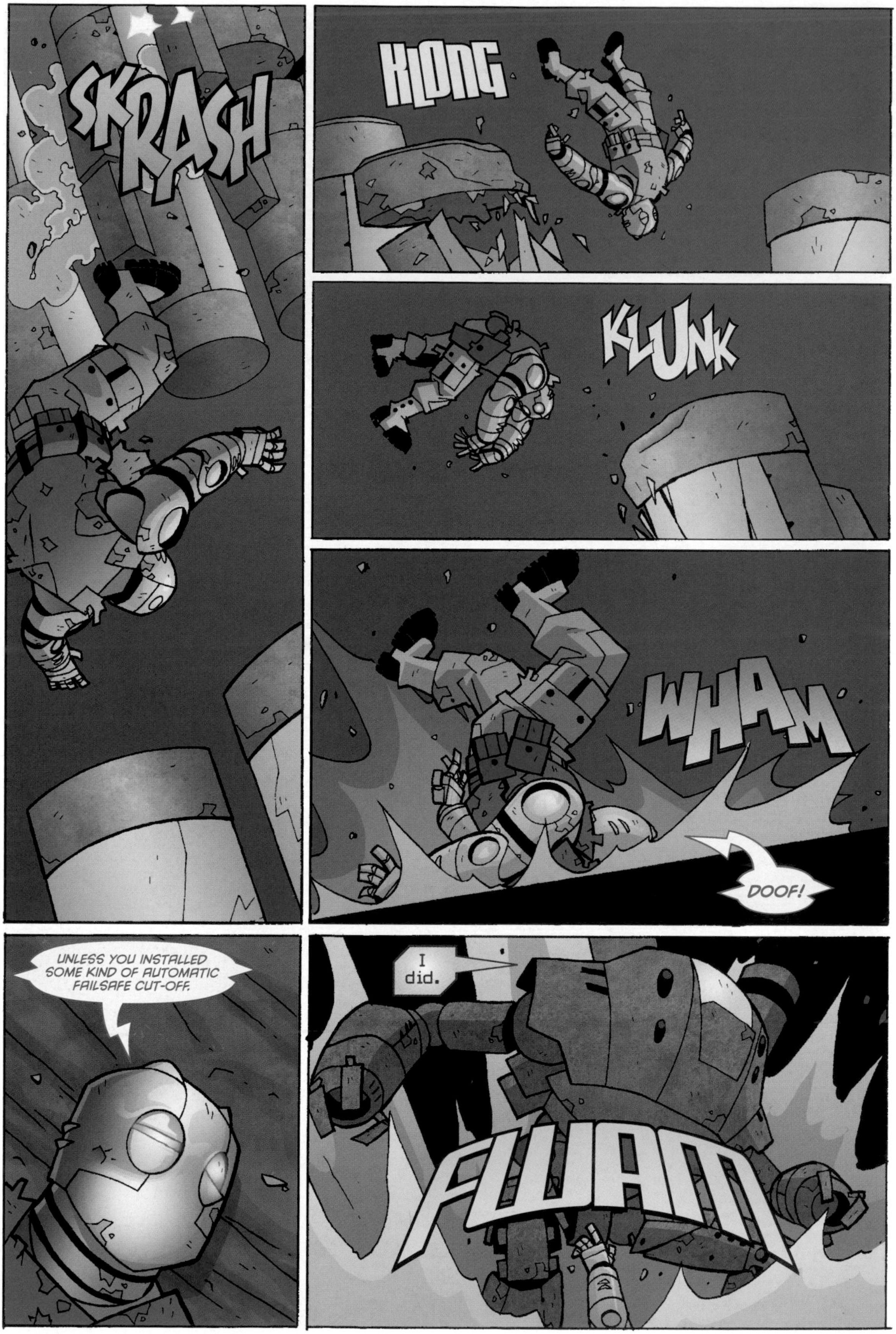
SKRASH
KLONG
KLUNK
WHAM
DOOF!
UNLESS YOU INSTALLED SOME KIND OF AUTOMATIC FAILSAFE CUT-OFF.
I did.
FWAM

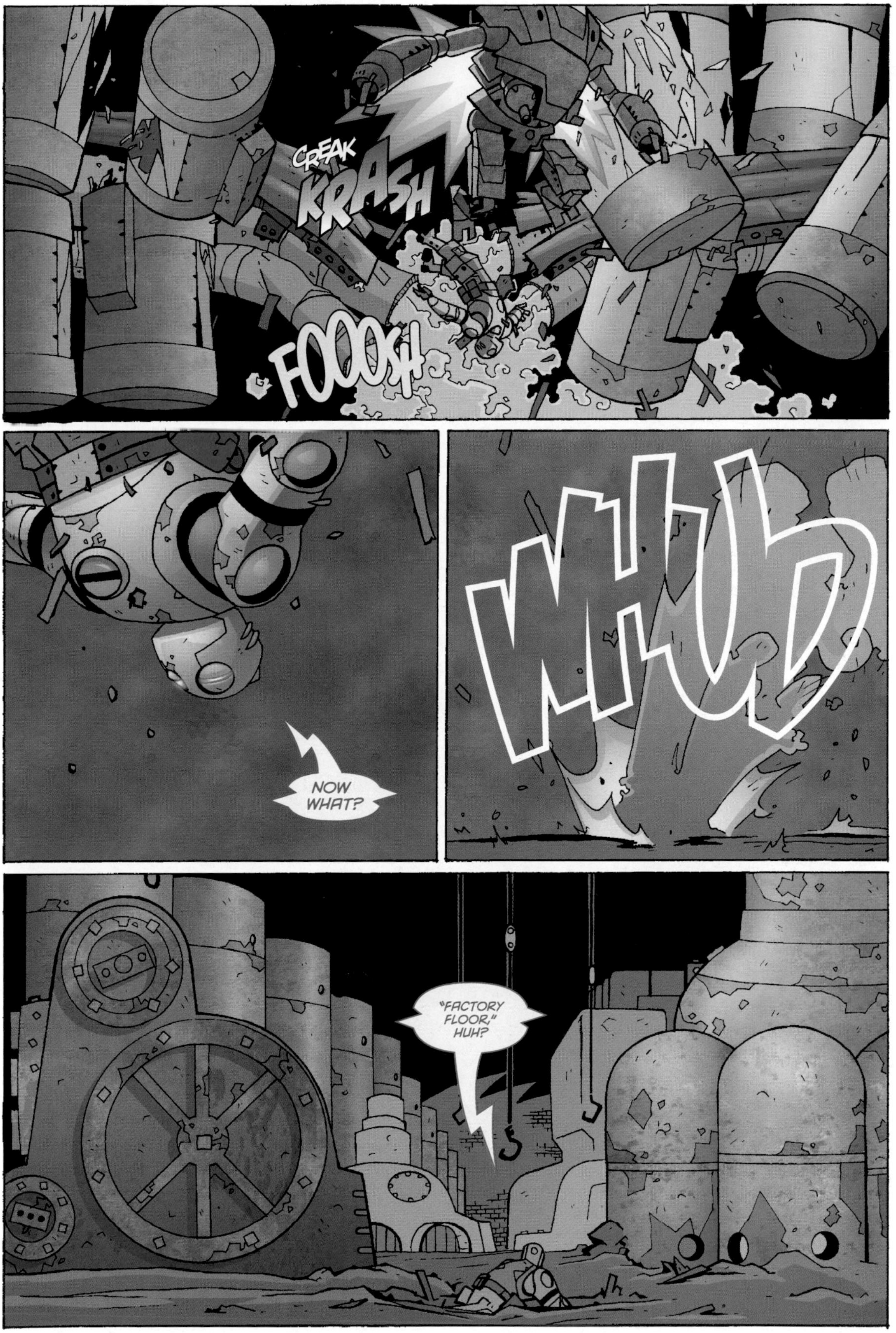
CREAK
KRASH
FOOOSH
NOW WHAT?
WHUD
"FACTORY FLOOR," HUH?

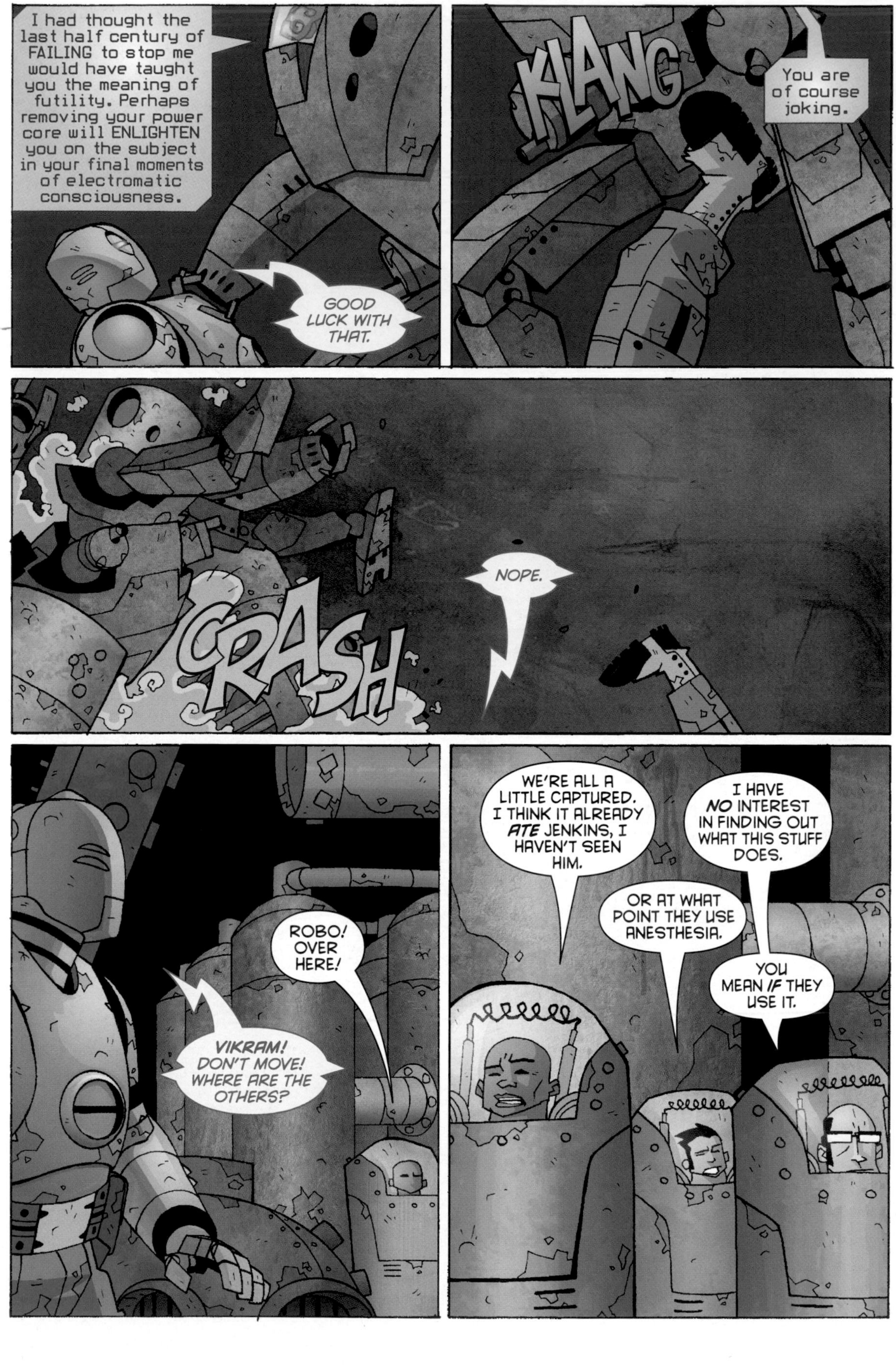
I had thought the last half century of FAILING to stop me would have taught you the meaning of futility. Perhaps removing your power core will ENLIGHTEN you on the subject in your final moments of electromatic consciousness.
GOOD LUCK WITH THAT.
KLANG
You are of course joking.
CRASH
NOPE.
VIKRAM! DON'T MOVE! WHERE ARE THE OTHERS?
ROBO! OVER HERE!
WE'RE ALL A LITTLE CAPTURED. I THINK IT ALREADY ATE JENKINS, I HAVEN'T SEEN HIM.
I HAVE NO INTEREST IN FINDING OUT WHAT THIS STUFF DOES.
OR AT WHAT POINT THEY USE ANESTHESIA.
YOU MEAN IF THEY USE IT.

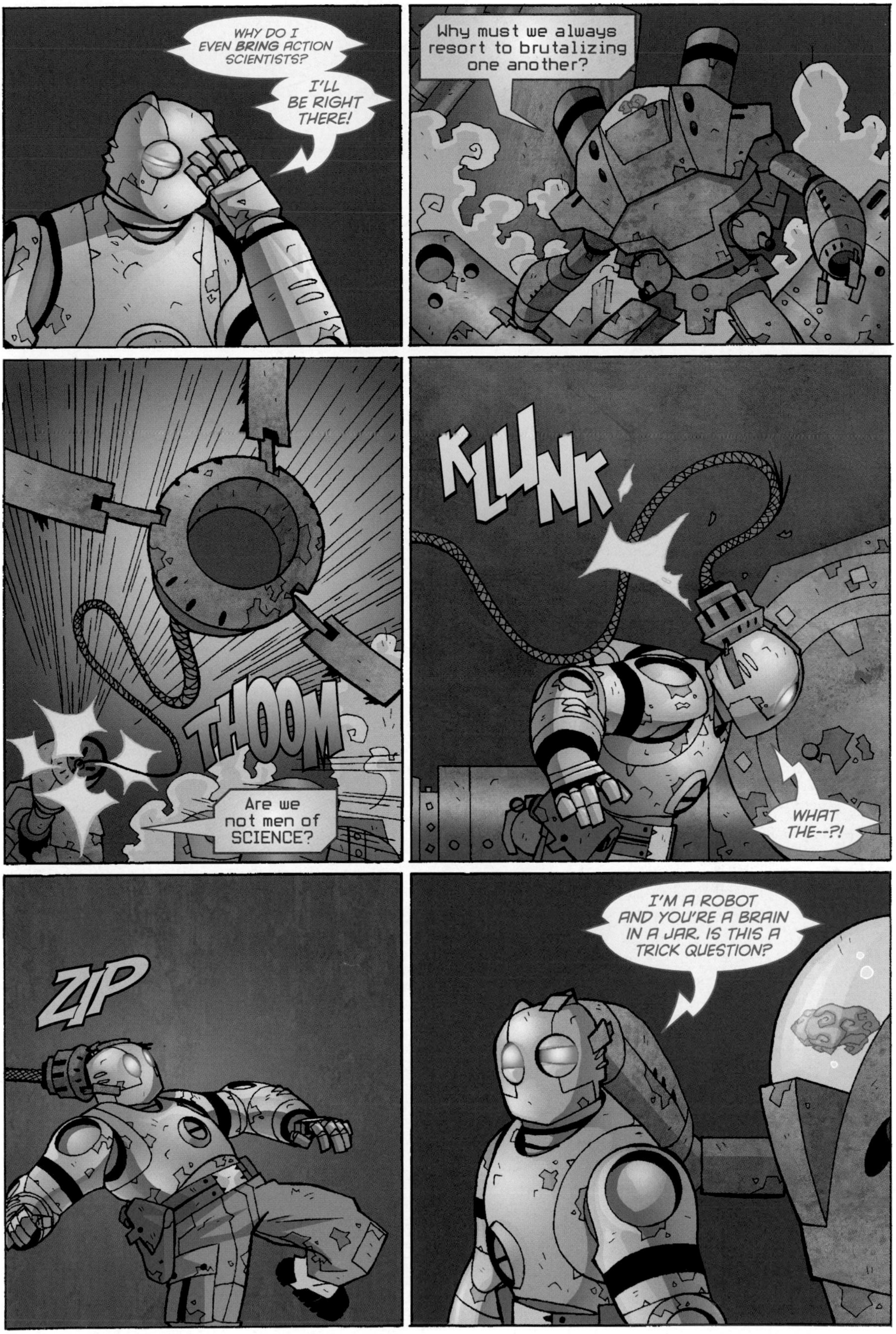
WHY DO I EVEN BRING ACTION SCIENTISTS?
I'LL BE RIGHT THERE!
Why must we always resort to brutalizing one another?
THOOM
Are we not men of SCIENCE?
KLUNK
WHAT THE--?!
ZIP
I'M A ROBOT AND YOU'RE A BRAIN IN A JAR. IS THIS A TRICK QUESTION?

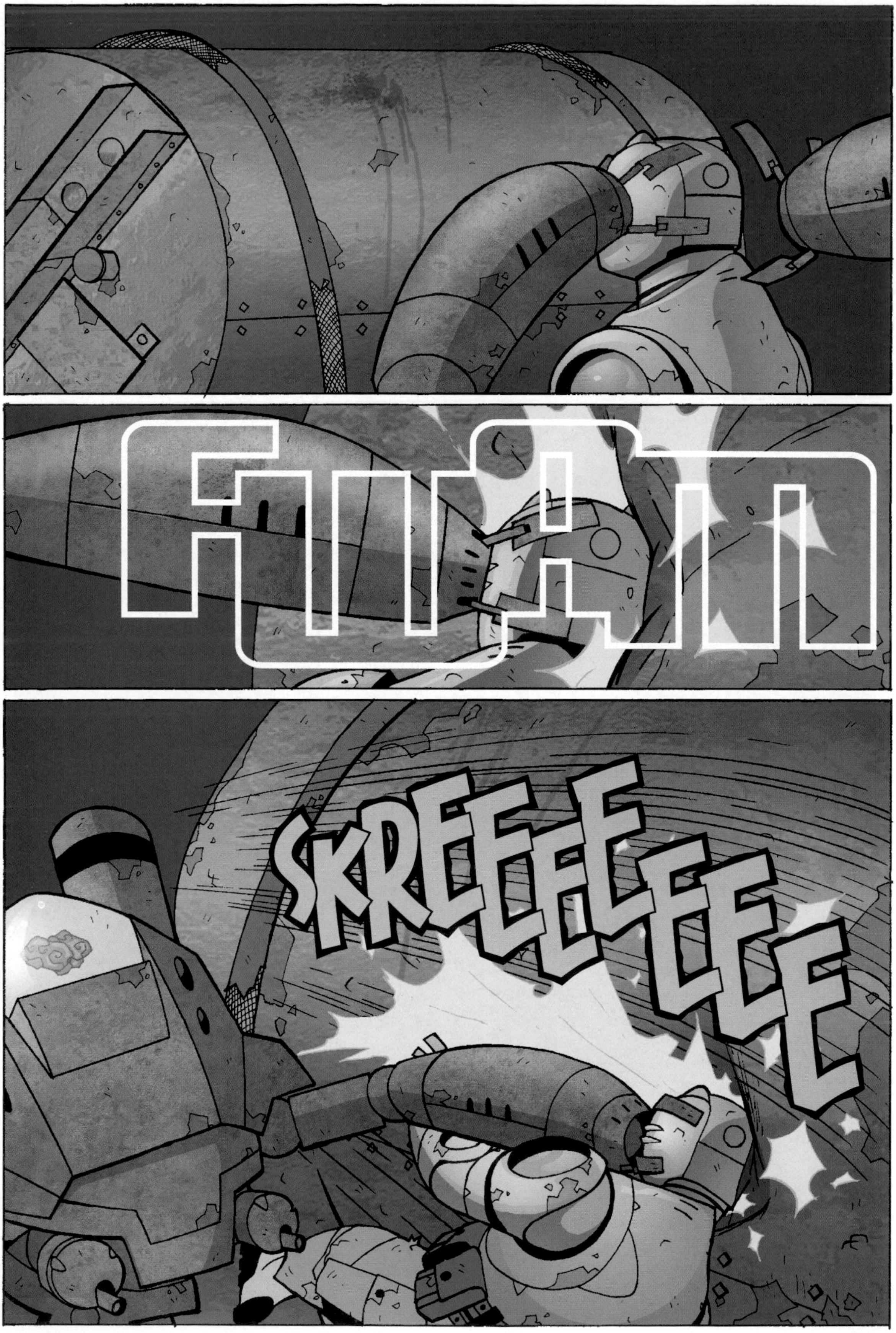
SKREEEEEEE

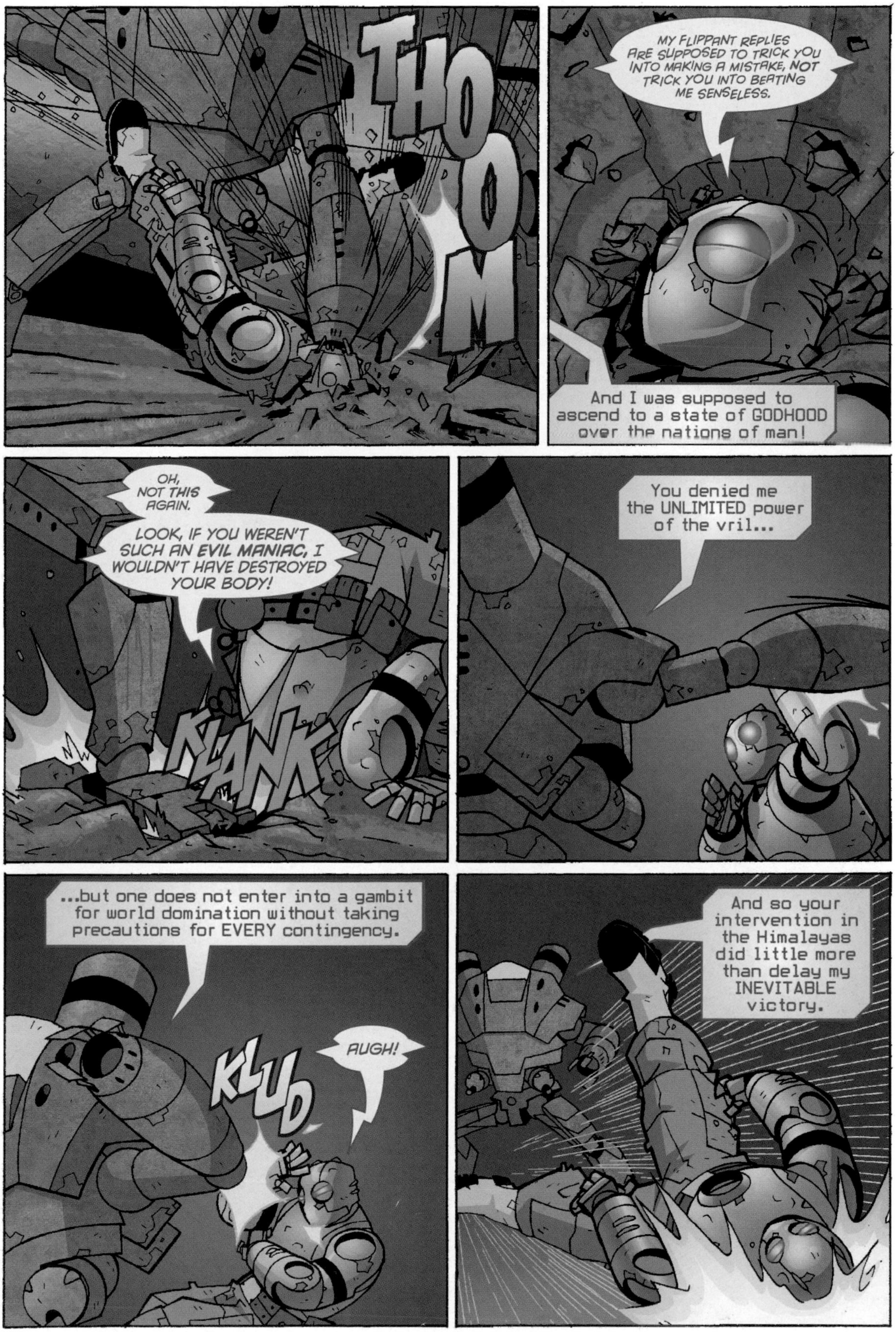
THOOM
MY FLIPPANT REPLIES ARE SUPPOSED TO TRICK YOU INTO MAKING A MISTAKE, NOT TRICK YOU INTO BEATING ME SENSELESS.
And I was supposed to ascend to a state of GODHOOD over the nations of man!
OH, NOT THIS AGAIN.
LOOK, IF YOU WEREN'T SUCH AN EVIL MANIAC, I WOULDN'T HAVE DESTROYED YOUR BODY!
KLANK
You denied me the UNLIMITED power of the vril...
...but one does not enter into a gambit for world domination without taking precautions for EVERY contingency.
KLUD
AUGH!
And so your intervention in the Himalayas did little more than delay my INEVITABLE victory.

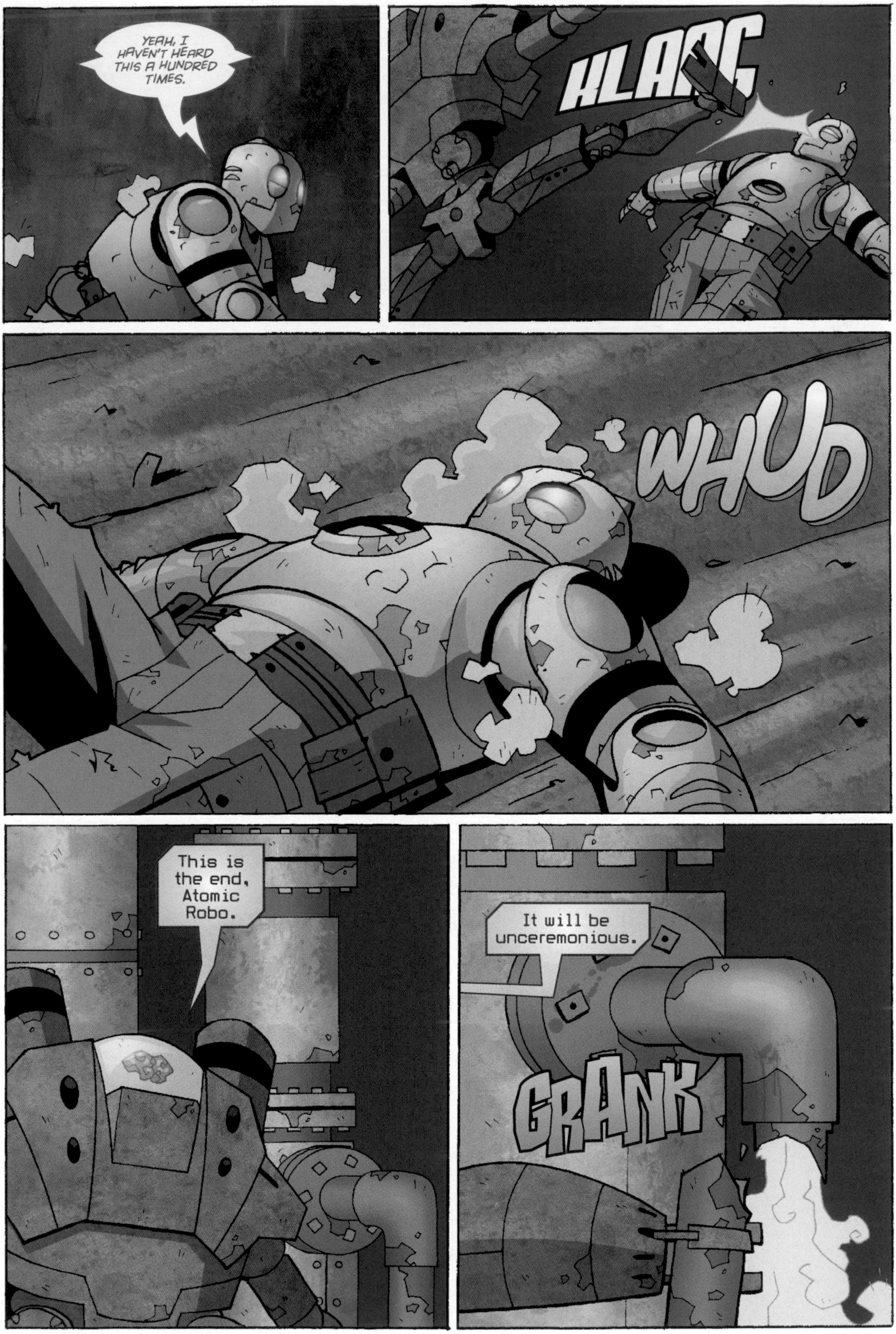
YEAH, I HAVEN'T HEARD THIS A HUNDRED TIMES.
KLANG
WHUD
This is the end, Atomic Robo.
It will be unceremonious.
GRANK

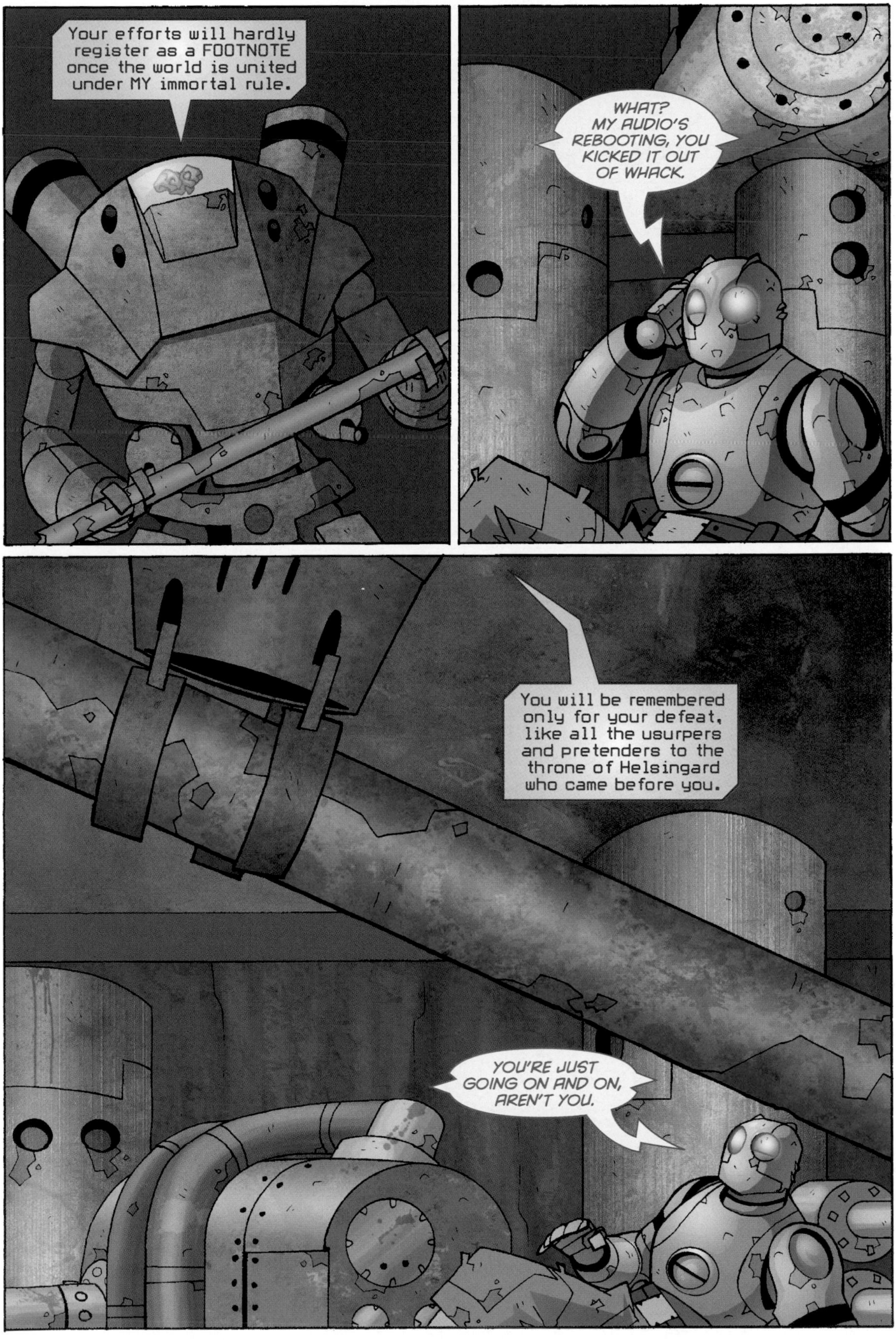
Your efforts will hardly register as a FOOTNOTE once the world is united under MY immortal rule.
WHAT? MY AUDIO'S REBOOTING, YOU KICKED IT OUT OF WHACK.
You will be remembered only for your defeat, like all the usurpers and pretenders to the throne of Helsingard who came before you.
YOU'RE JUST GOING ON AND ON, AREN'T YOU.

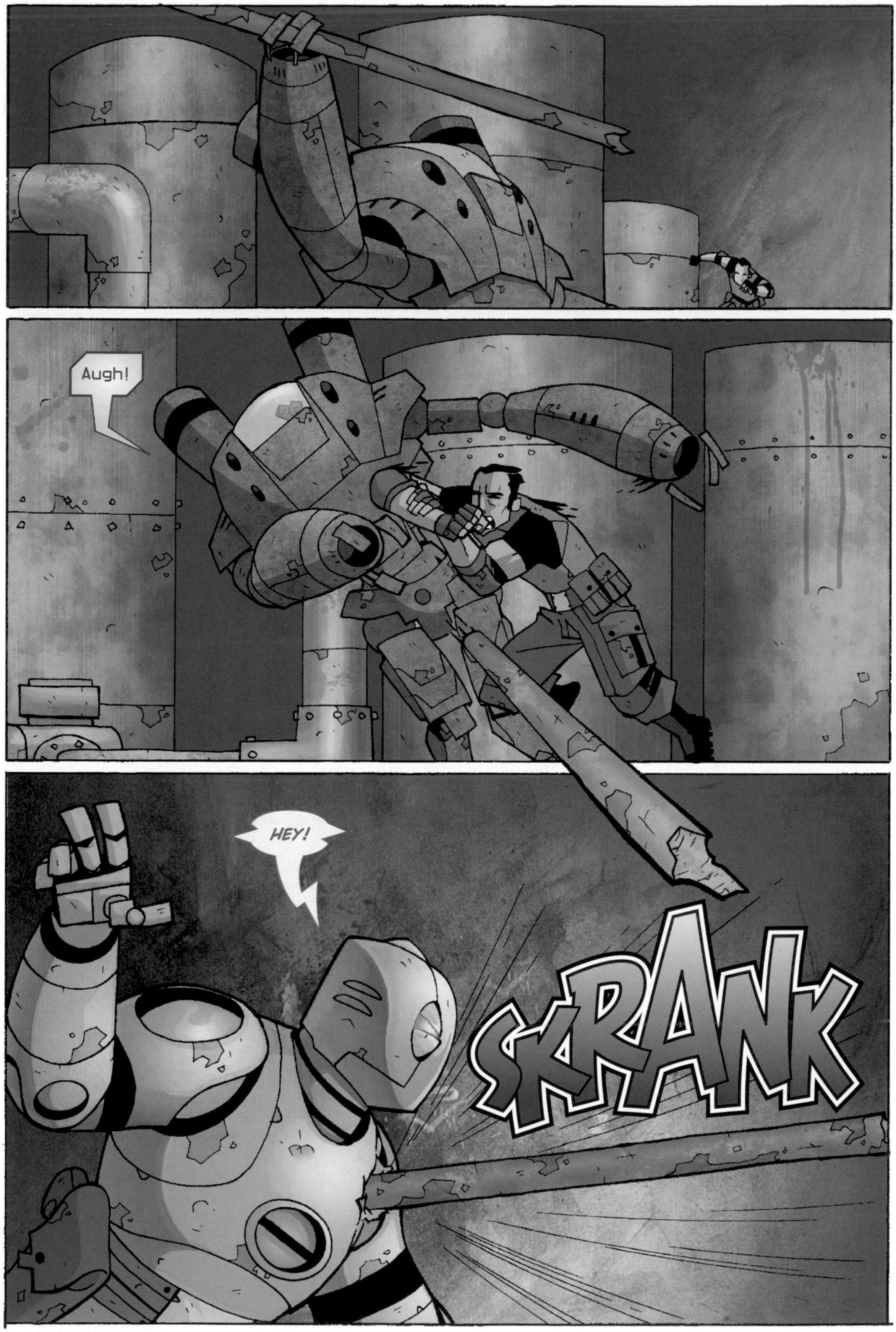
Augh!
HEY!
SKRANK

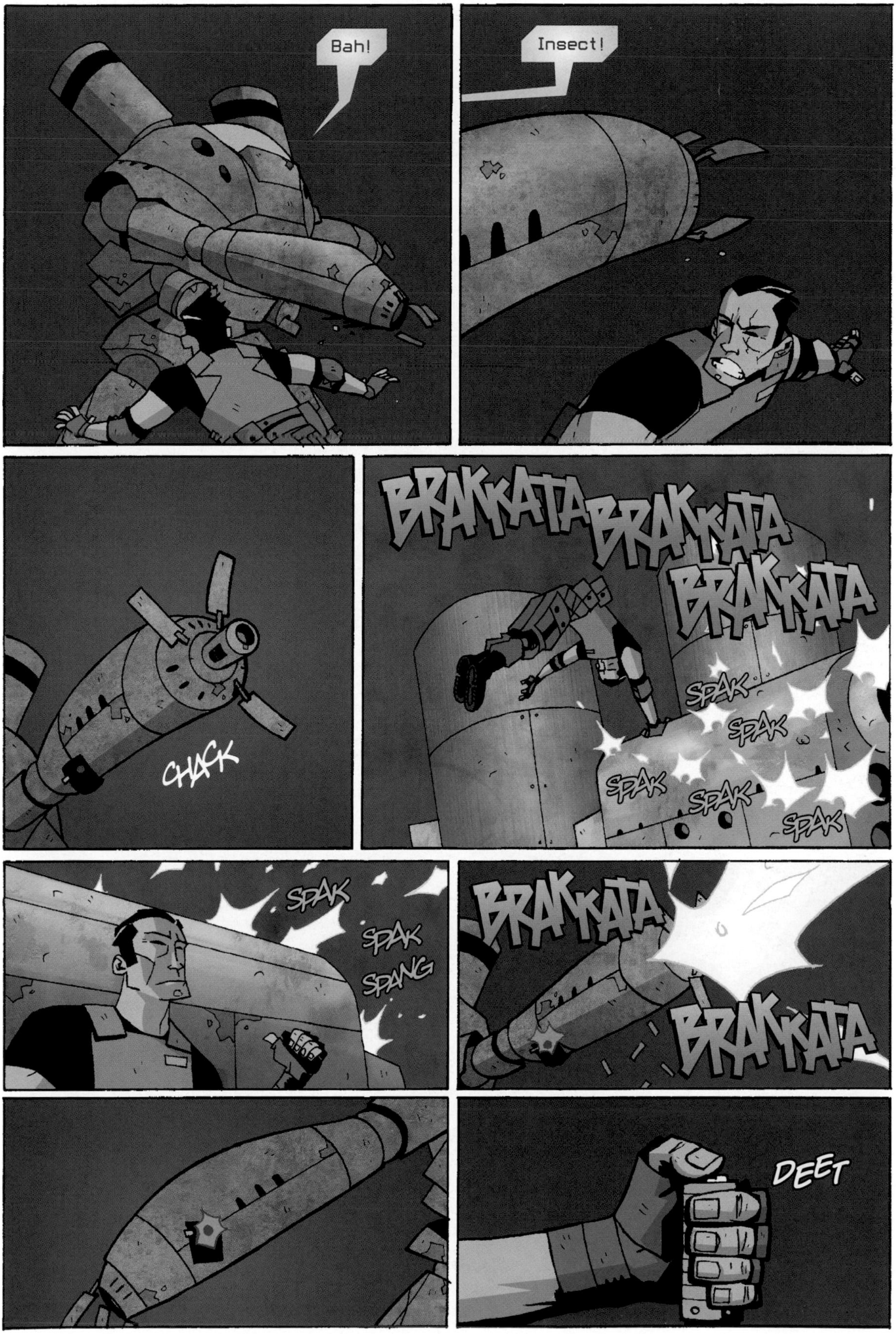
Bah!
Insect!
CHACK
BRAKKATA BRAKKATA
BRAKKATA
SPAK
SPAK
SPAK
SPAK
SPAK
SPAK
SPAK
SPANG
BRAKKATA
BRAKKATA
DEET

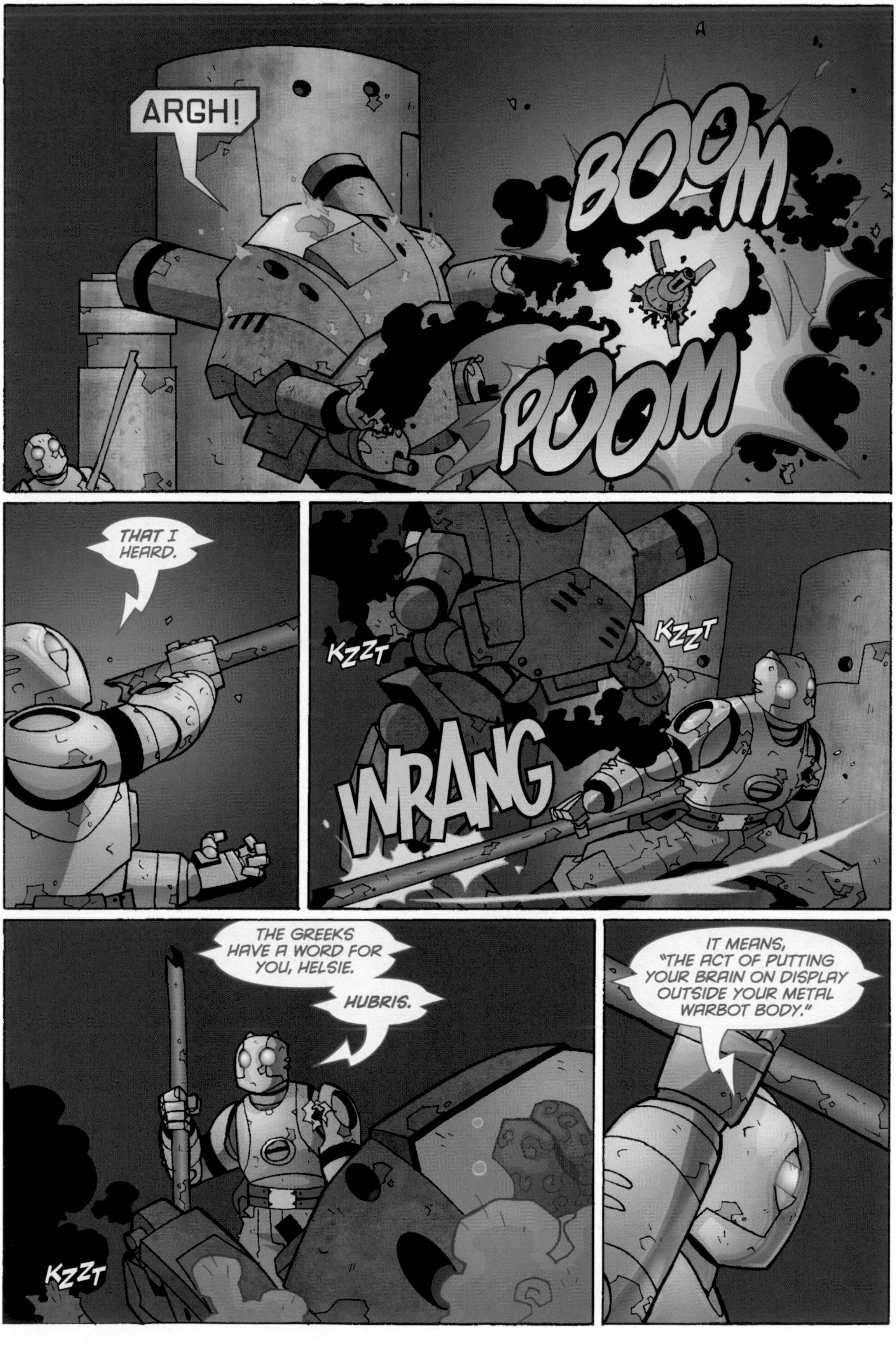
ARGH!
BOOM
POOM
THAT I HEARD.
KZZT
KZZT
WRANG
THE GREEKS HAVE A WORD FOR YOU, HELSIE.
HUBRIS.
KZZT
IT MEANS, "THE ACT OF PUTTING YOUR BRAIN ON DISPLAY OUTSIDE YOUR METAL WARBOT BODY."

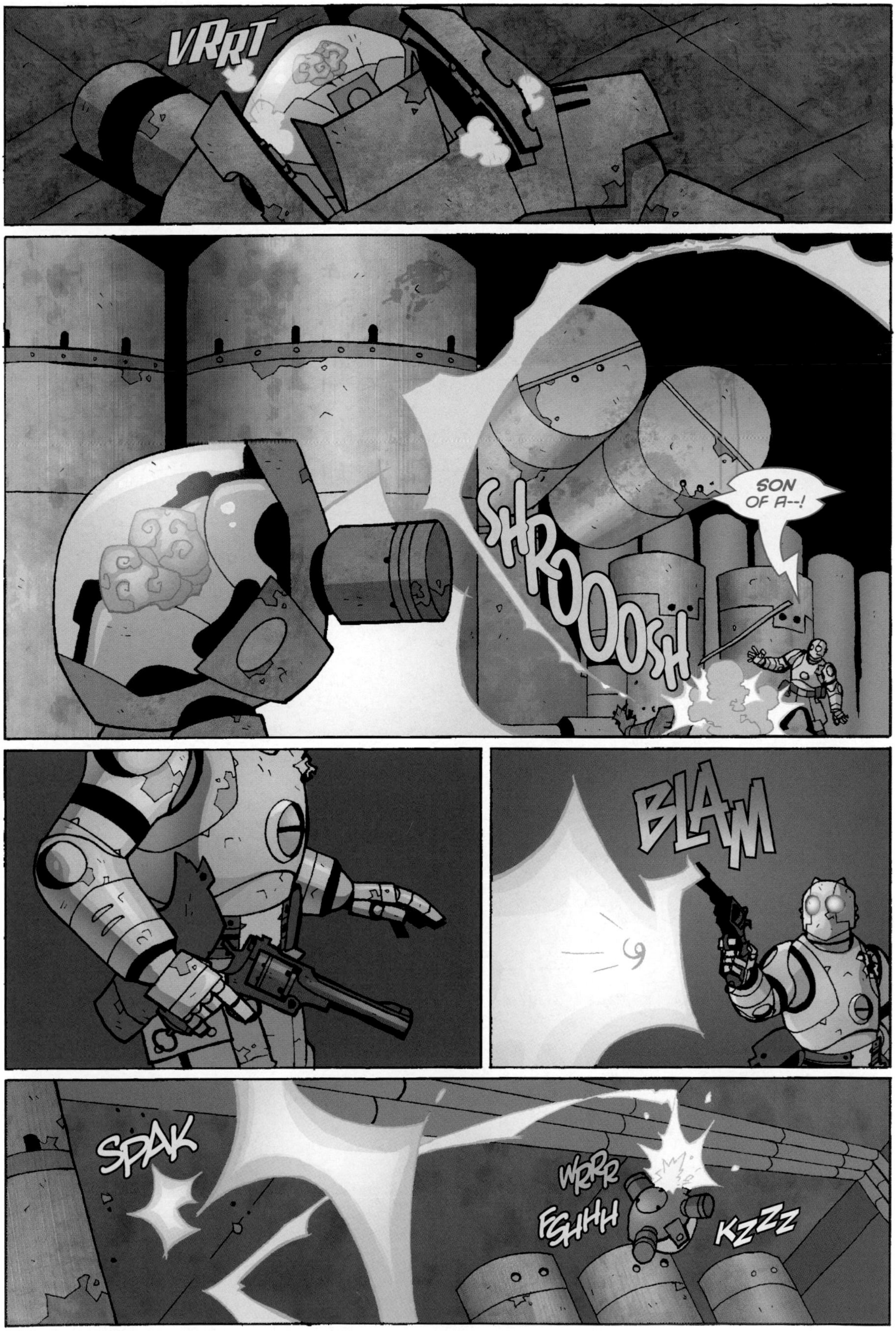
VRRT
SHROOOOSH
SON OF A--!
BLAM
SPAK
WRRR
FSHHH
KZZZ

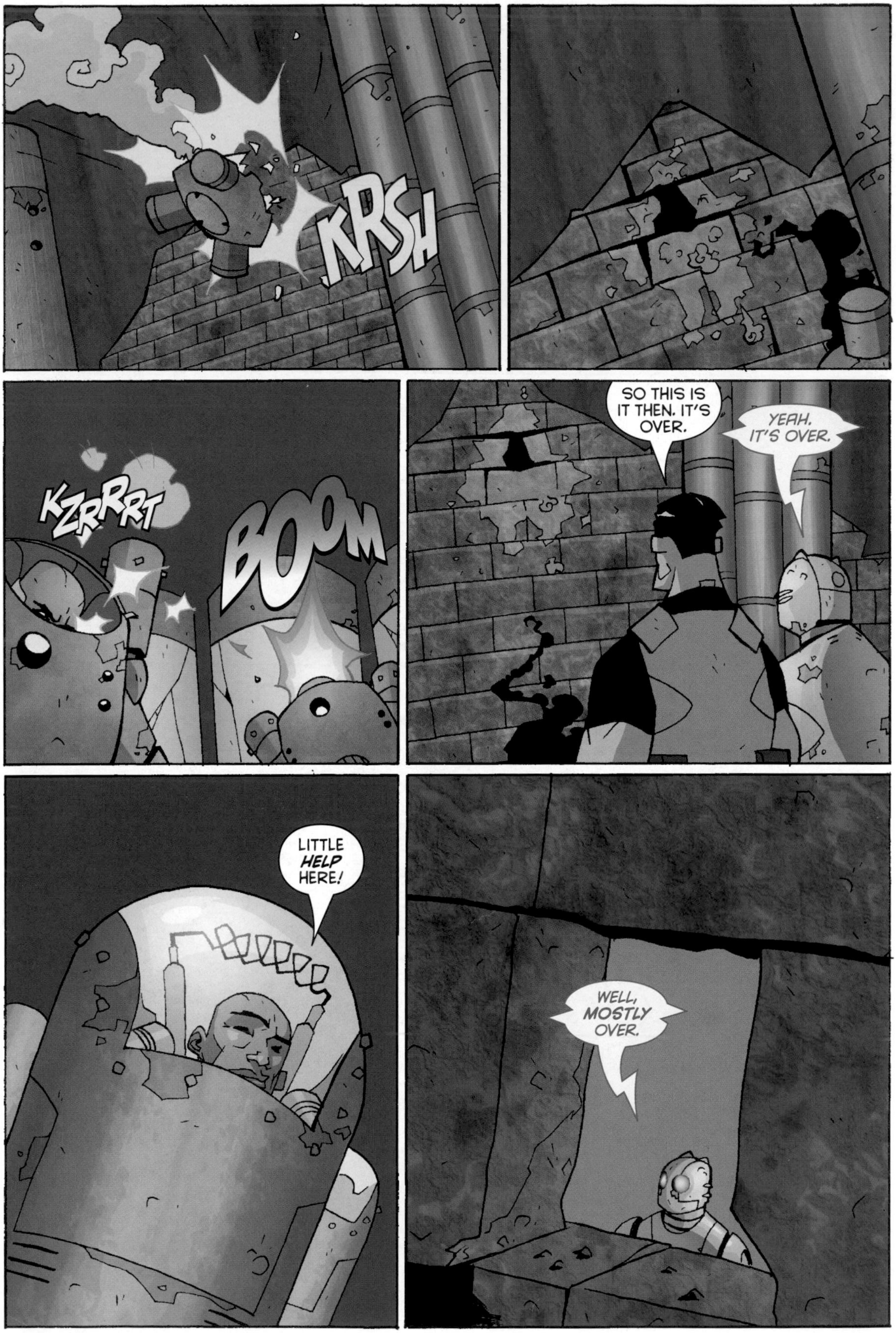
KRSH
KZRRRT
BOOM
SO THIS IS IT THEN. IT'S OVER.
YEAH. IT'S OVER.
LITTLE HELP HERE!
WELL, MOSTLY OVER.

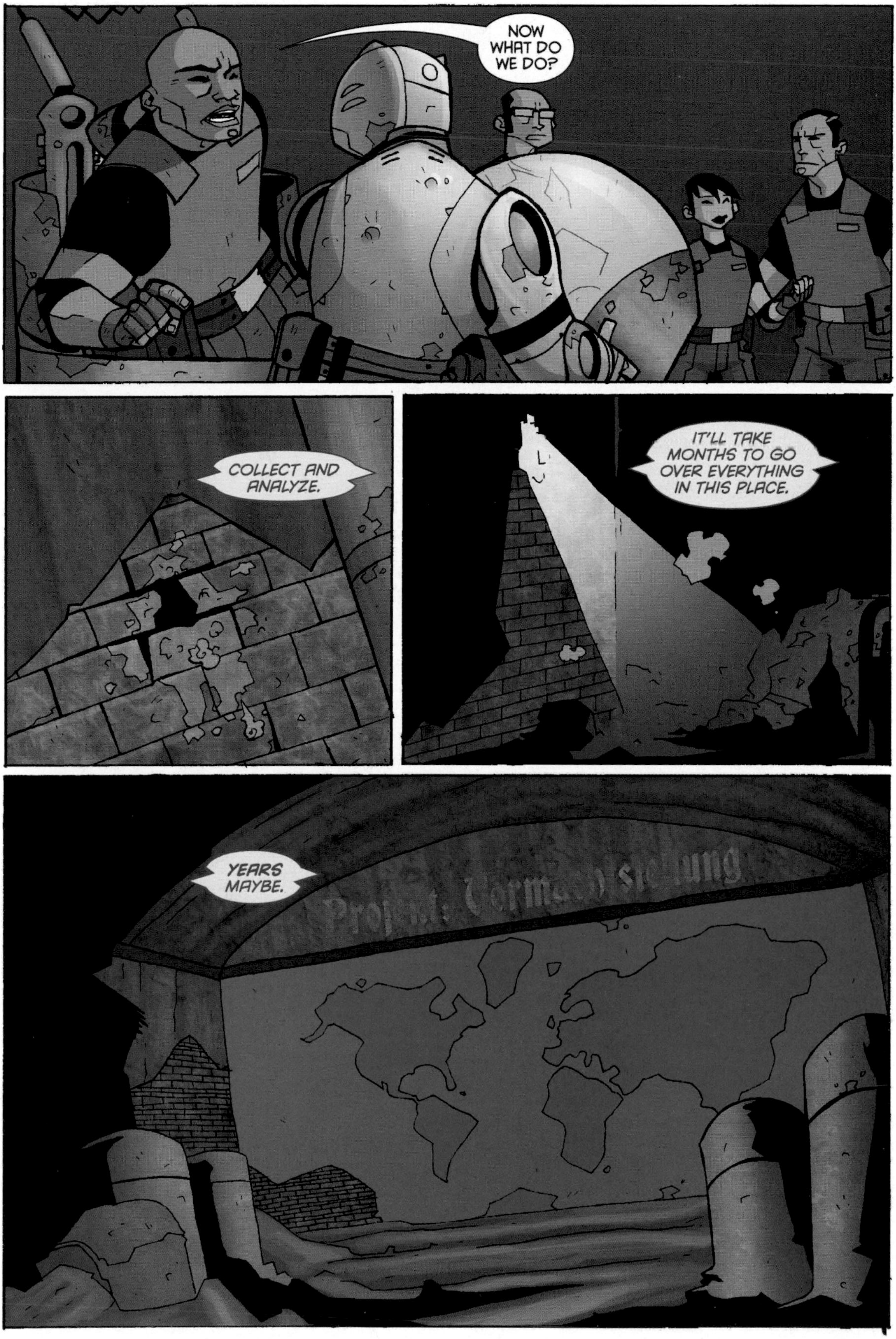
NOW WHAT DO WE DO?
COLLECT AND ANALYZE.
IT'LL TAKE MONTHS TO GO OVER EVERYTHING IN THIS PLACE.
YEARS MAYBE.

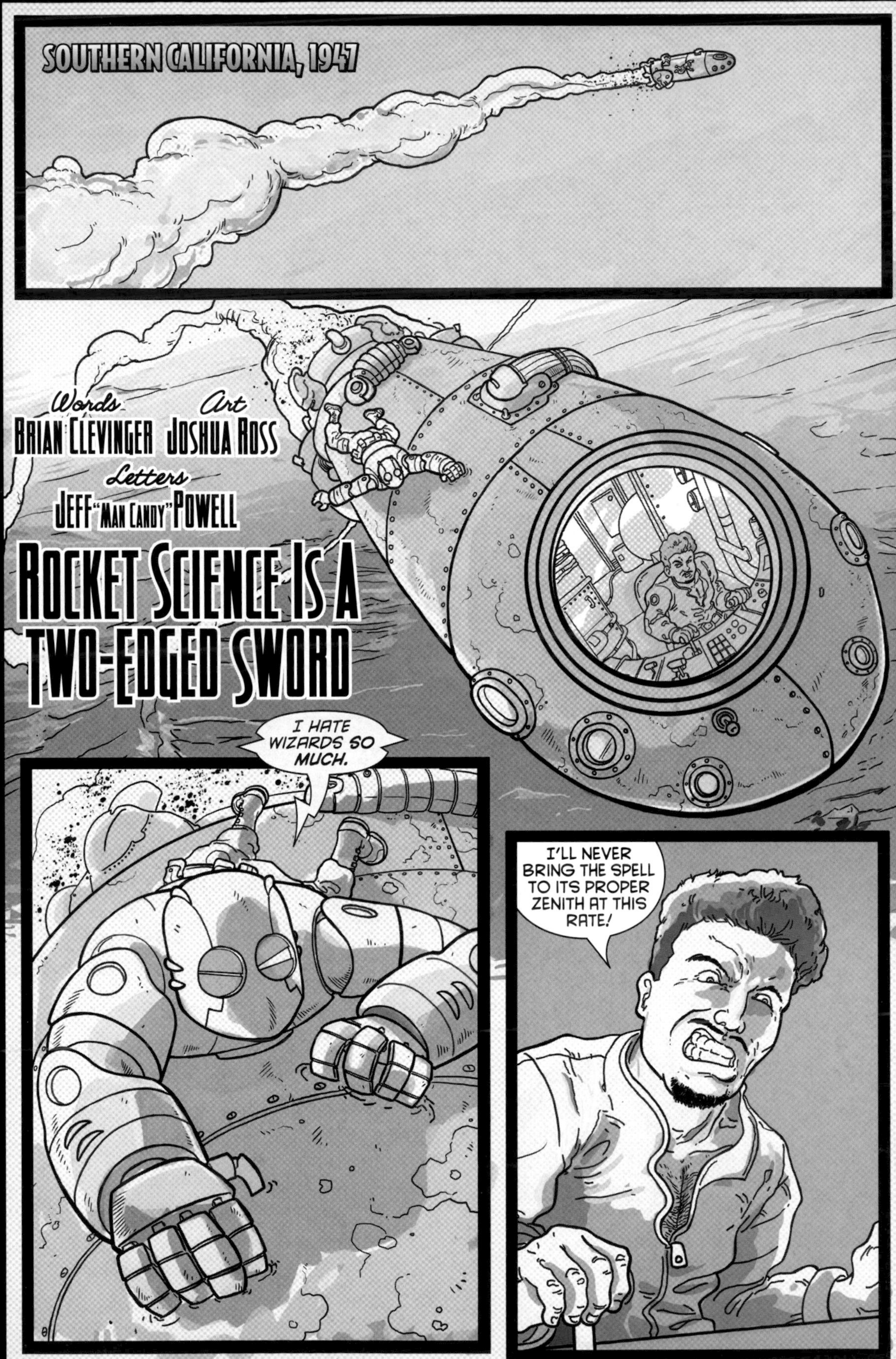
SOUTHERN CALIFORNIA, 1947
Words BRIAN CLEVINGER Art JOSHUA ROSS
Letters JEFF "MAN CANDY" POWELL
ROCKET SCIENCE IS A TWO-EDGED SWORD
I HATE WIZARDS SO MUCH.
I'LL NEVER BRING THE SPELL TO ITS PROPER ZENITH AT THIS RATE!

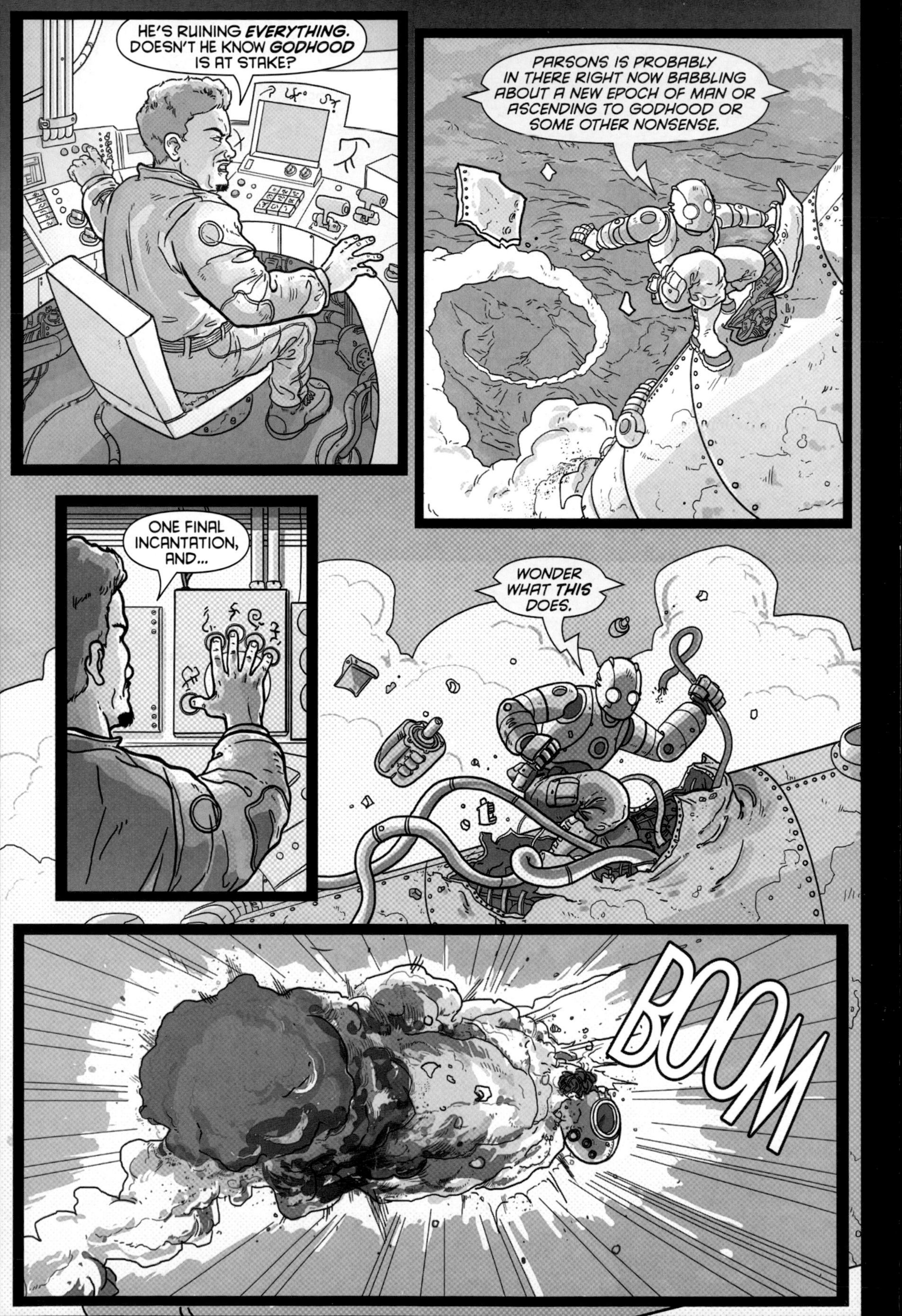
HE'S RUINING EVERYTHING. DOESN'T HE KNOW GODHOOD IS AT STAKE?
PARSONS IS PROBABLY IN THERE RIGHT NOW BABBLING ABOUT A NEW EPOCH OF MAN OR ASCENDING TO GODHOOD OR SOME OTHER NONSENSE.
ONE FINAL INCANTATION, AND...
WONDER WHAT THIS DOES.
BOOM

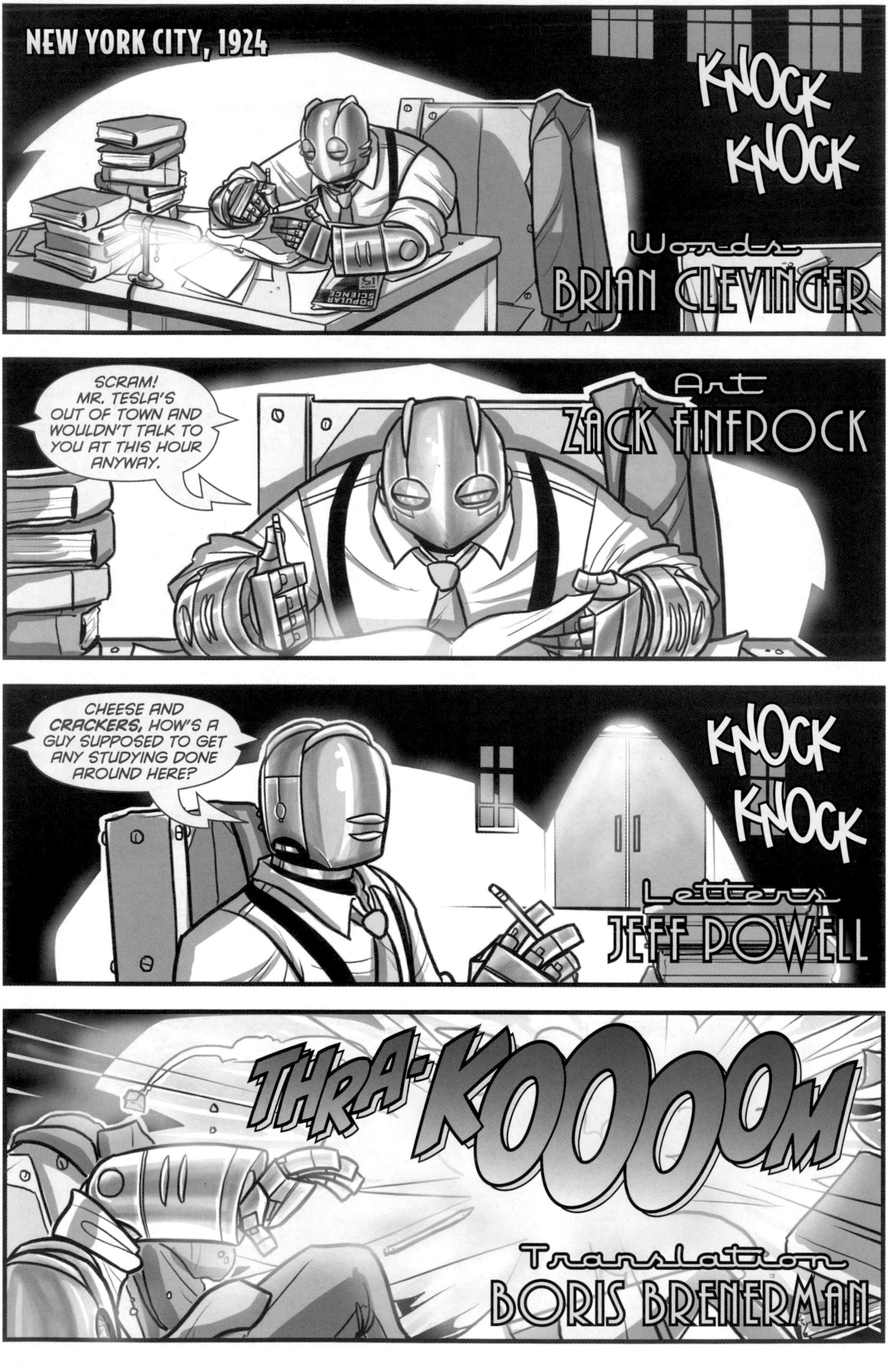
NEW YORK CITY, 1924
KNOCK KNOCK
Words
BRIAN CLEVINGER
POPULAR SCIENCE
SCRAM! MR. TESLA'S OUT OF TOWN AND WOULDN'T TALK TO YOU AT THIS HOUR ANYWAY.
Art
ZACK FINFROCK
CHEESE AND CRACKERS, HOW'S A GUY SUPPOSED TO GET ANY STUDYING DONE AROUND HERE?
KNOCK KNOCK
Letters
JEFF POWELL
THRA-KOOOOM
Translation
BORIS BRENERMAN

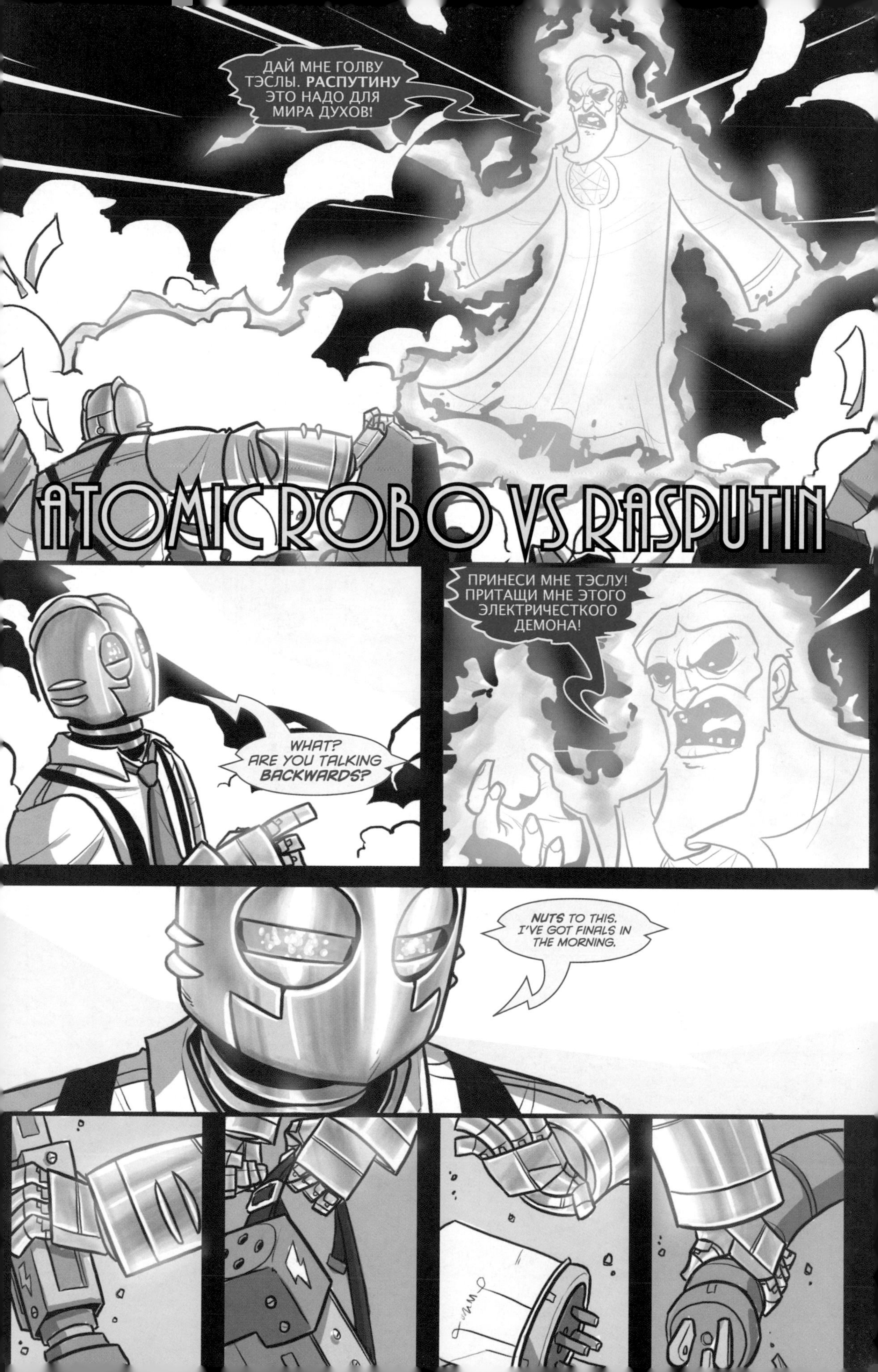
ДАЙ МНЕ ГОЛВУ ТЭСЛЫ. **РАСПУТИНУ** ЭТО НАДО ДЛЯ МИРА ДУХОВ!
ATOMIC ROBO VS RASPUTIN
WHAT? ARE YOU TALKING **BACKWARDS?**
ПРИНЕСИ МНЕ ТЭСЛУ! ПРИТАЩИ МНЕ ЭТОГО ЭЛЕКТРИЧЕСТКОГО ДЕМОНА!
NUTS TO THIS. I'VE GOT FINALS IN THE MORNING.

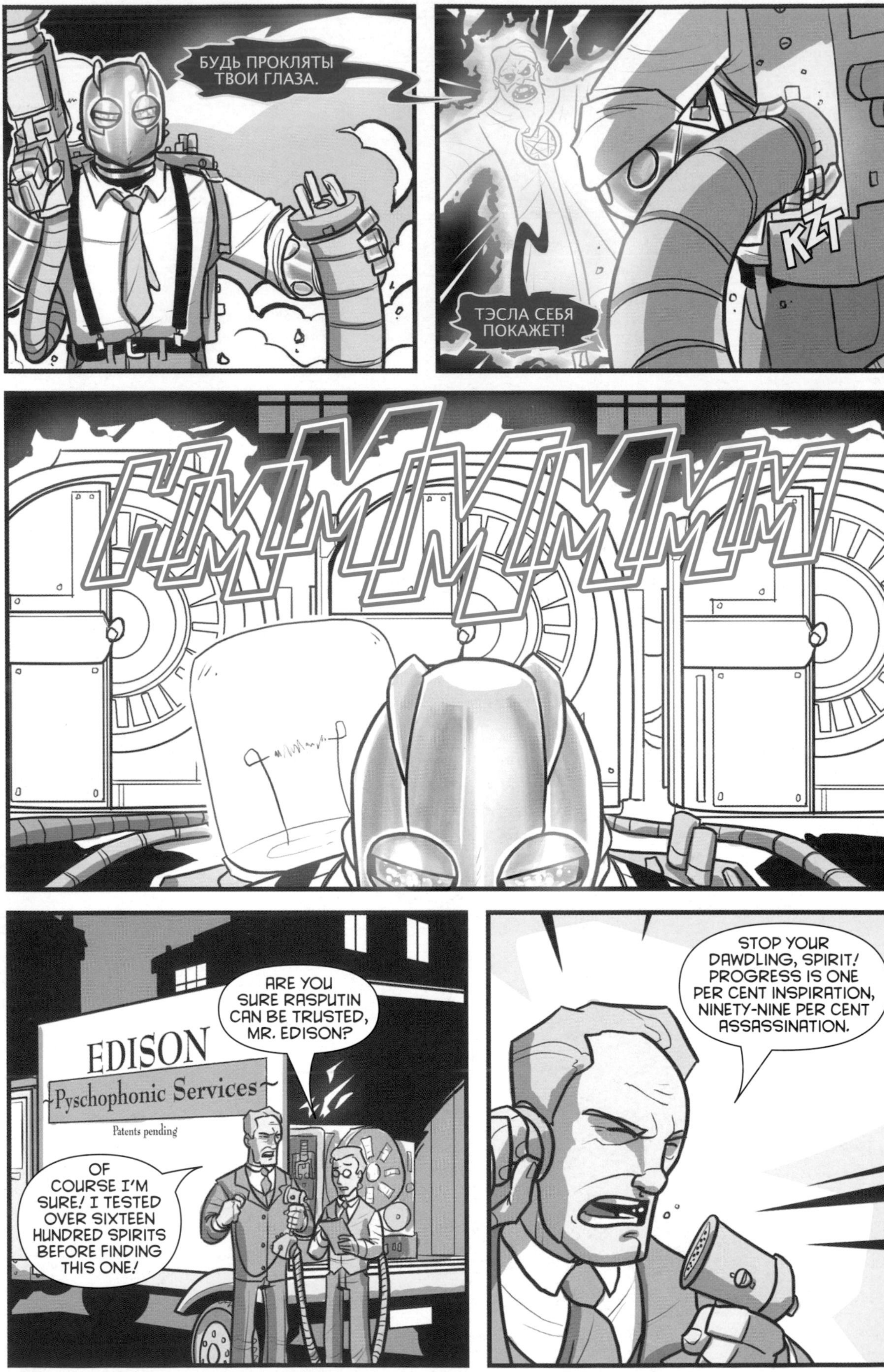

БУДЬ ПРОКЛЯТЫ ТВОИ ГЛАЗА.
ТЭСЛА СЕБЯ ПОКАЖЕТ!
KZT
HMMMMMMMMMMM
EDISON
~Pyschophonic Services~
Patents pending
ARE YOU SURE RASPUTIN CAN BE TRUSTED, MR. EDISON?
OF COURSE I'M SURE! I TESTED OVER SIXTEEN HUNDRED SPIRITS BEFORE FINDING THIS ONE!
STOP YOUR DAWDLING, SPIRIT! PROGRESS IS ONE PER CENT INSPIRATION, NINETY-NINE PER CENT ASSASSINATION.

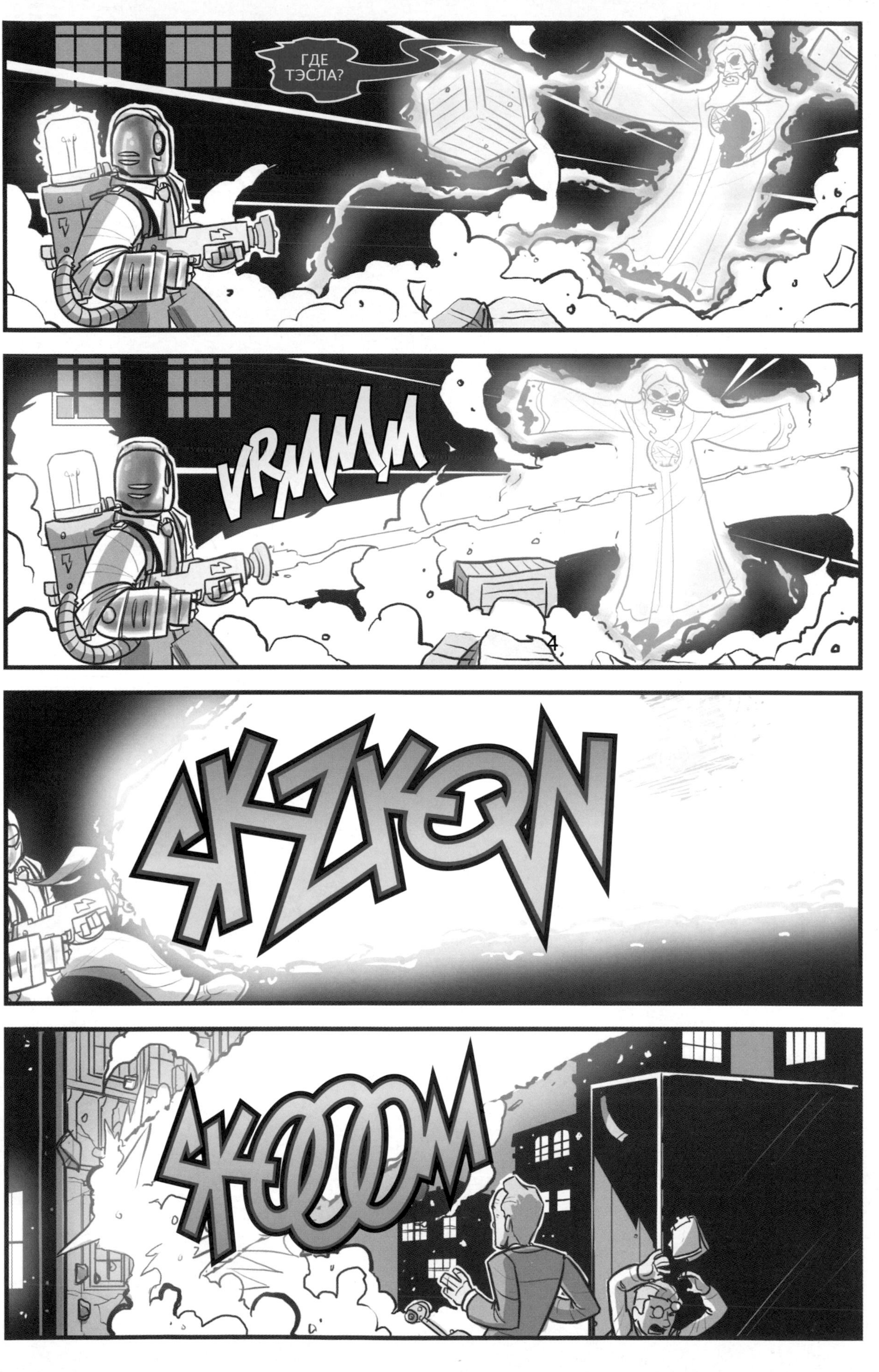
ГДЕ ТЭСЛА?
VRMMM

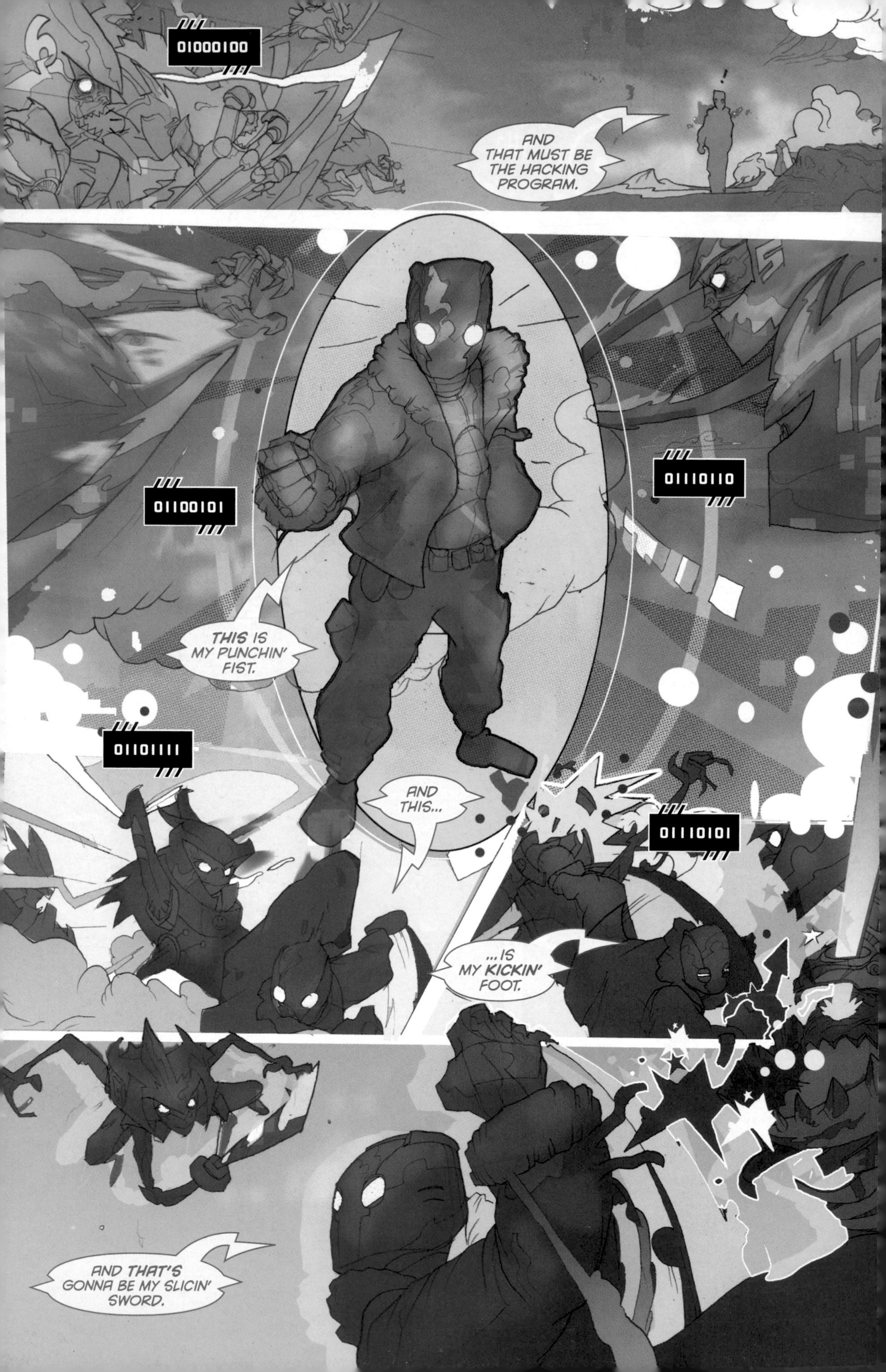

01000100
AND THAT MUST BE THE HACKING PROGRAM.
01100101
01110110
THIS IS MY PUNCHIN' FIST.
01101111
AND THIS...
01110101
...IS MY KICKIN' FOOT.
AND THAT'S GONNA BE MY SLICIN' SWORD.

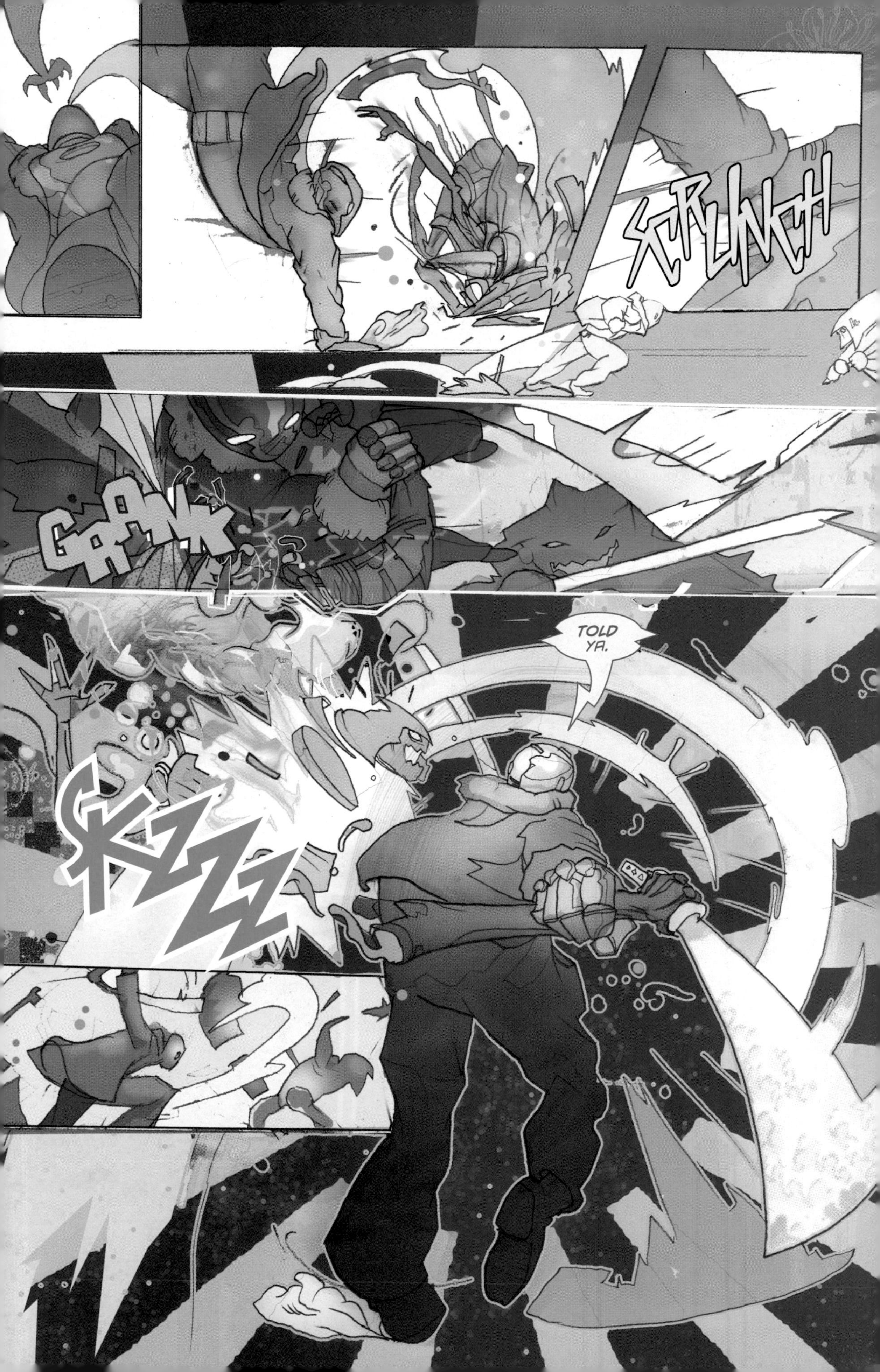
SCRUNCH
GRANK
TOLD YA.
SKZZZ

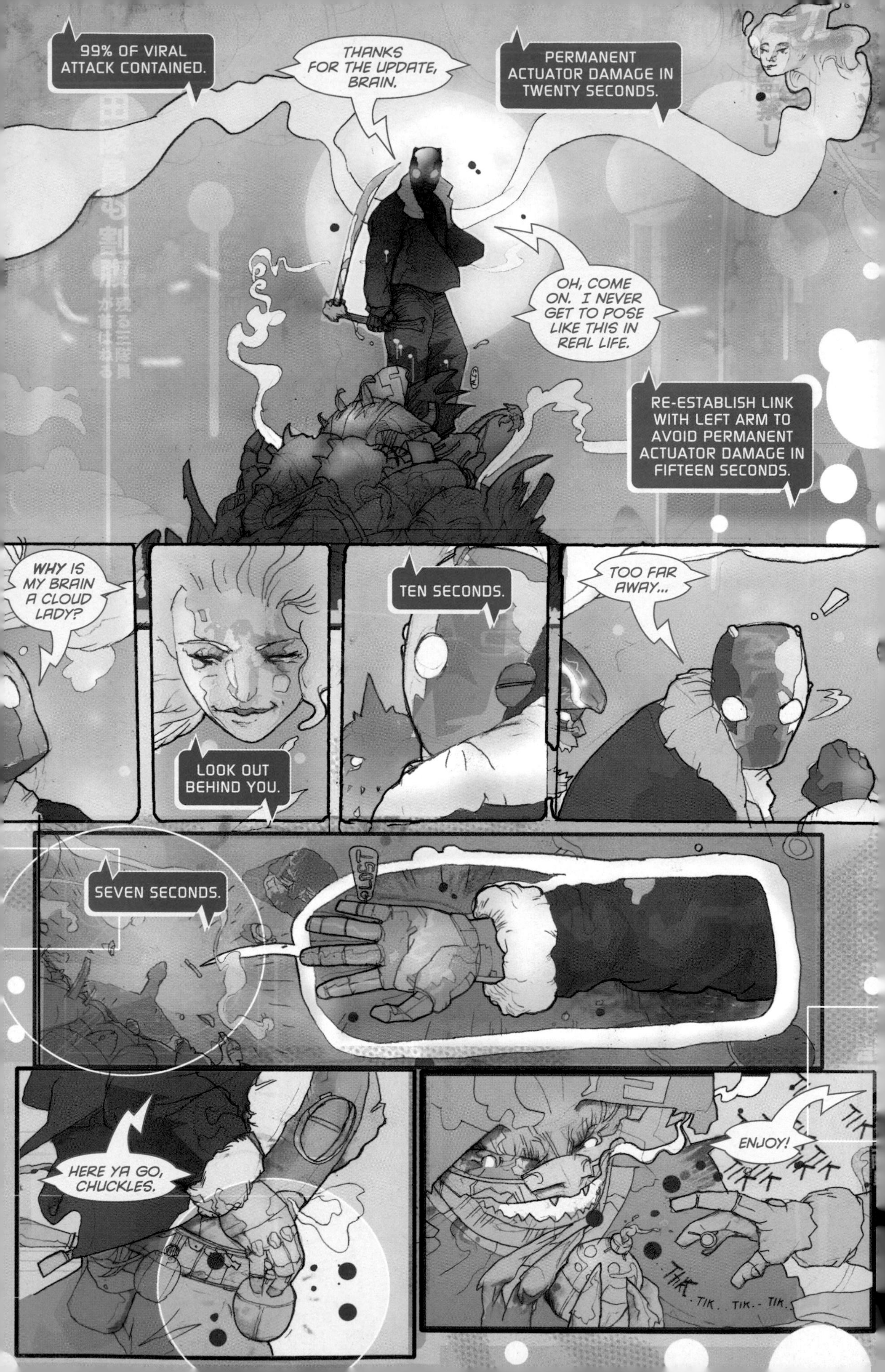

99% OF VIRAL ATTACK CONTAINED.
THANKS FOR THE UPDATE, BRAIN.
PERMANENT ACTUATOR DAMAGE IN TWENTY SECONDS.
OH, COME ON. I NEVER GET TO POSE LIKE THIS IN REAL LIFE.
RE-ESTABLISH LINK WITH LEFT ARM TO AVOID PERMANENT ACTUATOR DAMAGE IN FIFTEEN SECONDS.
WHY IS MY BRAIN A CLOUD LADY?
LOOK OUT BEHIND YOU.
TEN SECONDS.
TOO FAR AWAY...
!
LOST
SEVEN SECONDS.
HERE YA GO, CHUCKLES.
ENJOY!
TIK TIK TIK TIK
TIK.. TIK.. TIK.- TIK..

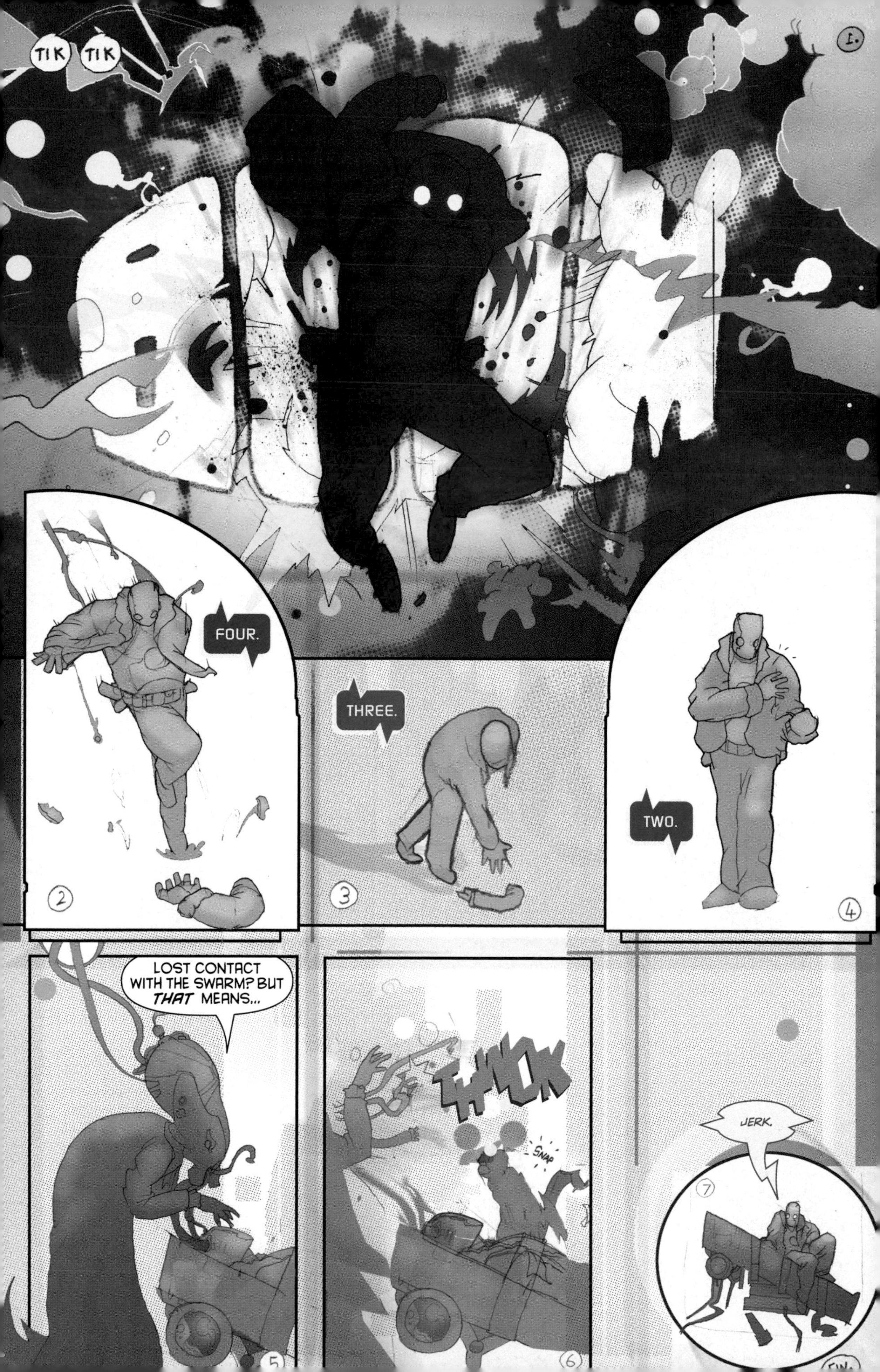
TIK TIK
FOUR.
THREE.
TWO.
LOST CONTACT WITH THE SWARM? BUT *THAT* MEANS...
THWOK
SNAP
JERK.
FIN.

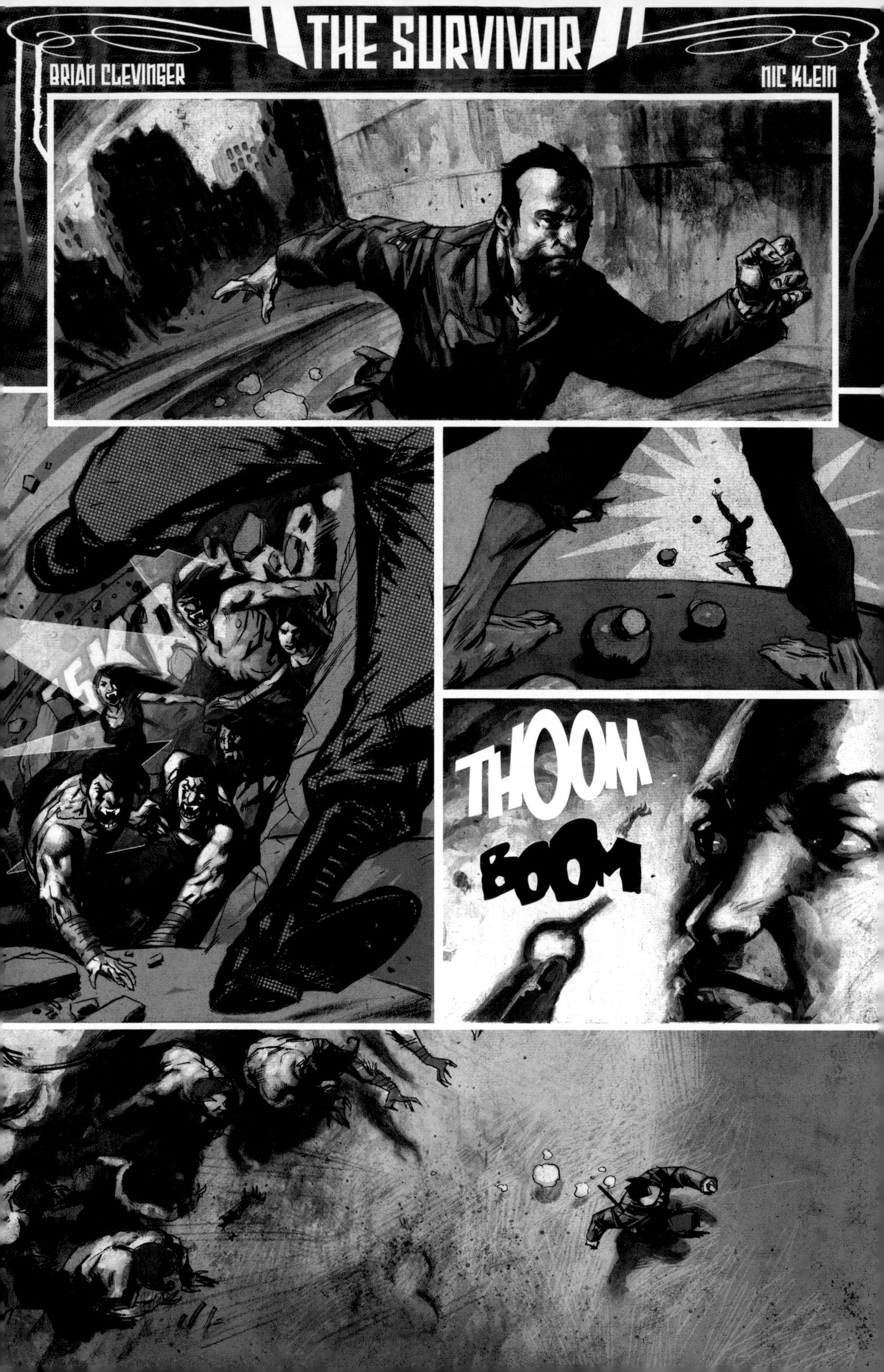
THE SURVIVOR
BRIAN CLEVINGER
NIC KLEIN
THOOM
BOOM

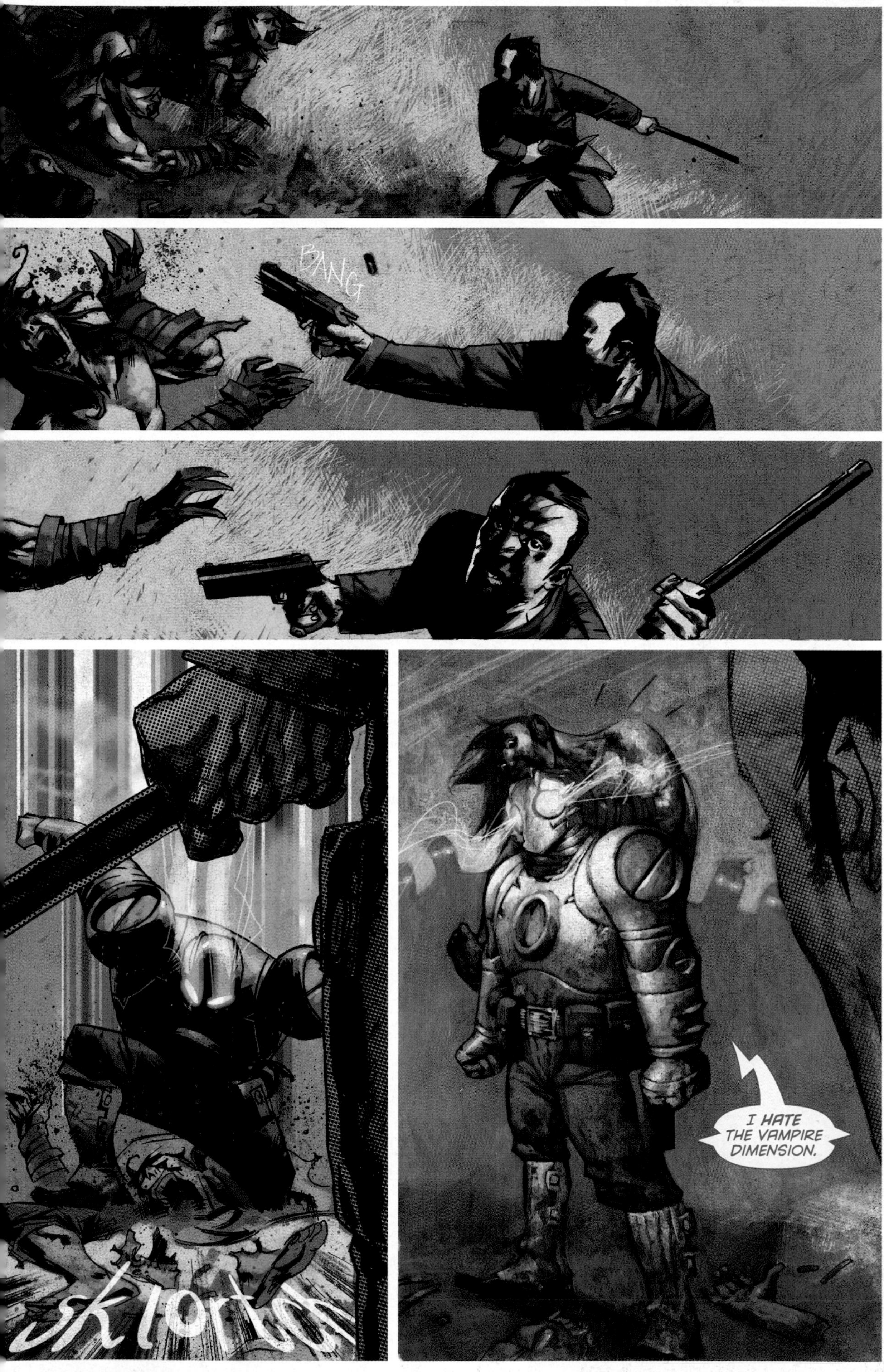
BANG
skloRtch
I HATE THE VAMPIRE DIMENSION.

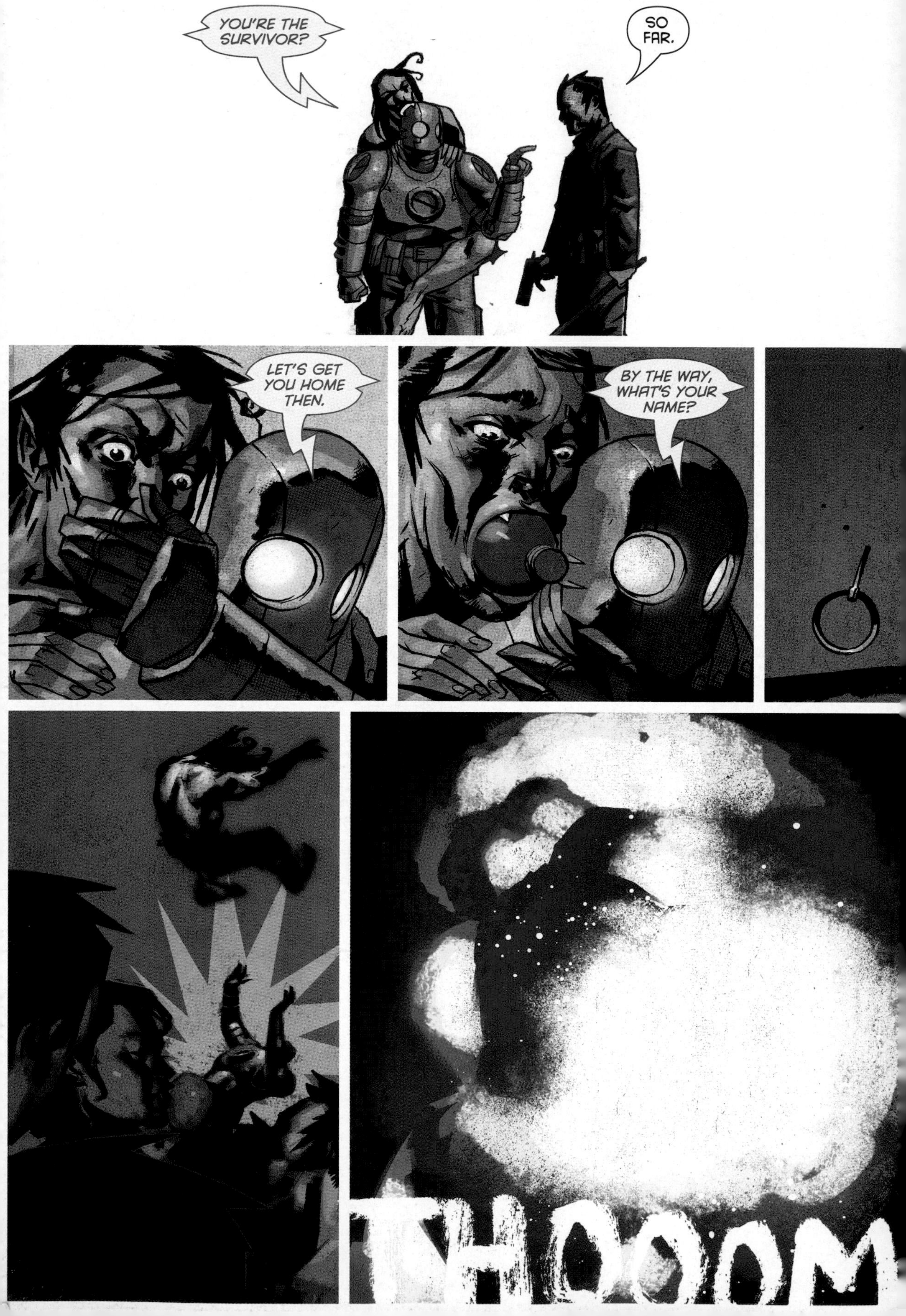
YOU'RE THE SURVIVOR?
SO FAR.
LET'S GET YOU HOME THEN.
BY THE WAY, WHAT'S YOUR NAME?
THOOOM

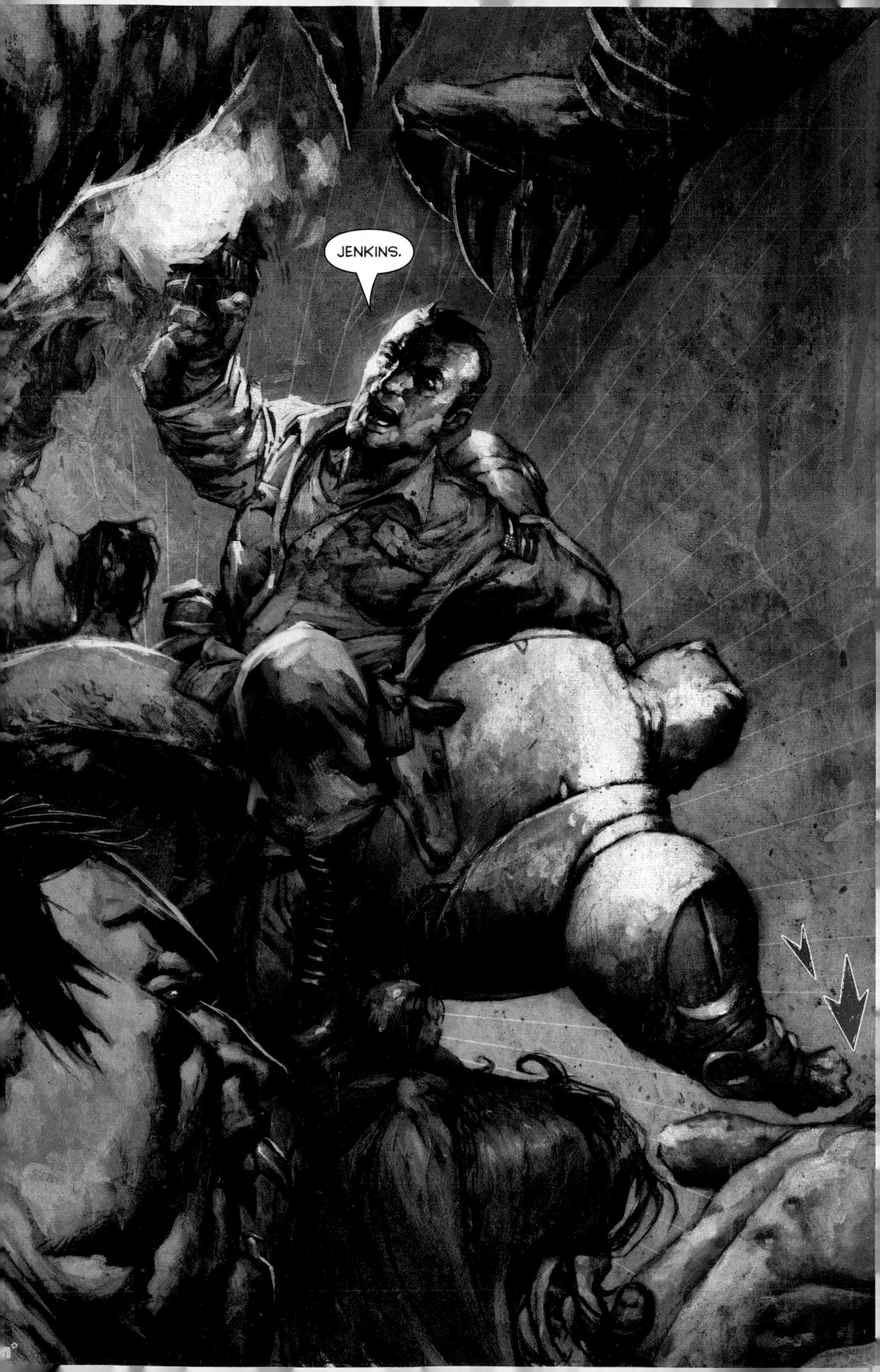
JENKINS.

ATOMIC ROBO

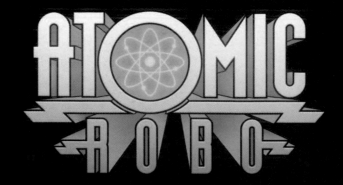

Pin-up Art

ROBO VISION by Zack Finfrock

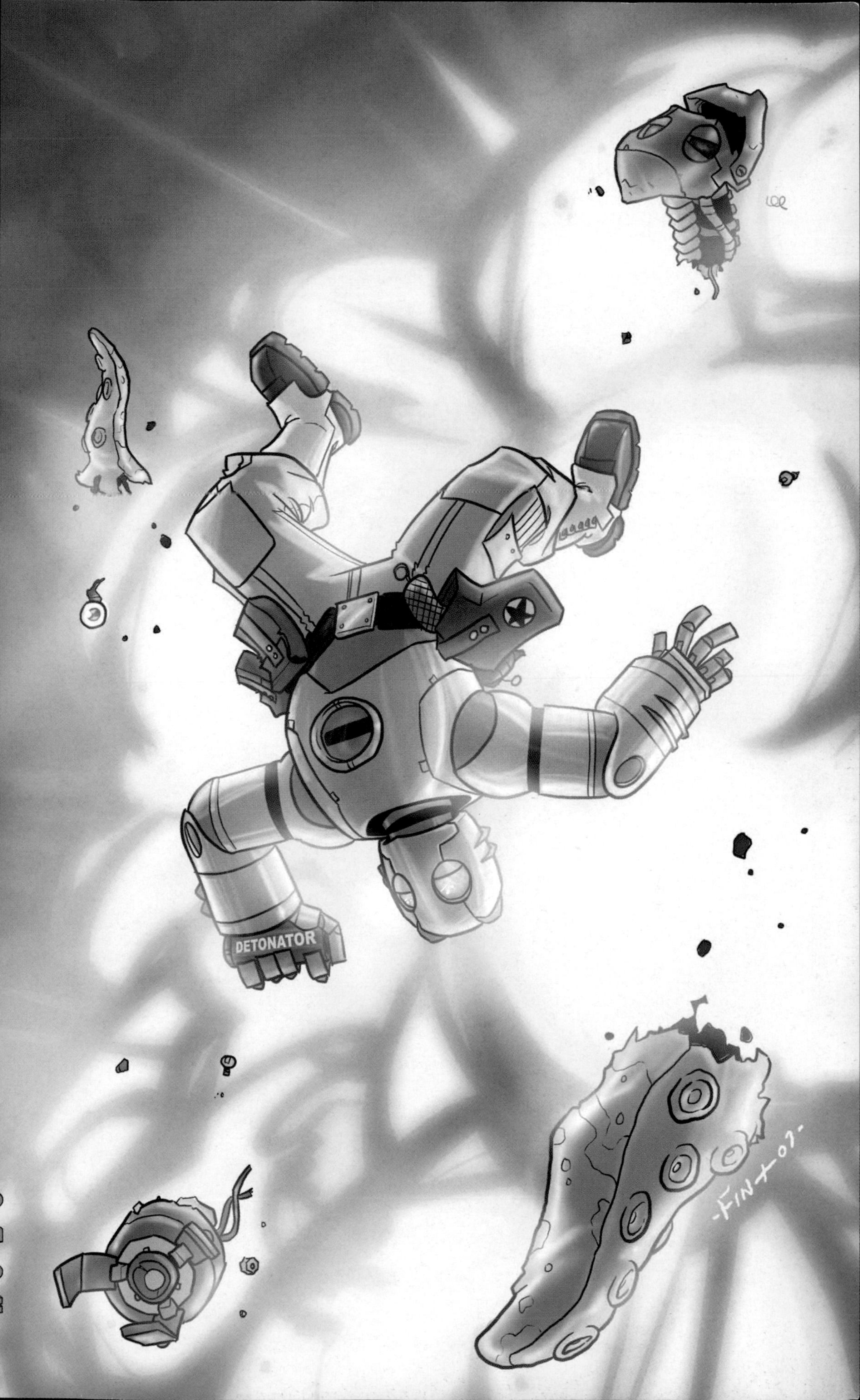
DETONATOR
-FIN+07-

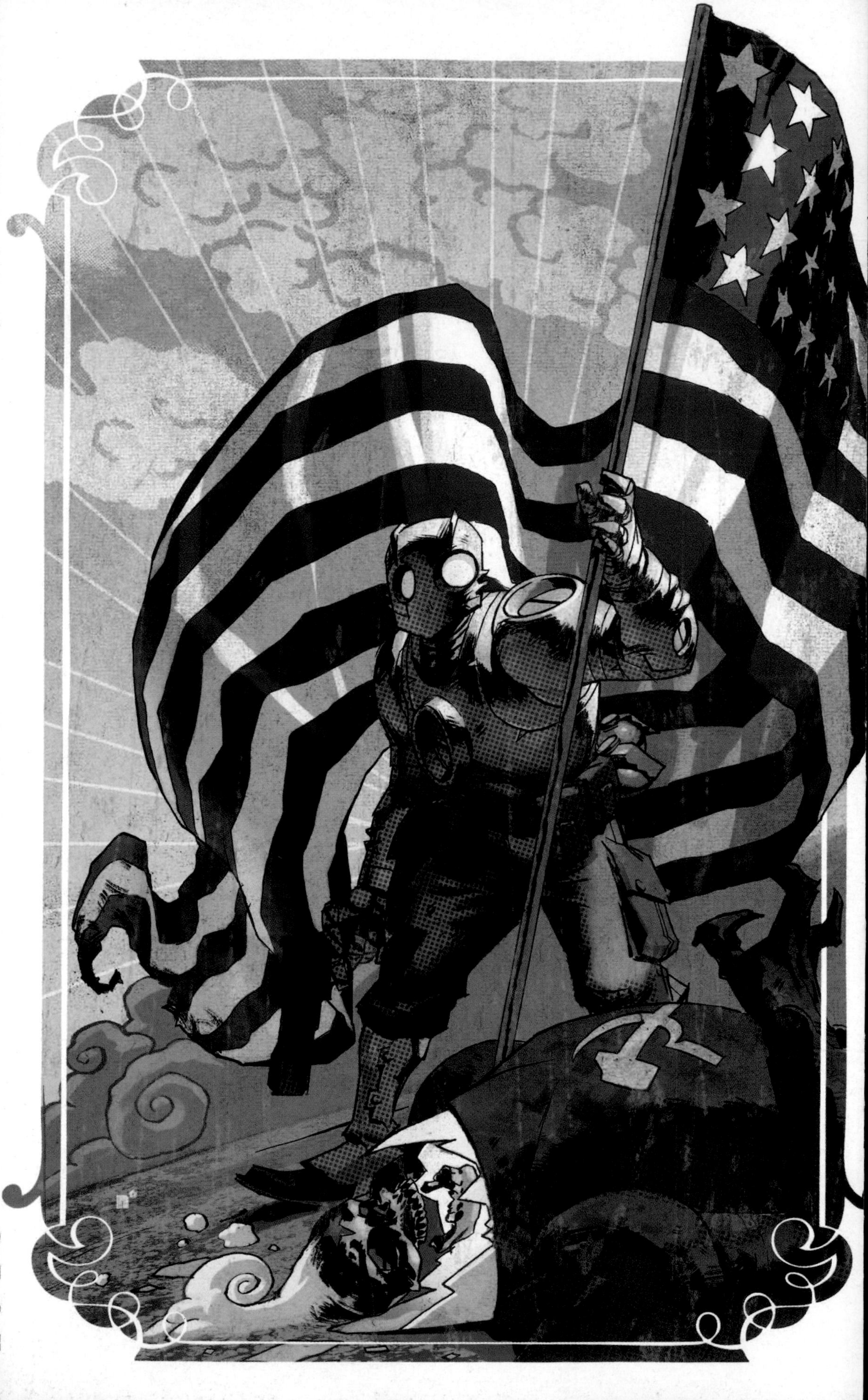

VISION by Nic Klein

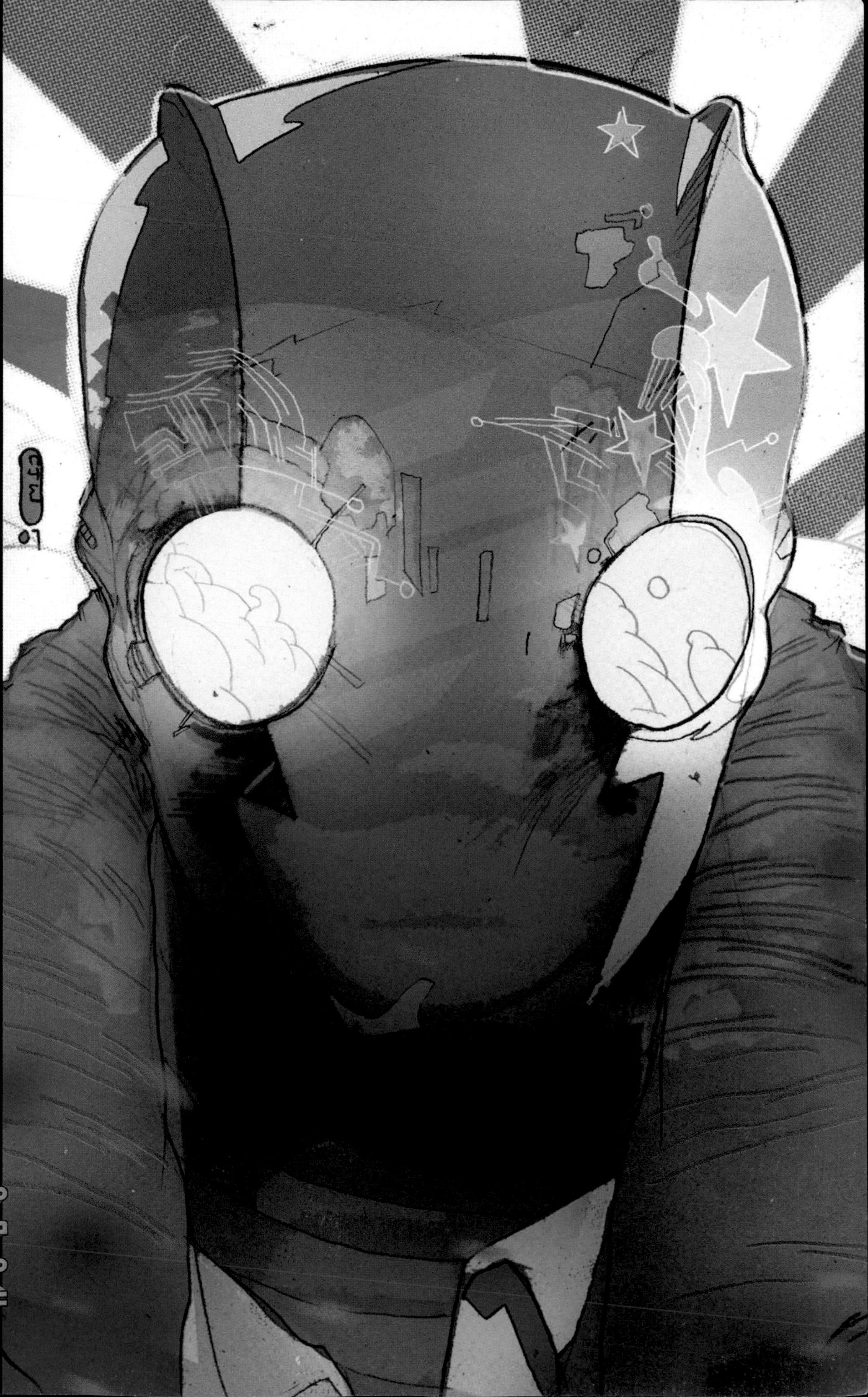

VISION by Christian Ward

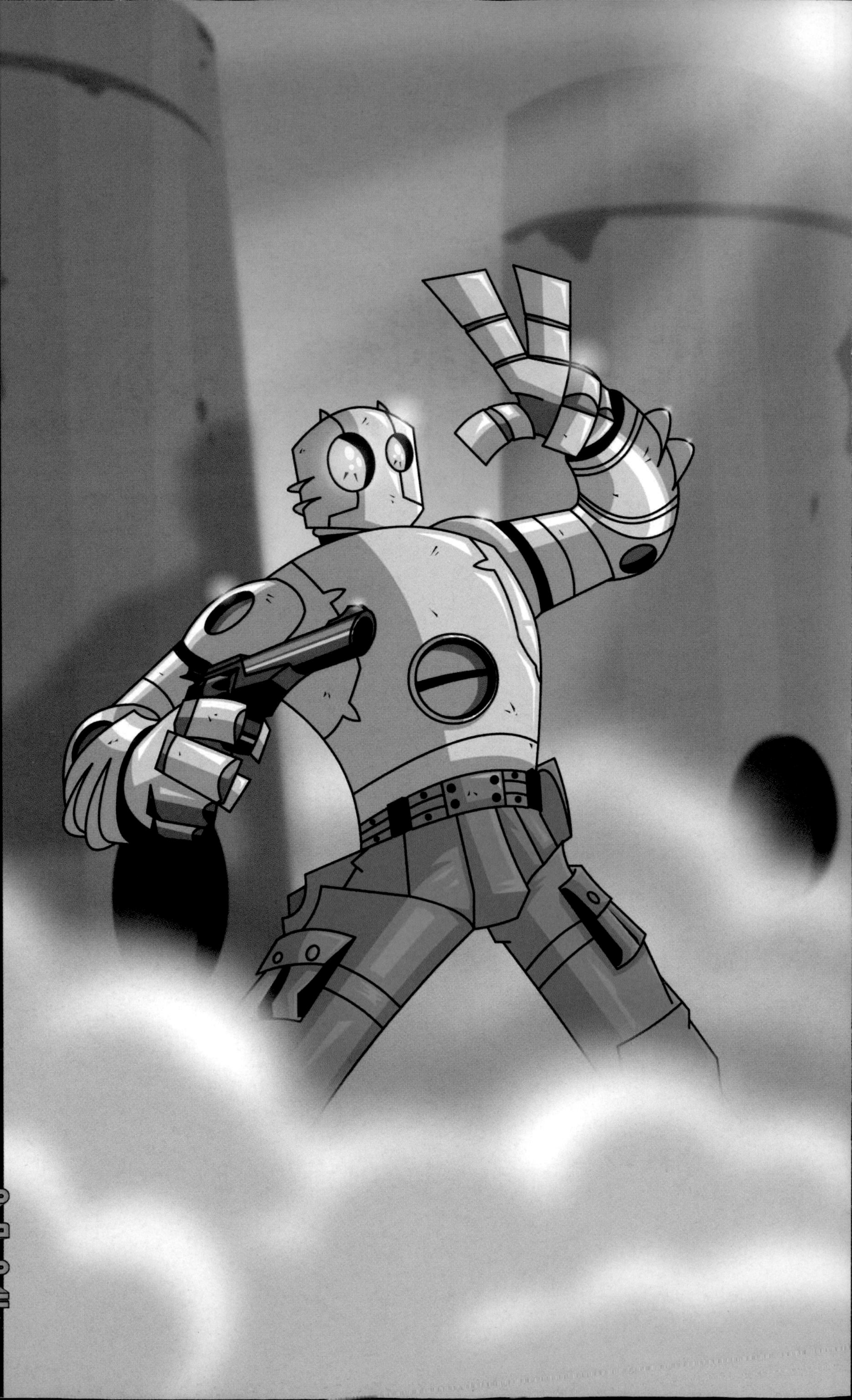

ROBO VISION by Geoff Munn

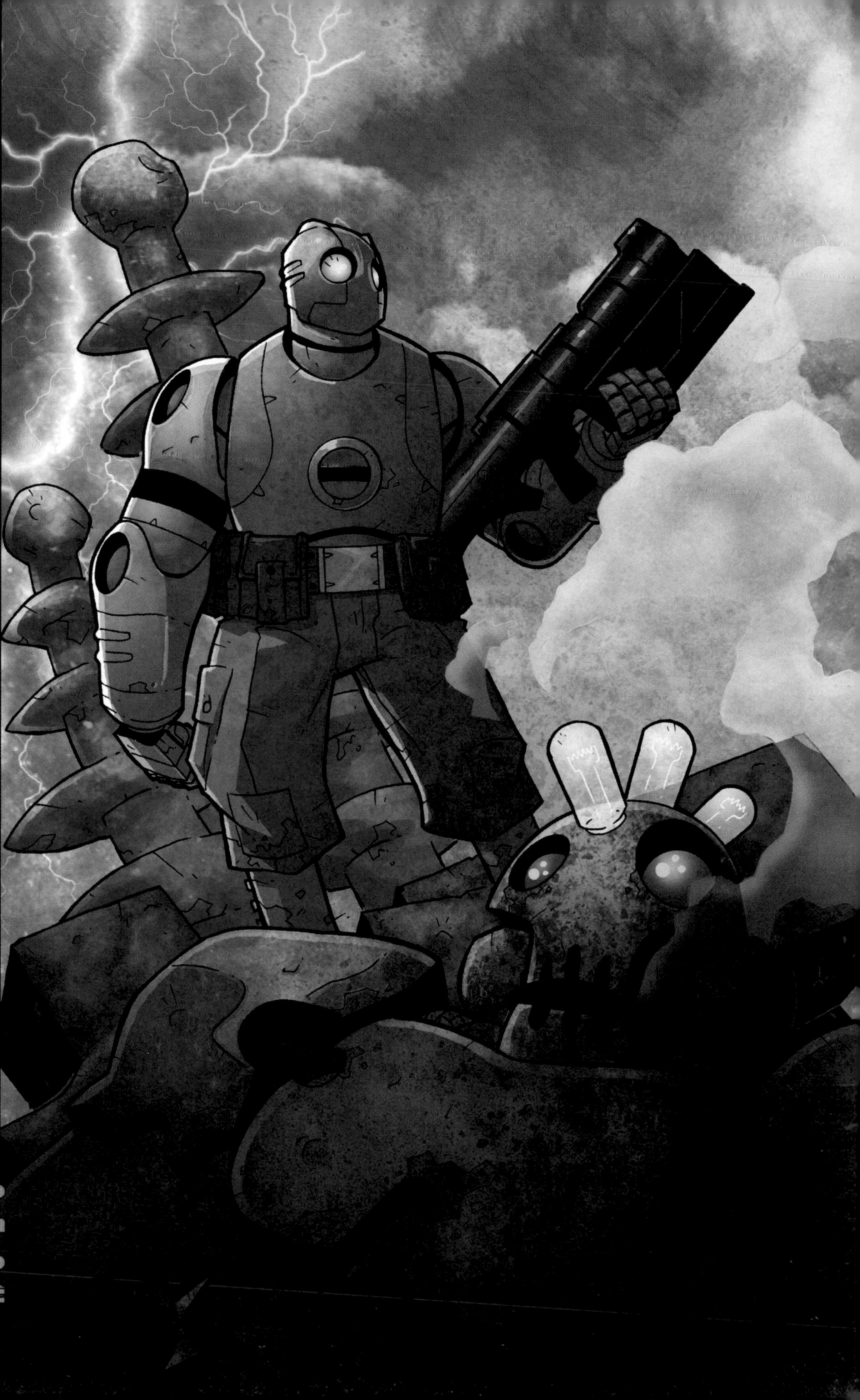

VISION by Scott Wegener

ROBO VISION by Rob Reilly

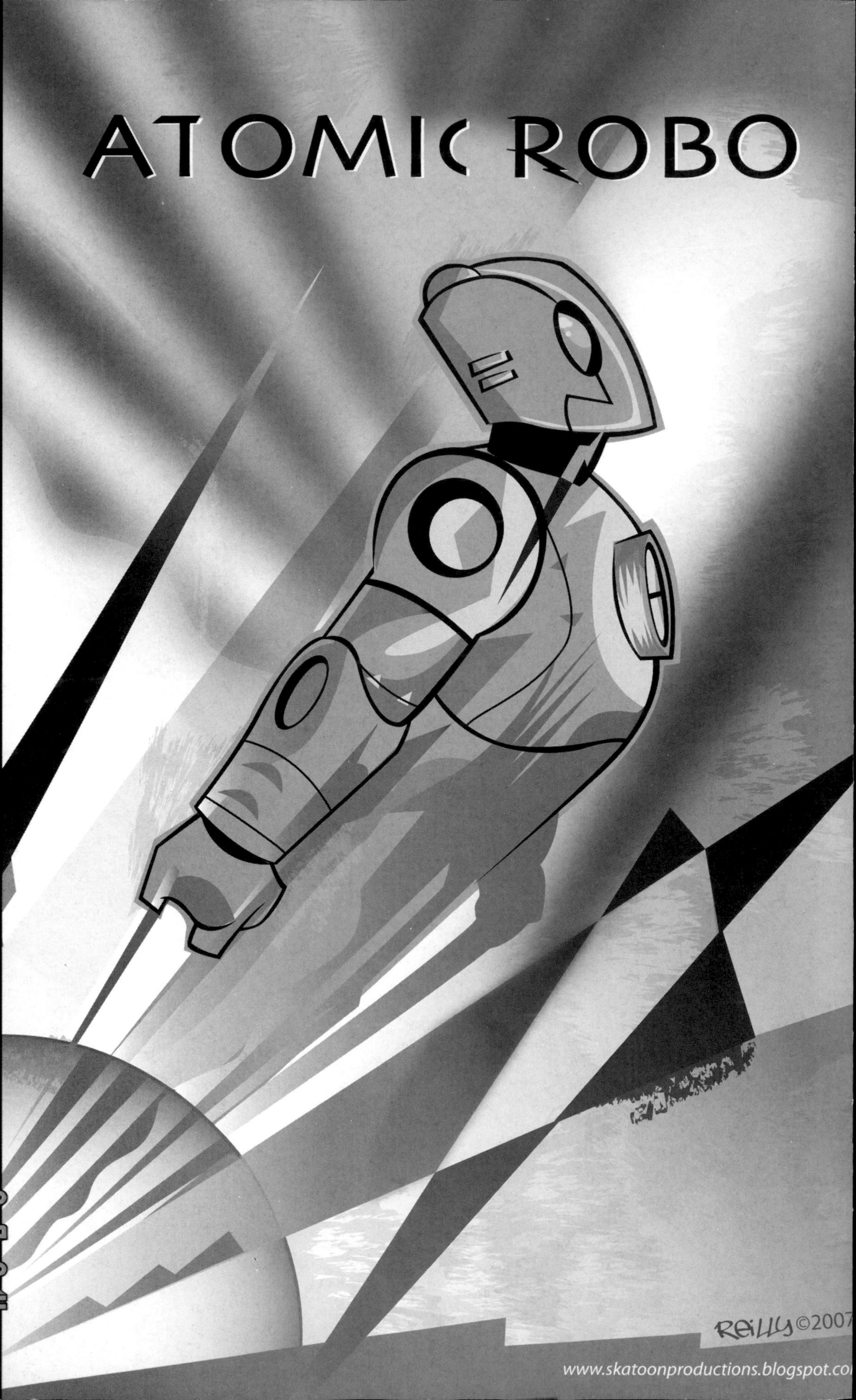
ATOMIC ROBO
REILLY ©2007
www.skatoonproductions.blogspot.co

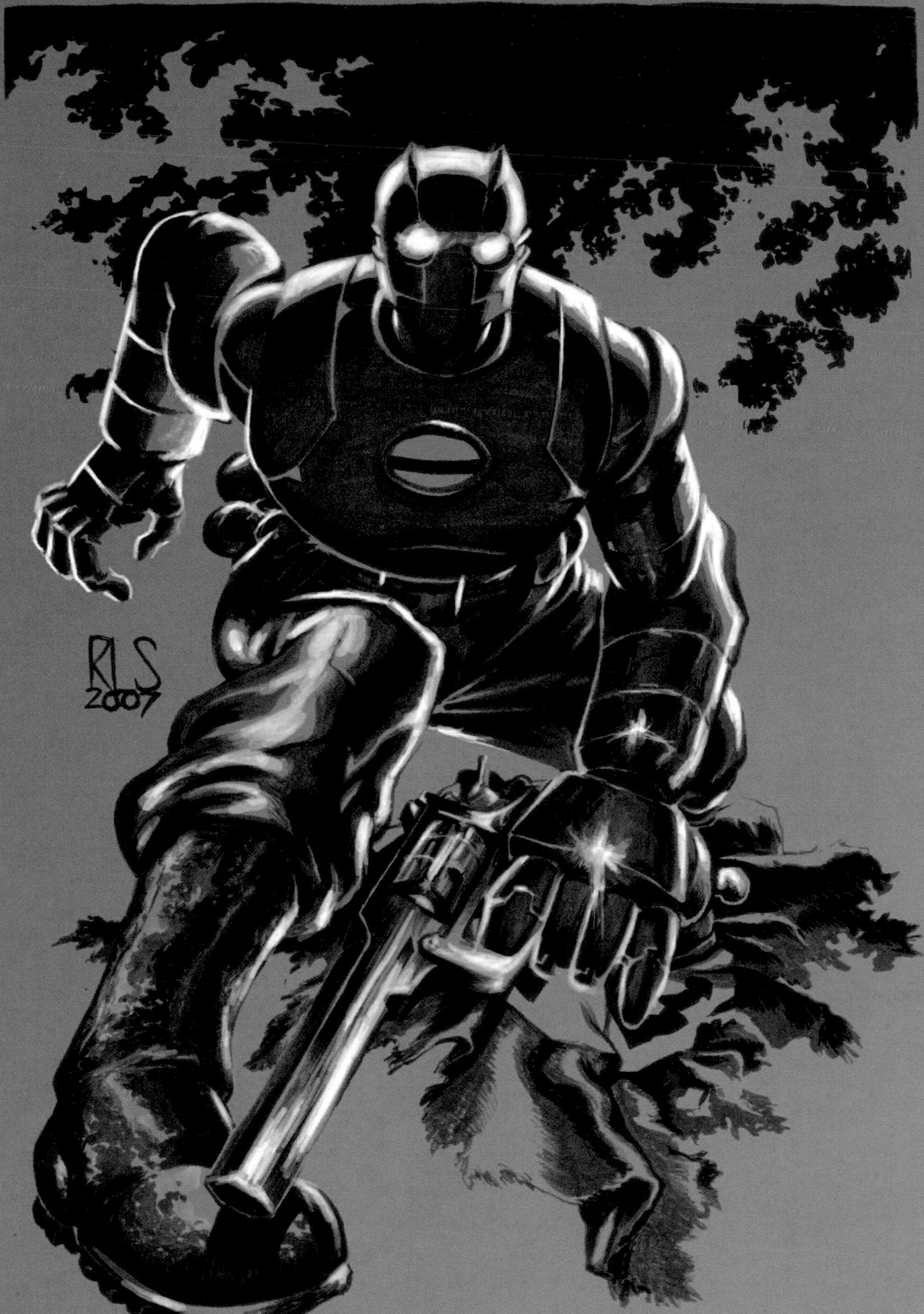
RLS
2007

ROBO VISION by Ronald Salas

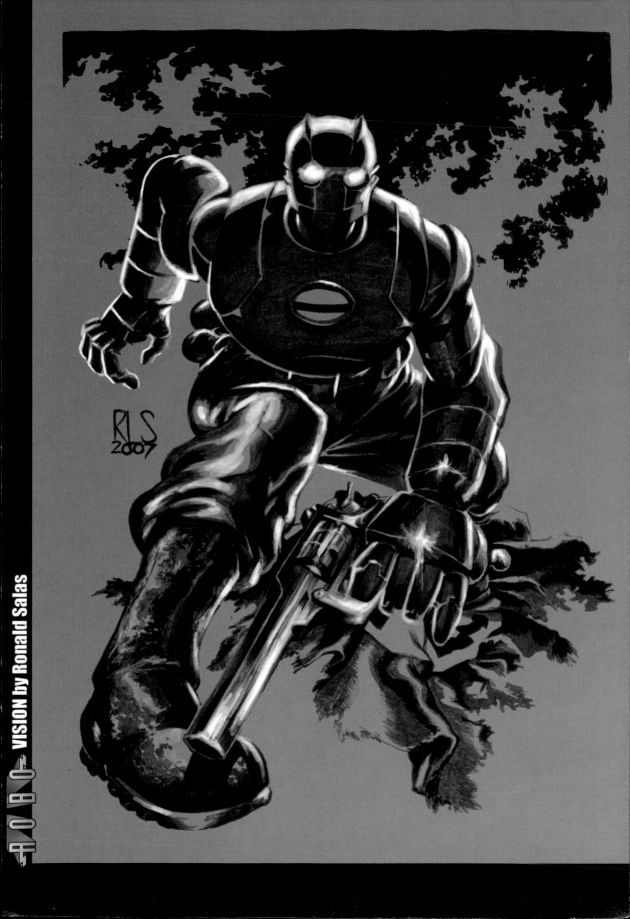

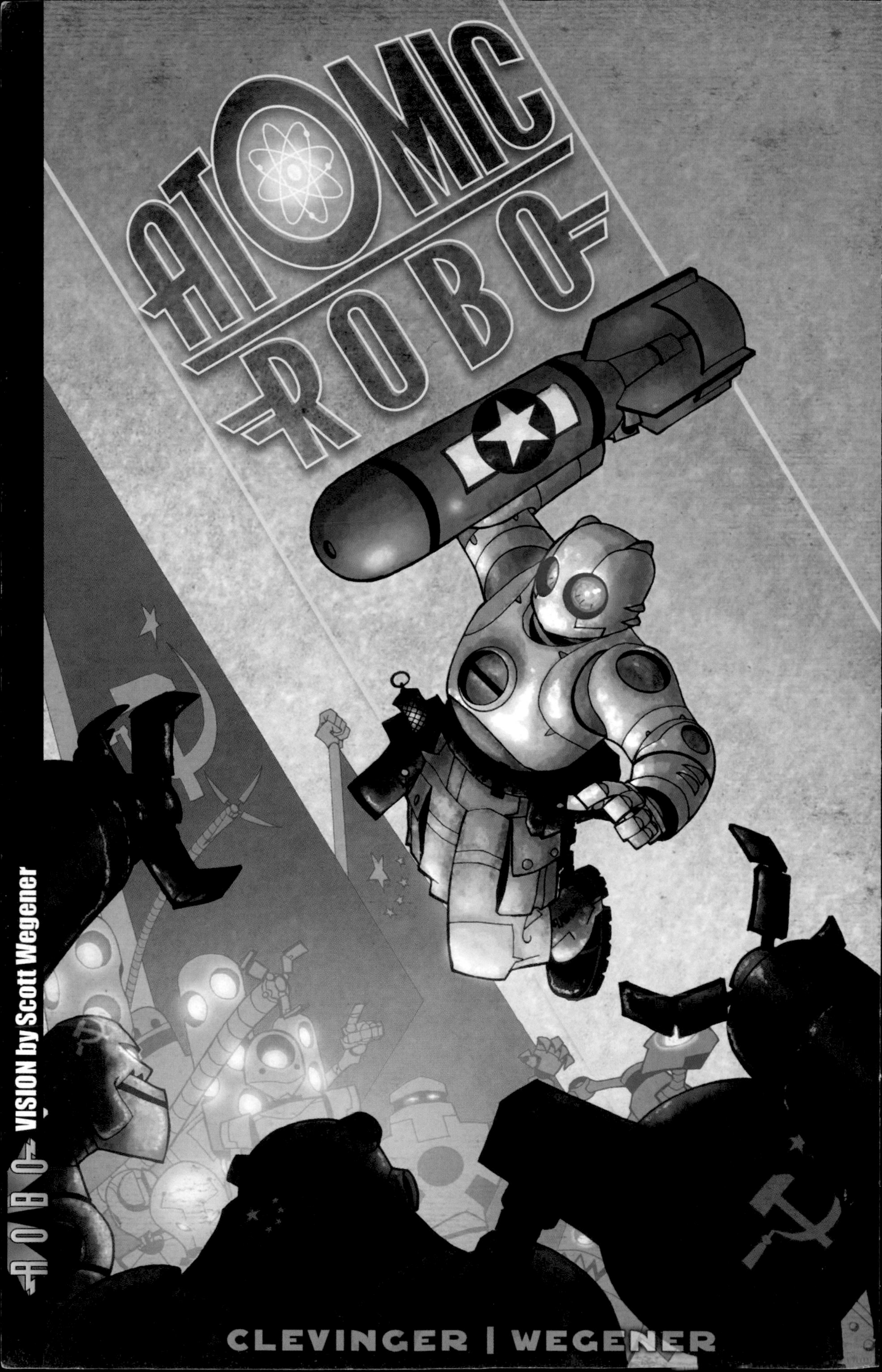
ATOMIC ROBO
CLEVINGER | WEGENER
ROBO VISION by Scott Wegener

ATOMIC ROBO

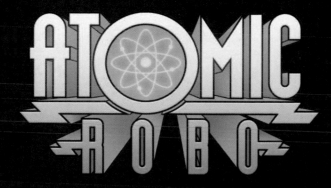

Concept Art

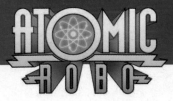

"*Extremely* early concept art for Robo. Possibly before I bothered to tell Scott that Robo wears clothes. So, we're talking prehistoric here."

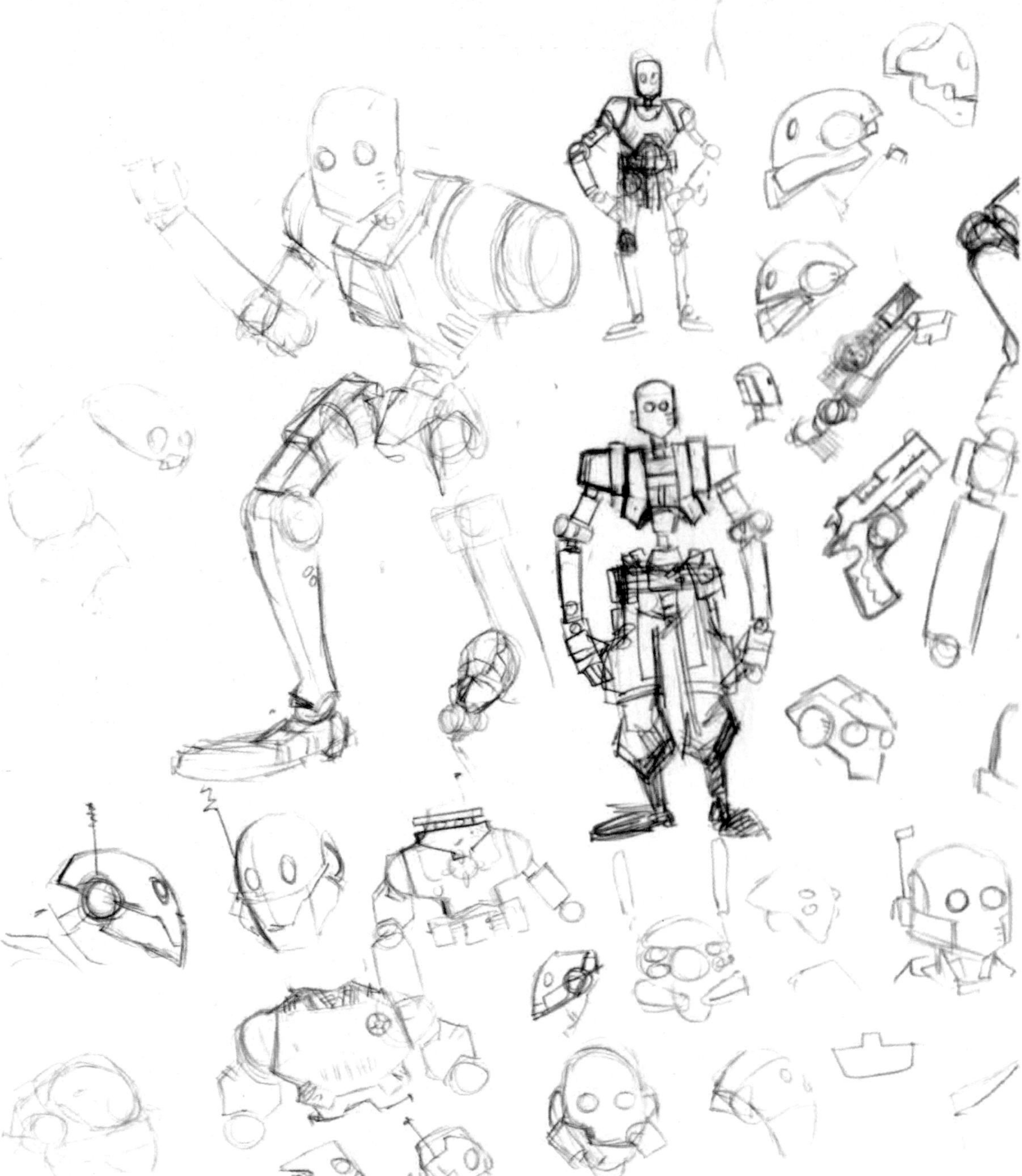

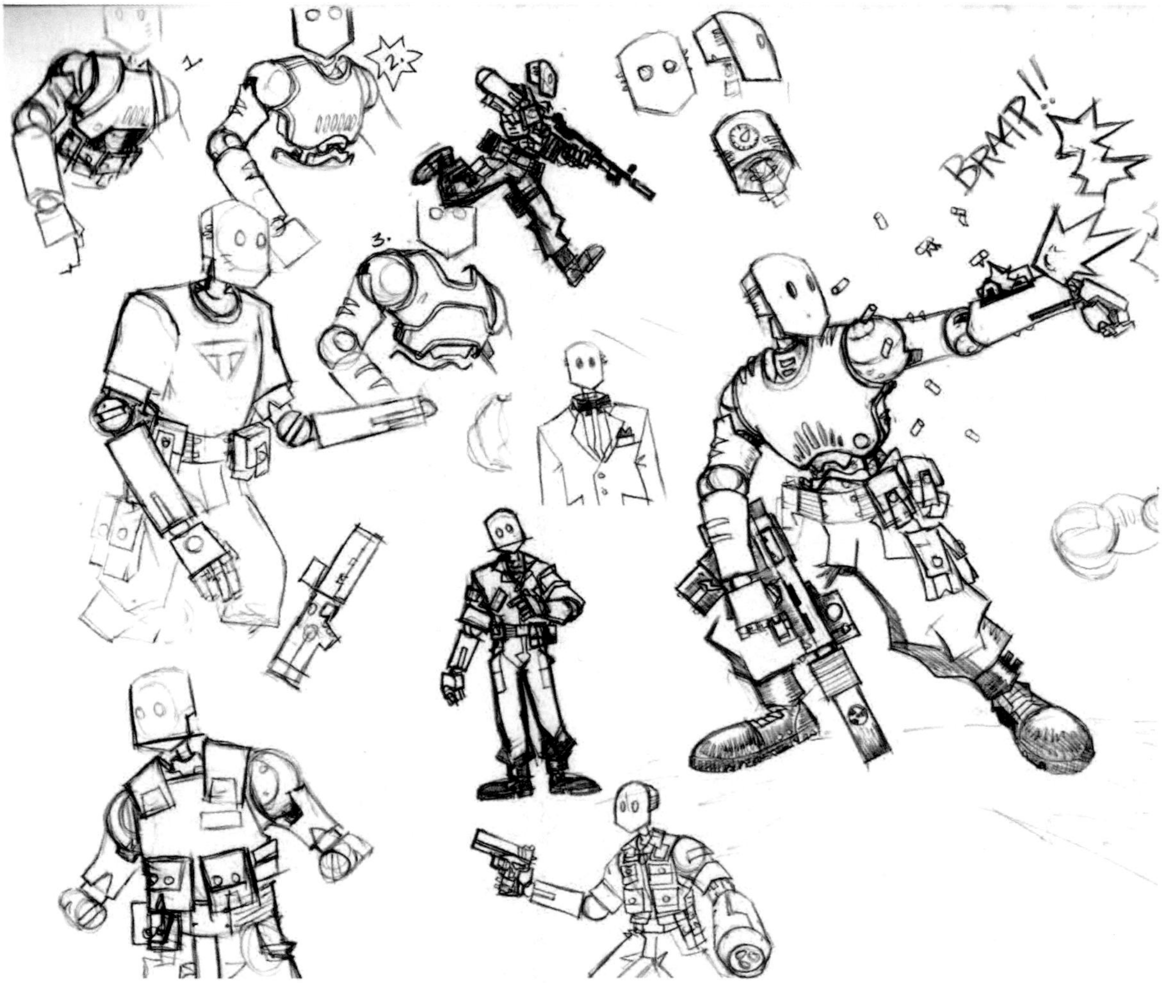
1.
2.
3.
BRAAP!!

"These are proto-Robo designs. He was originally to have arm blasters, so you see some of that here. These are all good designs, but I wanted Robo to be sturdier, stockier. Like he's stuffed with components. We'll probably steal from these designs from some bad guy 'bots eventually."

"Tons of head studies trying to figure out how to make a Rocketeer helmet not look like a Rocketeer helmet."

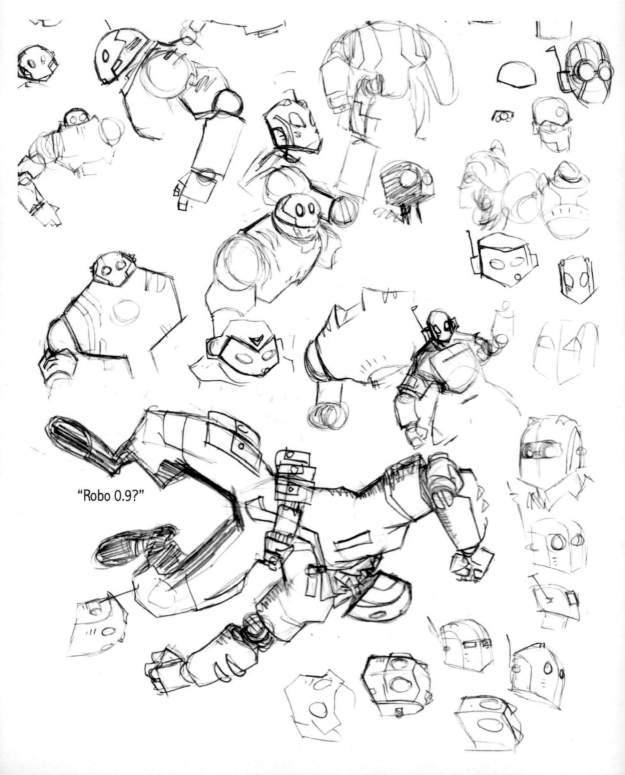

"Robo 0.9?"

"Oh, man. This brings back some memories. This is Atomic Robo 1.0, the first 'official' design that Scott and I were happy with. As much as I love our final design, I do miss the 'screw' elbows from this early iteration."

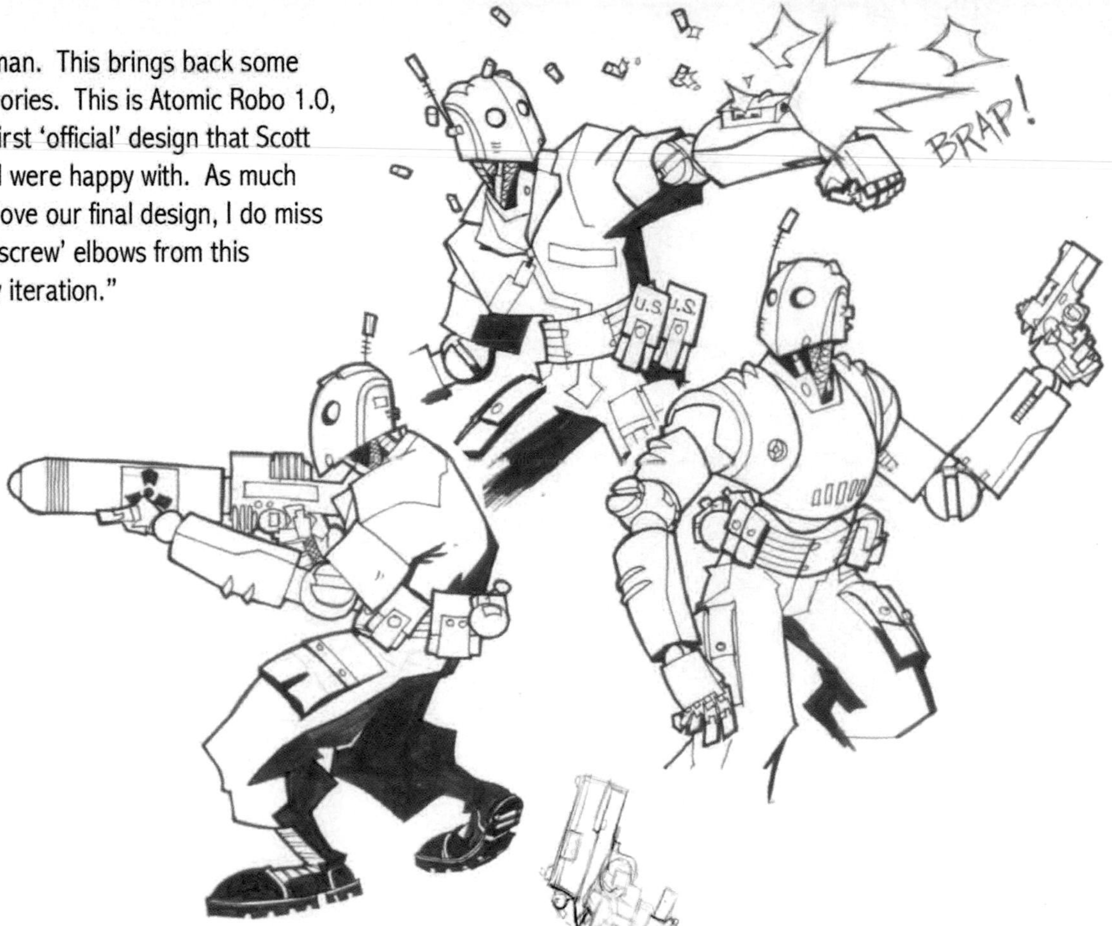
BRAP!
U.S.
U.S.

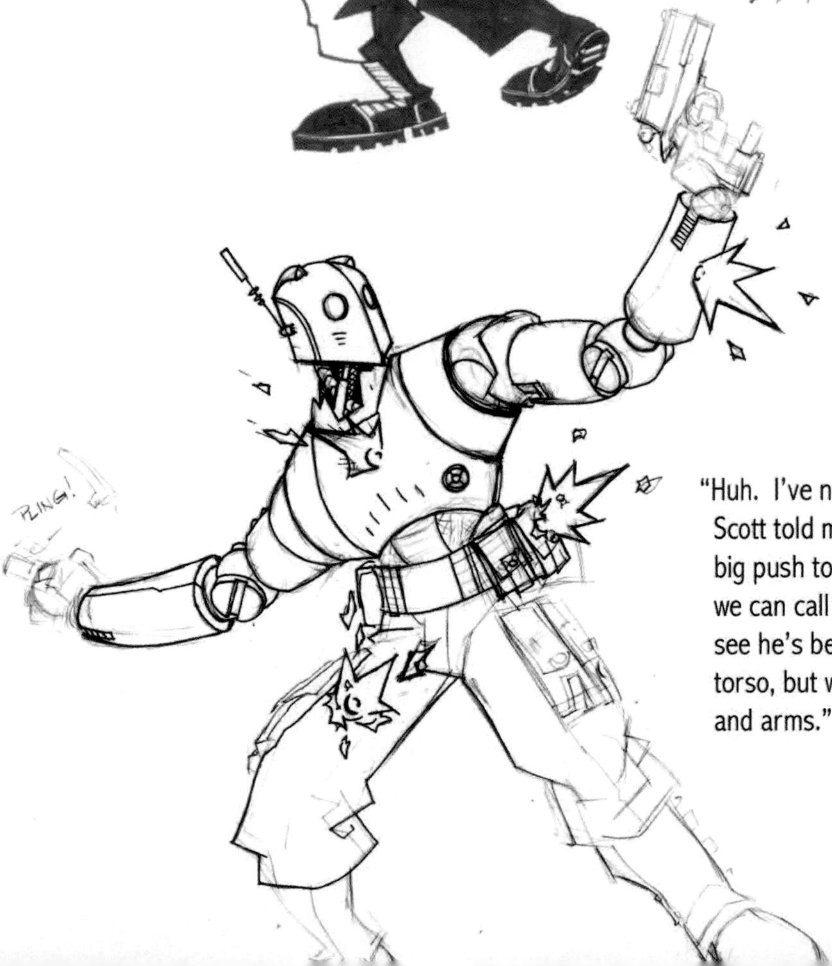
PLING!

"Huh. I've never seen this picture, but Scott told me about it just before his big push to the Robo 2.0 design. Guess we can call this Robo 1.5, then. You can see he's been bulked up a little in the torso, but we've still got the old chest and arms."

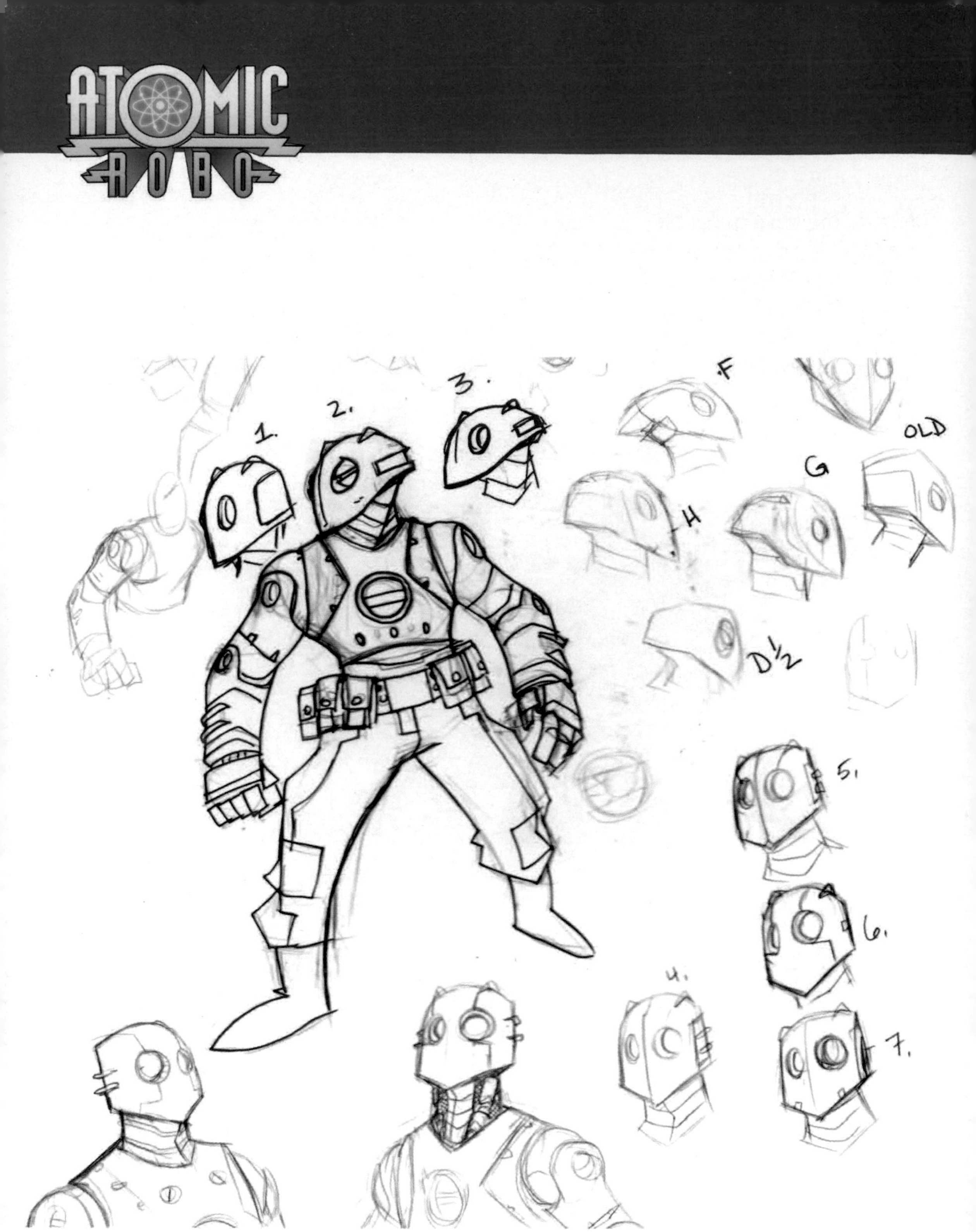
1.
2.
3.
F
OLD
G
H
D½
5.
6.
4.
7.

"And here's where Atomic Robo 2.0 came into being. Scott bulked up the original design (as per my original vision). We also decided that the eyes needed to be more prominent since they were his only facial feature. For those of you keeping score at home, we ended up going with the #6 head."

CONCEPT ART BY SCOTT WEGENER
WORDS BY BRIAN CLEVINGER

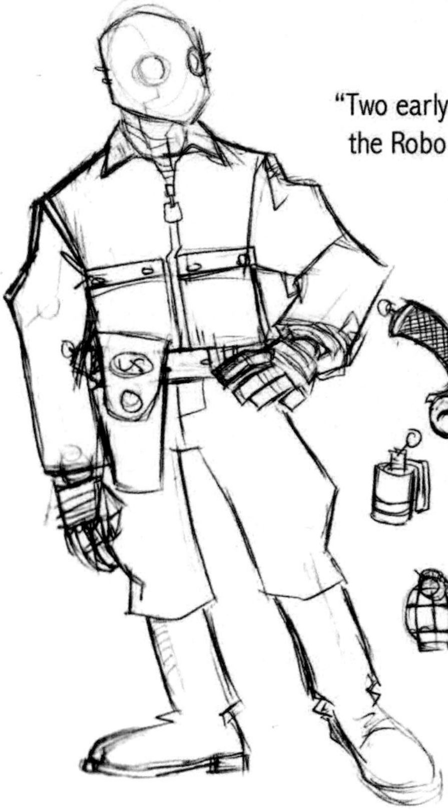

"Two early concept sketches of the Robo 2.0 design for issue 1."

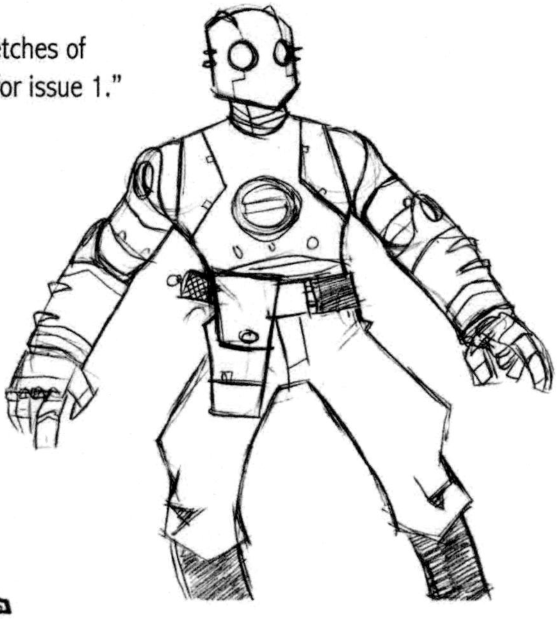

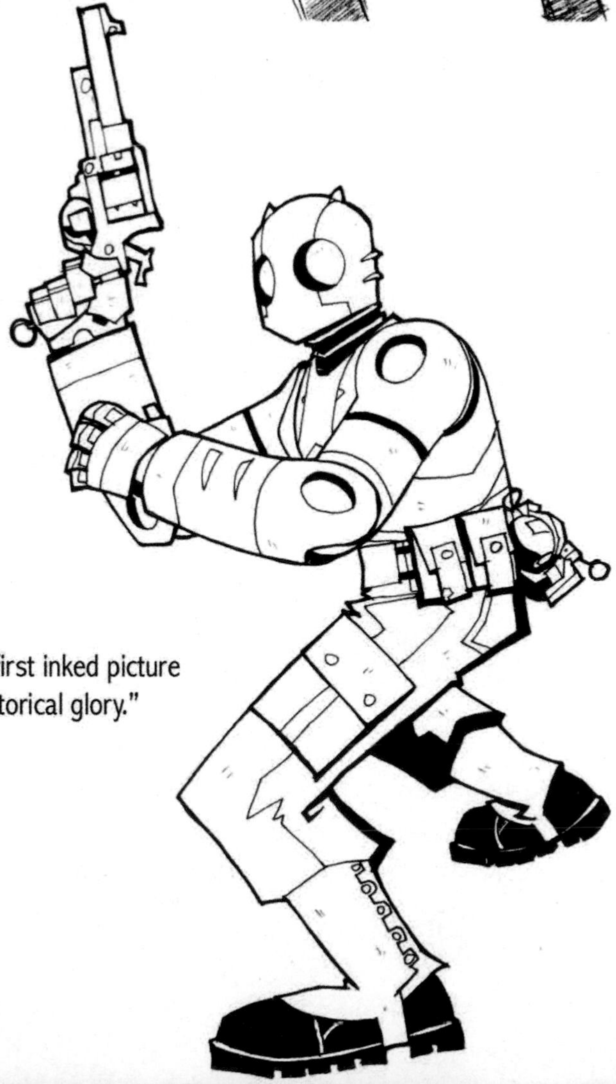

"Well, dang. This may actually be the first inked picture of Robo's 2.0 design. Bask in its historical glory."

Gentlemen,

Please find attached, for your information, the latest report by the Co-Chairs on Atomic Robot Study and Neutralization.

What little we know of Robo's construction has been pieced together by cataloguing nearly a century's worth of photographs, film and video, eyewitness reports, forensic evidence, and the scant details Robo himself has made public. It opens a frustratingly small window into potential exploitations.

Even in this cursory overview, it is immediately apparent that the central tenet of Robo's design is durability. He appears to be effectively immune to small arms fire. Higher caliber firearms cause some superficial damage, but it is likely for a "lucky shot" to impair a joint or sensor. Explosives fair little better depending on strength and Robo's distance from the epicenter. In theory, a direct hit with a powerful enough explosive would be certain to cause minor to crippling injuries. In practice, however, Robo is rarely more than stunned by

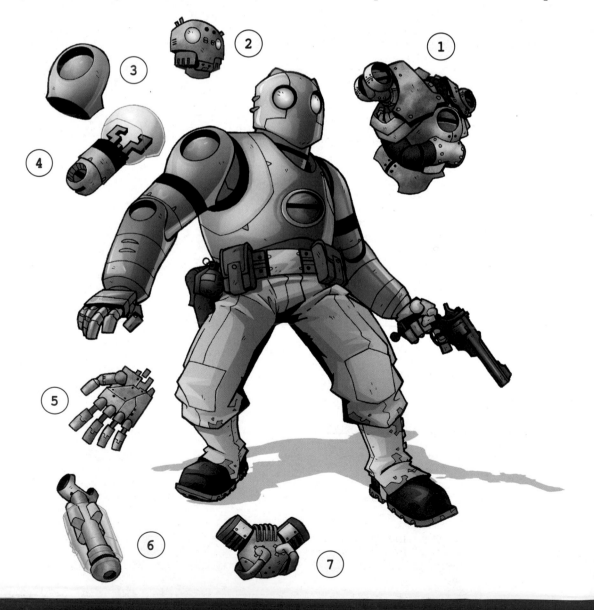

explosive attacks. Even this, it is theorized, has more to do with
the compression wave "rattling" his internal components than the raw
destructive force of the explosion itself. Robo's resilience to
temperature extremes remains a largely unexplored avenue of study. It
should be noted that the de-classified Viking I images show Robo in a
kind of environmental suit. More research is warranted.

1. Torso. Under Robo's external armor, we find a reinforced
breastbone and two ribs that provide a support cage for the interior
structures. Details beyond this point can only be speculated upon,
but the abundance of protective plating dedicated to this area - much
of it redundant - suggests that Robo's nuclear power core is located
somewhere in his mid- to lower-chest. The two large cables near his
"stomach" area most likely provide coolant.

Also note the reinforced shoulder joint. Robo has been observed to
lift and support significant weight, three to five tons on average,
which these joints must accommodate across the full range of motion.

2. Head. Atomic Robo's head has been referred to as "the most
advanced collection of technologies in the history of the world." It
is here that the secrets to automatic intelligence most likely reside
in addition to an impressive array of sensors. The full range of his
optical system is unknown, but it verifiably extends at least into
the infrared and ultraviolet. It is known that he can "hear" radio,
wi-fi, and blu tooth. He appears to have a limited ability to output
data along these frequencies as well.

3. Shoulder Armor. This external plating is the first line of
protection for Robo's shoulder joint.

4. Upper Arm. Reinforced C-clamps plug into the rotors in Robo's
shoulder joints. Note the "beach ball" armor covering the clamps. It
is segmented into two sections, most likely to provide a greater range
of motion.

5. Hand. Robo's grip possesses strength enough to bend gun barrels,
yet he can handle fragile and delicate items with ease. His manual
dexterity appears to fall within the upper range of human ability.
Much like the rest of his body, Robo's individual fingers and hands
are armored to withstand the forces he is able to exert. Even so, it
seems likely his hands must receive a great deal of maintenance due to
the frequency and intensity of his punches.

6. Forearm. This simply plugs into the elbow joint at one end and the
wrist joint at the other. The majority of this structure is dedicated
to armor plating and shock absorption to protect Robo from his own
strength. The four "lumps" near the elbow joint most likely suppress
vibrational stresses on the elbow.

7. Atomic Engine. Other than Robo's automatic intelligence, his
power core is the most mysterious system in his make-up. In fact,
some debate whether atomic energy is involved at all, citing that
a miniature atomic reactor built with 1920s technology would be no
more impossible than utilizing universal harmonics or other likewise
esoteric energy sources Tesla claimed to be able to harness toward
the end of his life. Still, atomic energy is the commonly accepted
source of Robo's power. What fuel(s) he may use, how often they must
be replaced, and the maximum energy output available to him remain
a mystery. The most likely fuel is Pu-238 or Pu-239, but further
speculation is beyond the ability of the committee at this time.